Foundations of Market Systems Science

Volume I

Foundations of Market Systems Science

Volume I

Understanding, Evolution, and Decision in Financial Markets

by

Saeed Mohammad

Founder, WallStreetDelta Institute

"Markets are not merely collections of prices. They are evolving systems whose behavior emerges through the continuous interaction of participants, information, incentives, uncertainty, and time."

First Edition

WallStreetDelta Institute

2026

Foundations of Market Systems Science, Volume I

This manuscript represents the first edition of an evolving body of work. The concepts, terminology, and frameworks presented herein are intended to support scientific inquiry into financial markets and should be interpreted as contributions to an open research program rather than statements of immutable fact.

The author and the WallStreetDelta Institute encourage scholarly critique, empirical testing, replication, and constructive refinement of the ideas presented in this volume.

Printed in the United States of America.

Dedication

To every curious mind that has ever looked at a market and asked not merely what happened, but why.

To the engineers who seek structure within complexity.

To the scientists who value evidence over certainty.

To the educators who believe understanding should outlive opinion.

And to my family, whose patience, encouragement, and unwavering support made this work possible.

May this volume serve as one small step toward a deeper understanding of financial markets as evolving systems.

About the Author

Saeed Mohammad is an engineer, systems thinker, entrepreneur, and founder of the WallStreetDelta Institute. His professional background spans biomedical engineering, medical device manufacturing, quality systems, process validation, and complex engineering operations.

Drawing on principles from systems engineering, decision science, statistics, and financial market analysis, he developed the conceptual foundations of **Market Systems Science**, an interdisciplinary framework that views financial markets as evolving complex adaptive systems rather than collections of isolated indicators or trading signals.

He is also the creator of the WallStreetDelta Observatory, a research platform designed to observe, measure, and investigate market structure through empirical evidence while emphasizing transparency, reproducibility, and scientific humility.

The views expressed in this volume represent an ongoing research program intended to invite investigation, critique, and refinement by the broader scientific and financial communities.

Foreword

Reserved for a future foreword by an invited scholar or practitioner.

The first edition is intentionally published without an external foreword. As the discipline matures and independent researchers contribute to its development, future editions may include perspectives from scholars, practitioners, or educators whose work has influenced or evaluated the evolution of Market Systems Science.

Preface

Why Another Book About Markets?

Financial markets have been studied for centuries. Economists, statisticians, mathematicians, physicists, psychologists, engineers, and practitioners have each developed valuable ways of understanding market behavior. Their collective work has produced powerful theories, sophisticated models, and practical tools that continue to shape modern finance.

Yet despite this rich body of knowledge, market participants often experience a persistent challenge. Information is abundant, but understanding is fragmented. Measurements are plentiful, but the relationships among them are frequently unclear. Models generate outputs, yet the reasoning that connects observation to judgment is often implicit rather than explicit.

This volume began with a simple question:

Can financial markets be studied as evolving systems through a structured scientific framework that separates observation, understanding, evolution, and decision-making?

The answer proposed in these pages is not a finished doctrine but an invitation to inquiry.

Market Systems Science does not seek to replace economics, finance, statistics, behavioral science, or systems theory. Instead, it seeks to integrate insights from these disciplines into a coherent framework for investigating markets as complex adaptive systems.

The framework rests on three foundational pillars:

- **Market Understanding** — how observations become evidence and evidence becomes understanding.
- **Market Evolution** — how market configurations change over time through transitions and evolving system states.
- **Market Judgment** — how understanding informs decisions within the context of objectives, constraints, uncertainty, and responsibility.

These pillars are intentionally separated because they answer different questions:

- *How do we know?*
- *What is the market doing?*

- *How should that understanding influence decisions?*

Throughout this volume, emphasis is placed on distinguishing observation from interpretation, evidence from opinion, and explanation from prediction. Readers will find repeated reminders that scientific progress depends not on certainty but on disciplined curiosity, transparent reasoning, and the willingness to revise conclusions when new evidence emerges.

This first volume establishes the conceptual and methodological foundations of the discipline. It introduces its vocabulary, principles, hierarchies, research methods, and philosophical commitments. Subsequent volumes are intended to expand these foundations into detailed treatments of market observation, configuration, state transitions, decision systems, and research governance.

No single book can fully explain markets. Markets continually evolve, and any scientific framework intended to study them must remain equally open to refinement. The objective of this work is therefore not to provide final answers but to offer a common language through which better questions—and ultimately better understanding—can emerge.

Acknowledgments

The development of this manuscript reflects the convergence of ideas from many disciplines. Systems engineering, economics, finance, statistics, complexity science, philosophy of science, decision theory, and software engineering have each contributed concepts that helped shape the framework presented in these pages.

The author is grateful to the educators, researchers, engineers, market practitioners, mentors, colleagues, and students whose questions, critiques, and discussions encouraged continual refinement of these ideas.

Special appreciation is extended to the growing community surrounding the WallStreetDelta Institute, whose commitment to disciplined inquiry and evidence-based market research continues to inspire the evolution of this work.

Finally, sincere gratitude is offered to the author's family for their patience, encouragement, and unwavering support throughout the many years required to transform an evolving collection of ideas into the beginnings of a structured scientific discipline.

Contents

Part I. Foundations of Market Systems Science

"Every scientific discipline begins not with answers, but with a disciplined way of asking questions."

Introduction to Part I

Before we can investigate financial markets scientifically, we must first establish a common language, define the scope of inquiry, and clarify the assumptions that guide our observations. Throughout history, markets have been examined through many different lenses, including economics, finance, mathematics, psychology, statistics, and engineering. Each perspective has contributed valuable insights while emphasizing different aspects of market behavior.

Market Systems Science does not seek to replace these disciplines. Instead, it provides an organizing framework through which their contributions can be integrated into a coherent understanding of markets as evolving systems.

The chapters in Part I establish the conceptual foundations upon which the remainder of this volume is built. They introduce the discipline, define its philosophical commitments, explain its scope, and establish the principles that distinguish observation from interpretation, evidence from opinion, and understanding from decision-making.

Readers should approach these chapters as the foundation of a scientific language. The terminology introduced here is used consistently throughout the remainder of this volume and in subsequent volumes of the series.

Chapter 1. Introduction to Market Systems Science

1.1 Why Study Markets as Systems?

Financial markets are among the most complex human systems ever created. Every trading day, millions of participants interact through countless transactions, continuously incorporating information, expectations, incentives, and uncertainty into prices. The resulting behavior reflects the collective actions of individuals and institutions operating under diverse objectives, constraints, and beliefs.

Despite the enormous volume of available data, understanding markets remains a significant scientific challenge. Prices, volumes, volatility measures, option positions, economic reports, and countless other observations provide information about market activity, yet no single observation fully explains why markets behave as they do or how they may evolve over time.

Traditional approaches frequently emphasize individual variables, isolated indicators, or specific models designed for particular purposes. While these methods have advanced both theory and practice, they often address only one aspect of a much larger system. Markets exhibit properties such as feedback, adaptation, emergence, and nonlinearity that cannot always be understood through isolated measurements alone.

Market Systems Science begins with a different premise: financial markets should be investigated as evolving systems whose observable behavior emerges from the interaction of many interconnected components operating across multiple temporal and structural scales.

Viewing markets through a systems perspective does not diminish the importance of established financial theory. Instead, it broadens the scope of inquiry by emphasizing relationships among observations, configurations, transitions, and participant decisions. This perspective encourages researchers to investigate not only individual measurements but also how those measurements collectively describe the evolving condition of the market itself.

The objective of this discipline is therefore not to replace existing knowledge but to organize it within a coherent scientific framework that supports observation, explanation, and disciplined decision-making.

1.2 The Need for an Organizing Framework

Scientific progress depends upon organization as much as discovery. Disciplines mature when they develop shared terminology, common methods of observation, transparent standards of evidence, and reproducible approaches to investigation.

Many fields—including physics, biology, chemistry, and systems engineering—possess well-established conceptual frameworks that enable researchers to communicate precisely, compare findings consistently, and build progressively upon previous work. Financial market research, however, often spans multiple disciplines whose terminology, assumptions, and methodologies differ substantially.

As a result, similar concepts may be described using different language, while identical terminology may refer to different underlying ideas. This fragmentation complicates communication, limits comparability across studies, and makes cumulative scientific progress more difficult.

Market Systems Science addresses this challenge by proposing an organizing framework that separates several fundamentally different activities:

- observing market activity,
- measuring observable phenomena,
- evaluating evidence,
- developing market understanding,
- investigating market evolution,
- and supporting participant judgment.

Separating these activities provides greater conceptual clarity while reducing the tendency to confuse observation with interpretation or explanation with prediction.

The framework presented throughout this volume therefore serves primarily as a scientific language rather than a predictive theory. Its purpose is to organize inquiry, establish consistent definitions, and encourage disciplined investigation of evolving market behavior.

1.3 What Is Market Systems Science?

Market Systems Science is the interdisciplinary study of financial markets as evolving complex adaptive systems through systematic observation, measurement, evidence evaluation, configuration analysis, state transition investigation, and decision support.

This definition contains several important ideas.

First, markets are regarded as **systems**, meaning that their behavior emerges from the interactions among numerous interconnected components rather than from isolated variables considered independently.

Second, markets are considered **adaptive**, reflecting the continual adjustment of participants as new information becomes available, expectations change, and incentives evolve.

Third, market behavior is viewed as **evolving** rather than static. The condition of the market changes continuously through sequences of observable configurations and transitions rather than occupying permanent equilibrium.

Fourth, the discipline emphasizes **systematic observation**. Scientific understanding begins not with opinion but with careful observation supported by transparent measurements and evidence.

Finally, Market Systems Science explicitly recognizes that understanding markets and making decisions are related but distinct activities. Scientific investigation seeks to improve understanding, whereas participants ultimately apply that understanding within their own Decision Environments to determine appropriate actions.

1.4 Scope of the Discipline

Market Systems Science investigates questions such as:

- How can market activity be observed systematically?
- Which measurements provide meaningful evidence about market behavior?
- How do multiple observations combine to improve understanding?
- How do market configurations change through time?
- What constitutes a market state?
- How can transitions between states be identified and characterized?
- Which observations appear most informative under different conditions?
- How should uncertainty influence confidence in market assessments?
- How can understanding support disciplined decision-making without eliminating human judgment?

Equally important are the questions that fall outside the discipline's primary scope.

Market Systems Science does **not** seek to identify guaranteed trading strategies, eliminate uncertainty, predict markets with certainty, or replace established disciplines such as economics, finance, or statistics. Rather, it seeks to provide a structured scientific framework within which those disciplines can contribute to a richer understanding of market behavior.

1.5 The Central Questions of This Volume

Throughout this volume, three foundational questions guide the development of the discipline:

1. **How do we know what we know about markets?**
2. **How do markets evolve through time?**
3. **How should understanding influence decisions under uncertainty?**

These questions correspond to the three foundational pillars introduced below and developed throughout the remainder of the book:

- **Market Understanding**
- **Market Evolution**
- **Market Judgment**

Each pillar addresses a distinct aspect of scientific inquiry while contributing to a unified framework for investigating financial markets as evolving systems.

1.6 Looking Ahead

The chapters that follow establish the conceptual architecture of Market Systems Science. Readers will encounter new terminology, formal definitions, organizing hierarchies, methodological principles, and research standards intended to support consistent investigation across diverse market environments.

No single framework can capture every aspect of financial markets, nor should it attempt to do so. Instead, the objective of this volume is to provide a disciplined foundation upon which future empirical research, theoretical refinement, and practical applications can be built.

The chapters that follow invite readers not merely to learn a new vocabulary but to participate in an ongoing scientific conversation about how markets can be observed, understood, and investigated with greater clarity, transparency, and intellectual humility.

Closing Reflection

Every scientific discipline begins by defining the questions it seeks to answer. Market Systems Science begins with a similar commitment: to investigate financial markets not as collections of isolated indicators or deterministic forecasts, but as evolving systems whose behavior can be observed, measured, understood, and studied through disciplined scientific inquiry.

Chapter 2. The Nature of Financial Markets

> *"Before a system can be understood, it must first be recognized as a system."*

Learning Objectives

After completing this chapter, the reader should be able to:

- Explain why financial markets are appropriately viewed as systems.
- Distinguish systems from collections of independent objects.
- Describe the characteristics of complex adaptive systems.
- Recognize the roles of emergence, feedback, adaptation, and nonlinearity.
- Understand why systems thinking provides a useful foundation for market investigation.
- Appreciate both the strengths and limitations of the systems perspective.

2.1 What Is a System?

The word *system* is widely used in everyday language, yet within science it carries a more precise meaning.

Across engineering, biology, ecology, physics, and systems science, a system is generally understood as **a collection of interacting components whose relationships give rise to behaviors that cannot be fully understood by examining the components independently.**

The defining characteristic of a system is therefore **interaction**, not merely composition.

A pile of sand is composed of many individual grains, yet the grains interact only minimally. Removing one grain rarely changes the overall behavior of the pile.

An ecosystem, by contrast, contains organisms whose interactions influence one another continuously. Removing a single species may alter predator-prey relationships, nutrient cycles, population dynamics, and ultimately the entire ecosystem.

The distinction lies not in the number of components but in the importance of their relationships.

Financial markets exhibit the latter characteristic. Prices emerge through the continual interaction of buyers, sellers, institutions, regulations, technologies, information, and expectations. Understanding the market therefore requires studying both its components and the relationships among them.

2.2 Financial Markets as Systems

Every observable market event is the consequence of numerous simultaneous interactions.

A change in interest rates may influence currency markets, equity valuations, bond prices, commodity demand, and derivatives positioning. Institutional responses affect liquidity. Liquidity influences execution quality. Execution quality affects subsequent participant behavior.

These interactions create feedback loops that propagate through the market in ways that cannot always be anticipated by examining any single variable.

Consequently, Market Systems Science adopts the following perspective:

Financial markets are dynamic systems whose observable behavior emerges from the continuous interaction of participants, information, institutions, incentives, technology, and time.

This definition emphasizes that market behavior is produced through interaction rather than isolated causes.

2.3 Components of a Financial Market System

Although market structures differ across exchanges and asset classes, several broad categories of components are consistently present.

Participants

Participants include individuals, institutions, market makers, hedge funds, banks, pension funds, governments, and algorithmic trading systems.

Each participant acts according to distinct objectives, constraints, information, and incentives.

Information

Information includes earnings reports, macroeconomic releases, geopolitical developments, order flow, corporate actions, regulatory announcements, and countless other observations.

Importantly, information influences markets only after it is interpreted by participants.

Trading Mechanisms

Markets require mechanisms through which buyers and sellers interact.

These include exchanges, electronic communication networks, matching engines, clearing systems, and settlement processes.

Incentives

Every participant responds to incentives.

Some pursue long-term investment.

Others pursue liquidity provision.

Others hedge risk.

Others speculate.

Different incentives produce different behaviors that collectively shape market activity.

Constraints

No participant operates without limitations.

Capital requirements, regulations, risk tolerances, mandates, technology, and available information constrain market behavior.

Constraints influence decisions just as strongly as objectives.

2.4 Interaction Creates Market Behavior

Perhaps the most important idea in this chapter is that **market behavior emerges through interaction**.

No single participant determines the market.

No single economic report determines the market.

No single indicator determines the market.

Instead, observable market behavior reflects the aggregate interaction of many simultaneous processes.

This principle has important consequences.

Suppose institutional buying increases while economic expectations deteriorate.

At the same time, volatility declines, dealer positioning changes, and liquidity becomes concentrated near key price levels.

None of these observations alone fully describes market conditions.

Together, however, they may reveal a coherent market configuration that could not have been inferred from any individual observation.

Market Systems Science therefore emphasizes relationships among observations rather than isolated measurements.

2.5 Complex Adaptive Systems

Financial markets belong to a broader class of systems known as **complex adaptive systems**.

Although definitions vary across disciplines, several characteristics appear consistently.

Large Numbers of Interacting Components

Markets contain millions of participants operating simultaneously.

Adaptation

Participants continuously modify their behavior as conditions change.

Strategies evolve.

Risk tolerances change.

Technology advances.

Regulations evolve.

Markets therefore adapt rather than remaining static.

Feedback

Actions influence markets.

Markets influence future actions.

This reciprocal relationship creates feedback loops that continually reshape system behavior.

Emergence

Many observable market phenomena arise only through collective interaction.

Liquidity.

Momentum.

Volatility clustering.

Market regimes.

These properties cannot be assigned to any individual participant.

They emerge from the behavior of the system as a whole.

Nonlinearity

Small events may occasionally produce large consequences.

Large events may sometimes produce surprisingly small effects.

Relationships between causes and observable outcomes are therefore often nonlinear.

2.6 Systems Thinking Versus Reductionism

Scientific progress frequently alternates between two complementary approaches.

Reductionism attempts to understand phenomena by studying their individual components.

Systems thinking attempts to understand phenomena by studying relationships among components.

Neither approach is sufficient independently.

Reductionism reveals important mechanisms.

Systems thinking reveals interaction.

Market Systems Science embraces both.

Individual measurements remain essential.

Yet understanding increasingly emerges through integrating those measurements into a broader representation of the evolving market system.

2.7 A Systems Perspective on Scientific Observation

Viewing markets as systems changes the nature of scientific observation.

Instead of asking:

"What does this indicator mean?"

we ask:

"What does this observation contribute to our understanding of the evolving market system?"

This shift is subtle but profound.

Individual measurements become evidence rather than conclusions.

Evidence contributes to understanding.

Understanding supports explanation.

Explanation informs judgment.

The emphasis moves away from isolated signals and toward structured reasoning grounded in multiple sources of evidence.

2.8 Limitations of the Systems Perspective

No scientific perspective is universally applicable.

Viewing markets as systems offers important advantages, but it also has limitations.

Systems models may oversimplify important details.

Relationships may change through time.

Some interactions remain unobservable.

Emergent behavior can be difficult to predict.

Consequently, Market Systems Science does not claim that systems thinking eliminates uncertainty or guarantees explanation.

Instead, it provides an organizing framework within which observations can be interpreted more coherently.

Recognizing these limitations is itself an essential component of scientific humility.

Chapter Summary

This chapter introduced the systems perspective that underlies the remainder of this volume.

Rather than treating financial markets as collections of independent variables, Market Systems Science views them as evolving systems whose behavior emerges through continual interaction among participants, information, incentives, institutions, and technology.

Several characteristics of complex adaptive systems—including emergence, adaptation, feedback, and nonlinearity—provide a conceptual foundation for later chapters on market observation, configuration, state, and evolution.

Most importantly, this chapter establishes that understanding markets requires studying relationships as carefully as individual observations. That systems perspective becomes the organizing principle for the scientific framework developed throughout the remainder of this volume.

Chapter 3. The Nature of Knowledge

How We Know What We Know About Markets

Chapter Purpose

Financial markets generate enormous quantities of observations, measurements, estimates, models, narratives, and forecasts. Yet the existence of information does not guarantee understanding. Before developing the analytical architecture of Market Systems Science, the discipline must establish how claims about markets are formed, evaluated, challenged, and revised.

This chapter introduces the epistemic foundation of the framework. It distinguishes market phenomena from recorded observations, data from measurements, measurements from evidence, evidence from inference, interpretation from assessment, judgment from decision, and models from the reality they represent.

It also establishes that uncertainty is permanent, confidence should remain proportional to evidence and claim type, and all material market understanding remains provisional. The objective is not skepticism for its own sake. It is to establish the conditions under which conclusions can become more defensible without being mistaken for final truth.

> **Governing Proposition:** Market knowledge is constructed through a traceable progression from recorded observation to controlled measurement, contextual evidence, inference, interpretation, assessment, judgment, and—only within a defined Decision Environment—action. Every stage adds assumptions and potential error; material conclusions therefore remain open to revision.

Learning Objectives

- Distinguish market phenomena from recorded observations and source-relative factual statements.
- Distinguish data, measurements, evidence, inference, interpretation, assessment, judgment, decision, and action.
- Explain why information is useful ordinary language but not a separate formal epistemic tier in this volume.
- Identify analytical statement types and understand inferential distance.

- Explain why measurements and models are selective representations rather than the market itself.
- Distinguish uncertainty, missingness, model dependence, and error.
- Explain why confidence should be claim-specific and proportional to evidence quality.
- Preserve competing, alternative, and null explanations.
- Explain why provisional knowledge does not imply relativism or refusal to conclude.
- Distinguish understanding from forecasting and predictive performance from causal explanation.
- Describe the iterative Market Inquiry Chain and the role of correction in disciplined inquiry.

3.1 The Pursuit of Understanding

Human inquiry begins with a simple act: something is noticed. From that observation come questions, comparisons, measurements, explanations, tests, and revisions. The tools change across disciplines and across generations, but the underlying pursuit remains recognizable. We observe patterns, ask why they may exist, construct representations, compare those representations with evidence, and revise them when they fail.

Financial markets deserve the same discipline. Markets are observed with extraordinary technical precision, yet they remain only partially understood. Prices, quotations, trades, order books, options, flows, and institutional reports can be recorded in enormous detail, but the mechanisms connecting those records to participant behavior and future outcomes are often incomplete, adaptive, or hidden.

The objective of Market Systems Science is therefore not to eliminate uncertainty. It is to improve the quality of understanding: to make observations more traceable, measurements more controlled, claims more proportional to evidence, models more explicit, and revision more routine.

> **Understanding Principle:** The goal of inquiry is not perfect certainty but progressively more defensible understanding under clearly stated evidence, methods, assumptions, and scope.

3.2 Market Reality, Observation, and Explanation

The market exists independently of any one data feed, indicator, model, or narrative. A transaction occurs in a particular institutional setting. A quotation is displayed or withdrawn. An order is executed, cancelled, or replaced. Participants hold exposures that may be directly reported, delayed, inferred, or entirely unobserved. These phenomena constitute the object of inquiry.

What researchers receive is a representation of selected aspects of that activity. An exchange may report a trade at a stated price and timestamp. A vendor may normalize, consolidate, correct, or enrich that record. A database may preserve the record with additional transformations. The resulting observation is useful, but it should not be confused with complete access to market reality.

Suppose an equity rises five percent during a trading session. The price change can be established under a defined price source and interval. Its explanation cannot. Earnings information, macroeconomic news, institutional demand, short covering, derivatives hedging, liquidity conditions, or several interacting forces may be relevant. The observed movement begins inquiry; it does not complete it.

> **Observation Principle:** A record can establish what an identified source reported under defined conditions without establishing why it occurred or whether the record fully represents the underlying phenomenon.

3.3 Data and Recorded Observations

Data are recorded representations of observable market activity or reported state. They answer a narrow but essential question: what did an identified source record?

- trade price and size
- bid and ask quotations
- quoted size
- trade and quote timestamps
- reported volume
- reported open interest
- reference prices and settlement values
- corporate-action records
- scheduled-event timestamps

Data quality depends on provenance. A value should be interpreted relative to its source, timestamp, schema, venue, revision behavior, and collection method. Records may be delayed, stale, corrected, cancelled, missing, or transformed by vendors. A feed value should therefore not be treated as an unqualified statement about the complete market.

A narrow factual statement can nevertheless be defensible. For example, "the identified exchange reported this trade at this price and time" is a source-relative factual claim. It does not establish participant intent, hidden liquidity, causal mechanism, or the complete market condition.

> **Provenance Principle:** The epistemic status of recorded data depends in part on knowing where the record came from, when

it applied, how it was represented, and whether it was later revised.

3.4 Measurement as Representation

Measurements are controlled representations constructed from data according to a defined method and purpose. They transform observations into quantities or classifications that can be compared, monitored, or analyzed.

A closing price is recorded data. A daily return calculated from successive closing prices is a measurement. Bid and ask quotations are data. Their difference is a spread measurement. A sequence of transaction prices is data; realized volatility calculated from those prices is a measurement.

Implied volatility requires particular care. The option premium is observed or quoted. Implied volatility is generally a model-dependent estimate obtained by solving a pricing relationship for the volatility parameter using that premium and other inputs. A vendor-provided implied-volatility field may itself be recorded as data in a database, but the economic quantity represented by that field remains derived and model-dependent.

Measurements depend on definitions, sampling, horizons, transformations, units, baselines, and assumptions. Two competent analysts can calculate different but defensible measurements from the same underlying records because they use different horizons or methods.

Measurement Principle: A measurement is a constructed representation of a phenomenon, not the phenomenon itself.

3.5 From Measurement to Evidence

A measurement does not possess a fixed evidentiary meaning by itself. It becomes evidence only when it is evaluated in relation to a question, proposition, comparison, or hypothesis.

A widening spread may be evidence relevant to a liquidity question. The same spread may be less informative about long-horizon valuation. Rising implied volatility may be relevant to questions about option pricing, uncertainty, hedging demand, or event sensitivity, but it does not by itself prove fear, predict realized volatility, or establish a particular causal mechanism.

Context therefore determines evidentiary value. Relevant context may include baseline, horizon, universe, market session, concurrent measurements, data quality, measurement validity, and competing explanations.

The word information remains useful in ordinary language for data or measurements organized so that relationships become easier to examine. In this volume, however, information is not treated as a separate formal epistemic tier between measurement and evidence.

Evidence Principle: A measurement becomes evidence only in relation to a defined question or proposition and within an explicit context.

3.6 Inference, Interpretation, and Assessment

Evidence still does not interpret itself. Analysts must reason from what is measured toward propositions that extend beyond direct observation. These extensions should be distinguished because they carry different inferential burdens.

Inference extends beyond direct measurement. If spreads widen, depth falls, and price impact increases, an analyst may infer that exchange conditions are becoming less resilient. That inference is not directly observed; it is supported by the combined measurements and the reasoning connecting them.

Interpretation organizes evidence and inference into meaning. It may describe a market as increasingly adjustment-sensitive, concentrated, or fragile under the stated framework. Interpretation is more assumption-dependent than the underlying measurements.

Assessment synthesizes evidence, alternative explanations, contradictions, missing information, confidence, and scope into a qualified view of current conditions. An assessment may conclude that short-horizon stress is developing while evidence of broader structural dysfunction remains incomplete.

Inference Principle: Claims that extend beyond measurement should make their reasoning, assumptions, and inferential distance visible.

3.7 Hypotheses, Alternatives, and Revision

A hypothesis is a proposed explanation structured so that evidence can support, weaken, restrict, or reformulate it. It is not simply a higher rung above interpretation. Hypotheses may be formed before evidence collection, after exploratory observation, or as alternatives to an existing explanation.

Responsible inquiry preserves more than one plausible account when evidence permits. A primary hypothesis may organize the current explanation. Alternative hypotheses capture competing mechanisms. A null or minimal explanation asks whether the apparent pattern can be explained by ordinary variation, measurement artifact, or a simpler process.

The discipline should also state revision conditions. What observation would reduce confidence? What result would narrow the scope? What new measurement would require the explanation to change? A claim becomes easier to defend when its possible failure is visible.

Alternative-Explanation Principle: The existence of one plausible explanation does not eliminate competing or null explanations.

3.8 Analytical Statement Types and Inferential Distance

Analytical statements differ in how far they extend beyond directly recorded observations. This difference can be described as inferential distance. Greater inferential distance does not automatically make a statement weaker or less useful, but it generally increases dependence on assumptions, models, context, and competing explanations.

Statement type	Meaning	Illustrative example	Does not establish
Recorded observation	What an identified source reported	Index closed at a stated level	Cause or complete reality
Measurement	Defined representation constructed from data	Realized volatility rose versus baseline	Meaning by itself
Evidentiary statement	Measurement related to a question	Variability is elevated for the stated horizon	Mechanism
Inference	Proposition extending beyond measurement	Adjustment intensity may be increasing	Causation
Interpretation	Organized account of evidence	Conditions appear increasingly fragile	Certain future outcome
Hypothesis	Testable proposed explanation	Concentrated exposure amplified selling	Confirmation
Assessment	Synthesis of evidence and uncertainty	Developing stress, moderate confidence	Universal decision
Judgment	Conclusion for a stated purpose	Risk merits greater caution	Universal action
Decision	Selection among alternatives	Reduce exposure under stated constraints	Correct outcome
Action	Implementation of decision	Position is reduced	Quality of the reasoning

INCREASING INFERENTIAL DISTANCE ↓

STATEMENT TYPE	DOES NOT ESTABLISH
Recorded observation	Cause or complete reality
Measurement	Meaning by itself
Evidentiary statement	Mechanism
Inference	Causation
Interpretation	Certain future outcome
Hypothesis	Confirmation
Assessment	Universal decision
Judgment	Universal action
Decision	Correct outcome
Action	Quality of the reasoning

Figure 3.1 — Analytical Statement Types and Inferential Distance

> **Claim-Boundary Principle:** Observation, measurement, evidence, inference, interpretation, hypothesis, assessment, judgment, decision, and action should not be treated as interchangeable.

3.9 Models and Reality

Markets cannot be studied without abstraction. The challenge is not to avoid models, but to remember what they are. A model is a purpose-specific representation of selected features or relationships within a system. It can be useful precisely because it omits complexity that is irrelevant to its purpose.

The epistemic chain can be written as market reality → observable activity → recorded data → measurement → model → output. At each transformation, some features are preserved, some are emphasized, some are compressed, and some are omitted.

A volatility model does not contain uncertainty itself. A liquidity score does not contain all available exchange capacity. A state classifier does not discover a single natural state of the market. These models may nevertheless provide disciplined, useful representations when their purpose, assumptions, inputs, limitations, and validation are explicit.

A useful model simplifies. An irresponsible model oversimplifies, conceals its assumptions, or permits its output to be interpreted beyond the evidence supporting it.

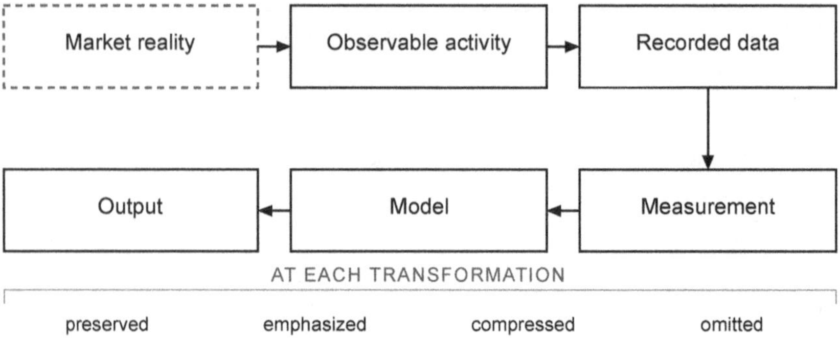

Figure 3.2 — Models and Reality

> **Representation Principle:** Every representation preserves selected features and omits others. Compression is useful only when those boundaries remain visible enough to challenge.

3.10 The Limits of Observation

Even exceptionally detailed market data leave important features unobserved. Participant intentions are rarely visible directly. True aggregate positioning may be incomplete or delayed. Hidden liquidity may not be displayed. Internal risk limits, funding constraints, hedging policies, and future decisions remain partly latent.

Some unknowns can be reduced with better data. Others are structural. Future information has not yet arrived. Future participants have not yet acted. Counterfactual paths were not observed. Even perfect historical recording would not convert these unknowns into certain forecasts.

The discipline should therefore distinguish what is unknown because evidence is currently missing from what may be inherently unknowable at the time a decision is made.

> **Observability Principle:** Better data can expand what is known without making the market fully observable.

3.11 Uncertainty, Unknowns, Missingness, and Error

Uncertainty is permanent, but not every analytical weakness should be called uncertainty. Several conditions must be distinguished.

Condition	Meaning	Illustrative consequence
Uncertainty	The relevant claim is not known with complete confidence	Confidence should be qualified
Missing information	Potentially relevant evidence is unavailable	Do not silently treat absence as neutral
Measurement uncertainty	The representation is imperfect or sensitive to method	Report method and sensitivity
Model uncertainty	Alternative model forms or assumptions remain plausible	Compare specifications or narrow claims
Future uncertainty	Future actions and events have not occurred	Use scenarios rather than certainty
Error	A value, calculation, or assertion is wrong	Correct it rather than merely lowering confidence

This distinction is important because uncertainty can be legitimate while error demands correction. Missing data should not be converted automatically into zero, unchanged, normal, or neutral. Unknown conditions should remain unknown unless a documented estimation method is applied.

> **Uncertainty Principle:** Better information can reduce uncertainty without eliminating it, while error should be corrected rather than disguised as uncertainty.

3.12 Confidence and Claim Strength

Confidence should be attached to a particular claim, not treated as a universal property of an analysis. An analyst may have high confidence that a price series is accurate, high confidence that realized volatility increased, moderate confidence that liquidity resilience deteriorated, low confidence about the causal mechanism, and low confidence about the next day's direction.

The strength of a conclusion should depend not merely on the quantity of supporting observations but on evidence validity, relevance, independence, completeness, inferential distance, contradiction, model dependence, and discriminating power relative to alternatives.

This is why confidence is multidimensional. Data confidence, measurement confidence, descriptive confidence, mechanistic confidence, classification confidence, and predictive confidence can differ materially within one analysis.

Confidence Principle: Confidence should remain proportional to evidence quality and appropriate to the type and inferential distance of the claim.

3.13 Intellectual Humility Without Relativism

Intellectual humility is sometimes misunderstood as reluctance to reach a conclusion. That is not the standard adopted here. Evidence can justify strong conclusions. Some explanations are better supported than others. Some measurements are more valid, some models are better calibrated, and some claims are simply incorrect.

Humility means recognizing the scope and conditions of a conclusion, preserving plausible alternatives where evidence remains incomplete, and being willing to revise when stronger evidence appears. It does not mean treating every interpretation as equally valid or suspending judgment indefinitely.

Humility Principle: Provisional knowledge is compatible with strong conclusions when evidence is strong. Humility requires willingness to revise, not refusal to conclude.

3.14 The Principle of Provisional Knowledge

Scientific understanding is rarely final. New data become available. Measurements improve. Hidden assumptions are exposed. Models fail outside their original scope. Market institutions change. Previously plausible explanations may become too narrow or incorrect.

Market Systems Science therefore treats knowledge as a current state of justified understanding rather than a claim of final certainty. A proposition becomes more credible when it survives appropriate examination, corroboration, replication where feasible, competing explanations, and changing evidence. Its credibility remains bounded by its scope.

Principle of Provisional Knowledge: Market understanding is the current best-supported representation permitted by available evidence, measurements, models, assumptions, and scope. It should remain open to revision when stronger evidence, improved measurements, superior explanations, or changed conditions justify correction.

This principle is institutional as well as analytical. The discipline values correction over consistency and refinement over institutional pride. A framework that cannot admit error eventually becomes a doctrine rather than a research program.

Correction Principle: Correction is evidence that disciplined inquiry is functioning. Preserving an outdated conclusion for the sake of consistency weakens knowledge.

3.15 Understanding and Prediction

Prediction is a legitimate scientific and practical purpose when its target, horizon, information set, model, uncertainty, and validation are specified. A predictive model may identify regularities that are useful even when the underlying mechanism is only partly understood.

Predictive success alone, however, does not establish causal understanding. A relationship can forecast well for a period because of correlation, institutional stability, hidden common causes, or temporary market structure. Conversely, a well-supported mechanism may not yield precise short-horizon forecasts in a noisy adaptive system.

For this reason, prediction is useful but not foundational to the Institute's philosophy. Understanding asks what the evidence supports about structure, relationships, constraints, and mechanisms. Prediction asks what may occur under a specified target and horizon. The two can complement one another without being confused.

> **Prediction-Boundary Principle:** Predictive performance does not by itself establish understanding, mechanism, or causal explanation.

3.16 Judgment, Decision, and Action

A disciplined market assessment still does not determine one universal action. Judgment forms a conclusion for a stated purpose. Decision selects among alternatives under objectives and constraints. Action implements the selected decision.

Two participants may agree completely about the current market assessment and act differently. A long-horizon investor may maintain exposure. A leveraged trader may reduce size. A market maker may adjust quoting. A risk manager may lower limits. The difference need not reflect disagreement about the market; it may reflect different Decision Environments.

Separating these layers prevents analytical outputs from being converted silently into generic buy, sell, risk-on, or risk-off instructions.

> **Decision-Boundary Principle:** A market assessment informs decisions but does not determine a participant-independent action.

3.17 The Market Inquiry Chain

The chapter's distinctions can be integrated into a single reasoning architecture. The sequence is not a rigid pipeline. Analysts may move backward when evidence is challenged, measurements are corrected, hypotheses fail, models change, or outcomes reveal new questions.

Conceptually, the Market Inquiry Chain is: market phenomenon → recorded observation/data → measurement → contextual evidence → inference and reasoning → interpretation → assessment → judgment → decision → action → outcome and review.

Outcome and review then feed back into inquiry. New observations may challenge the original measurement. A failed decision may reveal a poor assumption rather than a poor market assessment. A favorable outcome may conceal weak reasoning. Research may revise a model or narrow a claim. The chain is therefore iterative and self-correcting when governed well.

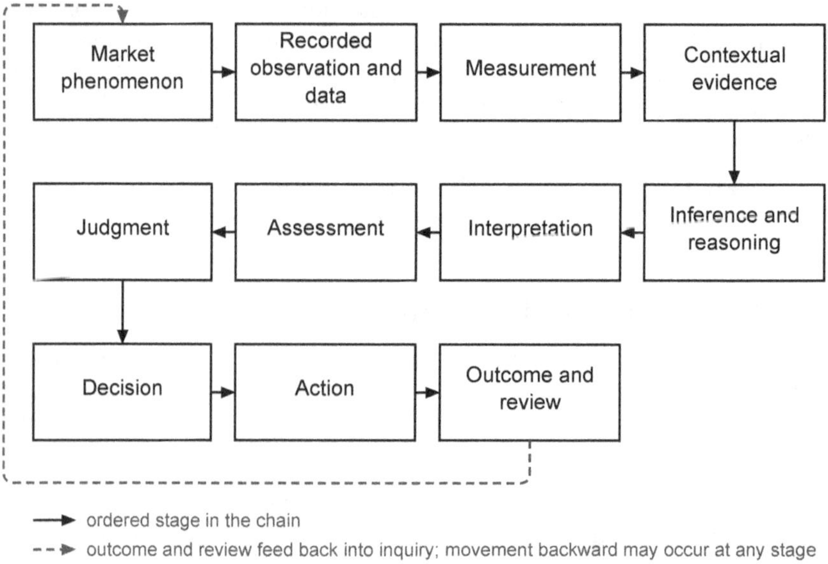

Figure 3.3 — The Market Inquiry Chain

> **Inquiry Principle:** The value of the chain lies in preserving the boundaries between stages while keeping every stage open to feedback and revision.

3.18 Worked Epistemic Example

Consider a hypothetical equity index that declines 1.8 percent during a trading session. The decline itself is not yet an explanation. A disciplined analysis separates what was recorded from what is measured, inferred, interpreted, and decided.

Layer	Illustrative statement
Recorded observation	The identified index source reports a 1.8% decline over the stated session.
Measurements	Realized variability rises; breadth weakens; quoted spreads widen moderately; displayed depth declines.
Evidence	Several measurements are relevant to the question of short-horizon market stress.
Inference	Exchange conditions appear less resilient than the selected baseline.
Interpretation	The decline appears broader and more adjustment-sensitive than an isolated price move.
Alternative hypothesis	A scheduled event produced temporary repricing without persistent structural deterioration.
Assessment	Short-horizon stress is developing; evidence of broader dysfunction remains incomplete; confidence is moderate.
Judgment	For a stated risk-management purpose, greater caution is warranted.
Decision	Participant-specific; depends on objectives, horizon, constraints, and risk capacity.
Action	May include maintaining exposure, reducing risk, hedging, waiting, or gathering more evidence.

The example demonstrates why the same underlying event can support a disciplined sequence without collapsing every layer into one narrative. It also shows where uncertainty enters and why participant action belongs downstream of market understanding rather than inside it.

Chapter Summary

Market knowledge begins with phenomena but reaches analysts through recorded observations. Those observations become useful through controlled measurements, and measurements become evidence only when they are interpreted relative to a defined question, baseline, horizon, and claim.

Inference, interpretation, assessment, judgment, decision, and action are distinct layers. Greater inferential distance generally increases dependence on assumptions and competing explanations. Hypotheses are testable proposed explanations rather than a higher grade of fact.

Models and measurements are selective representations. They can improve understanding precisely because they simplify, but they should never be treated as identical to the market. Derived quantities such as implied volatility retain the assumptions of the models used to construct them.

Uncertainty should be distinguished from missing information, model uncertainty, measurement uncertainty, and error. Confidence should be attached to specific claims and remain proportional to evidence validity, relevance, independence, completeness, and inferential distance.

Market Systems Science adopts a Principle of Provisional Knowledge. Strong conclusions are possible, but material understanding remains open to revision when evidence, measurements, models, or conditions change. Correction is therefore a normal feature of disciplined inquiry.

The Market Inquiry Chain connects market phenomenon, recorded data, measurement, evidence, reasoning, interpretation, assessment, judgment, decision, action, and review. Its purpose is not to make inquiry mechanical, but to preserve the boundaries that make claims traceable and revisable.

Established Knowledge

The epistemic principles in this chapter draw upon established work in epistemology, philosophy of science, scientific inference, measurement theory and metrology, statistics, empirical research methodology, causal reasoning, decision theory, model theory, uncertainty analysis, and systems science.

The Institute does not claim originality for the distinctions between observation and theory, provisional scientific knowledge, hypothesis testing, model uncertainty, measurement validity, Bayesian updating, causal inference, scientific replication, or decision theory. These are established intellectual traditions with extensive literatures and continuing debate.

Institute Perspective

The Institute's contribution is organizational and integrative. It applies established epistemic disciplines to a coherent market-analysis architecture that begins with observation rather than indicator-based recommendation and preserves the path from measurement to evidence, reasoning, assessment, judgment, and decision.

Within this architecture, provenance, inferential boundaries, uncertainty, competing explanations, participant dependence, and revision conditions are treated as part of the analysis rather than as optional disclaimers. Later chapters develop each layer in greater technical detail.

> **Institute Perspective:** Market education should begin with observation → measurement → evidence → reasoning → assessment → judgment → decision, not with indicator → forecast → trade.

Principles for Market Knowledge

Principle	Meaning
Observation Principle	Recorded observation establishes what an identified source reported, not complete meaning or cause.
Measurement Principle	Measurements are constructed representations, not the phenomena themselves.
Evidence Principle	A measurement becomes evidence only in relation to a defined question or proposition.
Inference Principle	Claims extending beyond measurement require explicit reasoning and assumptions.
Claim-Boundary Principle	Analytical statement types should not be treated as interchangeable.
Representation Principle	Every representation preserves selected features and omits others.
Scope Principle	Claims should identify material universe, horizon, method, and conditions.
Alternative-Explanation Principle	One plausible explanation does not eliminate competing or null explanations.
Uncertainty Principle	Better information can reduce uncertainty without eliminating it.
Confidence Principle	Confidence should be claim-specific and proportional to evidence quality.
Humility Principle	Intellectual humility means willingness to revise, not refusal to conclude.
Provisional-Knowledge Principle	Market knowledge remains open to revision when evidence, measurements, models, or conditions change.
Prediction-Boundary Principle	Predictive performance does not itself establish understanding or causation.
Decision-Boundary Principle	A market assessment does not determine one participant-independent action.
Correction Principle	Correction is evidence that disciplined inquiry is functioning.

Questions for Reflection

1. What distinguishes a market phenomenon from a recorded observation?
2. Why is an observed market event not automatically an explanation?
3. How does recorded data differ from a measurement?
4. Why is implied volatility a derived measurement rather than a directly observed market phenomenon?

5. When does a measurement become evidence?
6. Why does evidentiary meaning depend on the question being asked?
7. What distinguishes inference from interpretation?
8. What distinguishes interpretation from assessment?
9. Why is a hypothesis not simply a higher form of fact?
10. What is inferential distance?
11. Why may two analysts agree on measurements but disagree on interpretation?
12. Why should competing explanations be preserved?
13. What role should a null or minimal explanation play?
14. How can a model be useful while remaining incomplete?
15. What is lost or transformed as reality becomes data, measurements, and models?
16. What distinguishes uncertainty from error?
17. What distinguishes missing information from evidence that something is absent?
18. Why should confidence be claim-specific?
19. What does it mean for knowledge to be provisional?
20. Why does provisional knowledge not imply that all interpretations are equally valid?
21. Why should predictive success not automatically be interpreted as causal understanding?
22. What distinguishes judgment from decision?
23. Why can the same market assessment support different decisions?
24. What should cause a previously accepted interpretation to be revised?
25. Why does correction strengthen rather than weaken a scientific discipline?

Chapter 4. Universal Principles of Financial Markets

Durable Propositions for Studying Evolving Market Systems

Chapter Purpose

Financial markets change continuously. Instruments are created and retired. Trading venues evolve. Regulations shift. Technologies alter the speed, visibility, and cost of exchange. Participants develop new strategies, and those strategies change the environment in which later decisions are made.

Yet beneath this variation, certain broad propositions remain useful. Markets continue to organize exchange among heterogeneous participants. Prices continue to emerge through interaction. Behavior remains constrained, adaptive, and uncertain. Feedback can stabilize the system or amplify instability. Current conditions continue to depend partly upon the path through which they developed.

This chapter identifies a set of durable principles for studying financial markets as evolving systems. These principles are not presented as deterministic laws of price movement. They do not forecast the next return, identify a guaranteed strategy, or eliminate uncertainty. Their purpose is more fundamental: to establish boundaries for responsible explanation.

A valid market explanation should remain consistent with the realities of exchange, heterogeneity, interaction, constraint, adaptation, feedback, nonlinearity, path dependence, multidimensionality, scale, uncertainty, and continuous evolution. Explanations that ignore these properties may occasionally appear successful, but they remain incomplete representations of the system.

Learning Objectives

- Distinguish a principle from a tendency, recurring mechanism, empirical regularity, hypothesis, and scientific law.
- Explain why durable market principles should survive changes in instruments, institutions, and technology.
- Describe how exchange, heterogeneous participation, constraints, adaptation, and feedback shape market behavior.

- Explain why market effects may be nonlinear, path dependent, multidimensional, and horizon dependent.
- Recognize uncertainty as a permanent property of market inquiry rather than a defect to be eliminated.
- Use broad principles to evaluate explanations without treating the principles as mechanical predictions.

4.1 What Is a Market Principle?

The word principle is often used loosely. It may refer to a rule of conduct, a recurring observation, a mathematical relationship, a causal claim, or a personal belief. A scientific discipline requires greater precision.

Within Market Systems Science, a principle is a broad proposition that organizes understanding across many market contexts while remaining open to refinement. A principle identifies a durable feature of the system or a boundary that responsible explanations should respect. It is broader than a single empirical result, but weaker than a universal deterministic law.

A principle may remain useful even when its specific expression changes. For example, participants have always faced constraints, but the relevant constraints differ across an open-outcry commodity exchange, a modern electronic options market, a pension portfolio, and a decentralized digital-asset venue. The form changes. The underlying proposition—that behavior is constrained—remains useful.

Table 4.1 Types of Scientific and Analytical Claims

Claim Type	Meaning	Example of Appropriate Use
Principle	A broad proposition that organizes understanding across contexts.	Market behavior is shaped by participant constraints.
Tendency	A pattern that occurs frequently but not invariably.	Thin liquidity tends to increase price sensitivity to order imbalance.
Recurring mechanism	A process that repeatedly contributes to outcomes.	Leveraged losses can trigger forced selling through margin constraints.
Empirical regularity	A relationship repeatedly observed in data under stated conditions.	Volatility often clusters over particular samples and horizons.
Hypothesis	A proposed explanation that remains subject to testing.	A specific positioning imbalance may contribute to intraday acceleration.
Law	An exceptionally strong, clearly scoped, repeatedly validated relationship.	The term should be used sparingly in adaptive financial systems.

These categories should not be confused. A recurring mechanism can exist without producing the same outcome every time. An empirical regularity can weaken when institutions or participant behavior change. A hypothesis can be plausible without being established. A principle can guide inquiry without specifying a numerical prediction.

The discipline should therefore avoid converting useful tendencies into laws merely because they are familiar. Scientific language should reflect the strength, scope, and uncertainty of the underlying claim.

> Institute Distinction: A market principle defines a durable boundary for explanation. It does not guarantee a specific market outcome.

4.2 The Principle of Exchange

> **Financial markets exist to facilitate the exchange of financial claims, capital, and risk.**

At the most basic level, a market enables participants to transfer ownership, funding, exposure, or contractual obligations. A share transfers a claim on a corporation. A bond transfers capital in return for promised payments. A futures contract reallocates exposure to a future price. An option redistributes nonlinear risk. A foreign-exchange transaction exchanges one monetary claim for another.

The forms of exchange differ, but a transaction requires a mechanism through which willing participants can express and reconcile intentions. That mechanism includes instruments, rules, venues, clearing arrangements, settlement processes, information flows, and conventions for forming prices.

This principle prevents a common reduction: treating the market as merely a price series. Prices are important outputs of exchange, but the system also performs allocation, financing, hedging, inventory transfer, risk transformation, and information aggregation.

Exchange is therefore both an economic function and a systems process. The market converts intentions into observable activity through transactions, orders, quotations, positions, and changes in exposure.

> What is being exchanged, by whom, through which institutional mechanism, and under what constraints?

4.3 The Principle of Heterogeneous Participation

> **Market participants differ in objectives, information, beliefs, constraints, resources, and time horizons.**

A transaction does not require the buyer and seller to hold identical beliefs. It requires only that both accept the transaction terms at a particular moment. Their reasons may be entirely different.

A long-term investor may buy because expected future cash flows appear attractive. A dealer may sell the same instrument to manage inventory. A corporation may transact to hedge an operating exposure. An index fund may trade because of portfolio rules. A leveraged trader may reduce a position because of a risk limit. Each action can occur at the same price while reflecting a different decision environment.

Heterogeneity is not noise surrounding an otherwise uniform market. It is one of the conditions that makes exchange possible. Differences in valuation, timing, mandate, liquidity need, tax position, risk tolerance, and information create potential counterparties.

The same heterogeneity also complicates interpretation. Observed buying does not reveal one universal motive. A price increase does not prove that all participants became more optimistic. Market activity aggregates unlike decisions made for unlike reasons.

> Which classes of participants may be acting, and how might their objectives or constraints differ?

4.4 The Principle of Interactive Price Formation

> **Prices emerge from interaction among participants within institutional and liquidity constraints.**

Price is not discovered by observing an independent object called true value. It emerges through a process in which participants submit, revise, accept, or withdraw terms of exchange.

That process is shaped by the available market mechanism. An auction, dealer market, limit-order book, request-for-quote system, dark pool, and bilateral negotiation do not expose or reconcile intentions in the same way. Tick size, trading hours, queue rules, margin, clearing, transparency, and transaction costs can all influence the observed price path.

Prices therefore contain information, but they do not contain all information. They summarize completed or currently available terms of exchange. They do not directly reveal the full distribution of participant beliefs, hidden liquidity, unexpressed demand, latent constraints, or future reactions.

The principle also distinguishes price from value. Participants may estimate value differently, and those estimates may change. The market price is an outcome of interaction; value is an interpretation or model-dependent assessment.

What interaction produced the observed price, and what important conditions remain outside the price itself?

4.5 The Principle of Constrained Behavior

Market behavior is shaped not only by preferences, but also by capital, leverage, mandates, risk limits, collateral, regulation, time, and available liquidity.

Participants do not act in an unconstrained environment. An investor may prefer to hold an asset but still sell to meet redemptions. A dealer may believe a position is attractive but reduce it because inventory limits have been reached. A fund may recognize long-term value but remain unable to buy because its mandate, benchmark, or liquidity policy prohibits the exposure.

Constraints can transform opinions into actions that appear inconsistent with those opinions. Forced liquidation is the clearest example. A participant may sell not because expected value declined, but because leverage, margin, collateral, or funding conditions changed.

Constraints also vary across participants and through time. Rising volatility can tighten risk limits. Falling prices can increase margin requirements. Reduced liquidity can make the same desired trade more costly. Regulatory changes can alter permissible behavior. The system can therefore reorganize even when beliefs change only modestly.

This principle is essential for causal reasoning. Explanations that refer only to sentiment or information may miss the mechanisms through which constraints convert conditions into transactions.

What could participants want to do, what are they able to do, and what might they be forced to do?

4.6 The Principle of Adaptation

Participants modify behavior in response to information, incentives, outcomes, and the observed behavior of others.

Financial markets are populated by learning agents. Participants test strategies, imitate successful behavior, abandon failing approaches, change execution methods, alter risk limits, and respond to new technologies or regulations.

Adaptation means that a relationship observed in the past may change after it becomes widely recognized. A profitable strategy can attract capital, which can reduce the opportunity, shift the timing of the effect, or create new vulnerabilities. Market makers can adjust pricing when order flow changes. Institutions can redesign hedges after a stress event. Regulators can modify rules after a failure.

Adaptation also occurs at different speeds. Algorithms may respond in milliseconds. Portfolio managers may adjust over days or months. Institutions and regulation may evolve over years. These overlapping timescales create complex interactions.

A model that treats participant behavior as fixed may therefore perform well only while the environment remains sufficiently similar to the one in which it was developed.

> How might participants change their behavior because this relationship is known, exploited, regulated, or experienced?

4.7 The Principle of Feedback

> **Market actions alter the conditions to which participants subsequently respond.**

Feedback exists when an action changes the environment and the changed environment influences later action. This creates circular rather than purely linear causality.

Negative feedback tends to oppose movement. A price decline may attract value-oriented demand, reduce supply, or trigger stabilizing hedges. Positive feedback tends to reinforce movement. Rising prices may attract momentum demand, increase leverage capacity, or force short covering. Falling prices may trigger stop-losses, margin calls, redemptions, or defensive hedging.

The same mechanism can stabilize one configuration and destabilize another. Dealer hedging, for example, may oppose price movement under one exposure profile and reinforce it under another. The mechanism cannot be interpreted responsibly without context.

Feedback also connects market understanding to market evolution. A condition is not merely observed; participant responses to that condition can change the configuration itself.

> Does the observed response dampen the original movement, amplify it, or change character as conditions evolve?

4.8 The Principle of Nonlinearity

> **The magnitude of a market response need not be proportional to the magnitude of the initiating change.**

A small information update may produce little movement when liquidity is deep, positioning is balanced, and volatility is contained. The same update may produce a large movement when liquidity is thin, leverage is high, positioning is concentrated, and participants are near risk limits.

This is nonlinearity: equal inputs do not necessarily produce equal outputs. Thresholds, saturation, interaction effects, and feedback can cause the response function to change across configurations.

Nonlinearity helps explain why markets can appear stable for extended periods and then reorganize rapidly. The visible catalyst may be modest, while the underlying configuration has become fragile. The catalyst initiates the adjustment, but the system condition determines the scale and pathway of the response.

Nonlinearity also cautions against simple extrapolation. A relationship estimated during ordinary conditions may not remain proportional during stress.

> What features of the current configuration could amplify, suppress, delay, or redirect the response?

4.9 The Principle of Path Dependence

> **Current market behavior depends partly upon the sequence through which the present configuration developed.**

Two markets can display similar current prices and volatility while possessing different histories of positioning, liquidity, participation, and prior stress. Those histories may influence how participants respond next.

A gradual advance supported by broad participation may create a different configuration from a rapid rebound driven by short covering, even if both end at the same index level. A volatility decline following genuine stabilization may differ from a volatility decline caused by temporary suppression of realized movement. Current measurements must be interpreted in relation to the pathway that produced them.

Path dependence arises through memory embedded in positions, reference prices, gains and losses, institutional responses, collateral conditions, and learned behavior. Participants remember prior events. Portfolios carry exposures accumulated earlier. Rules and risk controls may have been changed because of past stress.

The present is therefore not fully described by a snapshot. Historical sequence can influence present sensitivity and future transition pathways.

> How did the market arrive here, and what residual exposures, reference points, or institutional memories remain?

4.10 The Principle of Multidimensional Conditions

No single variable can adequately represent the condition of a financial market.

Price alone cannot reveal whether movement is supported by deep liquidity or occurring through a thin market. Volume alone cannot reveal execution capacity. Volatility alone cannot distinguish orderly repricing from unstable stress. Positioning alone cannot determine whether concentrated exposure will persist, unwind, or remain inert.

Market condition emerges from the arrangement and interaction of multiple dimensions. A trend can be strong while liquidity deteriorates. Volatility can remain low while positioning concentration rises. Liquidity can appear adequate at ordinary trade sizes while becoming fragile under larger demand.

This principle prepares the observational architecture developed in Part II. The Institute organizes evidence into four foundational observational domains—liquidity, positioning, volatility, and trend—not because they exhaust market reality, but because they provide a disciplined starting structure for multidimensional observation.

A multidimensional approach does not mean collecting every available metric. It means selecting measurements that represent distinct aspects of the system and interpreting their interaction rather than allowing one indicator to dominate the assessment.

> Which dimensions are represented, which are missing, and how might their interaction alter the conclusion?

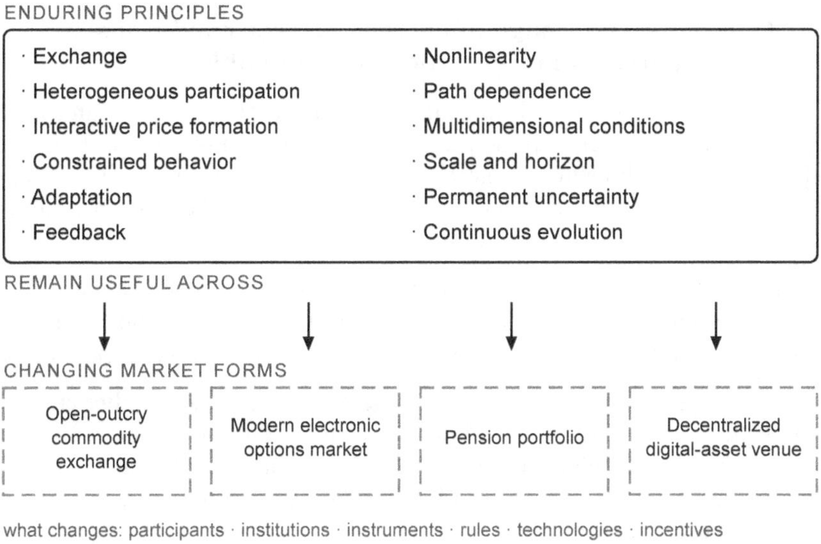

Figure 4.1 — Enduring Principles Across Changing Market Forms

4.11 The Principle of Scale and Horizon

> **Market relationships depend upon the instrument, level of aggregation, and time horizon being studied.**

A condition visible at one scale may be absent or reversed at another. An index may rise while many constituents fall. A market may display a long-term uptrend while undergoing a short-term liquidation. Liquidity may be deep for small orders but inadequate for institutional size. Volatility may be low on daily data while intraday instability increases.

Time horizon also changes the meaning of evidence. A short-term trader, pension fund, corporate treasurer, and market maker can observe the same market and reach different judgments because their objectives and exposure durations differ.

This does not imply that all interpretations are equally valid. Each claim must specify its scale, horizon, and purpose. A measurement appropriate for one question may be misleading for another.

The principle therefore supports disciplined scope. Analysts should avoid presenting a local relationship as a universal one or a short-horizon signal as a complete description of long-term condition.

> At what scale and horizon is the claim intended to hold, and would it remain meaningful if either changed?

4.12 The Principle of Permanent Uncertainty

> **Complete knowledge of current market conditions and future participant behavior is unattainable.**

Market observers work with incomplete, delayed, transformed, and model-dependent information. Hidden intentions remain unobserved. Future decisions cannot be known completely in advance. Relationships may change as participants adapt. Unexpected events can alter the system boundary itself.

Uncertainty is therefore not merely the absence of sufficient effort. Better data and models can reduce some uncertainty, but they cannot remove the openness of an adaptive system populated by decision-making participants.

This principle does not justify vague analysis. It creates a higher standard. Claims should identify what is known, what is inferred, what remains uncertain, and what evidence would cause revision. Confidence should be proportional to measurement quality, explanatory coherence, and the stability of relevant relationships.

Permanent uncertainty also separates disciplined assessment from prediction theater. The purpose of analysis is not to manufacture certainty. It is to produce the most defensible understanding permitted by available evidence.

> What remains unknown, how could it matter, and what evidence would change the assessment?

4.13 The Principle of Continuous Evolution

> **Markets evolve as participants, institutions, instruments, rules, technologies, and incentives change.**

Market structure is not fixed. New instruments create new exposures. Automation changes execution. Regulation alters permissible behavior. Clearing and margin arrangements redistribute risk. Data availability changes what participants can observe. Institutional growth changes who dominates activity.

A durable theory must therefore distinguish enduring concepts from temporary implementations. Liquidity is an enduring phenomenon; a particular order-book feed is one technology for observing it. Positioning is an enduring domain; a specific derivatives dataset is one incomplete representation. Price formation is enduring; the venue and matching protocol may change.

Continuous evolution means that classifications, measurements, and models require periodic revalidation. A framework should endure only to the extent that evidence continues to support its usefulness.

This principle also preserves the openness of Market Systems Science. The discipline is not committed to defending a fixed vocabulary or model against better evidence. It is committed to improving the quality of market inquiry.

> Which features are enduring system properties, and which depend upon the present institutional or technological implementation?

4.14 Principles Define Boundaries, Not Predictions

The principles in this chapter constrain explanation, but they do not mechanically determine outcomes. Knowing that participants are heterogeneous does not reveal which group will dominate the next interval. Knowing that feedback exists does not establish whether it will be stabilizing or destabilizing. Knowing that markets are nonlinear does not identify the location of a threshold.

The principles are most useful as questions imposed upon analysis. Does the explanation identify the exchange process? Does it account for participant differences and constraints? Does it consider adaptation and feedback? Is the relationship scoped by horizon and market structure? Does the conclusion acknowledge multidimensional evidence and uncertainty?

An explanation that satisfies these questions may still prove wrong. Scientific quality does not guarantee a correct forecast. It improves traceability, limits overstatement, and makes error more informative when outcomes differ from expectations.

The principles therefore belong primarily to the architecture of understanding. Some also describe market evolution, and several affect participant judgment. None should be converted directly into a universal trading instruction.

Table 4.2 Relationship to the Three Foundational Pillars

Foundational Pillar	Relevant Principles	Primary Contribution
Market Understanding	Exchange; heterogeneous participation; interactive price formation; multidimensional conditions; scale and horizon; permanent uncertainty	Defines what must be observed and how claims should be scoped.
Market Evolution	Constraints; adaptation; feedback; nonlinearity; path dependence; continuous evolution	Explains why configurations reorganize and why transitions may vary.
Market Judgment	Heterogeneous participation; constraints; scale and horizon; permanent uncertainty	Prevents universal recommendations and supports participant-specific judgment.

4.15 A Worked Example: One Event, Different System Responses

Consider an unexpected policy announcement that is moderately unfavorable to risk assets. The information is identical in each of the following hypothetical markets, but the system configurations differ.

In Market A, liquidity is deep, leverage is moderate, positioning is balanced, volatility is already elevated, and participants have recently reduced risk. Prices decline modestly, buyers appear, and the market stabilizes.

In Market B, liquidity has deteriorated, leveraged exposure is concentrated, volatility has been suppressed, and many participants hold similar positions. The initial decline triggers risk limits, dealer hedging, stop orders, and forced selling. The visible announcement is moderate, but the response is large.

The difference cannot be explained by the information alone. The principles identify the missing structure. Participants are heterogeneous but constrained. Price forms interactively. Feedback changes as the move develops. The response is nonlinear. The path of prior risk accumulation matters. Multiple dimensions of condition must be considered.

This example demonstrates why a catalyst should not be confused with a complete explanation. Events interact with configurations. The same event can produce different outcomes because the system through which it propagates is different.

Chapter Summary

Financial markets vary across instruments, institutions, historical periods, and technologies, yet several broad propositions remain useful for disciplined inquiry.

Markets facilitate exchange among heterogeneous participants. Prices emerge through interaction. Participant behavior is constrained and adaptive. Actions alter later conditions through feedback. Responses may be nonlinear and path dependent. Market condition is multidimensional and dependent upon scale and horizon. Uncertainty cannot be eliminated, and the system continually evolves.

These propositions should be treated as principles rather than deterministic laws. They define boundaries for responsible explanation, not formulas for guaranteed prediction. Their purpose is to improve the structure, scope, and humility of market reasoning.

The next part of this volume converts these broad principles into an observational architecture. It begins by organizing market evidence into four foundational observational domains: liquidity, positioning, volatility, and trend.

Established Knowledge

The chapter synthesizes concepts that are well established across financial economics, market microstructure, behavioral finance, institutional analysis, and complex adaptive systems. These include heterogeneous agents, constrained optimization, price formation through interaction, feedback, nonlinearity, path dependence, scale dependence, adaptive behavior, and uncertainty. The specific organization of these ideas into a unified set of governing principles for Market Systems Science is a scholarly synthesis rather than a claim that each concept originated within the Institute.

Institute Perspective

The WallStreetDelta Institute treats these principles as a provisional foundation for disciplined market inquiry. They are intended to survive changes in data vendors, software, execution technology, and specific analytical models. Future research may refine the wording, add principles, divide existing ones, or demonstrate that certain propositions require narrower scope. Their value depends upon their continuing ability to organize evidence and improve explanation.

The Institute therefore adopts a principle of revision: governing principles should be retained only while they remain coherent, empirically defensible, and useful across relevant market contexts.

Questions for Reflection

1. Why is a principle different from a deterministic law?
2. How can two participants transact at the same price for entirely different reasons?
3. What information about the market is not contained in price alone?
4. How can constraints cause participants to act against their stated beliefs or preferences?
5. Why may a profitable relationship weaken after it becomes widely recognized?
6. What distinguishes stabilizing feedback from destabilizing feedback?
7. How can a modest catalyst produce a large market response?
8. Why can two markets with similar current measurements respond differently because of their histories?
9. What does it mean to describe market condition as multidimensional?
10. How can the same evidence support different judgments at different horizons?
11. Why can better data reduce uncertainty without eliminating it?
12. Which market properties are enduring, and which depend upon current technology or institutional structure?
13. How should an analyst use principles without converting them into trading rules?
14. What evidence would justify revising or rejecting one of the principles in this chapter?
15. Which additional principle, if any, would improve the framework, and how could it be tested?

Part II. Market Understanding

Chapter 5. The Four Foundational Observational Domains

An Organizing Framework for Market Observation

Chapter Purpose

The preceding chapters defined financial markets as evolving systems, explained why a systems perspective is necessary, established a philosophy of provisional knowledge, and identified broad principles that remain useful across instruments, periods, and technologies. This chapter begins the manuscript's observational architecture.

Modern markets generate immense quantities of data: transactions, quotations, order-book changes, holdings reports, option prices, open interest, volatility estimates, cross-asset movements, macroeconomic releases, and countless derived indicators. The analytical problem is not merely how to collect more information. It is how to organize diverse observations without confusing measurements with the phenomena they attempt to represent.

Market Systems Science proposes four foundational observational domains—liquidity, positioning, volatility, and trend—as a disciplined starting point for organizing evidence about market conditions. These domains are not presented as universal laws, exhaustive categories, independent causes, or predictive signals. They are proposed conceptual categories through which related measurements may be grouped, compared, and interpreted.

The purpose of this chapter is to define an observational domain, explain why these four domains were selected, clarify their distinct roles and permeable boundaries, disclose the assumptions and limitations of the framework, and establish standards by which future research may evaluate, revise, expand, or reject it.

Learning Objectives

- Define an observational domain and distinguish it from a phenomenon, measurement, indicator, model, and causal mechanism.
- Explain why complex market evidence benefits from a multidomain organizing architecture.

- Describe the foundational observational questions associated with liquidity, positioning, volatility, and trend.
- Recognize that a single measurement may contribute evidence to more than one domain.
- Explain why the domains are analytically distinct but not independent.
- Understand the difference between an organizing framework and a predictive model.
- Identify the design assumptions, intended benefits, limitations, and open research questions of the four-domain architecture.
- Describe how the framework may be verified and validated through future theoretical and empirical research.

5.1 Why Market Observation Requires an Organizing Architecture

Complex systems generate more observable detail than any analyst can interpret directly. A financial market contains participants, institutions, instruments, rules, technologies, incentives, constraints, information flows, and feedback processes. Each component produces observable activity, but the activity does not arrive preclassified according to meaning.

A trade record may indicate that an exchange occurred, but it does not by itself explain whether the market was liquid, whether a participant was forced to transact, whether uncertainty was rising, or whether the transaction contributed to a durable trend. A change in an option premium may reflect changing volatility expectations, altered supply and demand, interest-rate effects, time decay, or a shift in positioning. The same observation may therefore support several possible interpretations.

Without an organizing architecture, analysts often respond to complexity in one of two ways. The first is accumulation: more indicators, more dashboards, and more data feeds are added in the hope that quantity will produce understanding. The second is reduction: one favored indicator is treated as if it represents the entire market. Both approaches are inadequate.

Accumulation can produce informational overload without conceptual clarity. Reduction can create false confidence by assigning excessive meaning to a partial measurement. An organizing architecture addresses a different question: Which observations belong together, what dimension of market behavior do they illuminate, and how should their combined meaning be evaluated?

> **Institute Proposition:** Better market understanding requires not only more observations, but also a disciplined architecture

for relating measurements to phenomena and phenomena to system-level interpretation.

5.2 What Is an Observational Domain?

An observational domain is a conceptual category used to organize evidence concerning one dimension of market behavior. It provides a stable vocabulary for grouping related observations while preserving the distinction between what exists in the market and how that condition is measured.

Definition — Observational Domain

An observational domain is a conceptual category that organizes multiple forms of evidence describing one dimension of market behavior. An observational domain is not itself a measurement, indicator, causal force, or predictive model. It provides a structured context within which related observations may be interpreted.

This definition contains several boundaries. First, the domain is not identical to the phenomenon. Liquidity, for example, is a property of the market's capacity for exchange. The liquidity domain is the analytical category within which evidence about that property is organized.

Second, the domain is not a measurement. A bid–ask spread, quoted depth, market-impact estimate, or order-book recovery time may provide evidence concerning liquidity, but none is liquidity itself. Each measurement represents only selected characteristics of the broader phenomenon.

Third, the domain is not an indicator or index. An indicator combines or transforms measurements according to a rule. A domain remains a conceptual category even when no single numerical indicator has been assigned to it.

Fourth, the domain is not a causal force in the physical sense. Conditions within one domain may influence another, but the category itself does not act upon the market. The term force may be useful when describing pressure, influence, or feedback, but it should not replace the more precise scholarly term domain.

Finally, the domain is not a predictive model. Organizing evidence into liquidity, positioning, volatility, and trend does not by itself determine what price will do next. Prediction requires additional assumptions, definitions, estimation procedures, validation, and explicit treatment of uncertainty.

Concept	Meaning	Example
Phenomenon or system property	The aspect of market reality being studied.	The market's capacity to absorb transactions.

Concept	Meaning	Example
Data	Recorded events or reported values.	Bid, ask, size, trade price, timestamp.
Measurement	A defined representation constructed from data.	Bid–ask spread or estimated price impact.
Evidence	A measurement interpreted as relevant to a claim.	Persistently widening spreads support concern about weakening liquidity.
Observational domain	A conceptual category organizing related evidence.	Liquidity.
Interpretation	A reasoned statement about what the evidence may mean.	Exchange capacity is deteriorating at the current horizon.
Model	A selective representation used for description, estimation, classification, or prediction.	A liquidity-state classifier using spread, depth, and resilience.

5.3 From Market Activity to Domain-Based Understanding

The four-domain framework occupies a specific position within the hierarchy of market understanding. Market activity produces observable records. Those records become measurements only after selection, definition, transformation, and quality control. Measurements become evidence when they are judged relevant to a question or claim. Evidence is then organized within observational domains before being synthesized into broader market understanding.

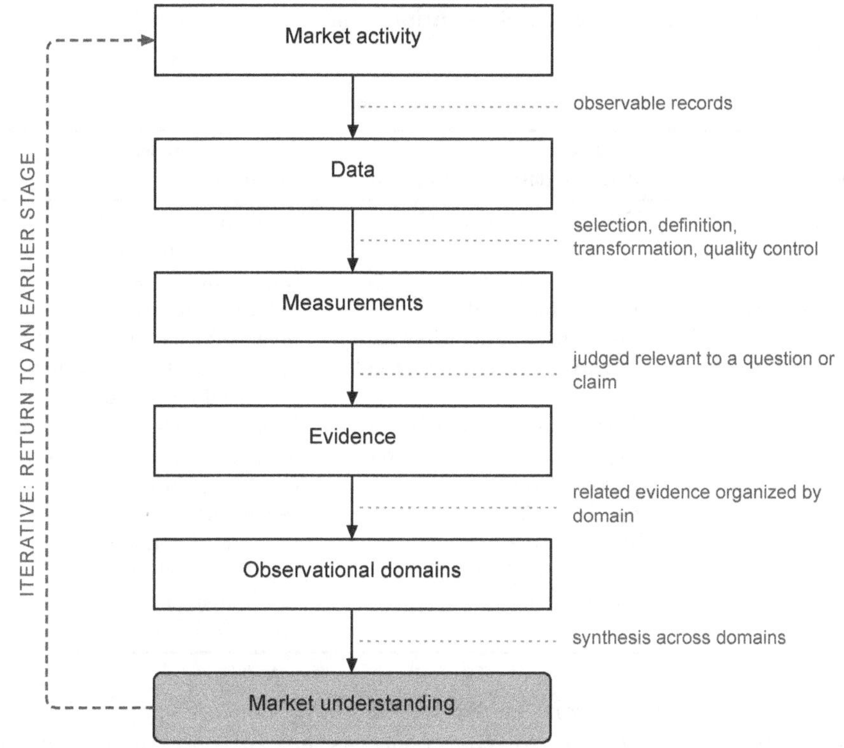

Figure 5.1 — Market Activity → Data → Measurements → Evidence → Observational Domains → Market Understanding

This sequence is not a rigid one-way pipeline. Research is iterative. A preliminary interpretation may reveal that a measurement is poorly defined, that additional data are required, or that the domain assignment is ambiguous. The analyst may return to an earlier stage, revise the measurement, reconsider the evidence, or redefine the question.

Chapter 11 will examine measurements in detail, and Chapter 12 will develop the standards by which measurements become evidence. The present chapter establishes the intermediate organizing function of observational domains: they make it possible to reason about multiple measurements without treating the collection as an undifferentiated list.

5.4 Why These Four Domains?

The selection of liquidity, positioning, volatility, and trend is a design proposition. It was not derived from a claim that all financial-market reality can be divided naturally and exclusively into four parts. The selection emerged from the attempt to identify a parsimonious set of categories broad enough to organize important market observations while distinct enough to preserve analytical meaning.

Each domain addresses a foundational observational question:

Domain	**Foundational observational question**	**Primary object of attention**
Liquidity	What is the market's current capacity to facilitate exchange?	Immediacy, cost, depth, counterparties, market impact, and resilience.
Positioning	How is financial exposure distributed, and where are sensitivities concentrated?	Holdings, leverage, inventory, hedging needs, option sensitivities, and potential response.
Volatility	How is uncertainty being expressed through prices, expectations, and variability?	Realized movement, implied expectations, asymmetry, term structure, and sensitivity.
Trend	What directional persistence is emerging through time?	Direction, persistence, breadth, participation, relative strength, and structural continuity.

The four questions are complementary. Liquidity concerns capacity. Positioning concerns exposure. Volatility concerns the expression of uncertainty. Trend concerns emergent direction. Together they create a multidimensional vocabulary for describing market conditions without reducing the market to price alone.

The selection also reflects an intended balance between parsimony and coverage. A framework with too few categories may collapse distinct phenomena into one label. A framework with too many categories may become difficult to use consistently, produce overlapping classifications, and obscure rather than organize understanding.

Parsimony, however, is not proof of completeness. Funding, collateral, credit transmission, information flow, participation, and institutional structure may in some contexts deserve separate treatment. Future research should determine whether such concepts are best treated as independent domains, subdomains, cross-domain influences, or external conditions.

5.5 Liquidity — Capacity for Exchange

Liquidity is the observational domain concerned with the market's capacity to facilitate exchange with acceptable immediacy, cost, depth, and resilience.

Every transaction depends upon a counterparty willing and able to exchange financial claims. Yet the ability to complete a transaction is not binary. Markets differ in how quickly transactions can occur, how much size can be exchanged, how much price must adjust, how costly execution becomes, and how readily conditions recover after an imbalance.

Liquidity is therefore broader than trading volume. High volume may coexist with poor execution quality when transactions occur under stress, spreads widen, depth disappears, or prices move sharply in response to modest orders. Low volume may coexist with adequate liquidity when available counterparties and market depth are sufficient for the size of intended transactions.

Measurements associated with the liquidity domain may include spreads, quoted and executed depth, market impact, turnover, order-book imbalance, cancellation behavior, trade-size distributions, execution shortfall, and resilience after shocks. No single measurement captures the domain completely.

Chapter 6 examines liquidity as a phenomenon, its observable manifestations, measurement approaches, interactions, limitations, and common misuses.

5.6 Positioning — Distribution of Exposure

Positioning is the observational domain concerned with the distribution of financial exposure, sensitivity, leverage, inventory, and potential participant response.

Markets contain participants with different holdings, liabilities, hedges, leverage, mandates, and sensitivities. These exposures influence how participants may respond when prices, volatility, funding conditions, or information change.

Positioning may remain latent. A concentrated exposure does not necessarily produce immediate price movement. Its importance may become visible only when a threshold is crossed, a hedge must be adjusted, collateral requirements change, losses accumulate, or liquidity deteriorates.

Observable evidence may include reported holdings, futures commitments, open interest, dealer inventory estimates, option sensitivity measures, short interest, fund flows, leverage proxies, cross-sectional concentration, and signs of forced or mechanical trading. Many positioning measures are incomplete, delayed, estimated, or model dependent.

The domain therefore concerns not merely where participants appear to be positioned, but also how the distribution of exposure may shape potential demand for liquidity and sensitivity to future market changes. Chapter 7 develops this domain in depth.

5.7 Volatility — Expression of Uncertainty

Volatility is the observational domain concerned with how uncertainty, changing expectations, disagreement, and sensitivity are expressed through market prices and derivative valuations.

Volatility is often treated as a synonym for risk or fear. That usage is too narrow. Realized volatility describes the variability of observed price movement under a specified method and horizon. Implied volatility reflects information embedded in option prices and depends upon model assumptions, supply and demand, expected events, hedging activity, and risk premia.

Volatility evidence may include realized and implied volatility, skew, term structure, volatility-of-volatility, gap frequency, intraday range, tail pricing, cross-asset volatility, dispersion, and the relationship between price movement and volatility changes.

The same level of volatility may carry different meaning under different market conditions. Elevated volatility with deep liquidity and balanced positioning may represent active adjustment. The same volatility with concentrated exposure and deteriorating liquidity may indicate fragility. Volatility must therefore be interpreted in context rather than ranked mechanically as good or bad.

Chapter 8 examines volatility as the observable expression of uncertainty and distinguishes its measurements, interpretations, interactions, and limitations.

5.8 Trend — Emergence of Direction

Trend is the observational domain concerned with the emergence, persistence, breadth, and organization of directional movement through time.

Trend differs from the other domains because it is primarily an emergent condition rather than a single underlying cause. Persistent directional movement may arise from repeated interactions among information, liquidity, positioning, volatility, expectations, and participant adaptation.

Trend evidence may include returns across horizons, moving relationships, breadth, participation, relative strength, persistence, autocorrelation, leadership, volume confirmation, and the stability of directional structure.

Once a trend becomes visible, it can influence the system that produced it. Participants may enter because they observe persistence. Risk managers may reduce exposure because losses accumulate. Dealers may adjust hedges. Volatility expectations may change. Liquidity providers may alter their willingness to quote. Trend is therefore both an emergent result and a subsequent source of feedback.

Trend should not be equated automatically with value, durability, causation, or future continuation. A strong observed trend may be broad and resilient, or narrow and fragile. Chapter 9 examines the emergence of direction and the evidence needed to distinguish among different forms of trend.

5.9 Domain Boundaries Are Useful but Permeable

The four domains are analytically distinct, but their boundaries are not perfectly sealed. A measurement may provide evidence concerning more than one domain, and the significance of one domain may depend upon the condition of the others.

Measurement or observation	Primary domain association	Possible cross-domain relevance
Bid–ask spread	Liquidity	May widen because volatility rises or market makers reduce risk due to positioning.
Open interest	Positioning	May alter future liquidity demand and affect volatility sensitivity.
Implied-volatility skew	Volatility	May also reflect protective positioning, dealer inventory, or event demand.
Market breadth	Trend	May reveal participation concentration and potential liquidity fragility.
Trading volume	Liquidity or trend, depending on use	May reflect exchange capacity, directional participation, repositioning, or forced activity.
Dealer gamma estimate	Positioning	May shape hedging flows, liquidity demand, realized volatility, and trend behavior.

Permeability does not make the framework meaningless. It reflects the interconnected nature of market systems. The purpose of classification is not to pretend that observations possess only one interpretation. It is to make the analyst explicit about which dimension is being examined and what alternative meanings remain possible.

A rigid classification rule may create false precision. An entirely unstructured approach may create inconsistency. The appropriate posture is disciplined flexibility: assign evidence according to a stated analytical purpose, disclose cross-domain relevance, and avoid double counting when measurements are later combined.

5.10 Domains Are Distinct but Not Independent

Markets do not experience liquidity, positioning, volatility, and trend separately. The domains interact continuously, often through feedback.

- Concentrated positioning may remain stable while liquidity is deep but become fragile when exchange capacity deteriorates.
- Rising volatility may be absorbed without major directional change when positioning is balanced and liquidity remains resilient.
- A persistent trend may attract additional exposure, increasing concentration and future sensitivity.
- Apparently calm volatility may coexist with weakening liquidity and increasingly one-sided positioning.
- A liquidity shock may force position reduction, intensify volatility, and transform a weak directional movement into a disorderly trend.
- A broad trend supported by participation and functional liquidity may behave differently from a narrow trend sustained by mechanical hedging.

These examples illustrate why isolated indicators are often misleading. A low volatility reading does not necessarily indicate stability. A strong trend does not necessarily indicate healthy participation. A large position does not necessarily imply imminent pressure. A high-volume market is not necessarily liquid for every transaction size.

> **Multidomain Principle:** The meaning of any observational domain depends partly upon the condition of the others. Market understanding therefore requires multidomain interpretation rather than isolated indicator reading.

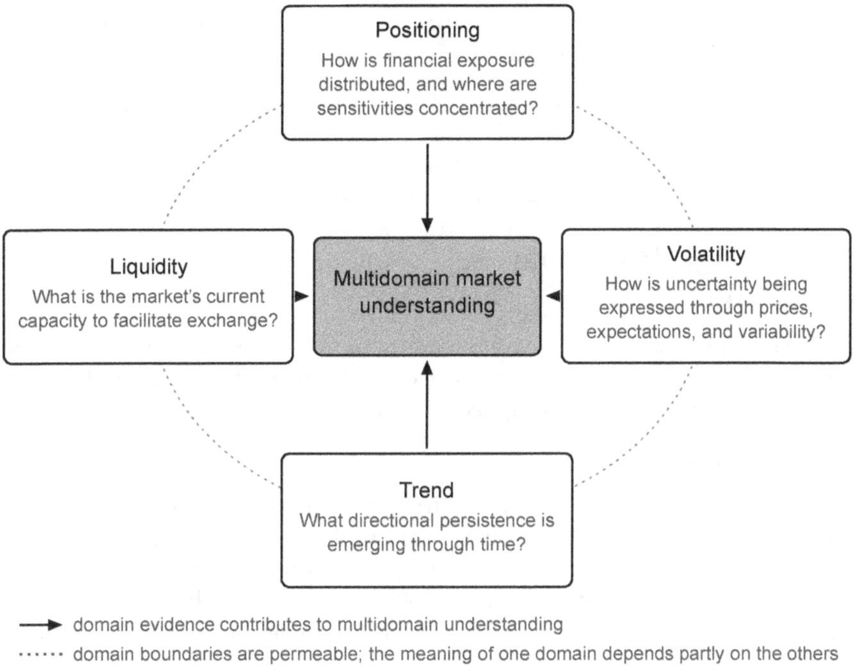

Figure 5.2 — The Four Foundational Observational Domains surrounding Multidomain Market Understanding

5.11 A Framework, Not a Formula or Model

The four-domain architecture is an organizing framework. It should not be confused with a formula, scoring system, state classifier, or predictive model.

By itself, the framework does not:

- calculate a market state;
- assign numerical weights to measurements;
- determine whether a domain is favorable or unfavorable;
- generate entry or exit signals;
- predict direction, return, or volatility;
- establish causation merely by categorizing evidence;
- guarantee completeness or eliminate uncertainty.

A later model may use evidence from the four domains to estimate a configuration, classify a state, detect a transition, or support a decision. That model must be defined separately. Its inputs, transformations, assumptions, thresholds, training procedures, validation data, failure modes, and uncertainty must be documented.

This boundary protects the conceptual framework from being judged by claims it does not make. It also protects models from borrowing unearned authority from foundational language. A model does not become valid merely because its inputs have been assigned to well-named domains.

5.12 Design Rationale

Design Objective

The design objective is to create a parsimonious but sufficiently broad architecture for organizing diverse market observations into conceptually meaningful categories that can support multidomain reasoning.

Problem Addressed

Market analysis frequently suffers from indicator accumulation, inconsistent terminology, isolated interpretation, and confusion among phenomena, measurements, and models. The framework is intended to create a common structure through which different forms of evidence can be related without claiming that one measurement represents the market as a whole.

Core Assumptions

1. Market condition is multidimensional and cannot be represented adequately by price or any single metric.
2. Related measurements can be organized into conceptually coherent observational domains.
3. Liquidity, positioning, volatility, and trend capture important but not exhaustive dimensions of market behavior.
4. Interactions among domains contain information that isolated measurements do not.
5. Domain assignments depend upon analytical purpose, definitions, horizon, and data quality.
6. The usefulness of the architecture must ultimately be evaluated through transparent theoretical and empirical research.

Intended Benefits

- Clearer separation of phenomena from measurements and model outputs.
- Reduced dependence on isolated indicators.
- A consistent vocabulary across instruments and analytical methods.
- A bridge from measurements and evidence to system-level understanding.
- An explicit basis for studying multidomain interactions.

- An extensible structure that can be revised as research and data improve.

5.13 Limitations and Failure Modes

The framework should be evaluated most carefully where it appears most foundational. Later analysis may inherit its errors, omissions, or ambiguities. The following limitations are therefore part of the framework, not objections to be concealed.

- Important market phenomena may not fit clearly within the four domains.
- Domain boundaries may become ambiguous, especially when one measurement reflects several mechanisms.
- The framework may produce redundant classifications or encourage double counting.
- A domain with abundant data may be overemphasized relative to a domain that is difficult to observe.
- The same measurement may have different meaning across instruments, venues, regimes, and time horizons.
- A domain label may create an appearance of understanding when the underlying measurements remain weak or model dependent.
- Interaction patterns may be unstable, nonlinear, or unobservable in real time.
- The four-domain architecture may not improve explanation, classification, or decision quality compared with alternative organizations.
- Commercial implementation may bias the framework toward data that are available rather than phenomena that are important.

These failure modes create a responsibility to distinguish unknown from unavailable, estimated from directly observed, and conceptually relevant from empirically validated.

5.14 Open Research Questions

- Should funding and collateral be treated as a distinct observational domain?
- Is credit transmission a subdomain of liquidity, an independent domain, or an external system condition?
- Should information flow be represented as a domain or as a cross-domain influence?
- Does participation or breadth belong entirely within trend?
- Can the sufficiency of the four domains be tested empirically?
- Do multidomain assessments improve description or state classification relative to isolated metrics?
- How stable are domain meanings across equities, futures, options, fixed income, foreign exchange, and digital assets?

- How should evidence be assigned when one measurement contributes materially to several domains?
- Can domain interaction be represented without imposing arbitrary weights?
- What failure cases would justify dividing, combining, extending, or rejecting the architecture?

5.15 Standards for Future Verification and Validation

The framework is a scholarly proposition, not a completed doctrine. Future research should evaluate both its conceptual coherence and its practical usefulness.

Evaluation dimension	Research question
Coverage	Can relevant market evidence be organized coherently without forcing important phenomena into unsuitable categories?
Discriminant usefulness	Do the domains represent meaningfully different conditions, or are they redundant?
Measurement reliability	Do domain assessments remain reasonably stable across valid measurement choices and data sources?
Interpretive value	Does domain organization improve the clarity and traceability of market reasoning?
Interaction value	Do multidomain relationships reveal information that isolated measurements omit?
Generalizability	Does the architecture remain useful across instruments, venues, periods, and technologies?
Predictive value	Where prediction is explicitly studied, does domain-based evidence improve out-of-sample performance under stated conditions?
Decision-support value	Does the framework improve decision quality after participant-specific constraints are considered?
Failure analysis	Where does classification create confusion, instability, or no analytical improvement?
Revisability	Can the architecture be refined without protecting existing terminology from evidence-based correction?

Verification asks whether the framework has been defined and applied as intended. Validation asks whether the framework is useful for its intended analytical purposes in real market contexts. A framework may be internally consistent yet fail to improve understanding. Conversely, practical usefulness does not excuse vague definitions or untraceable reasoning. Both standards are necessary.

5.16 Preparing for the Domain Chapters

Chapters 6 through 9 examine each domain separately using a common scholarly architecture. Each chapter will distinguish the phenomenon, observable manifestations, measurements, evidence, interpretation, interactions, limitations, common misuse, and Institute perspective.

That separation is necessary for clarity, but it is temporary. Chapter 10 will return to the central systems proposition: the market's condition cannot be represented adequately by any single domain because system behavior emerges from interactions among domains.

The four-domain architecture therefore serves two functions. It divides complexity so that each dimension can be studied carefully, and it prepares those dimensions to be recombined into multidomain understanding.

Chapter Summary

Market Systems Science proposes liquidity, positioning, volatility, and trend as four foundational observational domains for organizing the study of market conditions.

Liquidity describes the market's capacity for exchange. Positioning describes the distribution of exposure and sensitivity. Volatility describes the expression of uncertainty and variability. Trend describes the emergence and persistence of direction through time.

These domains are not presented as universal laws, exhaustive dimensions, independent causes, or predictive signals. They are a proposed observational architecture through which diverse measurements may be organized and interpreted.

Domain boundaries are useful but permeable. A measurement may contribute evidence to more than one domain, and the meaning of each domain depends partly upon the condition of the others. Market understanding therefore requires multidomain interpretation rather than isolated indicator reading.

The framework is provisional and testable. Its value should be judged by coverage, discriminant usefulness, measurement reliability, interpretive clarity, interaction value, generalizability, documented failure cases, and its capacity to remain open to correction.

Established Knowledge

Liquidity, positioning, volatility, and trend are not inventions of Market Systems Science. Each is deeply established within financial economics, market microstructure, asset pricing, derivatives research, portfolio and risk management, behavioral finance, and quantitative analysis.

Existing scholarship has developed extensive theories and measurements concerning transaction costs, market depth, price impact, inventory, leverage, holdings, open interest, volatility estimation, option-implied expectations, momentum, trend persistence, and market participation.

The distinction between a market phenomenon and any single measurement of that phenomenon is likewise consistent with broader scientific practice. Measurements are selective representations whose meaning depends upon definition, sampling, data quality, context, and purpose.

Institute Perspective

The Institute's proposed contribution is not the invention of the four concepts individually. It is the organization of liquidity, positioning, volatility, and trend as complementary observational domains within a unified market-reasoning architecture.

The framework further proposes that measurements should be interpreted as evidence concerning one or more domains, that domain boundaries may remain permeable, and that market understanding arises from relationships, interactions, and changes across domains rather than from isolated indicators.

This architecture should endure only to the extent that evidence continues to justify it. Future research may refine, divide, combine, expand, or reject the domains. Such revision would represent the maturation of the discipline rather than a failure of institutional consistency.

Questions for Reflection

1. Why does greater access to market data not necessarily produce better market understanding?
2. What distinguishes an observational domain from a market phenomenon?
3. What distinguishes an observational domain from a measurement or indicator?
4. Can one measurement contribute evidence to multiple domains? Give an example.
5. Why should the four domains not be described as universal market forces?
6. What important market phenomenon might not fit clearly within the proposed framework?
7. Why is liquidity broader than trading volume?
8. Why can positioning matter before it becomes visible in price movement?
9. Why should volatility not be equated automatically with risk or fear?
10. In what sense is trend an emergent condition?

11. How can an emergent trend later influence the conditions that produced it?
12. Why should domain boundaries remain permeable rather than rigid?
13. What evidence would suggest that the four-domain architecture is incomplete or redundant?
14. How might domain meanings change across instruments or time horizons?
15. What standards should be used to verify and validate an observational architecture?

Chapter 6. Liquidity: The Market's Capacity for Exchange

Chapter Purpose

Liquidity is one of the most frequently discussed and most easily oversimplified concepts in financial markets. It is often described as the ability to buy or sell an asset without materially affecting price. That description is useful, but incomplete. It does not specify transaction size, urgency, venue, time horizon, side of the market, or the conditions under which exchange must occur.

This chapter develops liquidity as the first foundational observational domain within Market Systems Science. Liquidity is treated as a multidimensional and conditional capacity of the market system rather than as a single number, a permanent property of an asset, or a synonym for trading volume.

The chapter distinguishes the liquidity phenomenon from its observable manifestations, measurements, evidence, and interpretations. It explains how liquidity arises from participant interaction, how it changes under stress, how it interacts with positioning, volatility, and trend, and why no single metric can represent the market's complete capacity for exchange.

Learning Objectives

- Define liquidity from economic, execution, and systems perspectives.
- Distinguish liquidity from volume, activity, and price stability.
- Explain why liquidity depends on transaction size, time horizon, venue, urgency, and market condition.
- Identify the principal dimensions of liquidity, including immediacy, cost, depth, breadth, impact, resilience, continuity, and replenishment.
- Distinguish observable manifestations, measurements, evidence, and interpretations of liquidity.
- Evaluate the uses and limitations of common liquidity measurements and proxies.
- Explain the differences among displayed, hidden, realized, latent, and committed liquidity.

- Understand how liquidity interacts with positioning, volatility, and trend.
- Recognize common analytical misuses and limitations of liquidity analysis.

6.1 Liquidity as a Market Phenomenon

Governing Definition

Liquidity is the market's capacity to facilitate exchange with a given degree of immediacy, cost, depth, price impact, and resilience under specified conditions.

The shorter expression—liquidity is the market's capacity for exchange—captures the central idea. The longer definition establishes the conditions under which that capacity must be evaluated.

Liquidity is a capacity, not an event. A completed transaction demonstrates that exchange occurred, but it does not by itself reveal how much additional exchange could have occurred, at what cost, how quickly, or with what market impact. Liquidity concerns the readiness and ability of the market to accommodate intended transactions.

Liquidity exists in degrees. A market may be highly liquid for one order size and poorly liquid for another. It may be liquid under ordinary conditions and impaired during stress. It may provide strong buying liquidity but weak selling liquidity, or vice versa. It may function well over several hours but poorly for a participant requiring immediate execution.

Liquidity is therefore neither permanent nor absolute. It is a conditional relationship between intended exchange and available market capacity.

Conditional Liquidity Principle: A valid liquidity claim must be scoped to the instrument, venue, transaction size, side, urgency, time horizon, and market condition being evaluated.

6.2 Why Liquidity Exists

Financial markets exist because participants possess different objectives, information, constraints, liabilities, beliefs, and time horizons. Some seek financing. Others seek investment. Some wish to transfer risk. Others are willing to assume it. Some rebalance portfolios, hedge exposures, manage inventories, arbitrage related instruments, or provide immediacy to other participants.

Liquidity emerges when these heterogeneous participants are willing and able to transact. Willingness alone is insufficient. Exchange capacity also depends upon available capital, inventory tolerance, funding, collateral, risk limits, information asymmetry, competition, regulation, venue design, expected volatility, and technological access.

> **Institute Distinction:** Willingness creates potential participation; capacity determines how much exchange can occur and under what conditions.

Without sufficient liquidity, capital allocation becomes more costly, risk transfer becomes more difficult, and price discovery becomes less reliable. Yet liquidity should not be treated as a moral good or as proof that prices are correct. It enables exchange; it does not determine the wisdom or value of the claims being exchanged.

6.3 Liquidity Is Not Volume

Trading volume records transactions that have already occurred. Liquidity concerns the market's capacity to accommodate current and future transactions. The two are related, but they are not synonymous.

A market may exhibit high volume because many participants transact under stress while spreads widen, depth disappears, and price impact increases. In such a case, high volume may be the consequence of deteriorating liquidity rather than evidence of abundant liquidity.

Conversely, a market may display modest volume while maintaining narrow effective costs, adequate depth for typical transaction sizes, low price impact, and rapid replenishment. That market may be more liquid for the intended transaction than a higher-volume market.

Characteristic	Market A	Market B
Daily activity	High volume	Lower volume
Spread	Wide	Narrow
Depth near current price	Shallow	Adequate for typical size
Price impact	Large	Small
Recovery after trades	Slow	Rapid
Interpretation	High activity but weak exchange capacity	Lower activity but stronger liquidity for typical transactions

Volume can become relevant evidence when interpreted with transaction cost, depth, impact, and resilience. It should not be treated as a standalone definition of liquidity.

6.4 Liquidity Is Conditional

Liquidity is not a universal property of an instrument. It is a conditional relationship between the exchange a participant intends to make and the capacity available to support it.

A liquidity assessment should specify at least seven conditions:

1. Instrument: What financial claim or contract is being exchanged?
2. Venue: Where can the exchange occur, and is liquidity fragmented across venues?
3. Transaction size: How large is the intended trade relative to available capacity?
4. Side: Is the participant buying, selling, borrowing, lending, or hedging?
5. Urgency: Must execution occur immediately, or can the order be worked through time?
6. Time horizon: Is the assessment concerned with seconds, minutes, a session, or a longer period?
7. Market condition: Are conditions ordinary, event-driven, stressed, or structurally impaired?

A stock may be liquid for a retail order but illiquid for a block sale. A futures contract may be liquid in the nearest expiration but thin in distant months. An option may be liquid at one strike and expiration but not another. A sovereign bond may trade efficiently under ordinary conditions yet become difficult to exchange during a funding shock.

This conditionality prevents the analyst from assigning a single permanent liquidity label to an asset or market.

6.5 The Dimensions of Liquidity

Liquidity is multidimensional. The principal dimensions may strengthen or weaken independently, which is why no single metric can fully characterize exchange capacity.

Dimension	**Question addressed**	**Illustrative manifestation**
Immediacy	How quickly can exchange occur?	Time to execution or probability of timely fill.
Transaction cost	What explicit and implicit cost accompanies exchange?	Spread, fees, slippage, and opportunity cost.
Depth	How much quantity is available near current prices?	Executable size at or near the best available prices.

Dimension	Question addressed	Illustrative manifestation
Breadth	How is available interest distributed across price levels?	Quantity available beyond the first price level.
Price impact	How much does execution move the market?	Temporary or persistent price response per unit traded.
Resilience	How quickly do price and liquidity conditions recover after disruption?	Restoration of spread, depth, and orderly trading.
Continuity	How consistently are counterparties and prices available through time?	Persistence of executable quotes and low frequency of gaps.
Replenishment	How rapidly does new liquidity appear after existing liquidity is consumed?	Replacement of executed or withdrawn size.

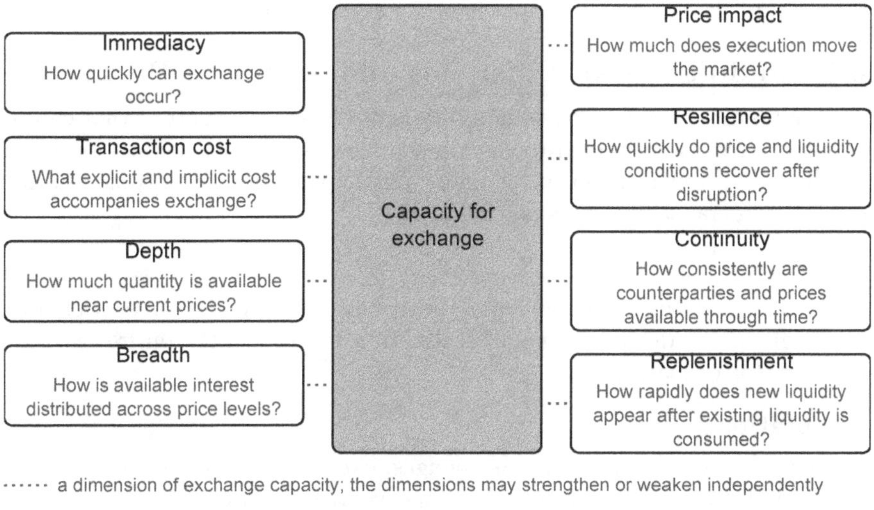

Figure 6.1 — The Dimensions of Liquidity surrounding Capacity for Exchange

A market may have narrow spreads but little depth. It may display substantial depth but recover slowly after large trades. It may offer rapid execution while imposing substantial price impact. The multidimensional framework makes such differences visible.

6.6 How Liquidity Arises

Liquidity does not arise from one participant class or one market mechanism. It emerges from the combined behavior of natural buyers and sellers, market makers, dealers, arbitrageurs, hedgers, institutions, algorithmic execution systems, and participants managing inventory or funding needs.

Liquidity suppliers accept several forms of risk. They may face inventory risk if prices move while they hold exposure, adverse-selection risk if counterparties possess superior information, funding risk if positions require financing, operational risk if systems fail, and volatility risk if market conditions change faster than positions can be adjusted.

Their willingness to provide capacity may decline when uncertainty rises, inventories become unbalanced, funding tightens, correlated markets become unstable, risk limits bind, or expected volatility increases. Liquidity can therefore disappear precisely when many participants need it most.

Liquidity demand is also adaptive. Participants may accelerate execution when prices move against them, reduce urgency when costs rise, split transactions across time and venues, or substitute related instruments. Both supply and demand respond to changing conditions.

6.7 Liquidity as an Emergent and Adaptive Property

Within a systems perspective, liquidity is not a static inventory that can be counted once and assumed to remain available. It is an emergent property produced by the interaction of many participants whose willingness and capacity to transact evolve continuously.

Emergence

System-wide liquidity arises from the combined behavior of participants. No single order, dealer, venue, or institution represents the entire market's capacity for exchange.

Adaptation

Participants modify quotes, sizes, hedges, execution methods, and risk limits as information, prices, inventory, and volatility change.

Feedback

Liquidity affects price movement. Price movement changes perceived risk and participant behavior. Those changes alter positioning, volatility, and subsequent liquidity. The market's response to exchange therefore changes the conditions under which later exchange occurs.

> **Systems Principle:** Liquidity is both a condition of exchange and a product of the market's evolving response to exchange.

6.8 Observable Manifestations

Liquidity cannot be observed completely through any single measure. Its manifestations appear through the conditions participants experience before, during, and after exchange.

Possible manifestations of weakening liquidity

- Widening effective transaction costs.
- Reduced executable depth near current prices.
- Greater price movement per unit of transaction.
- Longer execution times or lower fill probability.
- More frequent gaps or discontinuities.
- Withdrawal or shortening of quote duration.
- Slower replenishment after size is consumed.
- Slower recovery after order imbalance or shock.
- Greater variation in execution quality across venues, instruments, or time.
- Increasing asymmetry between buying and selling capacity.

Possible manifestations of strengthening liquidity

- Narrower effective costs under comparable conditions.
- Deeper executable interest for the relevant transaction size.
- Lower marginal price impact.
- Faster replenishment and recovery.
- Improved continuity of executable prices.
- Greater capacity to absorb two-sided activity without disruption.

These manifestations are evidence candidates, not proof of a single cause. Widening spreads, for example, may be temporary, venue-specific, event-related, or caused by stale data. Interpretation requires context and corroboration.

6.9 Liquidity Measurements

Measurements transform observable market data into structured representations of selected liquidity dimensions. They differ in directness, assumptions, scope, and sensitivity to data quality.

Measurement category	Examples	Primary dimension	Important limitation
Cost measures	Quoted spread, effective spread, realized spread, slippage, implementation shortfall	Transaction cost	May vary with order type, size, venue, and timing.

Measurement category	Examples	Primary dimension	Important limitation
Quantity measures	Displayed depth, executed depth, size across price levels, turnover, trade-size distribution	Depth and breadth	Displayed size may not be executable or may omit hidden interest.
Impact measures	Price impact per unit traded, temporary and permanent impact, impact asymmetry	Price impact	Usually model dependent and highly sensitive to horizon and trade classification.
Time measures	Execution time, fill probability, quote duration, cancellation rate, replenishment time	Immediacy, continuity, replenishment	Requires precise event data and may be venue specific.
Resilience measures	Spread recovery, price recovery, depth restoration, post-shock normalization	Resilience	Recovery baseline and shock definition may be arbitrary.
Composite estimates	Liquidity indices, latent-liquidity estimates, stress-capacity models	Multiple dimensions	Combines assumptions and may obscure conflicting components.

Direct observations, derived measurements, estimates, and model outputs should be labeled distinctly. Numerical precision does not guarantee conceptual or empirical reliability.

6.10 From Measurement to Evidence

A measurement becomes evidence only when it is relevant to a stated question or claim. The following sequence illustrates the distinction:

Stage	Liquidity example
Data	Recorded bid and ask quotations.
Measurement	Quoted spread.
Observation	The spread widens from 2 basis points to 8 basis points.
Evidence claim	Observable transaction cost appears to be increasing.

Stage	Liquidity example
Interpretation	Liquidity may be deteriorating for the evaluated size, venue, and horizon.
Qualification	The change may be temporary, venue-specific, event-driven, stale, or offset by hidden depth and rapid replenishment.

The interpretation is stronger when widening spreads coincide with reduced depth, greater price impact, slower replenishment, and impaired recovery. It is weaker when the change is brief, isolated, or inconsistent with other evidence.

> **Evidence Principle:** A liquidity interpretation should be proportional to the breadth, quality, persistence, and transaction relevance of the available evidence.

6.11 Interpreting Liquidity Evidence

A disciplined liquidity assessment should evaluate more than the current level of a metric. It should consider:

- Consistency across multiple liquidity dimensions.
- Persistence through time rather than a single observation.
- Comparison with an appropriate instrument- and regime-specific baseline.
- Relevance to the intended transaction size and execution method.
- Coverage across venues and related instruments.
- Data freshness, completeness, and timestamp alignment.
- Current volatility, event risk, and market regime.
- Alternative explanations for the observed change.
- Potential asymmetry between buying and selling capacity.
- Whether a model-based estimate remains valid under current conditions.

A market-wide statement should not be made from evidence that is narrow, stale, or specific to one venue or transaction size. Responsible interpretation states the scope and confidence of the conclusion.

6.12 Displayed, Hidden, Realized, Latent, and Committed Liquidity

The liquidity visible before execution is not necessarily the liquidity that will be experienced during execution.

Form of liquidity	Meaning	Interpretive caution
Displayed liquidity	Visible interest represented through quotes or orders.	May be cancelled, moved, fragmented, or unavailable by the time execution reaches it.
Hidden or non-displayed liquidity	Interest not fully visible before execution.	Cannot be inferred reliably from visible depth alone.
Realized liquidity	The execution conditions actually experienced.	Known only after or during execution and depends on order strategy.
Latent liquidity	Potential willingness to transact that may appear when price or conditions change.	Difficult to measure and often model dependent.
Committed liquidity	Capacity contractually or institutionally expected from dealers or facilities.	Commitment may have limits, conditions, or fail under extreme stress.

Displayed depth should not be treated as guaranteed executable capacity. Conversely, a thin displayed book does not prove that no additional liquidity will emerge. The distinction is important across order-driven, dealer-mediated, and hybrid market structures.

6.13 A Progressive Example

Stage 1 — Ordinary transaction

A participant wishes to sell 10,000 shares. The spread is narrow, depth is sufficient, execution occurs quickly, average price remains close to the initial market, and depth replenishes after the trade. The evidence supports a narrow claim: liquidity is functional for that transaction size, venue, and horizon under current conditions.

Stage 2 — Larger transaction

The same participant attempts to sell 500,000 shares. Available depth is insufficient, the order must be divided, average execution worsens, and price moves materially as size is completed. The asset has not changed, but the liquidity relationship has. The market is less liquid for the larger and more urgent transaction.

Stage 3 — Concentrated stress demand

Several participants attempt to sell simultaneously. Volatility rises, liquidity suppliers reduce quoted size, spreads widen, depth disappears, price impact becomes nonlinear, and recovery slows. The demand for exchange has become concentrated at the same time that risk-bearing capacity is declining.

The example demonstrates that liquidity depends upon size, urgency, participation, and system condition. Historical average volume or a previously narrow spread would not have captured the stressed capacity accurately.

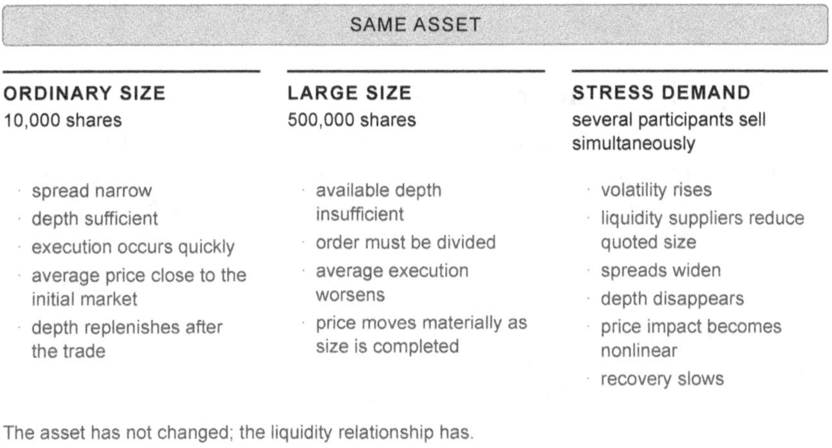

Figure 6.2 — Liquidity Across Ordinary Size, Large Size, and Stress Demand

6.14 Interaction with the Other Observational Domains

Liquidity and Positioning

Concentrated, leveraged, or mechanically sensitive positioning may create future demand for liquidity. If many participants need to hedge, rebalance, or reduce risk at the same time, available exchange capacity may be insufficient. Weak liquidity may also prevent orderly repositioning and increase the likelihood of forced execution.

Liquidity and Volatility

Lower liquidity can increase price sensitivity because less capacity is available to absorb transactions. Rising volatility can then cause liquidity suppliers to widen spreads, reduce size, or withdraw. The relationship may therefore operate in both directions and create reinforcing feedback.

Liquidity and Trend

A trend may attract participants and improve exchange capacity, or it may become increasingly one-sided and reduce available counterparties. Strong directional movement can coexist with either healthy or fragile liquidity. Trend direction alone does not reveal the quality of exchange capacity.

Multidomain illustration

Consider a market with concentrated long positioning, declining depth, rising implied volatility, and a mature upward trend. Price may still appear strong while the market becomes structurally fragile. A modest shock could produce disproportionate selling demand into weakening liquidity.

This example does not predict that a reversal must occur. It shows why liquidity gains meaning when interpreted with positioning, volatility, and trend.

6.15 Liquidity Under Stress

Liquidity often appears abundant until many participants attempt to use it simultaneously. Stress reveals whether apparently available capacity is independent or whether it depends on participants who will withdraw under the same conditions.

Stress may expose:

- Correlation among liquidity demands.
- Withdrawal of market-making or dealer capacity.
- Widening basis relationships across related instruments.
- Execution delays and reduced fill probability.
- Large gaps between displayed and executable prices.
- Forced selling, hedging, or deleveraging.
- Fragmentation across venues or instruments.
- Discontinuous price adjustment and slow recovery.

> **Stress Principle:** Liquidity should be evaluated not only by how it functions under ordinary activity, but also by how it responds when demand for exchange becomes concentrated.

Stress testing cannot reveal the future with certainty. It can, however, identify assumptions that are unlikely to remain valid when participation, volatility, funding, and risk-bearing capacity change together.

6.16 Common Misuses

Misuse	Why it is misleading	More disciplined approach
Treating volume as liquidity	Volume records completed activity, not future capacity.	Combine volume with cost, depth, impact, and resilience.
Treating narrow spreads as complete proof	Spreads may be narrow while depth and continuity are weak.	Evaluate multiple dimensions and transaction size.

Misuse	Why it is misleading	More disciplined approach
Ignoring transaction size	Liquidity may deteriorate nonlinearly as size increases.	Scope every claim to intended size.
Treating displayed depth as guaranteed	Displayed orders may cancel, move, or fragment.	Compare displayed and realized execution conditions.
Comparing instruments without normalization	Different prices, contract sizes, venues, and trading conventions distort comparison.	Normalize measurements and state the comparison basis.
Ignoring venue fragmentation	One venue may not represent total capacity.	Assess relevant venues and routing constraints.
Assuming historical liquidity remains available	Participation and risk capacity are adaptive.	Treat current and historical liquidity as conditional.
Assuming price stability proves liquidity	Prices may be stable because activity is low or latent risk is untested.	Evaluate capacity under relevant transaction demand.
Equating high volatility with low liquidity in every case	Volatility and liquidity are related but not identical.	Examine direct liquidity evidence.
Treating a model output as directly observed	Composite estimates embed assumptions and may fail.	Label estimates and inspect components.
Assuming symmetry	Buying and selling capacity may differ materially.	Evaluate both sides of the market.
Using current liquidity as a forecast	Liquidity can change rapidly under stress.	Separate present assessment from future scenario analysis.

6.17 Limitations

Liquidity explains an important dimension of market functioning, but it does not explain all market behavior. Liquidity analysis cannot by itself determine:

- Fair value or the correctness of market prices.
- Long-term economic growth or corporate fundamentals.
- The desirability of a position for a particular participant.
- The cause or meaning of an information event.
- Whether volatility will rise or fall.
- Whether a trend will continue or reverse.
- Whether displayed liquidity will remain available.
- Whether a market reaction will be temporary or permanent.

- Whether liquidity deterioration is the cause of a move, the consequence of it, or both.
- Future market direction.

Liquidity measurements may also be incomplete, venue specific, delayed, model dependent, or sensitive to execution methodology. These limitations should constrain the confidence and scope of any conclusion.

6.18 Why Liquidity Matters

Liquidity determines the market's capacity to transform intentions into transactions. It influences transaction cost, capital allocation, risk transfer, execution quality, and the reliability of price discovery.

> **Institute Proposition:** Liquidity determines not whether participants possess intentions, but whether those intentions can be expressed through exchange without disproportionate cost or disruption.

Even well-informed participants may struggle to express their views when liquidity is weak. Conversely, abundant liquidity can allow large changes in ownership and risk to occur with limited visible disruption.

Liquidity is therefore more than a technical execution characteristic. It is an essential dimension of market functioning and structural fragility. It should not, however, be treated as a complete measure of market health or as an independent predictor of direction.

Chapter Summary

Liquidity is the market's capacity to facilitate exchange with a given degree of immediacy, cost, depth, price impact, and resilience under specified conditions.

Liquidity is not synonymous with volume, narrow spreads, displayed depth, or price stability. It is multidimensional and conditional upon transaction size, time horizon, venue, urgency, side, and market condition.

Because no single measurement represents the complete phenomenon, liquidity must be assessed through multiple forms of evidence. Spreads, depth, execution costs, price impact, continuity, replenishment, and resilience illuminate different aspects of exchange capacity.

Liquidity emerges from the adaptive interaction of participants and can strengthen or deteriorate rapidly as positioning, volatility, trend, funding, information, and risk-bearing capacity change.

Liquidity improves understanding of market functioning, execution conditions, and structural fragility. It does not independently determine value, direction, or future outcomes.

Established Knowledge

The economic and institutional importance of liquidity is extensively documented within financial economics and market microstructure. Established areas of study include bid-ask spread theory, dealer inventory, adverse selection, market depth, price impact, immediacy, resilience, transaction costs, execution quality, liquidity risk, commonality in liquidity, and liquidity under market stress.

The distinction between liquidity and volume is well recognized, as is the principle that liquidity depends on transaction size and market condition. Research has also shown that liquidity can vary across instruments, venues, participants, and time, and that it may deteriorate sharply during periods of stress.

Institute Perspective

Market Systems Science treats liquidity as the capacity-for-exchange observational domain. The Institute's proposed contribution is not a new spread formula, order-book indicator, or execution technology. It is the organization of multiple liquidity manifestations and measurements as complementary evidence concerning a broader system property.

The Institute emphasizes conditionality by transaction size, horizon, venue, side, urgency, and market state. It also emphasizes that liquidity gains system-level meaning through its interactions with positioning, volatility, and trend.

Market-data feeds, venue protocols, order-book products, and software platforms are implementations used to observe liquidity. They should not be confused with the enduring concept. As technologies change, the measurements may change while the underlying question remains: What capacity does the market currently possess to facilitate exchange under the conditions being studied?

Questions for Reflection

1. Why is liquidity better described as a capacity than as an event?
2. Why is trading volume not equivalent to liquidity?
3. How can a high-volume market still be difficult to trade?
4. Why must liquidity be evaluated relative to transaction size?
5. How does execution urgency affect liquidity?
6. What is the difference between displayed and realized liquidity?
7. Why can narrow spreads coexist with weak depth?
8. What does resilience reveal that spread alone does not?
9. How can rising volatility reduce liquidity?
10. How can declining liquidity increase volatility?
11. Why may liquidity differ between buyers and sellers?

12. What alternative explanations may exist for widening spreads?
13. Why should one liquidity indicator not determine a system-level conclusion?
14. How can concentrated positioning create future demand for liquidity?
15. What evidence would show that a liquidity assessment was incomplete or incorrect?

Chapter 7. Positioning

The Distribution of Market Exposure

Chapter Purpose

Financial markets are often described through price movement. Yet prices reveal only the outcomes of completed transactions. They do not fully reveal the exposures that remain, the leverage supporting those exposures, the sensitivities embedded in derivative portfolios, the constraints facing participants, or the adjustments that may become necessary as conditions change.

Positioning is the second foundational observational domain within the Market Systems Science framework. Unlike liquidity, which concerns the market's capacity for exchange, positioning concerns how financial exposure is distributed across participants and how that exposure may respond to price, volatility, time, funding, liquidity, and other market variables.

This chapter defines positioning as a multidimensional and only partially observable market condition. It distinguishes positions from total economic exposure, gross from net exposure, positioning from flow, and exposure from sentiment or intent. It also explains why leverage, concentration, crowding, optionality, funding dependence, and participant constraints determine whether a position remains stable or becomes a source of adjustment pressure.

The purpose is not to claim that positioning predicts what markets will do next. Positioning improves understanding of market sensitivity and possible response pathways. Whether those pathways become observable activity depends upon triggers, constraints, liquidity, volatility, trend, and participant choice.

Learning Objectives

- Define positioning from financial, economic-exposure, and systems perspectives.
- Distinguish a recorded position from total economic exposure.
- Distinguish gross, net, concentrated, crowded, leveraged, and nonlinear positioning.
- Explain why identical nominal holdings may create different sensitivities and adjustment pressures.

- Distinguish positioning from price, transaction flow, sentiment, and participant intent.
- Identify direct, reported, inferred, delayed, and model-dependent positioning evidence.
- Explain how derivatives create nonlinear and time-varying exposure.
- Evaluate positioning evidence with appropriate treatment of uncertainty and alternative explanations.
- Understand positioning's interactions with liquidity, volatility, and trend.
- Recognize common misuses of positioning indicators and estimates.

7.1 Positioning as a Market Phenomenon

Every market participant holds or manages some form of financial exposure. An investor owns securities. A pension fund allocates capital among assets and liabilities. A hedge fund maintains leveraged positions. A market maker carries inventory. A corporation hedges currency, commodity, or interest-rate risk. A dealer offsets derivative sensitivities. A passive fund replicates an index. These exposures remain embedded in the market after transactions have occurred.

Definition — Positioning

Positioning is the distribution of financial exposure, sensitivity, leverage, concentration, and potential adjustment requirements across market participants under specified conditions.

The phrase under specified conditions is essential. The significance of a position depends on the instrument, participant, time horizon, financing arrangement, liquidity, volatility, risk limits, and the variables to which the exposure is sensitive.

A position is therefore not important merely because it is large. It becomes analytically important when its structure makes the participant or the market sensitive to changing conditions.

7.2 Position, Economic Exposure, and Sensitivity

Position, economic exposure, and sensitivity are related but distinct concepts.

Concept	Definition	Illustrative example
Position	A contractual, ownership, or inventory quantity held by a participant.	One million shares, 5,000 futures contracts, or a portfolio of option contracts.

Concept	Definition	Illustrative example
Economic exposure	The participant's overall gain-and-loss relationship after considering related holdings, hedges, financing, liabilities, and obligations.	A long equity holding offset by short futures may produce much lower net equity exposure than the share count suggests.
Sensitivity	The rate or manner in which position value or required management changes as market variables change.	An option portfolio's delta, gamma, vega, or time sensitivity.
Adjustment requirement	A condition under which a participant may need or choose to hedge, rebalance, finance, reduce, or increase exposure.	A margin call, target-allocation breach, volatility limit, or option-expiration effect.

A reported position may therefore differ materially from the participant's total economic exposure. A futures position may hedge a cash holding. An option position may be one leg of a spread. A dealer may offset customer exposure in another instrument or venue. A portfolio that appears directional in one dataset may be approximately neutral when the complete structure is considered.

For simple cash instruments, sensitivity may be approximately linear over a limited range. For options, leveraged products, structured notes, dynamically hedged portfolios, and multi-asset strategies, sensitivity can change with price, volatility, time, interest rates, correlation, dividends, path, and funding conditions.

7.3 Positioning Is Not Price

Price records the terms at which transactions have occurred. Positioning describes the exposures that remain after those transactions.

Rising prices do not prove that participants are broadly net long, and falling prices do not prove that positioning is uniformly bearish. A price increase may result from new long demand, short covering, dealer hedging, forced buying, or thin liquidity. A price decline may reflect new short selling, long liquidation, hedging, rebalancing, or a temporary absence of buyers.

Two markets may trade at the same price while possessing very different exposure structures. Likewise, positioning can change materially while price remains nearly unchanged when transactions transfer or offset risk without producing a large directional move.

Price–Positioning Distinction: Price is an observable transaction outcome. Positioning is the exposure structure that remains.

7.4 Positioning Is Not Flow

Flow describes orders and transactions occurring through time. Positioning describes the exposure structure that remains after activity has occurred.

A purchase may open a new long position, close a short position, hedge another exposure, rebalance an index, or facilitate a client transaction. The same observed flow can therefore produce different changes in economic exposure.

Open interest may rise when both sides establish new contracts, remain unchanged when exposure transfers from one participant to another, or decline when both sides close. Even then, the directional and economic meaning remains uncertain without knowing the complete position structure.

Flow–Positioning Distinction: Flow is activity through time. Positioning is the exposure structure that remains.

7.5 Positioning Is Not Sentiment or Intent

A position does not reliably reveal why it is held. Long exposure may reflect optimism, but it may also arise from index replication, liability matching, arbitrage, customer facilitation, inventory management, regulatory requirements, tax considerations, or a hedge against another liability.

Short exposure may reflect a negative directional view, but it may also hedge a long cash position, offset option risk, facilitate market making, or express a relative-value trade.

Participant intent is usually only partially observable. Responsible analysis should therefore avoid turning every reported long position into bullish sentiment or every reported short position into pessimism.

7.6 Dimensions of Positioning

Dimension	Meaning	Why it matters
Direction	Long, short, approximately neutral, or nonlinear exposure.	Indicates the sign and structure of sensitivity, but not the participant's motive.
Gross exposure	Total absolute exposure before offsets.	Large gross exposure may create substantial sensitivity even when net exposure is small.

Dimension	Meaning	Why it matters
Net exposure	Directional exposure after offsets.	Useful for broad directional assessment but may hide offsetting risk and crowding.
Concentration	Exposure held by relatively few participants, instruments, strikes, sectors, or strategies.	Concentrated exposure may create correlated adjustment pressure.
Dispersion	The breadth of exposure distribution across participants and instruments.	Broadly dispersed exposure may behave differently from exposure held by a small group.
Crowding	Similarity of exposures, assumptions, or adjustment rules across participants.	Crowding can create synchronized behavior without requiring identical positions.
Leverage	Exposure relative to capital, equity, collateral, or risk-bearing capacity.	Higher leverage reduces tolerance for adverse movement and may create forced adjustment.
Convexity and optionality	The degree to which sensitivity changes as conditions change.	Nonlinear exposures may generate accelerating or decelerating hedging needs.
Maturity and horizon	The period over which exposure remains relevant or must be managed.	Expiration, roll, and mandate horizons affect timing of adjustment.
Funding dependence	Reliance on borrowing, collateral, or continued financing.	Funding pressure can convert otherwise stable exposure into urgent liquidity demand.
Adjustment requirement	The likelihood that conditions will require hedging, rebalancing, liquidation, or new capital.	Links the current exposure structure to possible future activity.

7.7 Gross, Net, Concentrated, and Crowded Exposure

Net positioning is useful but can be misleading when treated alone. Consider one participant group holding \$10 billion of long exposure and another holding \$9.8 billion of short exposure. Net exposure is only \$200 million, but gross exposure is \$19.8 billion.

A nearly balanced net measure may therefore coexist with substantial leverage, financing needs, option sensitivities, and potential adjustment pressure on both sides.

Concentration and crowding are also distinct. Concentration concerns how exposure is distributed. Crowding concerns similarity in positions, assumptions, or response rules. A market may be concentrated without participants following the same strategy, or crowded across many participants even when no single participant is dominant.

Crowding does not guarantee immediate reversal. A crowded position may persist while capital, performance incentives, liquidity, and information continue to support it. Its importance lies in the possibility that many participants may respond similarly when conditions change.

7.8 Sources of Positioning

Positioning arises from heterogeneous objectives and institutional functions, including:

- long-term investment and asset allocation;
- short-term speculation and relative-value trading;
- portfolio rebalancing and liability matching;
- corporate financing and risk management;
- derivative hedging and volatility trading;
- market making and customer facilitation;
- index replication and passive fund flows;
- systematic trend-following, volatility-control, and risk-parity rules;
- arbitrage and basis trading;
- collateral optimization and funding management;
- tax-driven transactions;
- structured-product issuance;
- regulatory and capital requirements;
- issuer, sovereign, or central-bank activity.

Because participants operate with different objectives, horizons, constraints, and information, market positioning should not be interpreted as a single unified belief.

7.9 Positioning as Conditional Response Potential

Positioning may create latent demand to buy, sell, hedge, rebalance, finance, roll, cover, or reduce risk if relevant conditions change.

This idea is sometimes compared with stored potential energy. The analogy is useful only if its limits are explicit. A market position does not contain a predetermined quantity of future movement, and exposure does not guarantee a particular response.

Potential adjustment becomes activity only when a trigger, constraint, or participant decision activates it:

- price thresholds or drawdown limits;
- changes in volatility or correlation;
- passage of time and option expiration;
- funding stress or collateral calls;
- risk-budget or mandate limits;
- index changes and scheduled rebalancing;
- liquidity deterioration;
- redemptions or investor inflows;
- new information or policy action.

Conditional Response Principle: Positioning influences future behavior through possible adjustment requirements, not through deterministic mechanical necessity.

7.10 Observable Manifestations

Positioning changes may become visible through:

- changes in open interest;
- sustained creation, redemption, or fund-flow patterns;
- changes in short interest or securities-borrowing demand;
- concentration at particular strikes, maturities, sectors, or instruments;
- repeated hedging activity or price-insensitive transactions;
- dealer inventory imbalance;
- futures-basis and rollover behavior;
- margin utilization and collateral pressure;
- forced liquidation or short covering;
- divergence between price movement and participation;
- persistent response near contractual or risk thresholds.

These are manifestations, not proof of a single mechanism. A change in open interest, for example, may reflect new directional exposure, hedging, spreads, market-making activity, or structured-product issuance.

7.11 Positioning Data and Measurements

Evidence class	Examples	Principal limitations
Direct or reported	Regulatory holdings, institutional filings, futures commitment reports, fund allocations, short interest, securities-lending records, exchange open interest.	Often delayed, aggregated, incomplete, or unable to show related hedges.
Transaction-derived	Open-interest changes, creation and redemption activity, block trades, estimated opening versus closing activity, rollover patterns, flow persistence.	Transactions do not reveal complete intent or remaining economic exposure.
Derivative sensitivity	Delta, gamma, vega, theta, vanna, charm, and portfolio-level sensitivities.	Model dependent; sensitivities change with market variables and do not reveal motive.
Model-based estimates	Dealer exposure, trend-following exposure, volatility-control exposure, risk-parity rebalancing, liquidation thresholds, option-hedging demand.	Depend on assumptions about ownership, strategy rules, hedging behavior, and portfolio composition.
Market manifestations	Basis behavior, borrowing cost, price response near strikes, forced activity, participation concentration.	May have multiple competing explanations and may reflect liquidity or volatility as well as positioning.

Every positioning claim should disclose whether the underlying information is directly observed, reported, inferred, estimated, delayed, aggregated, or model dependent.

Observability Principle: Observed positions are not necessarily equivalent to total economic exposure, and reported exposure is not necessarily equivalent to participant intent.

7.12 Derivatives and Nonlinear Positioning

Derivatives can create exposures whose sensitivity changes continuously. The position quantity may remain unchanged while the economic exposure evolves.

- Delta describes sensitivity to a change in the underlying price.
- Gamma describes how delta changes as the underlying price changes.
- Vega describes sensitivity to changes in implied volatility.
- Theta describes sensitivity to the passage of time, subject to model and convention.
- Vanna links delta sensitivity to changes in volatility.
- Charm describes how delta changes as time passes.
- Other sensitivities may become relevant for complex instruments or large moves.

A Greek is a model-based sensitivity of an instrument or portfolio. It is not itself a trade, a participant motive, or proof that a participant must hedge in a specified way.

Dealer-positioning estimates are especially conditional when transaction side, customer identity, offsetting positions, internal netting, and actual hedging policy are unknown.

7.13 From Measurement to Evidence

Worked Evidence Chain: Increasing Option Open Interest

1. Data: contract-level open interest rises at selected strikes and expirations.
2. Measurement: concentration of open interest increases relative to prior levels and nearby contracts.
3. Possible evidence: exposure has accumulated in those contracts.
4. Unknowns: which participants hold each side, whether positions are hedged, whether they are part of spreads, whether they are opening or transferred positions, and how dealers manage inventory.
5. Interpretation: the market may possess increased sensitivity around those strikes, but direction and future hedging demand remain uncertain.
6. Revision condition: the interpretation should change if new data reveal offsets, closures, altered volatility, or different ownership assumptions.

A measurement becomes evidence only in relation to a stated claim. Even then, the claim should remain proportional to the quality and completeness of the information.

7.14 Interpreting Positioning Evidence

A disciplined positioning assessment should consider:

- gross and net exposure;
- concentration and dispersion;
- crowding and strategy similarity;
- leverage and funding dependence;
- participant type and objective;
- time horizon and maturity;
- instrument relationships and hedge structure;
- optionality and nonlinear sensitivity;
- liquidity and exit capacity;
- data age, coverage, and reporting method;
- model assumptions and parameter sensitivity;
- possible adjustment triggers;
- alternative explanations;
- the participant's ability to maintain the exposure.

Interpretive Principle: The significance of a position depends not only on its size, but also on its sensitivity, concentration, leverage, constraints, and capacity to remain in place.

7.15 Progressive Worked Example

Stage 1 — Initial Transaction

An institution purchases one million shares of a company. Price rises modestly and volume increases. The transaction confirms that shares transferred from sellers to the institution.

The transaction does not reveal:

- whether the institution will continue buying;
- whether sellers were closing long positions or establishing hedges;
- whether a dealer temporarily absorbed inventory;
- whether options or futures were used to offset the exposure;
- whether the trade was strategic, tactical, passive, or liability driven.

Stage 2 — New Exposure Structure

After the transaction, the institution holds a concentrated long position. A dealer may hold temporary short inventory. Derivative hedges may have been created. Gross positioning may have increased even if the market's net directional exposure changed only modestly.

Stage 3 — Market Declines

A later price decline may produce several different responses:

- the long-term institution may remain inactive;
- a leveraged fund may reduce exposure;
- dealers may hedge changing sensitivities;
- short sellers may cover;
- passive funds may rebalance;
- liquidity providers may reduce quoted size.

The same price decline produces different behavior because participants face different exposures, financing arrangements, objectives, and constraints.

Stage 4 — Liquidity Weakens

If many participants attempt to adjust while exchange capacity is limited, price impact may become nonlinear. Volatility may rise, forced execution may increase, and the decline may become self-reinforcing.

The example demonstrates the appropriate conclusion: positioning influences possible response, but it does not determine market behavior independently.

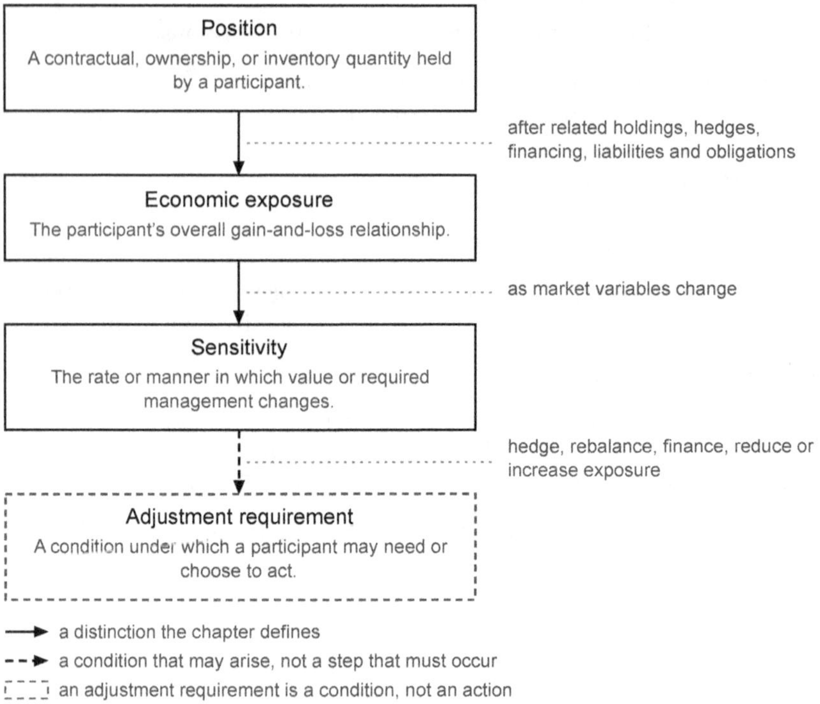

Figure 7.1 — From Position to Economic Exposure

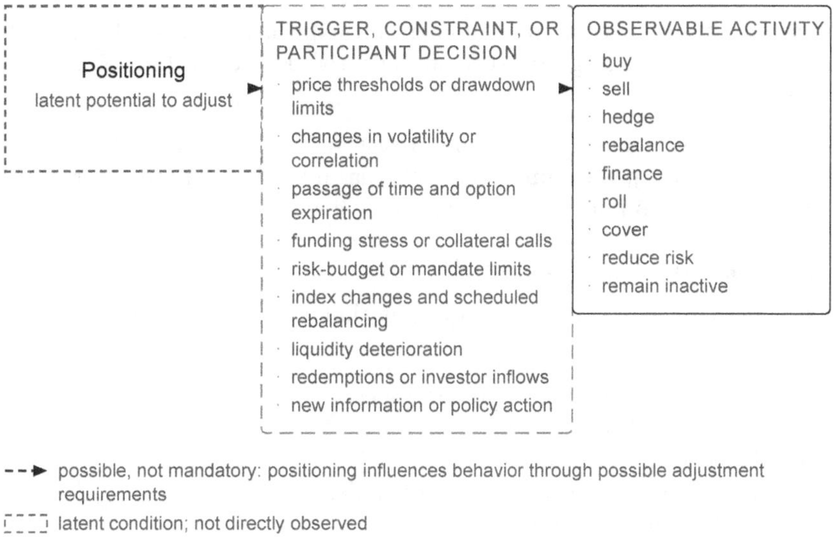

Figure 7.2 — Positioning as Conditional Response Potential

7.16 Positioning and Liquidity

Large, leveraged, crowded, or time-sensitive positions may create substantial demand for liquidity. Liquidity determines whether participants can establish, hedge, rebalance, roll, finance, or exit exposure at acceptable cost.

A position that appears manageable under deep liquidity may become destabilizing when exchange capacity deteriorates. Conversely, deep and resilient liquidity may absorb large adjustments without producing disorderly price movement.

7.17 Positioning and Volatility

Volatility can alter option sensitivities, collateral requirements, risk estimates, position limits, leverage, hedging frequency, and participant tolerance.

Positioning can also shape volatility when many participants respond similarly to changing conditions. The relationship is bidirectional and conditional rather than fixed.

7.18 Positioning and Trend

Persistent trends may attract momentum exposure, passive flows, performance chasing, hedging adjustments, and risk reduction by losing participants.

Positioning may reinforce a trend, resist it, or create conditions for reversal. Crowded positioning does not guarantee immediate reversal, and uncrowded positioning does not guarantee continuation.

7.19 Positioning Under Stress

Stress often reveals exposure structures that appeared stable during ordinary conditions.

- margin calls and collateral shortages;
- stop-loss and drawdown rules;
- volatility-targeting adjustments;
- redemptions and investor withdrawals;
- dealer inventory limits;
- option-expiration and maturity effects;
- funding withdrawal;
- correlated risk reduction;
- basis convergence or divergence;
- loss of liquidity in related instruments.

> **Stress Principle:** Positioning becomes most consequential when many participants face similar adjustment pressures while liquidity is insufficient to absorb them.

7.20 Common Misuses

Misuse	Why it is misleading
Treating price direction as a direct measure of positioning	Price is a transaction outcome and may reflect many mechanisms.
Treating flow as equivalent to remaining exposure	A transaction may open, close, transfer, or hedge exposure.
Inferring sentiment from every long or short position	Positions may arise from hedging, replication, arbitrage, regulation, or facilitation.
Relying only on net exposure	Net measures may hide large gross, leveraged, or offsetting exposures.
Ignoring concentration and crowding	Distribution and similarity of response rules may matter more than aggregate size.
Treating open interest as directional	Open interest records outstanding contracts, not which side holds the directional view.

Misuse	Why it is misleading
Assuming derivative exposure is unhedged	Participants may offset risk across instruments, maturities, or venues.
Treating Greeks as guaranteed future trades	Greeks are model sensitivities, not mandatory behavior.
Inferring dealer exposure without disclosing assumptions	Ownership, transaction side, netting, and hedging policy are often unknown.
Ignoring offsetting positions	Single-instrument data may misrepresent total economic exposure.
Comparing position sizes without normalization	Capital, volatility, liquidity, and leverage determine significance.
Assuming crowding must reverse immediately	Crowded positions can persist while supporting conditions remain.
Using delayed reports as current conditions	Positioning can change before reports are published.
Confusing model precision with observational certainty	Numerical detail does not remove assumption or data uncertainty.
Using positioning alone to predict direction	Future outcomes depend on triggers, liquidity, volatility, trend, information, and choices.

7.21 Limitations

Positioning analysis cannot independently determine:

- participant intent;
- complete ownership across the entire market;
- hidden or offsetting exposures;
- future participant decisions;
- whether hedging will occur;
- whether a trigger will be reached;
- whether liquidity will remain available;
- future market direction;
- fair value;
- the duration of crowding;
- whether a model-based estimate is correctly specified.

Positioning data are often weakest where exposures are most complex: private portfolios, cross-instrument hedges, structured products, rapidly changing dealer books, and funding relationships.

7.22 Why Positioning Matters

Positioning connects prior decisions to possible future responses. It shows how exposure, leverage, sensitivity, and constraints remain embedded in the market after transactions have occurred.

Positioning does not determine what participants will do. It helps explain why the same new information, price change, or volatility shock can produce very different outcomes under different market conditions.

For this reason, positioning is essential to understanding market sensitivity, fragility, and possible response pathways. Its meaning becomes strongest when interpreted jointly with liquidity, volatility, and trend.

Chapter Summary

Positioning is the distribution of financial exposure, sensitivity, leverage, concentration, and potential adjustment requirements across market participants under specified conditions.

Positioning is not equivalent to price, flow, sentiment, intent, or a simple long-versus-short count. The same nominal position may carry different significance depending on leverage, liquidity, time horizon, financing, optionality, and participant constraints.

Because positioning is only partially observable, researchers rely on reported holdings, open interest, futures data, securities lending, fund flows, derivative sensitivities, transaction-derived evidence, and model-based estimates. Each source captures only part of the exposure structure and may be delayed, aggregated, incomplete, or assumption dependent.

Positioning creates conditional response potential. Participants may hedge, rebalance, reduce risk, cover exposure, increase exposure, or remain inactive as conditions evolve. The resulting behavior depends on triggers, constraints, liquidity, volatility, trend, and participant choice.

Positioning improves understanding of market sensitivity and possible adjustment pressure. It does not independently predict direction or eliminate uncertainty.

Established Knowledge

The importance of positioning is well established across portfolio theory, derivatives, market making, dealer inventory, leverage, margin, institutional holdings, futures commitments, short selling, securities lending, fund flows, open interest, systematic strategies, crowding, deleveraging, and financial contagion.

Existing research also recognizes that exposure may be nonlinear, that gross and net measures convey different information, and that leverage, funding, collateral, and liquidity can transform ordinary price movement into forced adjustment.

Institute Perspective

The Institute treats positioning as the distribution-of-exposure observational domain. Its purpose is to integrate holdings, sensitivities, leverage, concentration, crowding, financing, and potential adjustment requirements within one coherent analytical category.

Reported positions are not assumed to equal total economic exposure. Derivative sensitivities are treated as conditional evidence rather than deterministic flow. Direct, reported, inferred, delayed, and model-dependent information should be labeled honestly.

Positioning should be interpreted jointly with liquidity, volatility, and trend. The framework is intended to improve understanding of possible market response, not to convert incomplete exposure estimates into claims of certain future direction.

Questions for Reflection

1. What distinguishes a recorded position from total economic exposure?
2. Why can two participants with identical holdings face different risks?
3. What is the difference between gross and net positioning?
4. Why can low net exposure coexist with high market sensitivity?
5. What distinguishes positioning from transaction flow?
6. Why should long exposure not automatically be interpreted as optimism?
7. How does leverage alter the importance of a position?
8. Why can concentrated exposure remain quiet for a long period?
9. What triggers may convert latent exposure into observable market activity?
10. Why is open interest not inherently bullish or bearish?
11. What does a Greek measure, and what does it not reveal?
12. Why are dealer-positioning estimates model dependent?
13. How can liquidity determine whether positioning becomes destabilizing?
14. Why does crowded positioning not guarantee immediate reversal?
15. What evidence would cause a positioning interpretation to be revised?

Chapter 8. Volatility

The Expression of Uncertainty

Chapter Purpose

Financial markets are inherently uncertain. Future outcomes, probability distributions, participant responses, policy decisions, information quality, and market mechanisms are never known completely. Participants continuously form beliefs, revise expectations, manage exposure, and react to changing conditions. These processes become visible partly through the variability of market prices and option valuations.

Volatility is among the most widely measured and most frequently misinterpreted concepts in finance. It is often treated as a synonym for uncertainty, risk, fear, instability, or expected direction. None of those equivalences is reliable. Volatility is a family of measurements and estimates describing the degree and structure of market variability under specified definitions, horizons, and methods.

Within Market Systems Science, volatility is the third foundational observational domain. The domain organizes evidence concerning realized variability, option-implied variability, asymmetry, term structure, volatility-of-volatility, jumps, dispersion, and correlation. It also examines how uncertainty, liquidity, positioning, information processing, and participant adjustment become expressed through market behavior.

The purpose of this chapter is to preserve the accepted statistical meaning of volatility while placing it within a broader systems context. It distinguishes observed prices from estimated or inferred volatility, volatility from uncertainty and risk, and realized volatility from implied and expected volatility. It also establishes standards for interpreting volatility without turning measurements into unsupported claims about fear, intent, causation, or future direction.

Learning Objectives

- Define volatility statistically and within a systems framework.
- Distinguish observed prices and returns from estimated or inferred volatility.
- Distinguish volatility from uncertainty, risk, fear, instability, and direction.

- Explain why every volatility statement must specify horizon, sampling, estimator, and market context.
- Distinguish historical, realized, implied, expected, forward, and risk-premium concepts.
- Identify major structural properties of volatility, including clustering, asymmetry, jumps, fat tails, and volatility-of-volatility.
- Interpret volatility term structure, skew, dispersion, and correlation carefully.
- Explain how volatility interacts with liquidity, positioning, and trend.
- Recognize model dependence, measurement limitations, and common analytical misuse.
- Evaluate volatility evidence proportionally to its quality, scope, and uncertainty.

8.1 Volatility as a Market Phenomenon

In conventional finance, volatility refers to the degree of variability in prices or returns over time. This statistical meaning is foundational and should be preserved.

Definition — Volatility

Volatility is the degree and structure of variability observed or implied in market prices over a specified horizon and under a specified measurement method.

The definition has four important elements. First, volatility concerns variability rather than direction. Second, it may be estimated from observed prices or inferred from option prices. Third, its value depends on the selected horizon and methodology. Fourth, volatility has structure: timing, asymmetry, persistence, cross-sectional dispersion, and correlation may matter as much as a single summary number.

Systems Interpretation: Within Market Systems Science, volatility is an observational domain organizing evidence about how uncertainty, sensitivity, disagreement, information processing, liquidity conditions, and participant adjustment become expressed through market variability and option valuation.

This interpretation does not claim that uncertainty is the sole cause of volatility. Variability may also reflect mechanical hedging, forced liquidation, weak liquidity, changing risk premia, market structure, leverage, scheduled activity, discontinuous information, or measurement choices.

8.2 Prices Are Observed; Volatility Is Measured or Inferred

Volatility is often described as observable, but that statement requires precision. Transactions, quotations, closing prices, and option prices are observed. Returns, ranges, variances, and volatility estimates are constructed from those observations.

Layer	What occurs	Example
Observed market data	Prices, quotes, trades, and option premiums are recorded.	A stock closes at $100 and then $102.
Constructed series	Observed prices are transformed into returns, ranges, or other inputs.	A 2% close-to-close return is calculated.
Volatility measurement or inference	A defined estimator or option model produces a volatility value.	Twenty-day realized volatility or one-month implied volatility.
Evidence claim	The measurement is evaluated relative to a question, baseline, or comparison.	Short-horizon realized variability has increased.
Interpretation	A reasoned conclusion is formed with stated qualifications.	The market is adjusting more actively, but the cause remains uncertain.

Measurement Principle: Market variability is observed through prices and returns; volatility is a measurement or model-conditioned estimate constructed from that variability.

A precise numerical output does not eliminate measurement uncertainty. Different sampling frequencies, windows, annualization conventions, price sources, option models, and data-cleaning rules may produce different volatility estimates from the same market.

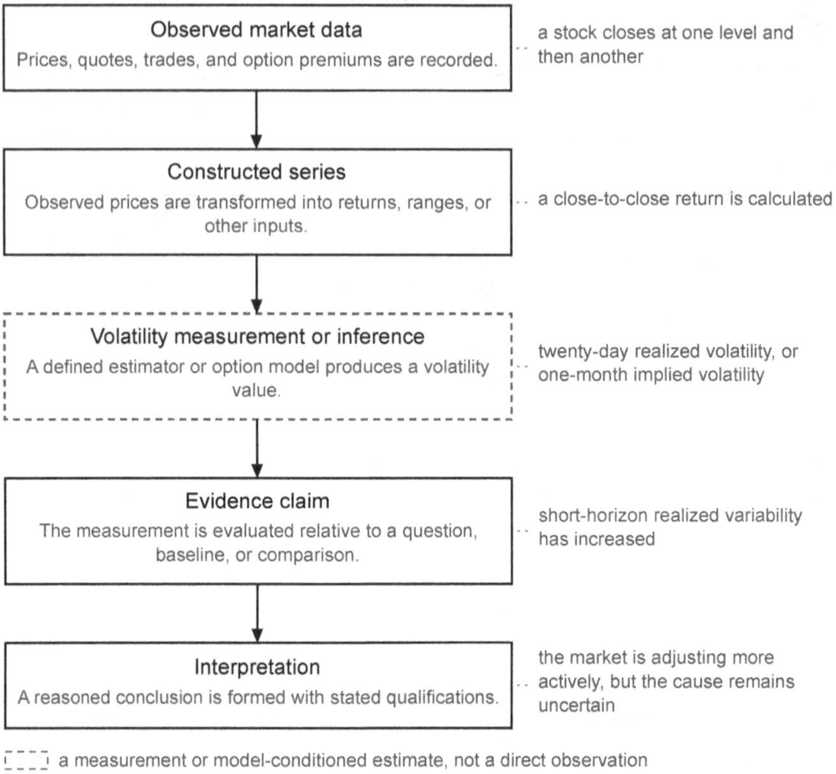

Figure 8.1 — From Price Observations to Volatility Interpretation

8.3 Uncertainty and Volatility Are Not the Same

Uncertainty concerns what is unknown or insufficiently knowable about future outcomes, probability distributions, mechanisms, information quality, and participant response. Participants form beliefs about uncertainty, but uncertainty is not confined to their mental states.

Volatility concerns observed or implied variability. The two may be related, but they need not move together.

Environment A — High uncertainty, limited realized volatility

Participants await a major policy announcement. The outcome is uncertain, but trading remains balanced, liquidity remains deep, and many participants reduce activity. Prices remain within a narrow range. Uncertainty may be substantial while realized volatility remains low.

Environment B — Volatility rises as uncertainty is resolved

The announcement arrives close to expectations, resolving one important unknown. Yet positioning is concentrated, liquidity is weak, and hedging demand accelerates. Prices move sharply. Realized volatility rises even though part of the original uncertainty has declined.

> **Uncertainty–Volatility Distinction:** Uncertainty may exist without immediate volatility, and volatility may rise even as one source of uncertainty is being resolved.

8.4 Volatility Is Not Risk

Volatility describes variability. Risk concerns the possibility and consequence of undesirable outcomes for a particular participant, portfolio, institution, or system.

Risk depends on position direction, leverage, funding, liabilities, horizon, liquidity, path, optionality, objectives, and loss tolerance. The same volatility can therefore create different risks for different participants.

- Upside volatility may benefit a long option holder while harming a short option seller.
- Downside volatility may threaten a leveraged investor more than an unleveraged long-term investor.
- A stable price series may conceal credit, liquidity, jump, or funding risk.
- A small, fully funded volatile position may pose less risk than a highly leveraged low-volatility position.
- Low realized volatility may encourage leverage that increases future fragility.

> **Risk Distinction:** Volatility describes variability. Risk concerns the consequences of possible outcomes for a particular participant or system.

8.5 Volatility Is Not Fear, Instability, or Direction

Concept	Meaning	Why it differs from volatility
Fear	A psychological or behavioral interpretation.	Volatility may rise for mechanical, informational, or liquidity reasons without demonstrating fear.
Instability	A condition of reduced resilience, fragile feedback, discontinuity, or susceptibility to disruption.	High volatility can occur in functional markets; low volatility can coexist with hidden fragility.
Direction	The sign and persistence of price movement.	Volatility measures variability, not whether prices rise or fall.
Uncertainty	What is unknown or insufficiently knowable about outcomes and mechanisms.	Volatility is one possible expression, not uncertainty itself.
Risk	The consequences of possible outcomes for a participant or system.	Risk is exposure-specific; volatility is a market or instrument measurement.

A market may exhibit high volatility without a sustained trend, high volatility within a strong upward trend, low volatility during a persistent decline, or rising implied volatility before meaningful realized movement occurs.

8.6 Why Volatility Arises

Volatility may arise from initiating influences and from the market conditions through which those influences are transmitted.

Potential initiating influences

- new economic, corporate, or policy information;
- changes in expectations;
- geopolitical developments;
- institutional rebalancing;
- order imbalance;
- technological disruption;
- changes in funding or collateral;
- unexpected market events.

Transmission and amplification conditions

- weak or fragmented liquidity;
- concentrated or leveraged positioning;
- dealer hedging and nonlinear exposure;

- correlated strategies and common risk limits;
- margin and collateral rules;
- feedback trading;
- market closures, reopenings, or gaps;
- changes in volatility risk premia.

The same initiating event may produce little market movement under one configuration and extraordinary movement under another. Volatility therefore cannot be understood from the event alone.

8.7 Volatility as a System Response

Volatility reflects how market prices adjust when information, expectations, exposure, liquidity demand, and participant constraints interact.

It is responsive because changing conditions alter variability. It is consequential because volatility itself changes option sensitivities, margin requirements, risk limits, position sizing, liquidity provision, and participant behavior.

- Rising volatility may widen spreads and reduce quoted size.
- Higher volatility may increase margin and collateral requirements.
- Option sensitivities may change, producing new hedging demand.
- Risk-control systems may reduce exposure as measured volatility rises.
- Demand for protection may increase implied volatility and skew.
- Volatility forecasts may affect capital allocation and execution choices.

Feedback Principle: Volatility is both a response to changing market conditions and a condition that can alter future market behavior.

8.8 Core Forms of Volatility

Form	What it represents	Principal limitation
Historical volatility	Variability calculated from past prices under a selected method.	Backward-looking and sensitive to window and estimator.
Realized volatility	Variability realized over a defined interval and sampling scheme.	Depends on sampling, microstructure noise, and treatment of jumps or gaps.
Implied volatility	The volatility parameter that reconciles an option-pricing model with an observed option price.	Model conditioned and affected by strike, maturity, supply, demand, liquidity, and risk premia.
Expected volatility	A forecast or belief concerning future variability.	Not directly observable and may be inaccurate.

Form	What it represents	Principal limitation
Implied variance	Option-derived market pricing of variance under a defined methodology.	Requires assumptions, option coverage, and implementation choices.
Forward volatility	Volatility inferred for a future interval from a term structure.	Highly dependent on model and term-structure assumptions.
Volatility risk premium	Compensation embedded in volatility-related prices relative to subsequently realized variability.	Definition, horizon, and measurement conventions vary.

8.9 Structural Properties of Volatility

Property	Description	Interpretive importance
Clustering	Large movements tend to occur near other large movements, and quiet periods often persist.	Volatility is not independent through time.
Mean reversion	Some volatility measures tend to move toward longer-run levels.	The long-run level may itself change; reversion is not guaranteed on a fixed schedule.
Asymmetry	Volatility may respond differently to price declines and increases.	Direction and variability can interact unevenly.
Leverage effect	Price declines may increase financial or perceived leverage and coincide with higher volatility.	Several mechanisms may contribute; the label does not prove one cause.
Jumps	Prices may change discontinuously rather than through small continuous steps.	Continuous models may understate abrupt movement.
Fat tails	Extreme returns occur more frequently than simple normal models imply.	Tail risk cannot be inferred reliably from standard deviation alone.

Property	Description	Interpretive importance
Volatility-of-volatility	Volatility itself varies and may become unstable.	Option and hedging sensitivities may change rapidly.
Horizon dependence	Short- and long-horizon measures may convey different information.	Volatility comparisons require matched horizons.
Dispersion	Individual assets may move differently even when aggregate index movement is moderate.	Index calm may conceal substantial internal variation.
Correlation	Aggregate volatility depends partly on how components move together.	Rising correlation can increase index volatility without equal changes in component volatility.

8.10 Realized Volatility

Realized volatility is estimated from observed price changes. Its meaning depends on methodology.

- arithmetic or logarithmic returns;
- sampling frequency;
- rolling-window length;
- overlapping or non-overlapping observations;
- close-to-close, high–low, or intraday estimators;
- inclusion or exclusion of overnight movement;
- annualization convention;
- treatment of missing data, market closures, and outliers;
- adjustment for microstructure noise.

A twenty-session daily estimate and a five-minute intraday estimate may both be valid while describing different aspects of the same market. The value should never be detached from its construction.

8.11 Implied Volatility

Implied volatility is inferred rather than directly observed. It is the volatility input that causes an option-pricing model to match an observed option price, given other inputs and assumptions.

- underlying price;
- strike price;
- time to expiration;
- interest rates and carry;
- dividends where relevant;
- exercise convention;
- model structure;
- transaction-price quality.

Implied volatility may reflect expected future variability, event risk, tail-risk pricing, protection demand, dealer inventory, option liquidity, hedging pressure, and the volatility risk premium.

> **Implied Volatility Principle:** Implied volatility is a model-conditioned market price of option exposure, not a pure or unbiased forecast of future realized volatility.

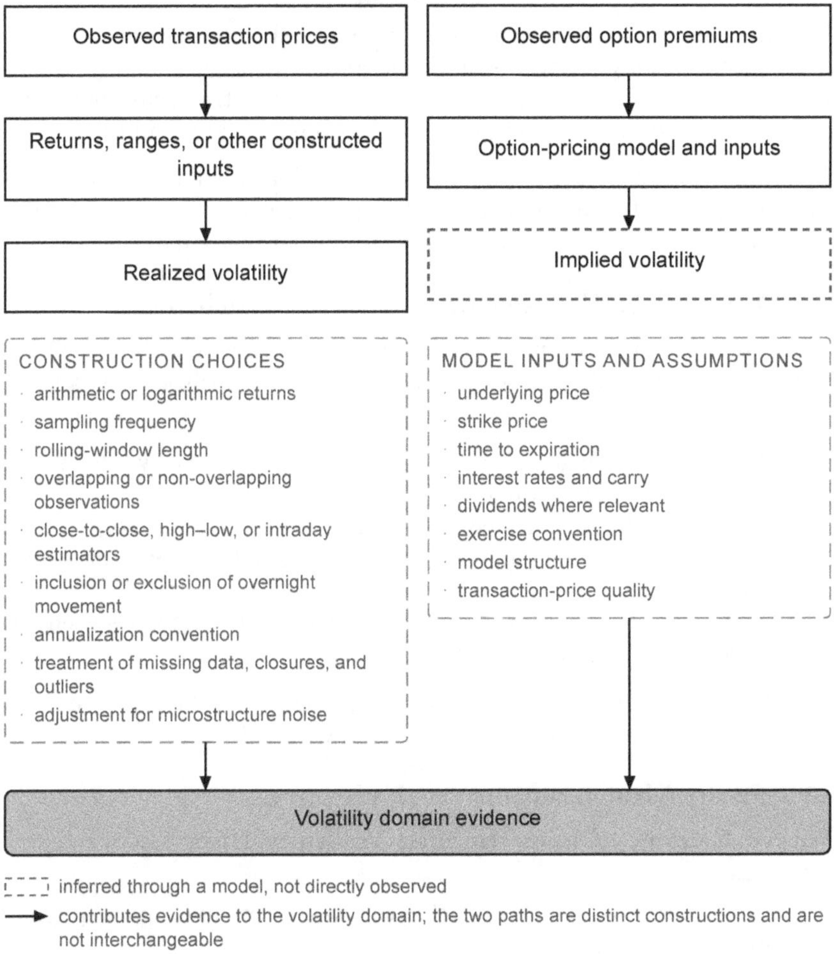

Figure 8.2 — Realized and Implied Volatility as Parallel Evidence Paths

8.12 Volatility Term Structure

Volatility term structure compares implied or expected volatility across maturities. Differences may reflect scheduled events, near-term uncertainty, long-horizon uncertainty, carry, supply and demand, mean-reversion expectations, liquidity, and risk premia.

An inverted term structure may accompany acute near-term demand or stress, but it does not prove panic, an imminent crash, or a specific directional outcome.

8.13 Volatility Skew and Smile

Skew and smile describe differences in implied volatility across strikes. These patterns may reflect asymmetric demand for protection, expected jump risk, leverage effects, dealer inventory, structured-product supply, crash-risk pricing, model limitations, or option-specific liquidity.

Skew is not a direct measure of sentiment and does not reveal participant intent by itself. Its meaning depends on maturity, moneyness, liquidity, event timing, and comparison with an appropriate baseline.

8.14 Volatility, Dispersion, and Correlation

Aggregate volatility does not reveal how movement is distributed within a market. Index volatility depends on component volatilities, weights, and correlations.

- Single-stock volatility may be high while index volatility remains moderate if correlations are low.
- Index volatility may rise sharply when correlations converge upward.
- Stable index movement may conceal substantial sector or security-level dispersion.
- Dispersion can create meaningful relative-value conditions even when aggregate volatility appears calm.

Aggregation Principle: Low aggregate volatility does not necessarily imply low internal market variability.

8.15 From Measurement to Evidence

Worked Evidence Chain: Implied Volatility Rises Before Earnings

1. Data: option prices rise relative to the current underlying price and other model inputs.
2. Measurement: near-term implied volatility increases, with possible changes in skew and term structure.
3. Possible evidence: the market is pricing greater near-term variability or greater compensation for bearing volatility exposure.
4. Alternative explanations: reduced option liquidity, one-sided demand, dealer inventory, event hedging, model-input error, or a wider volatility risk premium.
5. Interpretation: uncertainty or demand for protection may have increased, but the observation does not determine price direction or guarantee that realized volatility will exceed implied volatility.
6. Revision condition: the interpretation should change if option liquidity normalizes, the event passes, realized movement differs materially, or new information reveals a different mechanism.

8.16 Interpreting Volatility Evidence

A disciplined volatility assessment should identify:

- whether the measure is realized, implied, forecast, or risk-premium based;
- the estimator, option model, and data source;
- the horizon and sampling interval;
- the baseline and comparison period;
- persistence and rate of change;
- directional asymmetry;
- term structure and skew;
- volatility-of-volatility;
- dispersion and correlation;
- liquidity and option-market quality;
- positioning and potential hedging demand;
- event timing and market regime;
- model assumptions and alternative explanations.

Interpretive Principle: A volatility interpretation should identify what was measured, over what horizon, by what method, relative to which baseline, and with what uncertainty.

8.17 Progressive Worked Example

Session A — Controlled variability

The index trades within a narrow intraday range. Spreads remain narrow, depth is stable, realized intraday volatility remains low, implied volatility changes little, and participation remains balanced.

Session B — Same closing return, different path

The index finishes with the same net return as Session A, but the intraday range is much larger. Prices reverse repeatedly, spreads widen, depth declines, implied volatility and skew rise, and hedging activity accelerates.

The closing return is identical, but the volatility path and system condition are materially different.

Session C — Large directional move with controlled volatility

The index trends steadily, liquidity remains functional, pullbacks are limited, implied volatility remains stable or declines, and participation is broad. The total return is larger than in Sessions A or B, but the path is orderly.

A large return does not necessarily imply disorderly volatility, and a small closing return does not necessarily imply a calm market.

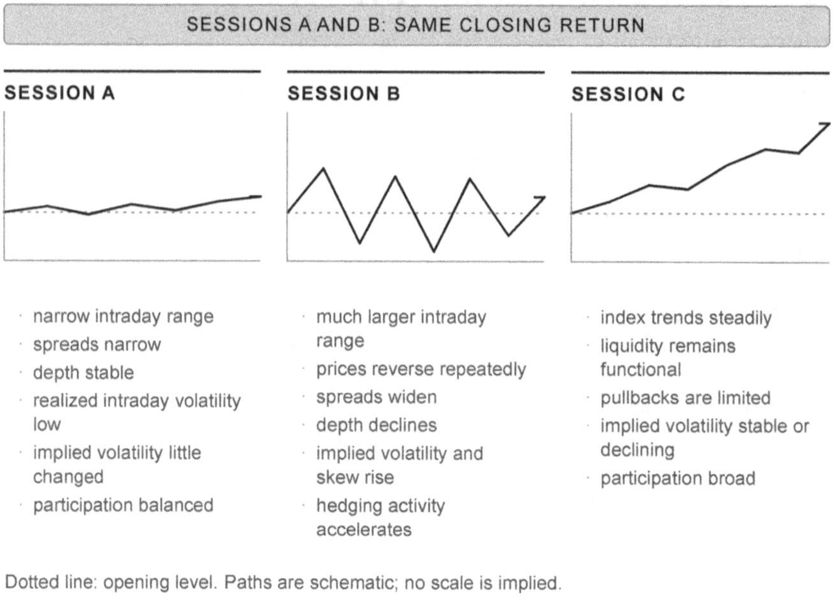

Figure 8.3 — Same Closing Return, Different Volatility Paths

8.18 Volatility and Liquidity

Weak liquidity may increase the price response to orders. Higher volatility may cause liquidity providers to widen spreads, reduce size, or withdraw. Widening spreads and reduced depth may then increase measured variability.

This feedback can become self-reinforcing, but high volatility can also coexist with functional liquidity during active information processing. The relationship is conditional rather than universal.

8.19 Volatility and Positioning

Positioning may affect volatility through leverage, margin calls, option convexity, dealer hedging, crowded strategies, volatility-control rules, redemptions, and correlated risk reduction.

Volatility may affect positioning through changing Greeks, risk limits, collateral requirements, position sizing, rebalancing, and the economics of hedging.

Dealer gamma and related estimates may provide useful evidence, but they do not determine realized volatility independently. Ownership, netting, liquidity, hedging policy, and alternative exposures remain important.

8.20 Volatility and Trend

Trend and volatility are not opposites. Markets may experience:

- a rising trend with falling volatility;
- a rising trend with rising volatility;
- a falling trend with rising volatility;
- a falling trend with declining volatility;
- a directionless market with high volatility;
- a directionless market with low volatility.

Meaning depends on persistence, path, participation, breadth, liquidity, positioning, and horizon.

8.21 Volatility Under Stress

Stress may be associated with:

- rapid expansion in realized volatility;
- jumps and price gaps;
- steepening skew;
- term-structure inversion;
- rising volatility-of-volatility;
- correlation convergence;
- widening option spreads;
- reduced executable liquidity;
- model instability;
- higher margin and collateral requirements.

No single feature proves systemic stress. Stress assessment requires multidomain evidence and explicit attention to data quality, horizon, and alternative explanations.

8.22 Common Misuses

Misuse	**Why it is misleading**
Treating volatility as uncertainty itself	Uncertainty may remain high while realized variability is low, and volatility may rise as uncertainty is resolved.
Treating volatility as risk	Risk depends on participant exposure, leverage, horizon, and consequences.
Treating volatility as fear	Variability may arise from mechanical, informational, or liquidity mechanisms.
Assuming high volatility is always harmful	Effects depend on position, purpose, and market functioning.

Misuse	Why it is misleading
Assuming low volatility means safety	Low measured variability may conceal leverage, jump, credit, or liquidity risk.
Comparing unmatched measures	Different horizons, sampling intervals, and estimators answer different questions.
Treating implied volatility as a direct forecast	It is model conditioned and includes supply, demand, liquidity, and risk premia.
Calling a volatility index a fear gauge without qualification	The index measures option-derived variance pricing under a defined methodology.
Ignoring skew and term structure	A single at-the-money value may omit important asymmetry and maturity information.
Treating realized and implied volatility as interchangeable	One is estimated from historical prices; the other is inferred from option prices.
Inferring direction from volatility alone	Volatility describes magnitude and structure, not sign.
Ignoring option liquidity	Poor prices or wide spreads can distort implied measures.
Ignoring overnight gaps or sampling effects	Methodology can materially alter the estimate.
Treating annualized volatility as a literal one-year forecast	Annualization is a scaling convention, not a guaranteed future outcome.
Assuming a stable distribution	Clustering, jumps, fat tails, and structural change violate simple assumptions.
Confusing numerical precision with certainty	Exact outputs may rest on uncertain data and models.
Ignoring dispersion and correlation	Aggregate volatility may conceal internal movement.
Treating volatility or gamma positioning as deterministic flow	Sensitivity estimates do not mandate one participant response.

8.23 Limitations

Volatility analysis cannot independently determine:

- future market direction;
- fair value;
- participant intent;
- the complete cause of variability;
- whether uncertainty is increasing or decreasing;
- whether implied volatility is overpriced or underpriced;

- whether realized volatility will match implied volatility;
- whether a market is stable or fragile;
- whether liquidity will remain available;
- whether a pattern will persist;
- whether a model is correctly specified.

Volatility measurements are conditional representations. Their usefulness depends on the question, horizon, estimator, data quality, and the other market conditions within which they are interpreted.

8.24 Why Volatility Matters

Volatility matters because it describes the magnitude, timing, asymmetry, persistence, and market pricing of variability.

It influences execution, option valuation, hedging, leverage, margin, risk management, capital allocation, and participant behavior.

Within a systems framework, volatility is most informative when interpreted jointly with liquidity, positioning, and trend. It improves understanding of market variability and sensitivity without independently revealing cause, intent, value, direction, or future outcome.

Chapter Summary

Volatility describes the degree and structure of variability observed or implied in market prices over a specified horizon and under a specified measurement method. Within Market Systems Science, volatility is interpreted as one observable expression of uncertainty, sensitivity, information processing, and participant adjustment.

Volatility is not uncertainty itself, nor is it synonymous with risk, fear, instability, or direction. Prices and returns are observed; realized volatility is estimated from historical observations; implied volatility is inferred from option prices through a model; expected future volatility remains uncertain.

Volatility is multidimensional. Its interpretation may require realized variability, implied volatility, skew, term structure, volatility-of-volatility, jumps, dispersion, and correlation. Each measurement addresses a different question and carries different assumptions.

Volatility interacts continuously with liquidity, positioning, and trend. It may arise as a response to market change and subsequently alter hedging, leverage, risk limits, liquidity provision, and participant behavior.

Volatility improves understanding of market variability and sensitivity. It does not independently reveal cause, intent, value, direction, or future outcome.

Established Knowledge

Volatility is one of the most extensively studied subjects in finance. Established areas include return variance and standard deviation, realized-volatility estimation, stochastic volatility, implied volatility, option pricing, volatility smiles and skew, volatility term structure, clustering, ARCH and GARCH models, jumps, fat tails, leverage effects, variance risk premia, volatility forecasting, correlation, dispersion, and volatility derivatives.

The manuscript relies on this scholarship and does not claim to replace the statistical or option-pricing definitions used within finance.

Institute Perspective

The Institute does not redefine volatility as something other than market variability. Its proposed contribution is organizational: treating volatility as an observational domain that integrates realized, implied, structural, and cross-sectional evidence within a broader market-reasoning framework.

Volatility is interpreted as one expression of uncertainty and system sensitivity, not as a direct measurement of uncertainty or a universal indicator of fear, risk, instability, or direction.

The Institute emphasizes the distinction among observation, estimation, model inference, evidence, and interpretation. Volatility should be analyzed jointly with liquidity, positioning, and trend, and every conclusion should remain proportional to the quality and scope of the underlying evidence.

Questions for Reflection

1. What is observed directly when volatility is estimated?
2. Why must a volatility statement specify its horizon and estimator?
3. How can uncertainty increase while realized volatility remains low?
4. How can volatility rise while uncertainty is being resolved?
5. What distinguishes volatility from participant-specific risk?
6. Why does low volatility not necessarily indicate safety?
7. What is the difference between realized and implied volatility?
8. Why is implied volatility not a pure forecast?
9. What information may be contained in volatility skew?
10. What can an inverted term structure indicate, and what can it not prove?
11. How can two sessions with the same closing return have different volatility conditions?
12. How do liquidity and volatility reinforce one another?
13. How may positioning amplify or suppress volatility?
14. Why are trend and volatility not opposites?
15. How can index volatility remain moderate while individual securities experience substantial variability?

16. What role does correlation play in aggregate volatility?
17. What evidence would cause a volatility interpretation to be revised?

Chapter 9. Trend

The Emergence of Direction

Chapter Purpose

Trend is among the most visible features of financial markets. Prices rise, decline, consolidate, reverse, and sometimes maintain directional persistence for extended periods. Participants often describe these movements using charts, moving averages, momentum indicators, relative-strength measures, and technical patterns.

Yet trend is frequently treated as if it were an independent force acting upon the market. A systems perspective requires greater precision. Prices are observed, but trend is inferred from persistence across observations, scales, and measurement rules. The same market can exhibit an upward long-horizon trend, a downward short-horizon movement, and a directionless intraday pattern without contradiction.

Within Market Systems Science, trend is the fourth foundational observational domain. It organizes evidence about sustained direction while recognizing that direction emerges through interactions among information, liquidity, positioning, volatility, participant behavior, and time.

The purpose of this chapter is to define trend as a measurable directional condition, distinguish it from isolated movement, return, momentum, and acceleration, and establish standards for assessing trend structure without turning directional evidence into deterministic prediction.

Learning Objectives

- Define trend statistically and within a systems framework.
- Distinguish observed price movement from inferred directional persistence.
- Distinguish direction, return, trend, momentum, and acceleration.
- Explain why trend depends on the selected variable, horizon, and measurement method.
- Evaluate breadth, participation, leadership, and rotation.
- Distinguish trend strength from trend structure.
- Identify multiple pathways through which trend may emerge.
- Distinguish trend deterioration, transition, failure, reversal, and broader market-state transition.

- Interpret trend jointly with liquidity, positioning, and volatility.
- Recognize measurement uncertainty, common misuse, and the retrospective nature of trend classification.

9.1 Trend as a Market Phenomenon

In ordinary market language, trend refers to the general direction in which a market variable moves over time. In this chapter, the primary focus is price-direction trend, although volatility, spreads, yields, volume, breadth, positioning, and other variables may also exhibit trends.

Definition — Trend

Trend is sustained directional persistence in a market variable over a specified horizon, identified through a stated measurement method and interpreted within the surrounding market conditions.

Systems Interpretation: Within Market Systems Science, price trend is treated as an emergent directional condition produced and modified through interactions among information, liquidity, positioning, volatility, participant behavior, and time.

Trend exists in degrees. It does not require uninterrupted movement, and it may coexist with pullbacks, gaps, or temporary countertrend activity. Its classification depends on scale, method, and analytical purpose.

9.2 Price Movement Is Not Necessarily Trend

Every transaction can change price, but not every price change creates persistent direction.

Case A — Isolated movement

A security trades at $100. A large market order pushes it to $101, but the price quickly returns to $100. Movement occurred, but persistence did not.

Case B — Retained level shift

The security moves from $100 to $101 and remains near the new level. The market may have accepted a step change, but a continuing trend has not yet been established.

Case C — Persistent advance

The security advances from $100 to $101, then $102, then $103 across multiple observations, with repeated retention after pullbacks and broader participation. Evidence of trend becomes stronger.

Persistence Principle: Magnitude alone does not establish trend; persistence and path matter.

9.3 Prices Are Observed; Trend Is Classified

Prices, quotations, and transactions are observed. Trend is classified from a sequence of observations using an explicit method.

Layer	What occurs	Example
Observed data	Prices, returns, volume, and related market data are recorded.	Daily closing prices for an equity index.
Directional features	Returns, slopes, highs and lows, or other directional measures are constructed.	A positive 12-week cumulative return and rising regression slope.
Persistence measurement	The continuity, duration, or consistency of direction is assessed.	The index remains above a rising reference level for most observations.
Trend classification	A rule or model labels the directional condition.	Medium-horizon upward trend under the selected method.
Structural interpretation	Breadth, leadership, liquidity, volatility, and positioning are evaluated.	The trend is persistent but increasingly concentrated.

Trend rules may use moving-average relationships, slope thresholds, cumulative returns, sequences of highs and lows, breakout retention, persistence scores, filters, or regime models. Different defensible methods may classify the same period differently.

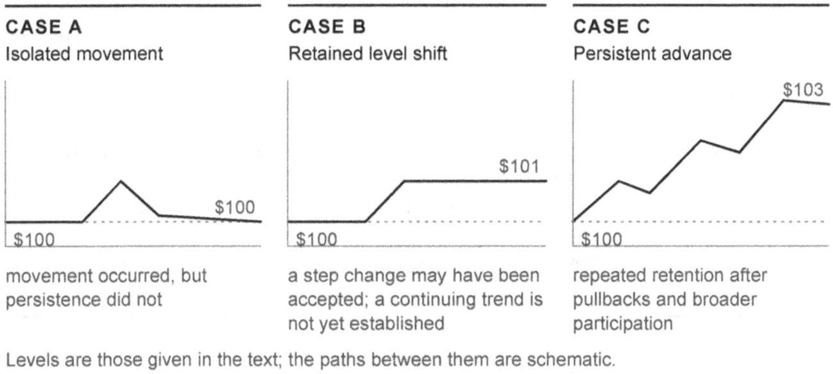

Figure 9.1 — Isolated Movement, Retained Level Shift, and Persistent Trend

9.4 Trend Depends on Variable and Horizon

A market may rise over several months, decline over several days, and consolidate over several hours. These descriptions can all be correct because market behavior is nested across time horizons.

A complete trend statement should identify:

- the instrument or market;
- the variable being evaluated;
- the direction;
- the horizon;
- the measurement method;
- the breadth or participation;
- the relevant qualification or uncertainty.

> **Example of a disciplined statement:** The capitalization-weighted equity index maintained positive 12-week price-direction persistence, while five-session momentum, equal-weight participation, and small-cap relative strength weakened.

This is more informative than saying simply that the market is bullish or trending upward.

9.5 Direction, Return, Trend, Momentum, and Acceleration

Concept	Meaning
Direction	The sign of movement over a specified interval.
Return	The magnitude of gain or loss over a specified interval.
Trend	Persistence of direction across multiple observations or a defined horizon.
Momentum	Recent directional strength or return persistence under a stated method.
Acceleration	A change in the rate or strength of movement under a stated measure.
Countertrend movement	Temporary movement against the prevailing trend.
Reversal	An observed change from one sustained direction to another.

Momentum has several established meanings in finance. It may refer to recent return, time-series persistence, relative performance, or a ranked cross-sectional strategy. The method must be stated.

Acceleration is also method dependent. It may refer to a change in return, a change in slope, a second difference in price, or a change in a momentum score.

Illustrative weekly sequence

Week	Closing Price	Weekly Change
1	100	—
2	104	+4
3	107	+3
4	109	+2
5	110	+1

Price continues to rise each week, so upward direction persists. The weekly gain declines, so recent directional strength weakens. The trend may remain intact while momentum slows.

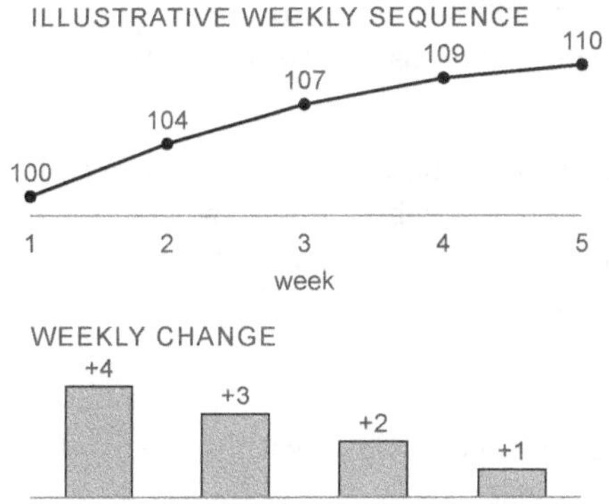

Direction persists each week while the weekly gain declines: the trend may remain intact while momentum slows.

Direction	The sign of movement over a specified interval.
Return	The magnitude of gain or loss over a specified interval.
Trend	Persistence of direction across multiple observations or a defined horizon.
Momentum	Recent directional strength or return persistence under a stated method.
Acceleration	A change in the rate or strength of movement under a stated measure.
Countertrend movement	Temporary movement against the prevailing trend.
Reversal	An observed change from one sustained direction to another.

Figure 9.2 — Direction, Trend, Momentum, and Acceleration

9.6 Trend as an Emergent Condition

Trend does not require one universal cause. Several pathways may create or sustain directional persistence.

Pathway	Illustrative mechanism
Information-led	New information changes expectations or valuation and produces sustained demand or supply.
Liquidity-led	Withdrawal of bids or offers allows one-sided price movement to persist.
Positioning-led	Short covering, liquidation, or rebalancing produces repeated directional flow.
Hedging-led	Derivative sensitivities generate recurring buying or selling.
Allocation-led	Gradual institutional, systematic, or passive capital movement sustains direction.
Feedback-led	Performance, narratives, risk capacity, and trend-following behavior reinforce persistence.

Emergence Principle: Trend may emerge through several pathways whose importance changes across instruments, periods, and horizons.

A simple information-to-buying sequence may be pedagogically useful, but it is only one possible pathway. Markets may also trend without a discrete information event, through slow allocation, mechanical rebalancing, liquidity withdrawal, or cross-asset transmission.

9.7 Persistence and Path

Trend concerns persistence, but persistence can take several forms.

- a smooth directional advance or decline;
- a stepwise progression with consolidations;
- a trend containing repeated but contained pullbacks;
- a trend with volatility contraction;
- a trend with volatility expansion;
- a gap-driven repricing followed by continued movement;
- a persistent slope that remains statistically weak but directionally consistent.

Persistence may be evaluated through:

- frequency of directionally consistent returns;
- slope stability;
- duration above or below reference levels;
- retention after pullbacks;
- proportion of observations in directional structure;
- consistency of highs and lows;
- model-based persistence probabilities.

No single form is universally superior. The appropriate measure depends on the decision problem and horizon.

9.8 Participation and Breadth

An index can rise even when many components decline because aggregate indexes are often weighted unevenly. Breadth describes how widely directional behavior is distributed across a defined universe.

- advancing versus declining securities;
- percentage above selected moving averages;
- new highs versus new lows;
- equal-weighted versus capitalization-weighted performance;
- sector or industry participation;
- volume breadth;
- contribution concentration;
- cross-sectional return dispersion.

Breadth depends on universe definition, index membership, weighting, threshold, horizon, and data treatment. A broadly supported trend may have a different structure from a narrowly supported one, but breadth does not guarantee continuation.

> **Breadth Principle:** Breadth describes how widely directional behavior is distributed; it does not independently determine whether the trend will continue.

9.9 Leadership and Rotation

Markets rarely move uniformly. Certain securities, industries, factors, or asset classes often display stronger directional persistence than others.

Leadership may be defined through absolute return, relative return, risk-adjusted return, persistence, benchmark contribution, or another stated method. Rotation describes changes in which groups lead or lag.

Leadership analysis asks:

- which instruments or groups lead;
- relative to which benchmark;
- for how long;
- with what breadth and liquidity;
- whether leadership is broadening, rotating, narrowing, or weakening;
- whether the leaders account for an increasing share of aggregate return.

Leadership is observational evidence. It may reveal where capital and attention are migrating, but it does not prove causality or future continuation.

9.10 Trend Strength and Trend Structure

Trend strength and trend structure answer different questions.

Dimension	Question addressed	Possible evidence
Trend strength	How large, steep, persistent, or statistically distinct is the directional movement?	Slope, cumulative return, persistence score, time above reference levels, drawdown behavior.
Trend structure	What market conditions accompany and sustain the direction?	Breadth, leadership, liquidity, volatility, positioning, cross-asset consistency, path.
Trend quality	A practical summary assessment of the observed structure.	A qualified interpretation, not an objective guarantee of durability.

Trend Structure Principle: Trend quality is an interpretive assessment of the conditions associated with directional movement, not a guaranteed measure of durability or desirability.

9.11 Feedback and Self-Reinforcement

Persistent direction may alter participant behavior and create feedback.

Reinforcing feedback

- momentum-oriented participation;
- short covering;
- performance chasing;
- systematic allocation;
- improving collateral or risk capacity;
- narrative reinforcement.

Limiting feedback

- valuation constraints;
- position crowding;
- risk limits;
- liquidity exhaustion;
- profit taking;
- adverse information;
- volatility escalation.

Feedback Qualification: Feedback may extend a trend, but the same feedback may also increase fragility by concentrating exposure and reducing marginal participation.

9.12 Observable Measurements

Category	Examples	Principal limitation
Direction and persistence	Cumulative return, slope, moving-average relationships, highs and lows, time above reference levels.	Highly dependent on horizon and parameters.
Momentum	Rate of change, rolling return, time-series momentum, relative strength.	May capture recent strength without durable persistence.
Participation	Breadth, equal-weight confirmation, volume breadth, sector participation.	Depends on universe and weighting choices.
Leadership and rotation	Relative performance, contribution concentration, sector or factor rotation.	Leadership may persist, rotate, or narrow without a predictable outcome.
Statistical measures	Autocorrelation, serial dependence, trend filters, regime probabilities.	Sensitive to sample, model assumptions, and structural breaks.
Cross-asset consistency	Related markets moving in compatible or divergent ways.	Relationships may change and divergence may be structurally justified.

Each measure captures one aspect of directional persistence. None is trend itself, and no single measure defines trend in every setting.

9.13 From Measurement to Evidence

Worked Evidence Chain: Price Above a Rising Moving Average

1. Data: daily closing prices for a specified instrument.
2. Measurement: price is above the 50-day moving average, and the average has a positive slope.
3. Possible evidence: medium-horizon upward directional persistence under the selected parameterization.
4. Alternative explanations: a recent price gap, narrow leadership, temporary liquidity effects, parameter sensitivity, or survivorship in the selected sample.
5. Interpretation: an upward trend may be present under the selected method, but breadth, stability, and durability require additional evidence.

6. Revision condition: the classification should be reconsidered if price repeatedly fails to retain the structure, the slope changes materially, or alternative measures provide stronger contrary evidence.

9.14 Interpreting Trend Evidence

A disciplined trend assessment should identify:

- instrument and variable;
- direction and return;
- horizon;
- method and parameters;
- magnitude and persistence;
- momentum and any stated acceleration measure;
- breadth and contribution concentration;
- leadership and rotation;
- path and pullback behavior;
- liquidity;
- positioning;
- volatility;
- cross-asset consistency;
- alternative classifications;
- possible transition evidence.

Interpretive Principle: A trend interpretation should distinguish what is measured from how the directional structure is being sustained.

9.15 Same Return, Different Trend Structure

Market A

- An index rises 10% over four months.
- Participation is broad.
- Liquidity remains stable.
- Volatility is moderate.
- Pullbacks are orderly.
- Leadership rotates among several sectors.
- Positioning expands gradually.

Market B

- The index also rises 10% over four months.
- Only a few large securities drive most of the gain.
- Liquidity deteriorates during declines.
- Volatility rises as prices advance.
- Leadership narrows continuously.
- Positioning becomes increasingly concentrated.

The final return is identical, but the underlying system conditions are not. Market A may be described as broadly supported. Market B may be directionally strong but increasingly sensitive to disruption.

> **Structural Principle:** Direction describes where the market has moved; the other domains help explain how that movement is being sustained.

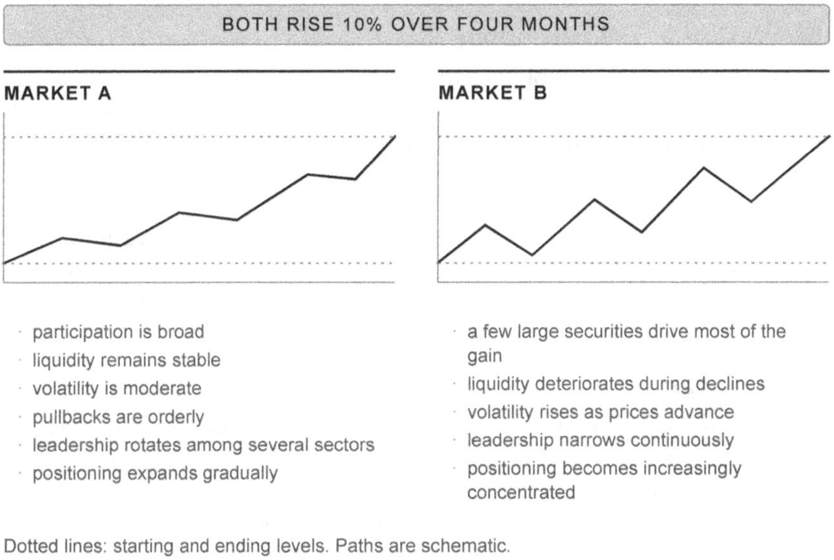

Figure 9.3 — Same Return, Different Trend Structure

9.16 Detailed Example: Broad Index Advance

Consider a hypothetical broad equity index that advances from 5,000 to 5,400 over eight weeks.

Observation 1 — Price

The index has risen 8%. Directional persistence is present under the selected eight-week horizon.

Observation 2 — Breadth

During the first four weeks, 75% of constituents trade above their intermediate moving averages. By the eighth week, only 48% remain above those averages. The index continues upward, but participation narrows.

Observation 3 — Leadership

Early in the advance, industrial, financial, technology, and consumer groups participate. Later, a small group of large technology companies accounts for most of the aggregate gain. Leadership becomes concentrated.

Observation 4 — Liquidity

Spreads remain normal during advances but widen materially during brief declines. The market absorbs buying more readily than selling.

Observation 5 — Positioning

Option prices and available positioning evidence are consistent with increasing upside exposure and concentrated risk in the leading securities. Participant identity and future hedging behavior remain uncertain.

Observation 6 — Volatility

Index realized volatility remains moderate, while implied volatility for several leading stocks rises. This may reflect event risk, protection demand, option-market conditions, or increased pricing of future variability; it does not directly prove that uncertainty has increased.

Interpretation

> The upward price trend remains intact under the selected horizon and method. However, breadth has narrowed, leadership has concentrated, downside liquidity has weakened, and exposure appears increasingly concentrated. These conditions may increase sensitivity to adverse information without determining whether or when reversal will occur.

9.17 Trend Deterioration, Transition, Failure, and Reversal

Condition	Meaning	What it does not prove
Trend deterioration	Supporting evidence weakens while prevailing direction persists.	That reversal is imminent.
Trend transition	Directional organization changes; persistence weakens or becomes ambiguous.	That a new sustained direction already exists.
Trend failure	A breakout or continuation attempt does not retain directional structure.	That the opposite trend must follow.
Trend reversal	A new sustained direction becomes established.	That the reversal will persist indefinitely.

Condition	Meaning	What it does not prove
Market-state transition	The broader multidomain configuration changes.	That price trend must reverse at the same time.

A trend transition is not equivalent to a full market-state transition. A market state may change before price direction reverses, and directional structure may change while the broader system remains within the same classified state.

Deterioration, transition, failure, and reversal do not form a universal linear sequence. Markets may stabilize, resume the original trend, or reconfigure in several ways.

9.18 Trend and Liquidity

Trend can persist through deep liquidity or thin liquidity. Stable liquidity may support orderly directional movement. Thin liquidity may amplify movement without demonstrating broad conviction.

Asymmetric liquidity can be especially informative. A market may absorb buying efficiently while becoming less resilient during selling, or the reverse. Liquidity helps characterize the path and resilience of trend but does not independently determine durability.

9.19 Trend and Positioning

Persistent direction changes profits, losses, exposure, and risk capacity. Profits may permit participants to add exposure; losses may force reduction. Short covering, systematic trend following, rebalancing, or liquidation may reinforce movement.

Crowded positioning may extend a trend or increase sensitivity to reversal. Crowding is therefore structural evidence, not a timing signal.

9.20 Trend and Volatility

Trend and volatility are not opposites. Markets may exhibit:

- strong trend with low volatility;
- strong trend with high volatility;
- weak trend with high volatility;
- weak trend with low volatility;
- trend with rising volatility;
- trend with falling volatility.

Volatility characterizes how direction is expressed. It does not determine whether direction exists.

9.21 Trend and Cross-Asset Relationships

Related markets may move consistently, diverge, lead, lag, or reflect different horizons and constraints.

- equities may rise while credit spreads widen;
- large-cap indexes may rise while small caps weaken;
- commodities may rise while producer equities lag;
- currency and interest-rate movements may support or complicate an interpretation.

Cross-asset consistency may strengthen an interpretation, while divergence may reveal fragility, timing differences, or legitimate structural distinctions. Divergence is evidence requiring explanation, not automatic proof of reversal.

9.22 Common Misuses

Misuse	Why it is misleading
Treating any price movement as trend	Movement can be isolated and nonpersistent.
Treating a large return as proof of trend	A single jump can create a large return without sustained direction.
Ignoring horizon	Different horizons may support different trend classifications.
Treating one indicator as the definition of trend	Indicators are measurement methods, not the phenomenon itself.
Confusing momentum with trend	Recent strength can be high without durable persistence, and trend can persist while momentum weakens.
Treating slowing momentum as confirmed reversal	Direction may continue at a slower rate.
Treating breadth deterioration as a certain sell signal	Narrow trends can persist.
Assuming broad participation guarantees continuation	Broad trends can still reverse.
Treating cross-asset divergence as automatic invalidation	Relationships may change or reflect different structures.
Treating moving-average parameters as objective truth	Parameter choices materially affect classification.
Ignoring transaction costs and implementation delay	A historical signal may not translate into executable returns.
Using hindsight to classify trends too cleanly	Real-time trend identification is uncertain and lagged.
Treating technical patterns as causal mechanisms	Patterns describe behavior; they do not independently explain cause.
Treating trend as independent of other domains	Liquidity, positioning, and volatility help shape directional behavior.

Misuse	Why it is misleading
Treating trend as prediction	Observed persistence does not guarantee continuation.
Using bullish or bearish without definition	The variable, horizon, and method remain unspecified.
Confusing trend transition with market-state transition	Directional change and multidomain reconfiguration are related but distinct.

9.23 Limitations

Trend analysis cannot independently determine:

- the cause of directional movement;
- fair value;
- participant intent;
- future continuation;
- reversal timing;
- structural stability;
- liquidity resilience;
- positioning vulnerability;
- the optimal parameter choice;
- whether historical persistence will survive costs;
- whether the same method generalizes across instruments.

Retrospective Limitation: Trend analysis is inherently retrospective to some degree because persistence can only be identified after observations accumulate.

9.24 Why Trend Matters

Trend matters because persistent direction changes wealth, incentives, expectations, risk capacity, positioning, and participant behavior.

It summarizes where a market variable has been moving. Liquidity, positioning, and volatility help explain how that direction is being sustained, whether participation is broad or concentrated, and where sensitivity may be developing.

Trend is the most visible of the four observational domains, but not the most self-explanatory. Its value increases when directional evidence is interpreted within the broader system.

Chapter Summary

Trend is sustained directional persistence in a market variable over a specified horizon, identified through a stated measurement method and interpreted within the surrounding market conditions.

Trend differs from isolated movement because it requires persistence. It differs from return because a large gain or loss may occur without sustained direction. It differs from momentum because directional persistence may continue while recent strength weakens. It differs from acceleration because the rate of movement may change while the prevailing direction remains intact.

Prices are observed; trend is classified through measures of direction, slope, persistence, breadth, leadership, path, relative strength, and cross-asset consistency. Every measure is horizon and method dependent.

Within Market Systems Science, trend is treated primarily as an emergent condition rather than an independent causal force. It may arise through information, liquidity, positioning, hedging, allocation, and feedback pathways.

Trend reveals where the market has been moving. Liquidity, positioning, and volatility help explain how that movement is being sustained, whether participation is broad or concentrated, and where sensitivity may be increasing. Trend does not independently predict continuation or reversal.

Established Knowledge

Trend, momentum, serial dependence, relative strength, market breadth, leadership, and trend-following strategies have long been studied in finance, econometrics, behavioral finance, and technical analysis.

Established research areas include time-series momentum, cross-sectional momentum, moving-average rules, autocorrelation, underreaction and overreaction, limits to arbitrage, trend persistence across asset classes, regime classification, implementation costs, factor crowding, and the role of participation and market structure.

The persistence, causes, costs, and reliability of trend-related effects remain subjects of continuing study. No established measurement provides a universal or deterministic forecast.

Institute Perspective

The Institute proposes that trend should be understood as the emergence of direction within a market system rather than as a fully independent force.

Its contribution is organizational: distinguishing trend from movement, return, momentum, and acceleration; requiring explicit horizon and method; treating breadth, leadership, and cross-asset relationships as structural context; and integrating trend with liquidity, positioning, and volatility.

The Institute further distinguishes trend transition from broader market-state transition and rejects deterministic claims of continuation or reversal based on trend evidence alone.

Questions for Reflection

1. What distinguishes a price movement from a trend?
2. Why can a large return occur without sustained directional persistence?
3. Why must a trend statement identify its horizon?
4. Can a market be in a long-horizon uptrend and a short-horizon downtrend simultaneously?
5. What distinguishes direction from return?
6. What distinguishes trend from momentum?
7. What does acceleration mean, and why must its measurement be specified?
8. Why can a trend continue while momentum weakens?
9. What does breadth reveal that an index level may conceal?
10. Why can a narrow trend remain persistent?
11. What is the difference between leadership and benchmark contribution?
12. How can liquidity amplify trend without demonstrating broad conviction?
13. How can positioning reinforce a trend and later increase fragility?
14. Why are trend and volatility not opposites?
15. What is the difference between trend deterioration, transition, failure, and reversal?
16. Why does cross-asset divergence require interpretation rather than an automatic conclusion?
17. What evidence would cause a trend classification to be revised?
18. Why is trend analysis inherently retrospective to some degree?

Part III. Market Evolution

Chapter 10. Interactions Among the Observational Domains

From Isolated Measurements to Market Configurations

Chapter Purpose

Liquidity, positioning, volatility, and trend provide four distinct ways of organizing evidence about financial markets. Liquidity describes exchange capacity. Positioning describes the distribution of exposure and sensitivity. Volatility describes the degree and structure of variability observed or implied in market prices. Trend describes sustained directional persistence.

Markets do not experience these dimensions independently. Position adjustment creates demand for liquidity. Liquidity conditions influence price impact. Price movement alters volatility measurements and option sensitivities. Persistent direction changes profits, losses, incentives, and exposure. These interactions may reinforce movement, oppose it, delay it, redirect it, or change its meaning.

Chapter 10 builds upon the four observational domains developed in Part II and serves as the bridge into Part III, where measurements, evidence, state representations, and transitions are formalized. It explains how measurements become evidence, how evidence is organized into domain assessments, and how the domains are combined into a multidomain market configuration. It also distinguishes a detailed configuration from a higher-level market-state representation.

The chapter does not claim that four domains exhaust every influence on market behavior. Information, valuation, policy, macroeconomic conditions, technology, institutional design, and participant adaptation remain essential. The purpose of the four-domain architecture is to support transparent reasoning under uncertainty, not to reduce the market to four variables.

Learning Objectives

- Distinguish data, measurement, evidence, domain assessment, market configuration, and market state.
- Explain why domain evidence must be interpreted jointly rather than counted mechanically.

- Identify conditional relationships among liquidity, positioning, volatility, and trend.
- Distinguish interaction, correlation, and causation.
- Analyze reinforcing and balancing feedback loops.
- Distinguish strength, stability, resilience, fragility, stress, and failure.
- Explain configuration dependence, nonlinearity, path dependence, and time lags.
- Build a transparent multidomain assessment that preserves contradictory and missing evidence.
- Evaluate composite representations without losing component traceability.
- Connect current configuration to configuration change and later market-state analysis.

10.1 From Measurements to Multidomain Configuration

Market analysis often begins with recorded data and constructed measurements. A spread widens. Open interest increases. Implied volatility rises. Price remains above a rising reference level. These observations do not become understanding merely because they are collected together.

Level	Meaning	Example
Market phenomena	The underlying market activity or process of interest.	Exchange, adjustment, repricing, hedging, allocation.
Observable data	Recorded representations of market activity.	Quotes, trades, option prices, reported holdings.
Controlled measurement	A defined construction based on data.	Spread, realized volatility, breadth, moving-average slope.
Contextual evidence	A measurement interpreted relative to a question, baseline, horizon, and uncertainty.	Depth is lower than its normal range for the current time of day.
Domain assessment	An organized view of one dimension of behavior.	Liquidity appears less resilient for large sell orders.
Market configuration	The detailed arrangement of conditions across domains.	Positive trend, narrow breadth, concentrated exposure, weakening downside depth.
Market-state representation	A higher-level summary of selected configuration features.	Fragile directional expansion.

Synthesis Principle: Measurements do not become understanding merely by being collected together. Synthesis requires attention to meaning, scale, quality, time, interaction, and alternative explanation.

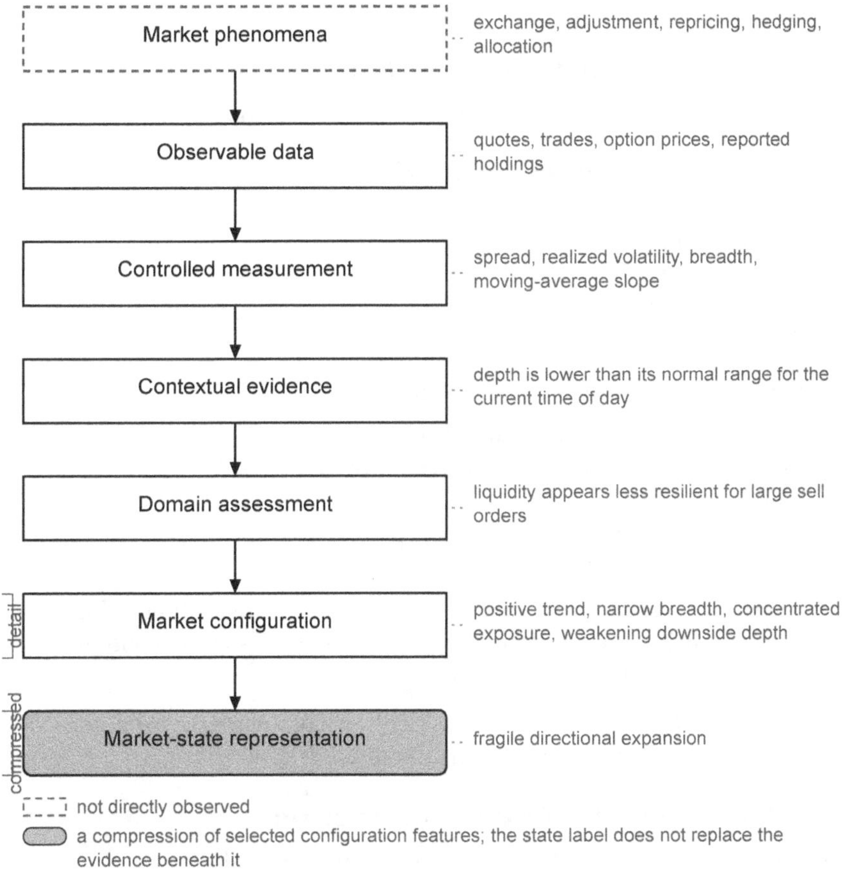

Figure 10.1 — From Market Phenomena to Market-State Representation

10.2 Measurements, Domains, Configurations, and States

A measurement is not the phenomenon it represents. A bid-ask spread is not liquidity itself. Open interest is not positioning itself. Implied volatility is not uncertainty itself. A moving average is not trend itself.

An observational domain is a conceptual category used to organize related evidence. A market configuration is the detailed arrangement of assessed conditions at a specified time and scale. A market state is a higher-level representation created for a stated analytical purpose.

> **Configuration–State Distinction:** A market configuration preserves detail. A market state compresses selected features of that configuration. The state label should never replace the evidence beneath it.

10.3 Why Isolated Indicators Often Fail

Suppose a broad equity index rises 1.5% in one session.

Environment A — Orderly expansion

- Liquidity remains deep and replenishing.
- Participation is broad.
- Realized variability remains proportionate.
- Exposure expands gradually.
- Pullbacks are absorbed efficiently.

Environment B — Fragile squeeze

- Liquidity is thin and asymmetric.
- A few large securities drive most of the move.
- Short exposure is reduced under pressure.
- Implied volatility rises.
- Downside depth replenishes poorly.

The return is identical, but the market configurations differ. The same outcome may arise from different mechanisms, and similar configurations may later produce different outcomes.

> **Systems Question:** Do not ask only what the market is doing. Ask under what configuration it is doing it.

10.4 Principles of Domain Interaction

1. Interactions are conditional rather than universal.
2. Relationships may be reciprocal rather than one-directional.
3. Co-movement does not identify causation.
4. Effects depend on horizon, scale, timing, thresholds, and participant adaptation.

Pairwise analysis is useful for learning, but actual markets involve simultaneous interaction among all four domains and other influences.

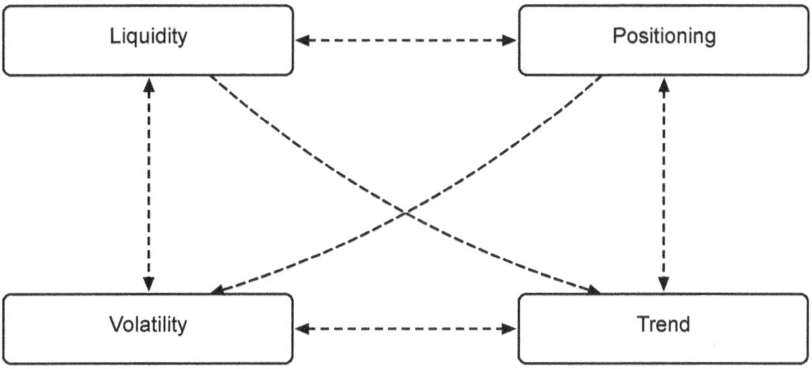

ALL SIX PAIRWISE RELATIONSHIPS

Liquidity — Positioning	adjustment demand and its transmission
Liquidity — Volatility	price impact and liquidity-provider response
Liquidity — Trend	efficiency of directional movement
Positioning — Volatility	sensitivities that may become active
Positioning — Trend	exposure, risk capacity, and concentration
Volatility — Trend	variability accompanying direction

◄ ► reciprocal but conditional: the relation may run in both directions and is not universal

Figure 10.2 — Six Reciprocal Pairwise Domain Relationships

10.5 Liquidity and Positioning

Liquidity conditions influence the cost, immediacy, depth, and price impact associated with establishing, modifying, hedging, or exiting exposure. Positioning may create potential future demand for liquidity, depending on price movement, constraints, leverage, hedging policy, and participant response.

Dispersed exposure with resilient liquidity

When exposure is distributed and exchange capacity is deep, adjustment may occur without disproportionate price disruption. This increases adaptive capacity but does not guarantee stability.

Concentrated exposure with weak liquidity

When many participants may need to adjust similar exposure while counterparties are limited, a small disturbance can create large price impact. Concentration alone does not cause the move, and weak liquidity alone does not determine direction. Sensitivity emerges from their interaction.

> **Conditional Demand Principle:** Positioning creates potential adjustment demand; liquidity influences how that adjustment is transmitted into price.

10.6 Liquidity and Volatility

Reduced executable liquidity can increase price impact for a given order flow. Larger price changes may raise realized-volatility estimates. Higher measured volatility can alter risk limits and cause liquidity providers to widen spreads or reduce size, producing a reinforcing loop.

1. Executable liquidity declines.
2. A given order produces greater price impact.
3. Observed price variability increases.
4. Risk limits and liquidity-provider behavior change.
5. Liquidity may decline further.

A balancing pathway is also possible. Wider spreads may attract counterparties, price deviations may invite arbitrage, and depth may replenish. Volatility may remain high while market functioning improves.

10.7 Liquidity and Trend

Trend identifies sustained direction; liquidity helps describe how efficiently the market travels in that direction. An orderly advance may involve repeated replenishment of offers. A squeeze may involve withdrawal of supply and discontinuous price movement. Both produce rising prices, but they have different structures.

Thin liquidity may exaggerate apparent trend strength. Persistent trend does not, by itself, establish exchange resilience.

10.8 Positioning and Volatility

Positioning creates sensitivities that may become active as prices, volatility, time, and constraints change. In derivatives markets, a position may have changing delta, gamma, vega, and other exposures.

Consider an illustrative case in which investors purchase protective puts and dealers are net short the relevant optionality. If those dealers hedge dynamically, if alternative exposures do not offset the sensitivity, and if liquidity is limited, a market decline may require additional selling. None of these conditions should be assumed without evidence.

> **Positioning Principle:** Positioning creates sensitivities and potential adjustment pathways; it does not predetermine participant behavior or market direction.

10.9 Positioning and Trend

Persistent direction changes gains, losses, risk capacity, benchmark pressure, and incentives. Trend-following systems may increase exposure, short participants may reduce exposure, and profitable positions may gain capacity to expand.

Continuation can also increase concentration. A trend may become stronger while the configuration becomes more sensitive to disruption. Crowding is structural evidence, not a timing signal.

> **Strength–Fragility Distinction:** Strength describes the magnitude or persistence of a current condition. Fragility describes sensitivity to disturbance. A market can possess both at the same time.

10.10 Volatility and Trend

Trend condition	Volatility structure	Possible interpretation
Rising	Low and stable	Orderly persistence, muted variability, or latent leverage.
Rising	Expanding	Rapid repricing, speculation, event response, or unstable participation.
Declining	Expanding	Stress, forced adjustment, information shock, or disorderly repricing.
Declining	Falling	Controlled weakness, drift, or reduced participation.
Mixed	High	Range instability or repeated repricing.
Mixed	Low	Compression, balance, or limited participation.

Each interpretation is conditional. Volatility characterizes the magnitude and structure of variability; trend characterizes directional persistence.

10.11 Multidomain Interaction Beyond Pairs

Pairwise analysis is an educational simplification. A multidomain sequence may involve concentrated exposure, adverse movement, rising adjustment demand, declining liquidity, greater price impact, expanding volatility, trend deterioration, and further repositioning. The order may differ, and several changes may occur simultaneously.

> **Causation Caution:** Observed co-movement among domains does not, by itself, identify the direction or mechanism of causation.

10.12 Reinforcing and Balancing Feedback

Illustrative reinforcing loop — downside adjustment

1. Prices decline.
2. Losses increase and some participants reduce exposure.
3. Selling consumes available liquidity.
4. Price impact and realized variability increase.
5. Risk limits tighten.
6. Additional exposure is reduced.

Illustrative balancing loop — liquidity restoration

1. Prices decline.
2. Some investors perceive improved prospective compensation.
3. New demand enters.
4. Depth replenishes.
5. Price impact declines.
6. Volatility stabilizes and forced selling becomes easier to absorb.

Feedback loops are analyst representations, not directly observed objects. Multiple loops may compete, change direction, or operate with delays. Stabilization need not restore the previous configuration.

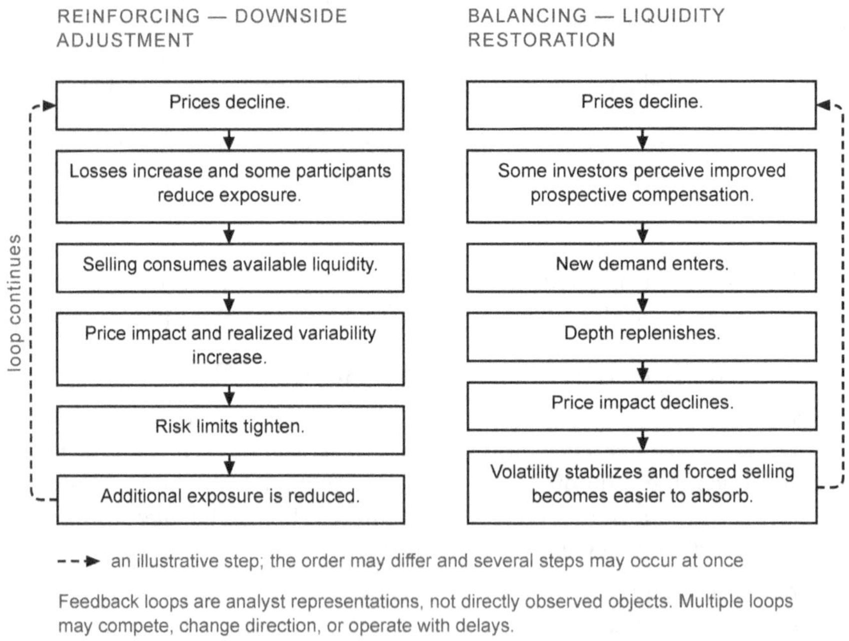

Figure 10.3 — Reinforcing and Balancing Feedback Loops

10.13 Strength, Stability, Resilience, Fragility, Stress, and Failure

Quality	Definition	Core question
Strength	Magnitude, persistence, or intensity of an observed condition.	How strong or persistent is it?
Stability	Degree to which organization is maintained under ordinary variation.	Does the configuration remain organized?
Resilience	Capacity to absorb disturbance, continue functioning, and recover or reorganize.	Can the system adapt without disproportionate impairment?
Fragility	Sensitivity arising from limited adaptive capacity, concentration, leverage, weak liquidity, or nonlinear exposure.	How vulnerable is the configuration to disturbance?
Stress	Observable strain, forced adjustment, impaired exchange, or reduced resilience.	What strain is present?
Failure	Material breakdown in a market function, mechanism, or institution.	Has a critical function broken down?

A market may be strong but fragile, volatile but resilient, calm but adjustment-sensitive, or stressed while continuing to function.

10.14 Hidden Fragility

Visible calm does not guarantee resilience. A market may show low realized volatility, narrow ranges, and a persistent advance while leverage, concentration, narrow leadership, weak depth, and volatility-sensitive exposure accumulate.

Such evidence may be consistent with greater fragility, but it does not prove that an abrupt transition is inevitable. The inference should remain conditional and revisable.

10.15 Visible Stress with Underlying Resilience

High volatility and large price movement do not necessarily imply market dysfunction. After a major policy announcement, prices may move sharply while transactions continue, spreads widen proportionately, depth replenishes, clearing and settlement function, and price discovery remains two-sided.

The market may be stressed but resilient. The quality of exchange matters as much as the magnitude of movement.

10.16 Detailed Scenario: Downside Adjustment

Consider an illustrative equity-index configuration: the long-horizon trend is positive, realized volatility is low, exposure is substantial, protective-option demand is elevated, and ordinary market depth appears adequate.

Initial disturbance

An unexpected economic report produces a 1% decline. The price change alone does not determine the broader response.

Conditional positioning response

Some participants may reduce exposure. Some volatility-sensitive strategies may rebalance, depending on mandate and horizon. Dealers may adjust hedges if their net exposure, netting relationships, and policies require it.

Liquidity and volatility response

Sell orders may consume bids. Some liquidity providers may reduce size. Intraday ranges and realized volatility may expand, while option prices may imply higher volatility.

Directional response

Short-horizon trend may turn downward while long-horizon trend remains positive. Continued adjustment could weaken intermediate directional structure.

Possible stabilization

Long-term demand may enter, hedge requirements may diminish, option supply may increase, and depth may recover. Volatility can remain elevated while the decline stabilizes.

> **Scenario Qualification:** This pathway is illustrative, not universal. The same initial disturbance may produce different outcomes under different configurations and adaptive responses.

10.17 Same Outcome, Different Mechanisms

Suppose an index declines 5% over one week.

Path	Mechanism	Indicative configuration
Fundamental revaluation	New information reduces expected earnings or cash flows.	Orderly adjustment, functional liquidity, moderate volatility expansion.

Path	Mechanism	Indicative configuration
Forced deleveraging	Losses trigger risk limits and simultaneous selling.	Concentrated adjustment demand, weak liquidity, rapid volatility expansion.
Policy uncertainty	Participants reduce activity because fair-value estimates become less reliable.	Lower participation, thinner liquidity, large movement from modest flow.
Liquidity discontinuity	Bids withdraw or market access becomes limited.	Discontinuous movement disproportionate to ordinary transaction volume.

Mechanism Principle: Outcome does not identify mechanism.

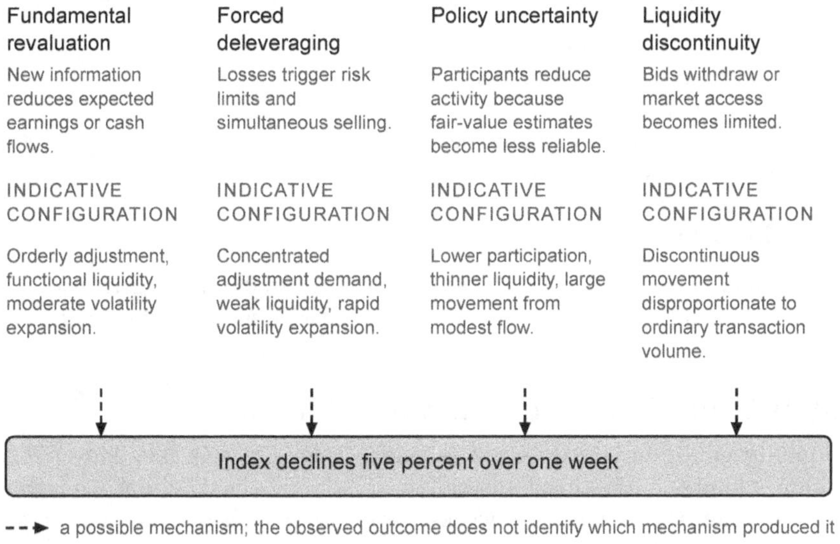

Figure 10.4 — Same Five-Percent Decline, Different Mechanisms

10.18 Similar Conditions, Different Outcomes

Two markets may begin with concentrated long exposure, low volatility, and a mature upward trend. After the same adverse event, one may remain contained because demand and liquidity persist. The other may accelerate because liquidity providers withdraw, leverage constraints activate, and volatility-sensitive strategies reduce exposure.

Initial conditions matter, but participant adaptation, institutional constraints, timing, and threshold effects shape the pathway. Markets are path-dependent.

10.19 Configuration Dependence

Definition — Configuration Dependence

Configuration dependence means that the effect of information, order flow, or disturbance depends on the market configuration in which it occurs.

A modest earnings disappointment may have little effect in a deeply liquid, lightly positioned market and a large effect in a crowded, illiquid market. This is a market-systems application of the broader concept of state dependence.

10.20 Nonlinearity and Thresholds

Market response is often nonlinear. A change may produce little visible effect until a threshold is crossed, after which the response increases rapidly.

- order-book depth depletion;
- margin or collateral breach;
- stop-order activation;
- volatility-control rebalancing;
- market-maker risk limits;
- funding withdrawal;
- circuit breakers or trading halts.

Thresholds may be unknown, changing, distributed across institutions, or activated at different times. A disturbance twice as large does not necessarily produce twice the effect.

10.21 Time Lags and Temporal Alignment

Liquidity can deteriorate within seconds. Intraday volatility may change within minutes. Reported institutional holdings may update quarterly. Long-horizon trend may take weeks to reclassify. These differences create temporal mismatch.

- timestamp;
- observation window;
- sampling interval;
- update frequency;
- publication delay;
- persistence horizon;
- freshness or staleness.

Temporal Alignment Principle: Evidence from different horizons may coexist, but it should not be treated as temporally equivalent.

10.22 Cross-Market Transmission

Strength or stress may transmit through funding relationships, collateral valuation, common dealers, portfolio rebalancing, currencies, derivative hedging, ETF creation and redemption, basis relationships, volatility targeting, common ownership, and global time-zone sequencing.

Cross-market co-movement does not prove a particular transmission mechanism. The proposed pathway should be supported by timing, institutional evidence, and alternative explanations.

10.23 Building a Multidomain Assessment

Domain	Core question	Illustrative evidence
Liquidity	What exchange capacity appears available, for what size, urgency, venue, side, and horizon?	Spreads, depth, price impact, execution quality, replenishment.
Positioning	What exposure, sensitivity, leverage, concentration, and adjustment requirements are evident or inferred?	Open interest, leverage, reported holdings, short interest, estimated sensitivities.
Volatility	What degree and structure of variability is realized or implied, under what horizon and method?	Realized volatility, implied volatility, skew, term structure, ranges, volatility-of-volatility.
Trend	What directional persistence is present, under what method, and with what breadth and structure?	Slope, returns, persistence, breadth, leadership, cross-asset consistency.

Final Synthesis Question: How do these conditions interact, and what alternative explanations remain?

10.24 Practical Market-Configuration Matrix

Domain	More adaptive configuration	Mixed configuration	More adjustment-sensitive configuration
Liquidity	Deep, replenishing, resilient.	Uneven or normal.	Thin, asymmetric, deteriorating.
Positioning	Dispersed, lower leverage, adaptable.	Unclear or balanced.	Concentrated, leveraged, nonlinear.

Domain	More adaptive configuration	Mixed configuration	More adjustment-sensitive configuration
Volatility	Proportionate and structurally stable.	Transitional or mixed.	Rapidly expanding, dislocated, unstable.
Trend	Persistent, broad, orderly.	Range-bound or mixed.	Narrowing, deteriorating, disorderly.

The matrix is a reasoning aid, not a trading signal. Conditions should not be counted mechanically. A severe liquidity impairment may matter more than several mild observations elsewhere.

10.25 Example of a Written Market Assessment

A weak assessment might state: "The market is bullish because price is above the 50-day moving average and volatility is low."

> **More disciplined assessment:** The intermediate price trend remains upward under the selected method. Realized volatility remains contained, and observed liquidity appears adequate for ordinary transaction sizes. However, breadth has narrowed, exposure appears increasingly concentrated among a small group of leaders, and downside depth has replenished less effectively during recent pullbacks. The current configuration is therefore directionally persistent but less broadly supported and potentially more adjustment-sensitive than earlier in the advance. This assessment does not determine whether or when reversal will occur.

10.26 Contradictory, Missing, and Stale Evidence

Evidence may conflict because of transition, genuine multidimensional coexistence, horizon mismatch, universe mismatch, data error, stale reporting, missing observations, or model disagreement.

1. Verify data, definitions, and provenance.
2. Align horizons where possible.
3. Preserve unresolved disagreement.
4. Reduce confidence when evidence is incomplete or stale.
5. Do not replace missing evidence with assumptions.
6. State what additional observation would resolve the ambiguity.

Unknown, unavailable, stale, estimated, and model-dependent are legitimate evidence states.

10.27 Composite Representations

Composite scores can simplify communication and reveal change over time, but they may conceal opposing domains, unequal quality, missing data, nonlinear interaction, and horizon differences.

Design requirement	Purpose
Preserve component values	Allows decomposition and review.
Preserve timestamps and horizons	Prevents false temporal equivalence.
Represent missingness explicitly	Avoids fabricated completeness.
Document weights and normalization	Makes construction auditable.
Document thresholds and versions	Supports reproducibility.
Show uncertainty or confidence	Prevents false precision.
Test sensitivity to assumptions	Reveals dependence on design choices.
Separate description from decision rule	Prevents a summary from becoming an unexamined signal.

> **Composite Principle:** A composite should compress information without destroying traceability.

10.28 The Market as an Evolving Configuration

A market configuration is temporary. Liquidity changes, exposure is adjusted, volatility expands or contracts, and trend strengthens, weakens, or reverses. The objective is not to assign a permanent label but to observe how the arrangement evolves.

> **Provisional Evolution Hierarchy:** Current configuration → configuration change → possible state transition → possible transition pathway → visible price adjustment.

Later chapters will formalize market states and transitions. Chapter 10 establishes the observational bridge without treating every configuration change as a state transition.

10.29 Why Domain Interactions Matter

No observational domain independently explains the market. Liquidity describes exchange capacity. Positioning describes distributed exposure and sensitivity. Volatility describes variability. Trend describes directional persistence.

Their interaction supports a more complete representation of current market configuration, while uncertainty, missing evidence, and alternative mechanisms remain explicit. Understanding emerges from relationships, not from one universally dominant indicator.

Chapter Summary

Liquidity, positioning, volatility, and trend organize evidence about different dimensions of market behavior. Markets do not experience these dimensions independently, and their relationships are not fixed mechanical laws.

Measurements provide contextual evidence. Evidence informs domain assessments. Domain assessments are synthesized into a multidomain market configuration. A market state is a higher-level representation of selected configuration features. Neither a state label nor a composite score should replace the underlying evidence.

Domain interactions may be reciprocal, delayed, nonlinear, path-dependent, and configuration-dependent. The same outcome may arise from different mechanisms, while similar initial conditions may produce different outcomes because participants adapt.

Strength, stability, resilience, fragility, stress, and failure describe different qualities. A market may be directionally strong but fragile, volatile but resilient, calm but adjustment-sensitive, or stressed while continuing to function.

A disciplined assessment identifies measurements, horizons, data quality, interaction pathways, contradictory evidence, alternative explanations, and uncertainty. It asks not only what the market is doing, but under what configuration it is doing it.

Established Knowledge

The interaction of liquidity, positioning, volatility, and directional behavior is studied across financial economics, market microstructure, derivatives research, behavioral finance, systemic-risk analysis, network theory, and complex-systems research.

Established areas include market liquidity and price impact, inventory and adverse-selection models, leverage and margin cycles, volatility clustering, endogenous risk, forced liquidation, derivative hedging, momentum, trend following, contagion, feedback systems, systemic resilience, state dependence, nonlinearity, path dependence, regime change, stress testing, and composite-indicator design.

No universally accepted four-domain model exists. Interaction strengths, directions, and persistence vary across instruments, institutions, periods, regulations, and market structures.

Institute Perspective

The Institute proposes a practical observational architecture that organizes evidence into four complementary domains and then synthesizes those domains into an evolving market configuration.

Its contribution is not a claim that four domains explain every market outcome. The contribution lies in distinguishing measurements, domain assessments, configurations, and states; emphasizing conditional interaction rather than mechanical causality; preserving contradictory and missing evidence; and requiring composite representations to remain decomposable.

The framework treats markets as evolving configurations rather than fixed labels and uses those configurations as the evidentiary basis for later study of market states and transitions.

Questions for Reflection

1. What distinguishes a measurement from a domain assessment?
2. What distinguishes a market configuration from a market state?
3. Why can identical returns arise from different mechanisms?
4. Why can similar initial configurations produce different outcomes?
5. What is the difference between interaction, correlation, and causation?
6. How can positioning create conditional demand for liquidity?
7. How can declining liquidity amplify measured volatility?
8. Can rising volatility coexist with resilient market functioning?
9. How can a strong trend also be fragile?
10. What distinguishes stability from resilience?
11. What distinguishes fragility from observable stress?
12. Why does stress not necessarily imply market failure?
13. What is configuration dependence?
14. How do thresholds create nonlinear market responses?
15. Why must multidomain evidence be aligned by time and horizon?
16. What might contradictory evidence represent besides transition?
17. Why should missing or stale evidence remain explicit?
18. What information can be lost in a composite score?
19. What design requirements should govern a composite market representation?
20. How would you describe a positive trend with narrowing breadth, concentrated exposure, stable realized volatility, and weakening downside depth without predicting the next move?

Chapter 11. Market Measurements

Turning Market Activity into Observable Evidence

Chapter Purpose

Financial markets cannot be understood through direct access to every participant belief, intention, constraint, exposure, or future decision. Researchers instead observe recorded activity: prices, quotations, trades, orders, option premiums, reported positions, volumes, and timestamps. These records are selected, processed, and transformed into measurements.

Measurements make market activity analytically accessible, but they do so selectively and imperfectly. Every measurement reflects choices about data source, definition, sampling, aggregation, normalization, timing, model assumptions, and intended purpose. A numerical value may therefore be reproducible and precise while still being incomplete, stale, invalid for the intended use, or vulnerable to alternative interpretation.

This chapter establishes the measurement discipline of Market Systems Science. It explains how recorded data become controlled measurements, how measurements become contextual evidence, and how evidence supports domain assessment without being confused with the underlying phenomenon, a causal explanation, a prediction, or a decision.

The objective is not to eliminate uncertainty. It is to prevent uncertainty from being concealed by numbers.

Learning Objectives

- Define a governed market measurement and distinguish recorded data, processed data, measurement, evidence, interpretation, judgment, and action.
- Explain why measurements are selective representations rather than the phenomena themselves.
- Classify recorded observations, deterministic derivations, model estimates, proxies, and latent-condition inferences by inferential distance.
- Explain how timing, sampling, aggregation, normalization, benchmarks, and regime selection affect meaning.
- Evaluate validity, reliability, accuracy, precision, resolution, and fit for purpose.

- Recognize stale, delayed, unavailable, incomplete, estimated, model-dependent, superseded, and invalid measurement states.
- Identify missing-data mechanisms, historical research biases, model risk, and false precision.
- Apply sensitivity, scenario, robustness, and stress testing.
- Preserve provenance, lineage, auditability, reproducibility, and version control.
- Use triangulation and composite measurements without destroying traceability.
- Separate description, association, mechanism, causation, prediction, prescription, judgment, and action.
- Understand how measurement use can influence the market through crowding and reflexivity.

11.1 Measurement as Controlled Representation

Definition — Market Measurement

A market measurement is a systematically constructed representation of observable market activity, produced from identified data through a documented method for a stated analytical purpose, with explicit units, timing, assumptions, provenance, and limitations.

The shorter conceptual formulation is: a measurement is a controlled representation of market activity. Control means that the construction is defined, repeatable, reviewable, and governed. Representation means that the output captures selected characteristics while omitting others.

11.2 The Measurement Hierarchy

Level	Meaning	Illustrative example
Market phenomenon	A process or condition the analyst seeks to understand.	Liquidity, positioning, volatility, directional persistence, stress, resilience.
Recorded data	Values or messages captured from a source.	Trades, quotes, option prices, reported open interest.
Processed data	Records cleaned, mapped, consolidated, adjusted, or aligned.	Corrected trades, mapped contracts, synchronized timestamps.
Controlled measurement	A defined calculation, estimate, or classification.	Spread, realized volatility, breadth, dealer-exposure estimate.

Level	Meaning	Illustrative example
Contextual evidence	A measurement interpreted relative to a question and comparison.	Depth is below the normal time-of-day range.
Domain assessment	Organized interpretation within one observational domain.	Liquidity appears less resilient for the stated size and horizon.
Market configuration	Detailed arrangement across domains.	Positive trend, narrow breadth, concentrated exposure, weakening depth.
Judgment and action	Participant-specific evaluation and response.	Reduce order size, widen quotes, remain inactive, or seek opportunity.

Canonical Hierarchy: Market phenomena → recorded data → processed data → controlled measurements → contextual evidence → domain assessment → multidomain market configuration → judgment → action.

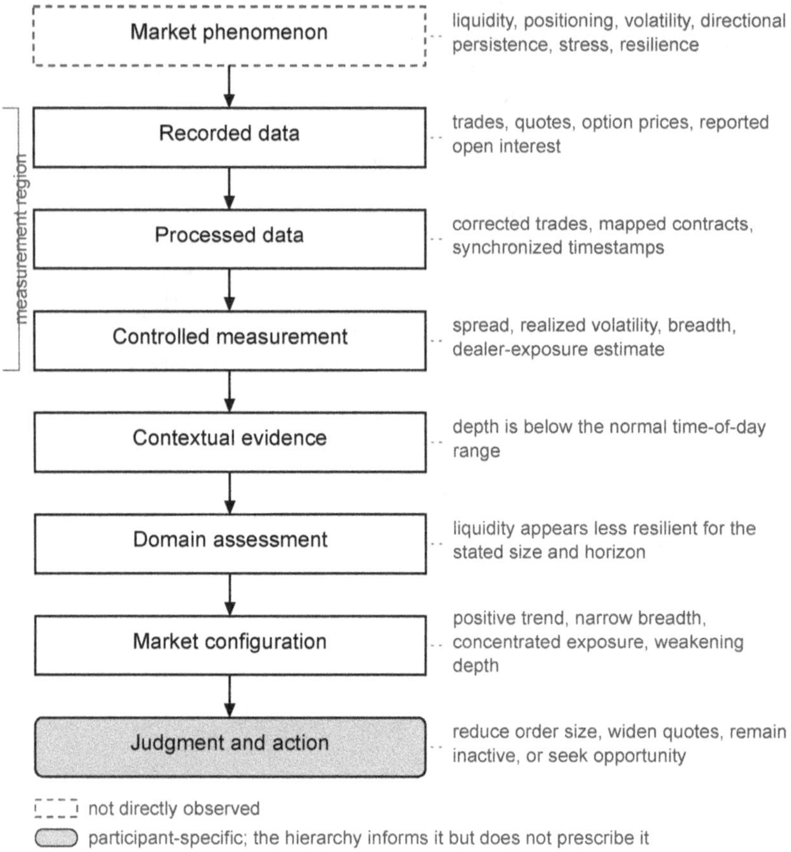

Figure 11.1 — The Measurement Hierarchy

11.3 Recorded Data, Processed Data, and Measurements

The phrase raw data should be used cautiously. Market records often contain prior decisions made by exchanges, vendors, consolidators, and software systems. A trade message may already include venue-specific conditions, corrections, sequencing rules, instrument mappings, and timestamp conventions.

Category	**Description**	**Example**
Recorded data	Values or events captured from a source.	Best bid, best ask, trade price, option premium.

Category	Description	Example
Processed data	Recorded data altered for usability or consistency.	Deduplication, symbol mapping, corporate-action adjustment, venue consolidation.
Measurement	A representation created to answer an analytical question.	Normalized spread, twenty-day realized volatility, participation breadth.

Data Qualification: Recorded data are not necessarily neutral, complete, or untouched. Their prior processing history is part of their meaning.

11.4 Measurement Is Not the Phenomenon

A bid-ask spread represents one dimension of visible transaction friction. It is not liquidity in its entirety. Open interest represents outstanding contracts. It does not directly reveal who owns each side, whether exposures are offset, or how participants will respond. A moving average summarizes prior prices. It is not the trend mechanism. Implied volatility is inferred from option prices through a model. It is not uncertainty itself.

Representation Principle: A measurement may represent an aspect of a phenomenon without being identical to that phenomenon.

11.5 Measurement Becomes Evidence Through Context

Definition — Evidence

Evidence is a measurement interpreted in relation to a defined question, comparison, context, and set of alternative explanations.

A four-basis-point spread may indicate impaired liquidity in one instrument and ordinary conditions in another. Its evidentiary meaning depends on market, venue, time of day, size, volatility, historical range, and executability. The number does not explain itself.

11.6 Classes of Measurement and Inferential Distance

Class	Description	Examples	Primary caution
Recorded observation	A directly reported value or event.	Trade price, quote, reported volume.	Still depends on reporting rules, timestamps, and coverage.
Deterministically derived	An explicit calculation from recorded data.	Spread, return, moving average, VWAP.	Definition and sampling choices shape meaning.
Model-estimated	An output dependent on a model or estimation procedure.	Implied volatility, impact coefficient, fair-value estimate.	Assumptions and input error affect the result.
Proxy measurement	A partial representation of a broader phenomenon.	Depth as a liquidity proxy; short interest as one positioning proxy.	Proxy substitution can overstate what is known.
Latent-condition inference	A higher-level classification from several measurements.	Stress, fragility, crowding, market-state classification.	Requires the strongest documentation and uncertainty controls.

Inferential Distance Principle: Greater inferential distance does not make a measurement unusable, but it requires stronger assumptions, documentation, validation, and uncertainty controls.

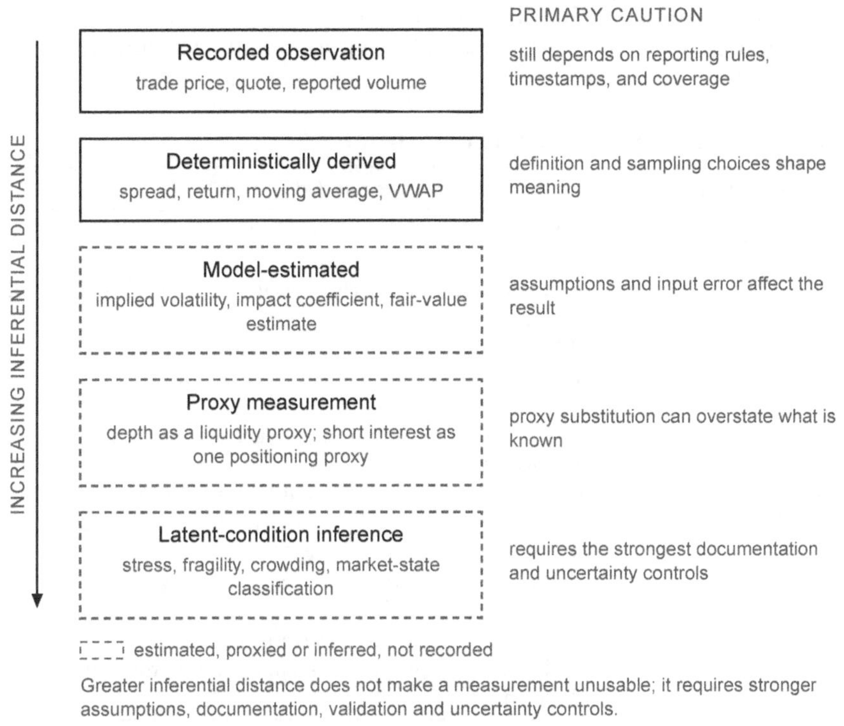

Figure 11.2 — Inferential Distance

11.7 Latent Variables and Proxies

Some concepts cannot be observed completely. Risk appetite, market stress, crowding, fragility, confidence, and uncertainty are latent conditions. They are inferred through related evidence such as spreads, depth, leverage, correlation, option prices, price impact, and adjustment behavior.

A proxy is useful only when the relationship to the intended phenomenon is justified and its limitations remain visible. Several complementary proxies may improve understanding, but agreement does not convert an inference into direct observation.

11.8 The Risk of Proxy Substitution

- Treating volume as liquidity.
- Treating open interest as directional positioning.
- Treating a volatility index as fear itself.
- Treating a moving average as trend quality.
- Treating an index return as the condition of the entire market.

Proxy Substitution Error: The analyst replaces a difficult question with an easier measurable question and then presents the easier answer as if it resolved the original phenomenon.

11.9 Measurement Design Choices

Design choice	Questions that must be answered
Underlying data	Which fields, vendors, venues, sessions, and corrections are included?
Transformation	What formula, algorithm, estimation, or classification rule is used?
Observation window	What period does the measurement represent?
Sampling interval	Tick, second, minute, daily, weekly, or another frequency?
Aggregation	Across time, instruments, venues, or participant categories?
Universe	Which instruments are included or excluded, and why?
Normalization	Percentage, basis points, z-score, notional, volatility scaling, or another method?
Benchmark	Compared with what historical, peer, seasonal, or model reference?
Units	What native and displayed units are used?
Regime relevance	Is the calibration period structurally comparable to the current market?

Design Principle: A measurement's meaning is inseparable from the design choices used to construct it.

11.10 Time, Sampling, and Temporal Alignment

Time concept	Meaning
Event time	When the underlying market activity occurred.
Exchange timestamp	When the venue recorded the event.
Receipt time	When the data consumer received the message.
Processing time	When the system handled, cleaned, or transformed the record.
Calculation time	When the measurement was produced.
Publication time	When the value became available to a user.
Effective period	The interval the measurement is intended to represent.

A daily close-to-close return may conceal a sharp intraday decline and recovery. A tick-level measure may reveal microstructure detail irrelevant to long-term allocation. Neither is universally correct. The appropriate sampling frequency depends on the question.

Temporal Alignment Principle: Evidence from different horizons may coexist, but it should not be treated as temporally equivalent.

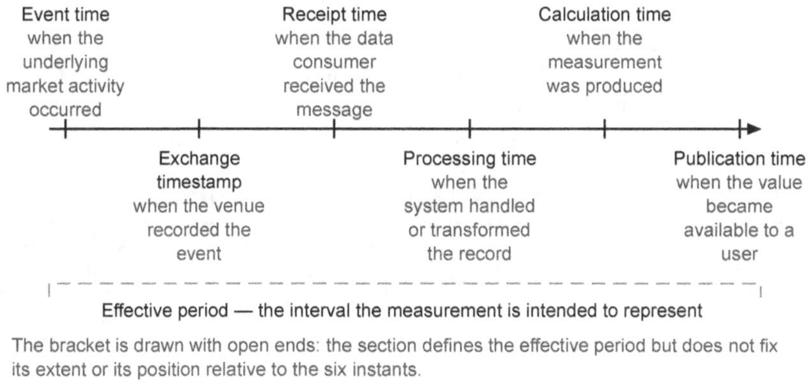

Figure 11.3 — Time Dimensions of a Measurement

11.11 Aggregation, Distributions, and Internal Variation

Aggregation can reveal broad patterns while concealing dispersion, concentration, sequencing, outliers, and internal instability. An index may remain stable while several components experience severe declines. Average liquidity may appear normal while one critical instrument becomes impaired.

Summary	What it reveals	What it may conceal
Mean	Central average.	Skew, tails, concentration, and subgroup divergence.
Median	Typical central observation.	Magnitude of extremes.
Percentiles	Distributional position.	Sequence and mechanism.
Dispersion	Variation across observations.	Direction and causal structure.
Concentration measure	Dependence on a small subset.	Liquidity and behavioral response.

Systems Principle: A stable average can coexist with unstable components.

11.12 Normalization, Benchmarks, and Regime Relevance

Normalization supports comparison across instruments and periods, but it can distort meaning when applied mechanically. A z-score describes unusualness relative to a selected historical distribution; it does not explain why the value changed or whether the historical period remains relevant.

Terms such as high, low, strong, weak, normal, or extreme are incomplete without a benchmark. The longest available history is not always the most appropriate baseline because market structure, regulation, tick size, technology, trading hours, and participant composition change.

11.13 Examples Across the Four Domains

Domain	Measurement	What it may indicate	What it cannot establish alone
Liquidity	Spread, depth, price impact, recovery time.	Visible friction, capacity, absorption, resilience.	Complete liquidity or future availability.
Positioning	Open interest, short interest, filings, leverage, exposure estimates.	Outstanding exposure, concentration, possible sensitivity.	Ownership, intent, net system direction, future adjustment.
Volatility	Realized volatility, implied volatility, skew, term structure.	Observed or option-implied variability structure.	Fear, direction, pure expectation, or risk for every participant.
Trend	Slope, moving averages, persistence, breadth, leadership.	Directional structure over a stated horizon.	Cause, durability, or future continuation.

11.14 Detailed Example: Measuring Liquidity

Suppose an analyst wants to determine whether liquidity in an equity-index futures market is deteriorating. The analyst examines spread, near-touch depth, price impact for comparable order sizes, recovery time after transactions, and cancellation behavior.

- The spread widens from one tick to two, suggesting greater visible transaction cost.
- Near-touch depth falls 40%, suggesting reduced displayed capacity.
- Comparable market orders move price farther, suggesting weaker absorption.

- The order book takes longer to rebuild, suggesting lower resilience.
- Displayed orders cancel more rapidly as price approaches, suggesting less dependable visible liquidity.

Disciplined conclusion: Liquidity appears to have deteriorated relative to the normal time-of-day baseline because spreads widened, near-touch depth declined, comparable price impact increased, and recovery slowed. Hidden liquidity and future participant response remain uncertain.

11.15 Detailed Example: Interpreting Rising Open Interest

Suppose open interest in index put options rises substantially. The recorded fact is that outstanding contracts increased. It does not directly establish bearish intent, net directional exposure, or dealer behavior.

- Investors may have bought protection.
- Other investors may have sold puts for income.
- New spreads may involve several strikes or expirations.
- Market makers may hold offsetting positions.
- Futures or other options may offset the apparent exposure.

A stronger analysis examines strikes, expirations, initiation estimates, implied-volatility changes, underlying activity, likely ownership, offsets, and sensitivity to ownership assumptions.

11.16 Validity, Reliability, Accuracy, Precision, and Resolution

Concept	**Core question**
Construct validity	Does the measurement reasonably represent the intended concept?
Content coverage	Does it include enough relevant dimensions?
Convergent validity	Does it behave consistently with other credible measures of the same phenomenon?
Discriminant validity	Can it be distinguished from different phenomena?
Criterion validity	Does it correspond with a trusted reference where one exists?
Predictive usefulness	Does it provide incremental information about a future outcome?
Reliability	Does it produce consistent results under comparable conditions?
Accuracy	Is it close to a trusted reference or best available representation, when one exists?
Precision	How detailed or repeatable is the reported value?
Resolution	What is the smallest detectable change or granularity?

Quality Distinction: A measurement can be reliable but invalid, precise but inaccurate, or descriptively valid without being predictively useful.

11.17 Data Quality and Measurement States

State	Meaning
Current	Within its defined validity window and supported by current inputs.
Delayed	Available later than the intended observation cadence.
Stale	Previously valid but older than its permitted freshness window.
Unavailable	No defensible value can be produced.
Incomplete	Required coverage or inputs are missing.
Estimated	Produced through an estimation procedure.
Model-dependent	Materially dependent on stated assumptions or model choice.
Superseded	Replaced by a corrected or newer controlled value.
Invalid	Fails validation or specification requirements.
Unknown	The status or value cannot be established.

Freshness Principle: A stale last-known value is not equivalent to a current observation.

Every time-sensitive measurement should preserve an observation or effective timestamp, calculation timestamp, expected validity window, freshness state, and stale-data policy.

11.18 Missing Data, Outliers, and Corrections

Missing data may result from technical failure, inactivity, nonexistence of an instrument, lack of reporting, invalid inputs, or deliberate withholding when assumptions are unmet. The reason for missingness affects interpretation.

Missingness Principle: Honest unavailability is preferable to unjustified fabrication.

Imputation should be used only with a stated method, fit-for-purpose justification, and uncertainty flag. Estimated values must not be presented as observed. Extreme values require investigation because they may represent genuine events, errors, delayed reports, unusual transactions, or structural change.

11.19 Historical Research Biases

Bias	Description	Example
Survivorship bias	Only entities still observable at the end are included.	Using today's index members for the full historical period.
Look-ahead bias	Information unavailable at the decision time is used.	Using end-of-day values in an intraday model before the close.
Selection bias	Observations are chosen in a way that favors a conclusion.	Testing only favorable periods or complete-data instruments.
Revision bias	Revised data replace the values originally available.	Testing with final economic releases instead of first releases.

Historical Integrity Principle: Every historical measurement should respect the information, universe, and definitions that were available at the time.

11.20 Model Risk, Sensitivity, and Robustness

Model-estimated measurements inherit assumptions about inputs, ownership, parameters, functional form, and aggregation. A dealer-exposure estimate may require contract mapping, open-interest data, option-pricing inputs, Greek calculations, ownership assumptions, dealer-side assumptions, and an aggregation method.

Inference Stack Principle: Mathematical correctness of a calculation does not establish behavioral correctness of its interpretation.

Method	Purpose
Sensitivity analysis	Change one or more assumptions and inspect the output.
Scenario analysis	Evaluate coherent alternative configurations.
Robustness testing	Test whether the conclusion survives reasonable changes in data, parameters, windows, and methods.
Stress testing	Evaluate behavior under extreme but plausible conditions.

11.21 Provenance, Lineage, Reproducibility, and Versioning

Concept	Meaning
Provenance	Where the source data or measurement originated.
Lineage	The sequence of transformations from source to output.
Auditability	The ability to inspect and reconstruct that sequence.
Reproducibility	The ability to obtain substantially similar results from the same inputs and method.
Version control	The controlled record of definitions, changes, effective dates, and supersession.

> **Traceability Principle:** Every governed measurement should be traceable backward to its source and forward through each transformation.

A formal change record should document purpose, design inputs, formula or algorithm, assumptions, expected behavior, boundary conditions, verification tests, validation evidence, known failure modes, approved version, effective date, supersession record, and retirement criteria.

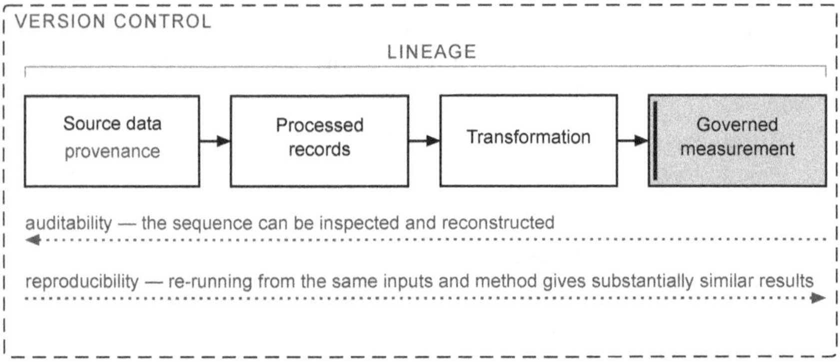

Every governed measurement should be traceable backward to its source and forward through each transformation.

Figure 11.4 — Measurement Lineage

11.22 Fit for Purpose

The relevant question is not whether a measurement is universally good. The question is whether it is sufficiently valid, reliable, timely, and interpretable for the specific purpose.

- A one-minute volatility measure may support intraday execution but not long-term allocation.
- An annual ownership filing may support structural research but not real-time positioning.
- A twenty-day realized-volatility measure may support option comparison while reacting too slowly for an intraday risk limit.

11.23 Triangulation, Independence, and Conflicting Evidence

Triangulation examines a phenomenon through several independent or partially independent measurements. It is not simple voting. Three transformations of the same price series do not provide the same evidentiary diversity as price, breadth, liquidity, and cross-asset evidence.

Conflicting measurements may reflect error, horizon mismatch, regime change, transition, risk premia, or genuinely multidimensional behavior. For example, falling realized volatility and rising implied volatility can coexist because they describe different windows and constructions.

> **Triangulation Principle:** The objective is not to maximize the number of indicators. It is to improve the diversity, independence, and relevance of evidence.

11.24 Composite Measurements and Classification

Composite measurements can summarize complex evidence, but they may conceal opposing conditions, unequal quality, missingness, redundant components, and nonlinear interaction.

Requirement	What must remain visible
Components	Underlying values and definitions.
Provenance and time	Sources, timestamps, horizons, and freshness.
Normalization and weights	Scaling choices, weights, and rationale.
Missingness	Unavailable components and substitution rules.
Thresholds	Calibration, boundary sensitivity, and ambiguity handling.
Uncertainty	Confidence, sensitivity, and model dependence.
Version and decomposition	Controlled definition and ability to reconstruct the score.

> **Composite Principle:** A composite should compress information without destroying traceability.

Continuous values should remain accessible when categories such as low, normal, high, stable, stressed, bullish, or bearish are used. Display precision should be proportional to epistemic confidence.

11.25 Measurement, Causality, and Decision Boundaries

Function	Question
Descriptive	What is happening now?
Comparative	How does the present differ from history or peers?
Diagnostic	What mechanisms may explain the condition?
Predictive	What future outcome may be more likely?
Prescriptive	What action should be taken?

These functions require increasing justification. Association does not establish mechanism, and mechanism does not automatically establish causation. A measurement that is descriptively useful should not be promoted to prediction or prescription without additional evidence.

> **Decision Boundary:** Measurements inform judgment within participant objectives and constraints. They do not prescribe universal action.

11.26 Measurement Use, Crowding, and Reflexivity

Measurements may influence the system they describe. Widely followed volatility thresholds can alter risk limits. Benchmark changes can cause rebalancing. Public positioning estimates can influence participants who anticipate the reactions of others.

When many participants use similar rules, their responses may become correlated. Widespread use can weaken a once-useful relationship, shift thresholds, create concentration, or make behavior strategically anticipated.

11.27 Measurement Governance and Retirement

Measurement governance is the controlled process through which analytical measures are defined, verified, validated, approved, monitored, changed, and retired.

- named ownership and purpose;
- documented design inputs and method;
- peer review and test cases;
- data-quality and freshness monitoring;
- model validation and sensitivity review;
- change approval and version control;
- performance and drift review;
- known limitations and failure modes;
- retirement and supersession criteria.

A measurement should be retired when its source becomes unreliable, market structure changes, its relationship to the intended phenomenon weakens, assumptions no longer hold, or a superior measure becomes available. Retirement is evidence of a functioning scientific process.

11.28 Formal Measurement Specification

Field	Required content
Measurement name	Unique controlled name.
Purpose	Question or function supported.
Primary domain	Liquidity, positioning, volatility, trend, or cross-domain.
Data provenance	Sources, fields, venues, vendor, and coverage.
Transformation	Formula, algorithm, model, or classification logic.
Units	Native and displayed units.
Time definition	Event time, sampling, lookback, cadence, and effective period.
Universe	Instruments, venues, sessions, and inclusion criteria.
Assumptions	Model, benchmark, ownership, or behavioral assumptions.
Interpretation	What the result may indicate.
Exclusions	What the result does not establish.
Quality controls	Validation, freshness, missingness, and error handling.
Uncertainty	Range, confidence, sensitivity, or classification.
Version	Effective controlled definition.
Verification	Evidence the calculation works as specified.
Validation	Evidence the measure is useful for its intended purpose.
Retirement criteria	Conditions under which it should no longer be used.

11.29 Complete Worked Example

At 10:30 a.m., a broad equity index is down 0.8%. The analytical question is whether the decline reflects ordinary weakness or developing short-horizon stress.

1. Price and trend: The index is down 0.8% from the prior close. Under the selected method, price remains above its intermediate moving average, short-horizon momentum is negative, and 70% of components are declining. This supports short-horizon deterioration within an intermediate upward trend.
2. Liquidity: Spreads have widened modestly, near-touch depth is 25% below the normal time-of-day range, comparable price impact has increased, and order books continue to recover after transactions. Liquidity has weakened but remains functional.

3. Positioning: Put open interest is elevated near current prices. Dealer-exposure estimates suggest greater downside sensitivity under the central ownership assumptions. Open interest is delayed and the exposure estimate is model-dependent.
4. Volatility: Realized intraday variability is rising. Short-dated implied volatility and downside skew have increased, while longer-dated implied volatility remains comparatively stable. The options market is pricing greater near-term implied variability, protection demand, event risk, or risk compensation; the measurement does not prove fear.
5. Data quality: Quote data are current. One options feed had a brief gap. Dealer estimates are model-dependent. Open-interest data reflect the prior reporting update. The evidence does not deserve equal weight.
6. Multidomain interpretation: The market is experiencing broad short-horizon selling within an intermediate upward price trend under the selected method. Liquidity measurements have deteriorated relative to the normal time-of-day baseline but remain functional. Realized intraday variability, short-dated implied volatility, and downside skew have increased. Model-dependent positioning estimates suggest possible additional downside sensitivity, but confidence is limited by ownership assumptions and delayed open-interest data. The configuration is consistent with developing short-horizon stress, not established market dysfunction.

Principles of Responsible Market Measurement

Principle 1: Define Before Measuring

Principle 2: Identify the Purpose

Principle 3: Preserve Provenance and Lineage

Principle 4: Distinguish Data, Measurement, Evidence, and Interpretation

Principle 5: Preserve the Distinction Between Proxy and Phenomenon

Principle 6: Match Time, Universe, and Method to the Question

Principle 7: Expose Assumptions and Inferential Distance

Principle 8: Represent Missingness and Staleness Honestly

Principle 9: Prefer Diverse Triangulation to Indicator Multiplication

Principle 10: Test Sensitivity and Robustness

Principle 11: Preserve Reproducibility and Version Control

Principle 12: Use Precision Proportional to Knowledge

Principle 13: Validate Continuously

Principle 14: Keep Composites Decomposable

Principle 15: Do Not Confuse Measurement With Judgment or Action

Chapter Summary

Market measurements transform recorded market activity into controlled representations. They are neither identical to source data nor identical to the phenomena they seek to describe.

A measurement becomes evidence only when interpreted in relation to a question, timeframe, universe, benchmark, context, and set of alternative explanations. Its meaning depends on provenance, transformation, sampling, aggregation, normalization, assumptions, and limitations.

Measurements vary in inferential distance. Recorded observations and deterministic calculations generally require fewer assumptions than model estimates, proxy representations, and latent-condition classifications. Greater inferential distance requires stronger documentation and uncertainty controls.

Data quality, timestamp integrity, freshness, missingness, historical bias, model risk, and regime change can invalidate otherwise sophisticated analysis. Unknown, unavailable, stale, estimated, and model-dependent are legitimate states and should remain visible.

Responsible measurement requires validity, reliability, provenance, reproducibility, robustness, version control, fit-for-purpose evaluation, and continuous governance. The objective is not to eliminate uncertainty, but to prevent uncertainty from being concealed by numbers.

Established Knowledge

Measurement theory, metrology, statistics, econometrics, market microstructure, data engineering, model risk management, and financial risk management provide extensive foundations for constructing and evaluating market measurements. Established concerns include sampling error, measurement error, proxy validity, missing-data mechanisms, survivorship bias, look-ahead bias, revision bias, benchmark sensitivity, aggregation effects, latent-variable modeling, reproducibility, composite-indicator construction, and model governance.

The Institute does not claim to originate these disciplines. Its contribution is to integrate them into a coherent market-systems architecture.

Institute Perspective

The Institute treats measurement as a governed process rather than a numerical output. A measurement is a controlled representation whose meaning depends on construction, context, purpose, and limitations.

The Institute formalizes the chain from phenomena to data, measurements, evidence, domain assessment, market configuration, judgment, and action. It requires explicit freshness and uncertainty states, applies engineering-style design control to analytical measures, keeps composites decomposable, and separates descriptive usefulness from predictive and prescriptive claims.

Computational systems may implement this discipline by collecting data, preserving provenance, validating inputs, constructing governed measurements, exposing freshness and limitations, organizing evidence by domain, and communicating uncertainty. Software is an implementation of measurement discipline, not a substitute for reasoning.

Questions for Reflection

1. What distinguishes recorded data from processed data and a measurement?
2. Why is a bid-ask spread not equivalent to liquidity?
3. When does a measurement become evidence?
4. What is inferential distance?
5. Why can a deterministically calculated value still be misleading?
6. What distinguishes a proxy from a latent-condition inference?
7. What is proxy substitution?
8. Why must sampling frequency match the analytical question?
9. How can aggregation conceal instability?
10. Why can a stable average coexist with unstable components?
11. What is the difference between validity and reliability?
12. How can a measurement be reliable but invalid?
13. Why may accuracy be difficult to establish for latent variables?
14. What is the difference between event time, calculation time, and publication time?
15. Why is a stale value not equivalent to a current value?
16. When should missing data remain unavailable rather than be estimated?
17. How can look-ahead or survivorship bias create misleading historical results?
18. Why does mathematical correctness not guarantee behavioral correctness?

19. What distinguishes sensitivity analysis from robustness testing?
20. Why must a composite remain decomposable?
21. How can widespread use of a measurement alter the market behavior it describes?
22. What evidence would justify retiring a measurement?
23. Why should numerical precision be proportional to epistemic confidence?
24. What information is needed to reproduce a governed market measurement?

Chapter 12. Evidence and Market Reasoning

From Observation to Defensible Interpretation

Chapter Purpose

Market analysis does not end when measurements are produced. A spread widens, implied volatility rises, open interest increases, breadth deteriorates, or price remains above a long-horizon moving average. These measurements may be accurate, yet they do not explain themselves.

The analyst must determine what the measurements establish, what they only suggest, which explanations remain plausible, how much confidence is justified, and what evidence would cause revision. This is the work of market reasoning.

Reasoning connects contextual evidence to inference, interpretation, and assessment. It also creates opportunities for error. A persuasive narrative may be unsupported. Correlation may be presented as mechanism. A plausible mechanism may be treated as proven causation. A valid observation may be extended beyond the scope of what it can establish.

This chapter establishes a governed discipline for moving from measurement to defensible interpretation. It integrates evidence quality, inferential distance, competing hypotheses, causal reasoning, confidence, contradiction, scenario analysis, auditability, and the Principle of Provisional Knowledge.

Learning Objectives

- Distinguish recorded observation, measurement, evidence, inference, interpretation, assessment, judgment, and action.
- Explain why evidence is question-dependent and context-dependent.
- Evaluate evidence quality separately from evidentiary value.
- Distinguish description, association, mechanism, contribution, causation, and causal weight.
- Construct primary, alternative, and null hypotheses.
- Seek discriminating, negative, and contradictory evidence.
- Use confidence labels appropriate to the claim being made.
- Preserve missing, stale, unknown, and unknowable information.

- Construct narratives and scenarios without converting them into certainty.
- Create auditable, revisable, contemporaneous market assessments.

12.1 From Measurement to Defensible Interpretation

A measurement becomes evidence only when it is placed in relation to a defined question. An increase in implied volatility from 18% to 24% is a measurement report. It becomes evidence when the analyst asks whether option prices reflect greater near-term implied variability, protection demand, event risk, reduced option supply, or another condition.

> **Governing Standard:** A defensible market interpretation must remain traceable to valid evidence, explicit about inference, aware of competing explanations, proportional in confidence, and open to revision.

Defensibility does not mean certainty. It means that the reasoning can be inspected, challenged, updated, and reconstructed.

12.2 The Canonical Reasoning Chain

Stage	Meaning
Market phenomenon	The characteristic or process being studied.
Recorded and processed data	Market events or values captured and prepared by data systems.
Controlled measurement	A governed representation created through a documented method.
Contextual evidence	A measurement interpreted relative to a proposition, horizon, universe, and baseline.
Inference	A reasoned step beyond what is measured directly.
Interpretation	An organized explanation of what the evidence may mean.
Multidomain assessment	A structured synthesis of evidence, interpretations, contradictions, gaps, and confidence.
Judgment	A decision-relevant conclusion formed within objectives and constraints.
Action	The response selected by a participant or system.

> **Reasoning Chain Principle:** Measurements support evidence; evidence supports inference; inferences are organized into interpretations; interpretations contribute to assessments; assessments inform judgment but do not prescribe action automatically.

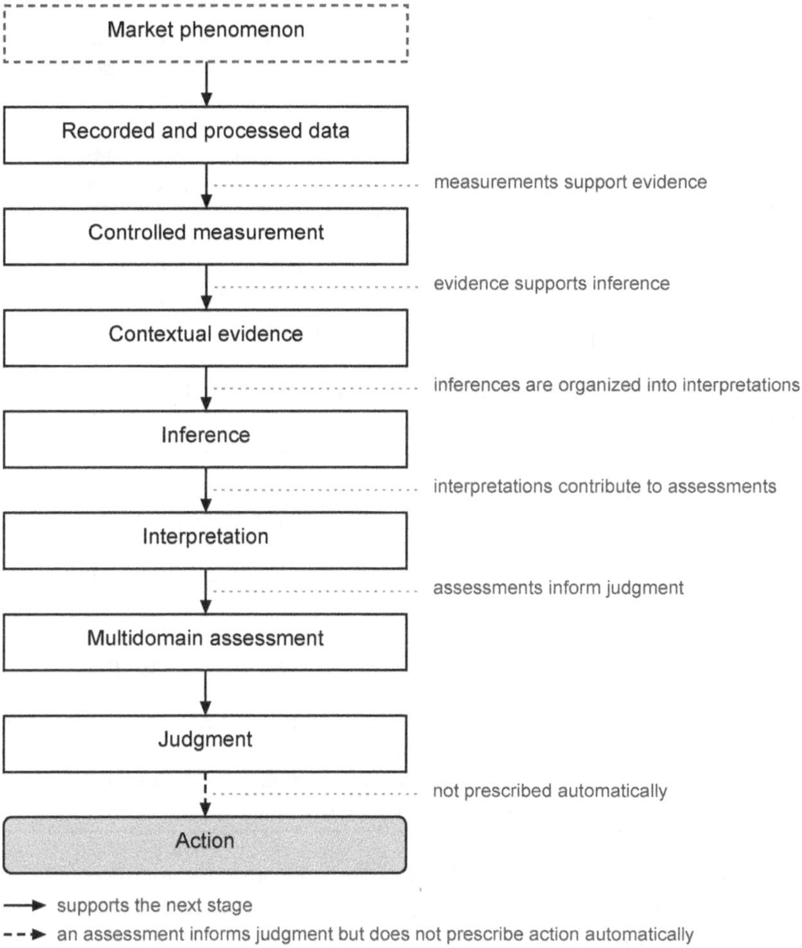

Figure 12.1 — The Market Reasoning Chain

12.3 Recorded Observation, Measurement, and Evidence

Level	Definition	Example
Recorded observation	A reported market event or value.	A trade occurred at $100.25.
Measurement	A controlled representation constructed from data.	Twenty-day realized volatility increased from 18% to 24%.

Level	Definition	Example
Evidentiary statement	A measurement placed in relation to a question and baseline.	Short-horizon realized variability has increased relative to the recent regime.
Inference	A proposition extending beyond direct measurement.	Market adjustment has become more intense.

A measurement does not carry a fixed meaning independent of context. A four-basis-point spread may be ordinary for one instrument, impaired for another, or expected immediately before a scheduled announcement.

12.4 Inference, Interpretation, Assessment, and Judgment

Term	Function
Inference	A reasoned proposition that extends beyond direct measurement.
Interpretation	An organized explanation of what a body of evidence may mean.
Assessment	A structured synthesis of current evidence, explanations, contradiction, uncertainty, and confidence.
Judgment	A conclusion formed for a particular decision purpose under stated constraints.
Action	A participant-specific response; not a universal consequence of the assessment.

> **Provisional Conclusion Principle:** A market conclusion is the current best-supported proposition under the available evidence and stated assumptions. It is provisional, not permanent.

12.5 The Standard of Defensibility

An interpretation is defensible when it:

- is traceable to valid and relevant evidence;
- separates recorded observations, measurements, estimates, and inferences;
- states its timeframe, universe, baseline, and assumptions;
- considers competing and null explanations;
- identifies contradictory and missing evidence;
- uses confidence proportional to support;
- states limitations and revision conditions;
- remains open to correction.

A compelling narrative that cannot meet these requirements may be rhetorically effective but analytically weak.

12.6 The Structure of a Reasoned Claim

A strong analytical claim contains:

1. The proposition being evaluated.
2. The evidence supporting it.
3. The reasoning connecting evidence to the proposition.
4. Competing explanations.
5. Limitations, gaps, and uncertainty.
6. A confidence statement.
7. Conditions that would cause revision.

Example — Liquidity deterioration

Proposition: Market liquidity deteriorated during the decline. Evidence: spreads widened, near-touch depth declined, price impact increased, and order-book recovery slowed. Reasoning: the measurements represent several dimensions of transaction friction, absorption, and resilience. Limitations: hidden liquidity is not observed completely, the change may be normal for the time of day, and venue coverage may be incomplete.

12.7 Evidence Quality and Evidentiary Value

Evidence quality	**Evidentiary value**
Validity	Relevance to the proposition
Reliability	Directness
Freshness	Independence
Completeness	Specificity
Provenance	Magnitude
Reproducibility	Persistence
Coverage	Discriminating power

A high-quality measurement may have little value for a particular question. Long-dated rate volatility may be measured accurately but provide limited evidence about whether an intraday equity advance is broadly supported.

> **Evidence Evaluation Principle:** Evaluate the trustworthiness of evidence separately from how strongly it distinguishes among competing explanations.

12.8 Inferential Distance and Pattern-Based Evidence

Level	Form of evidence	Typical qualification
1	Recorded market evidence	Closest to reported activity but may still be incomplete, delayed, or corrected.
2	Deterministically derived evidence	Transparent calculation; meaning remains method and context dependent.
3	Model-estimated evidence	Depends on model structure, inputs, and parameters.
4	Proxy-based inference	Represents a broader phenomenon only partially.
5	Latent-condition or behavioral inference	Requires substantial qualification because motives and complete system conditions are not directly observed.

Greater inferential distance generally increases assumptions. It does not automatically determine evidentiary strength. A validated model estimate may be useful, while a direct but stale report may be weak for a real-time question.

Pattern-based evidence combines several observations to support an inference when direct participant-level evidence is unavailable. The strength of the pattern depends on quality, coherence, independence, and the weakening of plausible alternatives.

12.9 Independence, Dependency, and Redundancy

Several indicators can appear to provide confirmation while relying on the same underlying information. A twenty-day moving average, twenty-day rate of change, trend regression, and momentum oscillator may all derive from the same price series and window.

- shared source data;
- shared transformation windows;
- shared model assumptions;
- common vendors;
- common market mechanisms;
- duplicated exposures.

> **Dependency Principle:** Indicator count is not evidence diversity. Confidence should reflect independent information, not the number of transformations displayed.

12.10 Description, Association, Mechanism, Contribution, and Causation

Claim level	Question	Example
Description	What occurred?	Price declined while realized volatility rose.
Association	What moved together?	Declines were accompanied by volatility expansion in the sample.
Temporal sequence	What preceded what?	The option repricing preceded the largest futures-selling interval.
Mechanism	Through what process could influence occur?	Changing hedge sensitivity could produce additional futures transactions.
Contribution	Did the factor materially influence the outcome?	Hedging flow appears to have amplified the move.
Causation	Would the outcome have differed materially without the factor?	The factor caused a measurable portion of the decline.
Causal weight	What role did the factor play?	Primary, amplifying, enabling, constraining, or incidental.

Causal Discipline: A coherent mechanism explains how an effect could occur; it does not establish that the mechanism occurred or dominated.

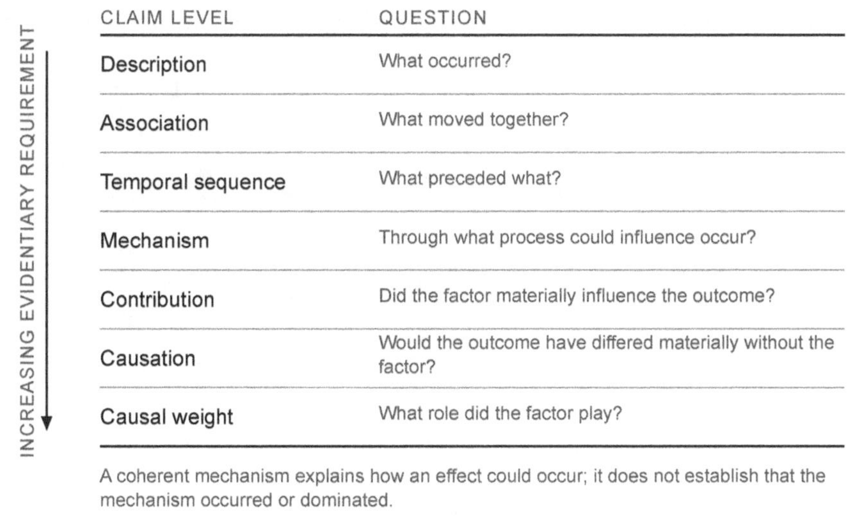

Figure 12.2 — Levels of Analytical Claims

12.11 Temporal Order and Causal Identification

A cause must generally precede its effect, but recorded market sequence may not reveal the true decision sequence. Prices, volatility, liquidity, and hedging activity may change almost simultaneously. Feeds may use different clocks, reports may be delayed, and participants may act before public events.

Temporal order is necessary for causal inference, but rarely sufficient. Causal identification also requires a plausible mechanism, evidence of contribution, alternatives, configuration dependence, and robustness across comparable cases.

12.12 Trigger, Mechanism, Structure, Feedback, and Outcome

Element	Meaning	Illustration
Trigger	The event associated with initiation.	An earnings surprise.
Proximate mechanism	The immediate transmission process.	Sell orders consume available bids.
Structural condition	The configuration influencing sensitivity.	Concentrated exposure and weak depth.
Feedback mechanism	The process reinforcing or limiting adjustment.	Volatility-sensitive deleveraging or liquidity replenishment.
Outcome	The observed result.	A disproportionate decline.

The trigger may explain why movement began at a particular moment. The market configuration helps explain why the response took its observed form.

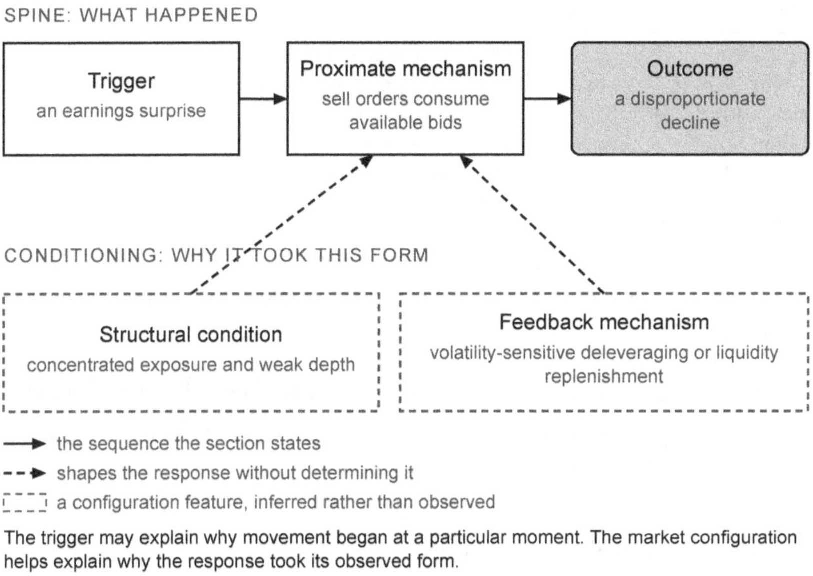

Figure 12.3 — Trigger, Structure, Feedback, and Outcome

12.13 Necessary, Sufficient, Contributory, and Constraining Conditions

- A necessary condition must be present for an outcome under the stated framework.
- A sufficient condition is enough to produce the outcome under stated assumptions.
- A contributory condition materially influences the outcome but is neither universally necessary nor sufficient.
- A constraining condition limits or opposes the outcome.

Few common market indicators are universally necessary or sufficient. Concentrated positioning is not sufficient for reversal, high volatility is not necessary for decline, and strong liquidity is not sufficient to prevent losses.

12.14 Multicausality and Causal Weight

Market outcomes frequently reflect several interacting factors. Multicausal reasoning should not become an unrestricted list of possibilities. Each material factor requires evidence and an appropriately limited role.

Role	Meaning
Primary	The principal factor initiating or explaining the outcome.
Contributing	A factor that materially adds to the outcome.

Role	Meaning
Amplifying	A factor that increases magnitude or speed.
Enabling	A condition that permits transmission.
Constraining	A condition that limits the response.
Incidental	A contemporaneous factor with little material influence.
Unsupported	A plausible factor for which available evidence is insufficient.

Multicausal Principle: A longer list of possible causes is not a stronger explanation. Evidence is required for each factor assigned material causal weight.

12.15 Competing, Null, and Alternative Hypotheses

A disciplined process compares more than one explanation. It should include a primary hypothesis, plausible alternatives, and a null or minimal explanation.

Example — Index rises while implied volatility also rises

- Primary hypothesis: concentrated upside option demand and associated hedging are amplifying the advance.
- Alternative hypothesis: investors participate in the advance while retaining downside protection.
- Alternative hypothesis: scheduled event risk raises option prices independently of directional conviction.
- Alternative hypothesis: reduced option supply increases required risk compensation.
- Null explanation: the observed combination reflects ordinary short-horizon variation rather than a distinct structural mechanism.

The objective is not to invent every imaginable story. It is to compare plausible explanations that imply meaningfully different expected observations.

12.16 Discriminating and Negative Evidence

Discriminating evidence is expected under one hypothesis more strongly than under another. Negative evidence occurs when an observation expected under a hypothesis does not appear.

- call versus put implied-volatility changes;
- skew and term-structure behavior;
- trade initiation estimates;
- underlying and futures response;
- breadth and sector participation;
- liquidity and price impact;
- scheduled-event timing;

- persistence after the suspected mechanism ends.

Negative evidence is strongest when the observation process was capable of detecting the expected condition. Failure to observe participant-level activity in an unavailable dataset is absence of evidence, not evidence of absence.

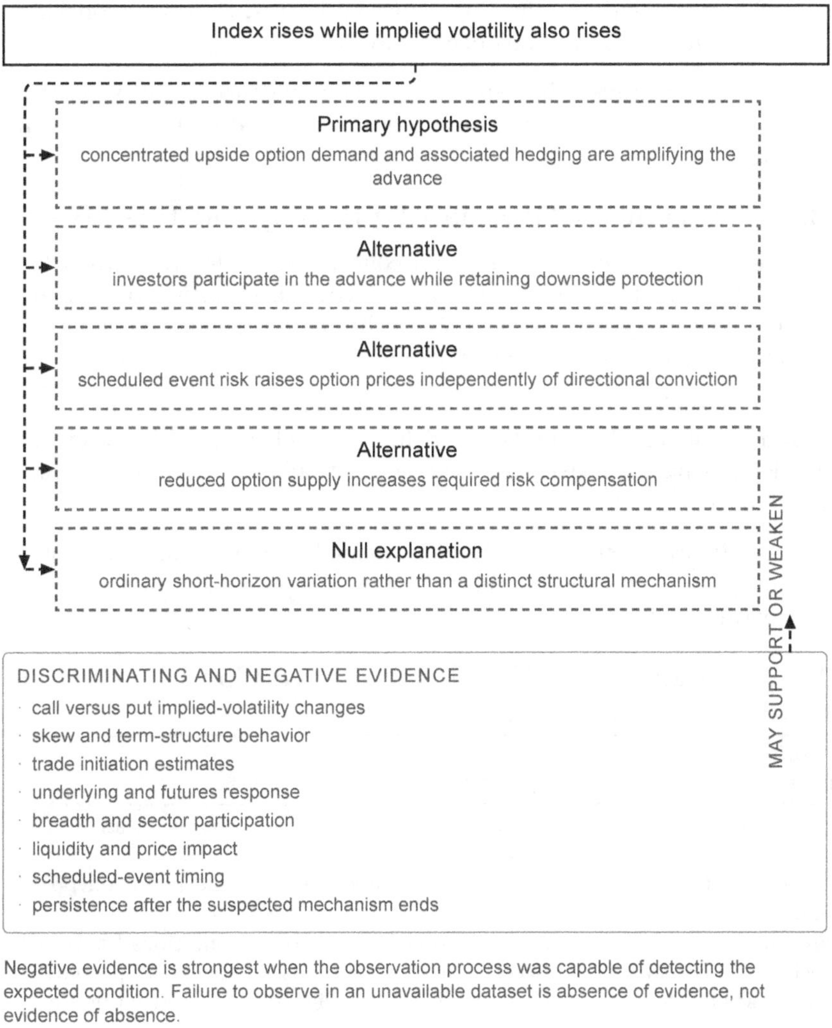

Figure 12.4 — Competing Hypotheses and Discriminating Evidence

12.17 Hypothesis Revision and Provisional Knowledge

A useful hypothesis should identify observations that would materially weaken, revise, or reject it. A claim that explains every outcome cannot be tested meaningfully.

> **Principle of Provisional Knowledge:** All market understanding is provisional and should remain open to revision when new evidence, improved measurements, superior models, or stronger explanations become available.

Changing an assessment in response to better evidence is not inconsistency. The discipline values correction over consistency and refinement over institutional pride.

12.18 Conceptual Bayesian Updating and Base Rates

Bayesian reasoning provides a useful conceptual model even when formal probabilities are not calculated. Begin with an explicit prior judgment, examine how likely the evidence would be under competing explanations, and update confidence according to the diagnostic value of the evidence.

Base rates provide historical discipline, but require comparable instruments, horizons, configurations, and event definitions. They must also be evaluated for selection bias, survivorship bias, look-ahead bias, regime change, and sample uncertainty.

> **Updating Principle:** Evidence should change confidence in proportion to how differently it would be expected under competing explanations.

12.19 Evidence Quality, Interpretive Confidence, and Predictive Confidence

Confidence dimension	Question
Data confidence	Are the source data current, complete, and trustworthy?
Measurement confidence	Is the method valid, reliable, and fit for purpose?
Descriptive confidence	How confidently can current conditions be described?
Mechanistic confidence	How strongly is a proposed process supported?
Classification confidence	How stable is the assigned configuration or state representation?
Predictive confidence	How strongly does the evidence support a future outcome?

A system may have high descriptive confidence, moderate classification confidence, low mechanistic confidence, and very low predictive confidence. These dimensions should not be collapsed into one undefined score.

Numerical confidence should be used only when its meaning, horizon, calibration population, historical reliability, version, and missing-data treatment are defined. Otherwise, qualitative labels with rationale are more defensible.

12.20 Contradictory, Missing, and Unknowable Evidence

Price may rise while breadth weakens, implied volatility increases, liquidity remains stable, and exposure becomes concentrated. This is not automatically an analytical failure.

- different horizons;
- different instrument universes;
- stale or delayed data;
- measurement error;
- shared but differently expressed mechanisms;
- genuine multidimensional coexistence;
- transition or structural divergence.

> **Contradiction Principle:** Mixed evidence should be preserved until its source is understood. It should not be forced into a premature bullish, bearish, stable, or stressed label.

Unknown information may become available later. Unknowable information may never be fully observable in real time, including private motives, future decisions, and unobserved counterfactual outcomes. The correct assessment may be that available evidence does not permit a reliable conclusion.

12.21 Narratives as Structured Hypotheses

Narratives help organize observations into sequences, but coherence is not proof. A responsible narrative should label each link as observed, measured, estimated, inferred, assumed, or unresolved.

> **Narrative Principle:** Narrative coherence is not evidentiary support. A narrative is a structured hypothesis whose links must be traceable and revisable.

A central-bank announcement followed by a decline may be relevant evidence, but temporal proximity alone does not establish cause. Positioning, liquidity, simultaneous events, prior expectations, and later reversals may alter the explanation.

12.22 Common Reasoning Failures

Failure category	Examples
Evidence selection	Confirmation bias, omission of contrary evidence, selective examples.
Temporal reasoning	Recency bias, hindsight bias, post hoc reasoning.
Narrative construction	Narrative fallacy, overfitted explanations, causal overreach.
Incentive and identity	Motivated reasoning, reputation protection, position-dependent interpretation.
Evaluation	Outcome bias, poor calibration, confusing a correct guess with sound process.
Complexity management	Overcomplication, indicator counting, failure to consider a simpler explanation.

A useful control is to record evidence supporting the current interpretation, evidence opposing it, and evidence that remains ambiguous.

12.23 Scenario Reasoning and Signposts

A scenario is a structured conditional pathway used to organize uncertainty, not a declaration that the pathway will occur.

Scenario	Conditional pathway	Illustrative signposts
Orderly continuation	Direction persists while participation broadens and variability stabilizes.	Stable spreads, improving breadth, moderate volatility.
Fragile continuation	Direction persists while concentration and sensitivity increase.	Narrow leadership, concentrated exposure, asymmetric liquidity.
Stress transition	Liquidity weakens, variability expands, and forced adjustment develops.	Widening spreads, rising impact, volatility expansion, forced selling.

Each scenario should identify a starting configuration, horizon, signposts, expected domain responses, and invalidating conditions. Probabilities should not be assigned unless calibrated.

12.24 Magnitude, Persistence, Breadth, and Horizon

- Magnitude: Is the change economically, operationally, or systemically meaningful?
- Persistence: Is the observation isolated, emerging, persistent, or established?
- Breadth: Is the condition local or distributed across instruments, sectors, or markets?

- Horizon: Do short-, intermediate-, and long-horizon measurements agree or diverge?

A statistically detectable change may be economically trivial. A one-minute anomaly should not be interpreted like a three-day condition. Cross-market breadth may strengthen generalization, while common exposure or mechanical rebalancing may create apparent breadth without independent mechanisms.

12.25 Building a Defensible Market Assessment

1. Define the proposition.
2. Define the horizon and market universe.
3. Identify the evidence required.
4. Validate data and measurements.
5. Separate recorded observations, measurements, estimates, and inferences.
6. Construct primary, alternative, and null hypotheses.
7. Seek discriminating and negative evidence.
8. Evaluate contradiction, dependency, and evidence gaps.
9. Assign multidimensional confidence.
10. State the provisional assessment.
11. Define revision conditions and monitoring signposts.
12. Preserve a contemporaneous record.

> **Assessment Principle:** The assessment should be the most defensible synthesis permitted by the available evidence, not the most forceful statement the analyst can make.

12.26 Complete Worked Example

At 11:00 a.m., a capitalization-weighted equity index is up 1.1%. Implied volatility is also higher. Only 42% of components are advancing, several large technology companies account for most of the gain, futures volume is elevated, visible spreads remain normal, and short-dated call activity is unusually high.

Question

Does the advance represent broad market expansion or a concentrated directional event?

Recorded observations and measurements

- The capitalization-weighted index is higher.
- Equal-weight and sector participation are weak.
- Leadership is concentrated.
- Short-dated implied volatility and call activity are elevated.

- Futures volume is elevated.
- Visible spreads remain normal; depth, impact, and recovery evidence remain incomplete.

Competing explanations

- Broad risk-on repricing.
- Large-cap leadership without broad participation.
- Short-horizon options-related amplification.
- Event-sensitive positioning ahead of a scheduled announcement.
- Ordinary short-horizon variation.

Additional evidence

- The equal-weighted index is nearly flat.
- Most sectors are unchanged or lower.
- Call activity is concentrated in same-week expirations.
- Model-dependent dealer estimates suggest negative gamma near current prices.
- Liquidity remains functional for observed transaction sizes.
- A major earnings announcement is scheduled after the close.

Provisional assessment

The capitalization-weighted index is advancing, but the move is narrowly concentrated and is not presently confirmed by equal-weight or broad sector participation. Short-dated option activity and model-dependent dealer-sensitivity estimates are consistent with possible options-related amplification, although trade initiation, ownership, and net exposure remain uncertain. Visible spreads remain normal, but broader liquidity evidence is incomplete. The current configuration is best described as a concentrated, event-sensitive advance rather than a broadly supported expansion. Interpretive confidence is moderate; causal and predictive confidence are lower.

Revision conditions

- The broad-expansion interpretation would strengthen if participation, equal-weight performance, and sector leadership broaden and persist after the event.
- The temporary-amplification interpretation would strengthen if call activity fades, leadership remains narrow, sensitivity estimates decline, and the index reverses after the event.
- Confidence would fall if option data become stale, ownership assumptions prove unstable, or liquidity evidence conflicts materially.

12.27 Language Proportional to Evidence

Claim condition	Appropriate language
Direct and well bounded	records, shows, establishes, confirms the measured fact
Supported but not proven	indicates, supports, is consistent with, increases confidence in
Limited or indirect	may reflect, could indicate, is compatible with, remains possible
Unresolved	cannot be determined, evidence is mixed, data are unavailable, conclusion remains provisional

Language must be matched to the subject and scope of the claim. Data may confirm that displayed spread widened; they generally cannot confirm that investors panicked.

Terms such as manipulation, panic, conviction, capitulation, accumulation, distribution, control, certainty, and inevitable require operational definition and supporting evidence.

12.28 Expert Judgment, Human Challenge, and Machine Assistance

Expert judgment can add contextual understanding but may introduce inconsistency, bias, or authority effects. It should be grounded in evidence, documented, open to contradiction, and reviewed over time.

A reviewer should ask:

- What evidence supports the conclusion?
- Which observations oppose or complicate it?
- Are the measurements independent?
- What assumptions are hidden?
- Is there a simpler explanation?
- What would weaken the hypothesis?
- Is the confidence level justified?
- Does the language exceed the evidence?

Computational systems and language models can organize observations, identify contradictions, generate candidate hypotheses, summarize evidence, and monitor signposts. They can also produce fluent but unsupported explanations.

> **Machine-Reasoning Principle:** An automated narrative should be trusted only to the extent that its claims, sources, timestamps, versions, assumptions, uncertainty, and revision conditions can be inspected.

Each machine-generated claim should be labeled as directly observed, deterministically measured, model estimated, proxy based, inferred, scenario based, stale, unavailable, or contradicted.

12.29 Auditability, Contemporaneous Records, and Calibration

A defensible assessment should preserve the measurements used, timestamps, versions, quality states, assumptions, alternatives, reasoning, confidence dimensions, and revision conditions.

A contemporaneous evidence record should include:

- question and proposition;
- horizon and universe;
- recorded observations and measurements;
- measurement-quality status;
- primary and competing hypotheses;
- supporting and contradictory evidence;
- evidence dependencies and gaps;
- confidence by claim type;
- signposts and revision conditions;
- timestamp and framework version.

Calibration must be evaluated separately for current-condition description, domain classification, market-configuration assessment, transition detection, causal attribution, conditional forecasting, and decision support.

12.30 Reasoning Failure Analysis

When an assessment fails, review the entire chain rather than judging only the outcome.

Failure stage	**Examples**
Data	Incorrect, incomplete, delayed, or stale input.
Measurement	Invalid method, wrong unit, unsuitable horizon, or model error.
Evidence selection	Irrelevant, redundant, or selectively chosen observations.
Inference	Unsupported extension beyond the measurement.
Interpretation	Narrative overreach or overlooked alternatives.
Assessment	Contradiction or uncertainty concealed.
Judgment	Confidence exceeded support or purpose was mismatched.
Action	Execution, sizing, timing, or constraints were mishandled.
External development	A genuinely unpredictable event changed the environment.

Process Principle: A correct outcome does not validate poor reasoning, and an adverse outcome does not automatically invalidate a sound process.

Standard Evidence Record

Field	Required content
Question or proposition	What is being evaluated?
Horizon and universe	When, where, and for which instruments?
Recorded observations	What was directly reported?
Measurements	What was constructed or estimated?
Measurement quality	Freshness, validity, completeness, and limitations.
Primary interpretation	What explanation currently has the strongest support?
Competing and null hypotheses	What alternatives remain plausible?
Supporting and contradictory evidence	What favors or complicates the primary interpretation?
Dependencies and gaps	Which inputs share assumptions, and what is missing or unknowable?
Causal role	Primary, contributing, amplifying, enabling, constraining, incidental, or unsupported.
Confidence	Data, descriptive, mechanistic, classification, and predictive confidence.
Revision conditions and signposts	What would strengthen, weaken, or reverse the assessment?
Timestamp and version	When and under which framework definition?

Principles of Responsible Market Reasoning

1. Define the proposition before evaluating it.
2. Separate recorded observation from measurement.
3. Separate measurement from inference.
4. Treat evidence as question-dependent.
5. Evaluate quality and diagnostic value separately.
6. Map evidence dependencies.
7. Distinguish association, mechanism, contribution, and causation.
8. Consider competing and null explanations.
9. Seek discriminating and negative evidence.
10. Distinguish trigger from structural condition.
11. Assign causal weight proportionally.
12. Preserve contradiction, missingness, and unknowability.
13. Use confidence appropriate to the claim type.
14. State revision conditions.
15. Treat narratives as structured hypotheses.

16. Preserve auditability and contemporaneous records.
17. Evaluate process separately from outcome.
18. Prefer correction over consistency.

Chapter Summary

Measurements become evidence only in relation to a defined question, timeframe, market universe, comparison, and set of alternatives. Evidence supports inference, inference contributes to interpretation, and interpretations are synthesized into provisional market assessments.

A defensible interpretation remains traceable to valid measurements, distinguishes observation from inference, exposes assumptions, evaluates competing explanations, uses confidence proportional to support, identifies limitations, and states what would cause revision.

Description, association, mechanism, contribution, and causation are different claim levels. A coherent mechanism may explain how an effect could occur without proving that it occurred or dominated. Market outcomes are often multicausal, but each proposed factor requires evidence and an appropriately limited causal role.

Contradictory, missing, stale, unknown, and unknowable evidence should remain visible. Confidence should be separated into data, measurement, descriptive, mechanistic, classification, and predictive dimensions rather than collapsed into an undefined score.

The objective of market reasoning is not to construct the most compelling narrative. It is to produce the most defensible interpretation permitted by the available evidence while remaining open to correction.

Established Knowledge

The principles in this chapter draw upon established work in philosophy of science, epistemology, scientific inference, causal inference, Bayesian reasoning, hypothesis testing, counterfactual analysis, decision theory, behavioral finance, cognitive psychology, model risk, expert judgment, forecast calibration, root-cause analysis, and human-machine decision systems.

The Institute does not claim originality for these disciplines. Its contribution lies in integrating them into a controlled market-analysis architecture that preserves measurement lineage, competing explanations, uncertainty, revision conditions, and the distinction between reasoning quality and realized outcome.

Institute Perspective

The Institute treats market reasoning as a governed evidentiary process. Its central contribution is to formalize the chain from measurement to evidence, inference, interpretation, assessment, judgment, and action.

It distinguishes trigger, mechanism, structural condition, feedback, and outcome; preserves competing explanations and contradiction; treats confidence as multidimensional; and requires every material assessment to remain auditable and revisable.

Within this framework, a market narrative is not an authoritative declaration. It is a transparent synthesis of evidence whose status, assumptions, limitations, and revision conditions remain visible.

Questions for Reflection

1. When does a measurement become evidence?
2. What distinguishes a recorded observation from a measurement?
3. What distinguishes inference from interpretation?
4. What distinguishes interpretation from assessment?
5. What makes a market interpretation defensible?
6. Why is evidence quality different from evidentiary value?
7. Why does inferential distance not automatically determine evidence strength?
8. Why are several indicators derived from the same data not independent confirmation?
9. What distinguishes association from mechanism?
10. What distinguishes mechanistic plausibility from causal contribution?
11. What is the difference between a trigger and a structural condition?
12. Why are market outcomes often multicausal?
13. What makes evidence discriminating?
14. What role should a null explanation play?
15. What observations would weaken a proposed market hypothesis?
16. Why should evidence quality and interpretive confidence remain separate?
17. Why may descriptive confidence be high while predictive confidence remains low?
18. What is the difference between absence of evidence and negative evidence?
19. Why should contradictory evidence sometimes remain unresolved?
20. How can a coherent narrative remain unsupported?
21. What makes a scenario different from a forecast?
22. Why should numerical confidence require calibration?
23. How can contemporaneous records reduce hindsight bias?
24. What should an automated market narrative disclose?

25. Why should reasoning quality be evaluated separately from outcome?
26. What evidence would justify revising a high-confidence assessment?

Chapter 13. Market States

Representing the Market as a Multidomain Configuration

Chapter Purpose

Financial markets continuously generate more evidence than any single label can preserve. Liquidity may remain functional while breadth narrows. Trend may persist while positioning becomes concentrated. Realized volatility may remain contained while short-dated implied volatility rises. A complete description of every measurement is often too detailed for communication, comparison, monitoring, or research.

Analysts therefore create higher-level representations that summarize selected features of a market configuration. These representations are useful only when their purpose, horizon, method, assumptions, and limitations remain visible.

This chapter defines market configuration and market state, distinguishes state from measurement, regime, signal, forecast, and decision, and establishes requirements for constructing state representations that remain decomposable, time-aligned, uncertainty-aware, governed, and open to revision.

Learning Objectives

- Define market configuration and market state and explain their relationship.
- Distinguish states from measurements, indicators, regimes, signals, forecasts, judgments, and actions.
- Explain why every state representation is selective, purpose-dependent, horizon-dependent, and provisional.
- Understand the Structural State Vector as a decomposable representation rather than a self-validating score.
- Understand the Market Compass as a communication layer rather than the state itself.
- Distinguish confirmed structural state from fast trajectory observations.
- Represent mixed, transitional, stale, unavailable, model-dependent, and low-confidence components.

- Evaluate state thresholds, hysteresis, validation, calibration, drift, and governance.
- Preserve the boundary between state description and participant-specific decision.

13.1 From Market Configuration to Market State

Chapters 10 through 12 established a controlled progression from measurements to evidence, interpretation, and multidomain assessment. Chapter 13 adds a further representational layer. A market configuration is the detailed arrangement of observed and inferred conditions at a particular time and scale. A market state is a higher-level representation of selected features of that configuration.

The distinction matters because the market does not arrive with a universally agreed label attached to it. Analysts and models select variables, define horizons, normalize measurements, establish thresholds, and create categories. The resulting state is therefore a controlled analytical representation, not a complete natural object discovered without judgment.

A useful state representation reduces complexity without concealing the evidence from which it was constructed.

Layer	Primary role
Controlled measurements	Represent observable market characteristics.
Contextual evidence	Relates measurements to a question, horizon, universe, and baseline.
Domain assessment	Organizes evidence within liquidity, positioning, volatility, trend, and related dimensions.
Market configuration	Describes the detailed multidomain arrangement.
Market state	Compresses selected configuration features for a stated analytical purpose.

Configuration-to-State Principle: The market possesses a configuration; the analyst or model assigns a state representation to selected features of that configuration.

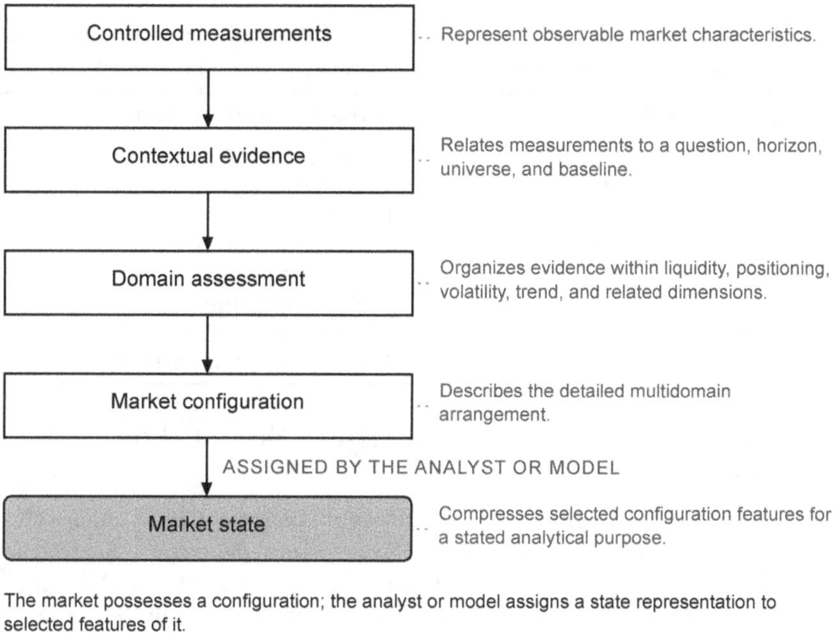

Figure 13.1 — Configuration to State Representation

13.2 What Is a Market State?

A market state is a controlled representation of selected market-configuration features at a specified time, scale, universe, and analytical purpose. The definition contains several safeguards.

First, a state represents selected features. It does not contain every variable that may affect the market. Second, it applies at a specified time and horizon. Third, it depends on a defined universe and method. Fourth, it exists for an analytical purpose such as description, comparison, transition monitoring, research, or decision context.

Two analysts can classify the same market differently without either necessarily making a calculation error if they use different horizons, universes, purposes, or state definitions. The difference must be documented rather than hidden.

> **Governing Definition:** A market state is a controlled, higher-level representation of selected features of a market configuration for a stated purpose, horizon, universe, and method.

13.3 What a Market State Is Not

Market-state language often acquires more authority than the underlying evidence supports. The following distinctions prevent that overreach.

A market state is	A market state is not
A structured representation	The complete market
A summary of selected evidence	A single indicator
Horizon-specific	Timeless
Model- and purpose-dependent	Universally objective
Provisional	Permanent
Decomposable	A black-box score
Descriptive or diagnostic	Automatically predictive
Decision-supporting	A universal action instruction

13.4 State, Configuration, Regime, Signal, Forecast, and Decision

Terms that appear similar perform different analytical functions. A configuration is the detailed arrangement of current evidence. A state is a higher-level representation of selected configuration features. A regime is a relatively persistent statistical, behavioral, or institutional environment identified under a stated method and horizon.

A signal is a rule-generated indication intended to inform a decision. A forecast concerns a possible future outcome. A judgment is a decision-relevant conclusion, and an action is the response selected by a participant subject to objectives, constraints, and risk capacity.

A state may inform a signal or forecast, but it is not identical to either. A state that is useful descriptively may possess little predictive value. A predictive relationship may still be unsuitable for action once transaction costs, constraints, or asymmetric risk are considered.

Concept	Primary question
Configuration	What is the detailed multidomain arrangement?
State	How should selected features be represented?
Regime	What relatively persistent environment appears to prevail?
Signal	Has a decision rule been activated?
Forecast	What future outcome may be more likely?
Judgment	What conclusion is appropriate for this participant and purpose?
Action	What response should be taken under the participant's constraints?

Boundary Principle: A state may inform a forecast, signal, or judgment, but it is not identical to any of them.

13.5 Why State Representations Are Needed

Without state representations, analysts must repeatedly process large numbers of measurements before communicating even a basic description. A controlled state can support comparison across time, monitoring, historical study, transition detection, scenario analysis, and platform implementation.

Compression also creates risk. Details may be lost, contradictory evidence may disappear, artificial boundaries may appear more real than they are, and missing values may be treated as neutral. A state representation is therefore useful only when it preserves a path back to its components.

- Communication and comparison across time.
- Historical research and transition study.
- Monitoring of multidomain change.
- Scenario and decision-context support.
- Model validation and platform implementation.

Compression Principle: A state may compress evidence, but it must not destroy traceability.

13.6 State Dimensions

A multidimensional state is more informative than a single bullish-bearish continuum. The four foundational observational domains provide the primary organizing structure: liquidity, positioning, volatility, and trend. Cross-domain dimensions may also be represented when they are defined and supported.

Possible cross-domain dimensions include breadth and leadership, resilience, fragility, stress, data quality, confidence, and temporal maturity. These dimensions are not necessarily independent. For example, fragility may be inferred partly from concentration, leverage, liquidity, and nonlinear sensitivity.

The state design should therefore identify both components and dependencies.

- Liquidity condition.
- Positioning structure and adjustment sensitivity.
- Volatility degree and structure.
- Trend direction, persistence, breadth, and leadership.
- Resilience and recovery capacity.
- Fragility or stress sensitivity.
- Data quality, freshness, and confidence.

13.7 The Structural State Vector

The Institute proposes the Structural State Vector as a decomposable representation containing selected domain and cross-domain variables at a defined time and horizon. An illustrative vector may be written as SSV(t) = [L, P, V, T, B, R, F, Q, C].

In this illustration, L represents liquidity condition, P positioning, V volatility, T trend, B breadth and leadership, R resilience, F fragility or stress sensitivity, Q data quality, and C confidence. The exact components, units, and methods must be specified by version.

The vector does not imply that every component is directly observable, independent, equally weighted, universally sufficient, or predictive. Some components may be measured directly, some derived, and others inferred from multiple proxies.

Component	Illustrative meaning	Required disclosure
L	Liquidity condition	Sources, horizon, venue coverage, size sensitivity
P	Positioning condition	Ownership assumptions, leverage, aggregation
V	Volatility condition	Realized or implied, horizon, model
T	Trend condition	Method, horizon, breadth
B	Breadth and leadership	Universe, weighting, concentration
R	Resilience	Disturbance and recovery definition
F	Fragility or stress sensitivity	Inference method and dependencies
Q	Data-quality state	Freshness, completeness, validity
C	Confidence	Claim type and calibration

> **Vector Principle:** The Structural State Vector is a governed representation of selected evidence, not a self-validating description of the entire market.

SSV(t) = [L | P | V | T | B | R | F | Q | C]

COMPONENT	REQUIRED DISCLOSURE
L — Liquidity condition	sources, horizon, venue coverage, size sensitivity
P — Positioning condition	ownership assumptions, leverage, aggregation
V — Volatility condition	realized or implied, horizon, model
T — Trend condition	method, horizon, breadth
B — Breadth and leadership	universe, weighting, concentration
R — Resilience	disturbance and recovery definition
F — Fragility or stress sensitivity	inference method and dependencies
Q — Data-quality state	freshness, completeness, validity
C — Confidence	claim type and calibration

The vector does not imply that every component is directly observable, independent, equally weighted, universally sufficient, or predictive.

Figure 13.2 — Structural State Vector

13.8 Continuous and Categorical Representation

Continuous values preserve magnitude and gradual change. Categories simplify communication. A liquidity-resilience percentile may distinguish modest from severe deterioration, while the category "impaired" communicates more quickly but creates a boundary.

A governed system should retain the continuous component where possible, display the category as a summary, and preserve the threshold used to create it. The category should not erase proximity to the boundary or uncertainty in the underlying value.

Continuous representation	Categorical representation
Preserves magnitude	Improves communication
Shows gradual change	Creates discrete boundaries
Supports sensitivity analysis	Supports rapid comparison
May be harder to interpret	May conceal near-boundary similarity

> **Representation Principle:** Continuous values preserve information; categories simplify communication. Retain both where possible.

13.9 The Market Compass

The Market Compass is a visual representation of selected multidomain state components. Its purpose is to communicate orientation, balance, divergence, confidence, and change without replacing the underlying evidence.

A responsible compass can show domain direction, condition, freshness, confidence, and trajectory. It should also identify mixed evidence and unavailable components. Color, position, and distance should not imply scientific precision beyond what has been validated.

The compass should never reduce all multidomain information to a single bullish or bearish arrow. It is a communication layer, not a universal signal.

- Display component values or categories.
- Show confidence and freshness.
- Distinguish confirmed state from trajectory.
- Expose mixed, stale, and unavailable components.
- Permit decomposition into source measurements.

> **Compass Principle:** The Market Compass communicates selected state components; it is not the market state itself and does not replace its measurements.

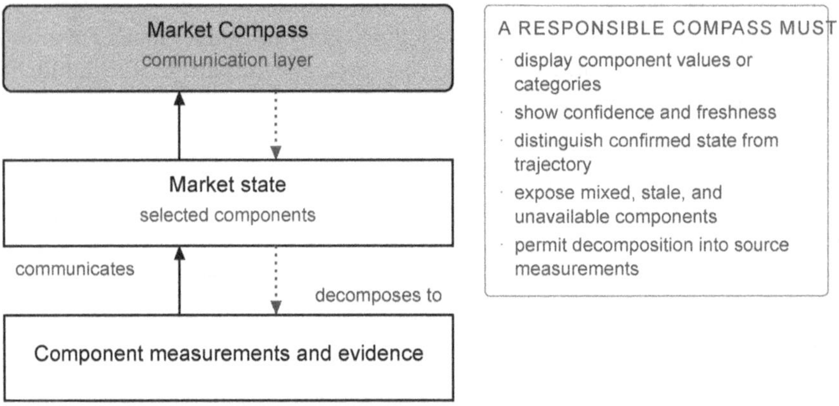

The Market Compass communicates selected state components. It is not the market state itself and does not replace its measurements.

Figure 13.3 — Market Compass as a Communication Layer

13.10 Confirmed Structural State

The confirmed structural state is the primary multidomain representation produced over a designated structural evaluation horizon after evidence-quality, freshness, and persistence requirements are satisfied.

The confirmed structural phase is evaluated over an implementation-defined confirmed structural evaluation horizon, together with implementation-defined persistence and confirmation requirements. The length of that horizon is an implementation choice, not a universal market law. Other instruments, purposes, or research designs may require different horizons.

The confirmed state describes the configuration under the designated method. It is not a prediction, permanent regime, or guarantee of stability. It remains dependent on data quality, model version, and the continued relevance of its components.

> **Confirmed-State Principle:** A confirmed state is established under a governed method; it is still provisional and subject to revision.

13.11 Fast Trajectory Observation

A fast trajectory observation describes recent multidomain movement relative to the confirmed structural state. Observations taken over implementation-defined sampling intervals shorter than the confirmed structural evaluation horizon may show intraday rotation before the structural phase changes.

Fast trajectory is valuable because it improves responsiveness. It is also more sensitive to noise, event effects, and temporary imbalance. It should not automatically replace the confirmed state.

The interface and narrative should display trajectory and confirmed phase together while labeling them distinctly.

> **Current implementation example:** In one WallStreetDelta implementation, five- and ten-minute observations describe fast trajectory, while a thirty-minute evaluation horizon governs the confirmed structural phase. These values are implementation parameters, not universal market laws.

Confirmed structural state	**Fast trajectory**
Primary structural representation	Recent path of multidomain change
Higher persistence requirement	Greater responsiveness
Lower sensitivity to temporary noise	Higher sensitivity to temporary noise
Used for structural description	Used for emerging rotation and monitoring
Not a forecast	Not a forecast or automatic transition signal

> **Trajectory Principle:** Fast observations describe trajectory; the confirmed phase represents established structural condition under the designated method.

DISPLAYED TOGETHER AND LABELED DISTINCTLY

CONFIRMED STRUCTURAL STATE	FAST TRAJECTORY
Primary structural representation	Recent path of multidomain change
Higher persistence requirement	Greater responsiveness
Lower sensitivity to temporary noise	Higher sensitivity to temporary noise
Used for structural description	Used for emerging rotation and monitoring
Not a forecast	Not a forecast or automatic transition signal

Fast trajectory should not automatically replace the confirmed state. A confirmed state is established under a governed method and remains provisional.

Figure 13.4 — Confirmed State Versus Fast Trajectory

13.12 State, Trajectory, Velocity, and Acceleration

State describes where the classified configuration currently stands. Trajectory describes the direction of recent component change. Velocity describes how quickly selected components are changing. Acceleration describes whether that rate of change is increasing or decreasing.

These concepts require explicit measurement definitions. A "rapidly deteriorating" liquidity trajectory is incomplete unless the analyst identifies the liquidity measurement, interval, baseline, and units.

A stable state can coexist with adverse trajectory if the recent movement has not yet met persistence or materiality requirements for reclassification.

Concept	**Question**
State	Where does the governed representation currently stand?
Trajectory	In what direction are selected components moving?
Velocity	How quickly are they changing?
Acceleration	Is the rate of change increasing or decreasing?

13.13 Mixed and Contradictory States

Markets frequently contain strength and sensitivity at the same time. A positive trend may coexist with narrow breadth. Realized volatility may remain low while short-dated implied volatility rises. Visible spreads may remain normal while depth weakens.

Mixed evidence should not be averaged automatically into "neutral." Neutral may imply balance, while the actual configuration may contain opposing but material conditions. More precise labels include mixed, divergent, transitional, indeterminate, and low-confidence.

The state summary should preserve the contradiction and explain which dimensions support each side.

- Coherent: most components support a similar interpretation.
- Mixed: meaningful supportive and adverse conditions coexist.
- Divergent: domains or horizons move in different directions.
- Transitional: evidence indicates material change but classification remains unsettled.
- Indeterminate: available evidence does not support a reliable state.
- Low-confidence: a state is assigned but support is limited.

Mixed-State Principle: Opposing evidence may be structurally informative. Do not erase it merely to produce a cleaner label.

13.14 Unknown, Unavailable, Stale, and Model-Dependent Components

Every component should carry a quality status. A missing component is not neutral, and a stale value is not current. Reusing a last-known value without disclosure can make an apparently complete state materially misleading.

Estimated and model-dependent values should remain distinguishable from directly observed or deterministically derived components. Contradicted or invalid components should not be silently averaged into a composite.

The state system should define how each quality status affects component use, confidence, and display.

Status	Meaning
Current	Within its defined validity window.
Delayed	Valid but not available in real time.
Stale	Outside its expected validity window.
Unavailable	No usable value is present.
Incomplete	Coverage is materially partial.
Estimated	Produced through estimation.
Proxy-based	Represents a broader condition indirectly.
Model-dependent	Sensitive to model assumptions.
Contradicted	Meaningful evidence conflicts.
Invalid	Fails quality or method requirements.
Unknown	Status or value cannot be determined reliably.

Quality-State Principle: A missing component is not neutral, and a stale component is not current.

13.15 State Confidence

Confidence should be separated by claim type. Data may be current and reliable while the state interpretation remains uncertain. A current state may be described confidently while transition or forecast confidence remains low.

One numerical confidence score can conceal these distinctions. Qualitative or multidimensional confidence is preferable unless probabilities or scores are defined and calibrated.

Confidence dimension	**Question**
Data confidence	Are the source observations current, complete, and trustworthy?
Measurement confidence	Are component methods valid and reliable?
Component-classification confidence	How stable is each component label?
Configuration confidence	How strongly does the evidence support the multidomain summary?
Transition confidence	How strongly does evidence support material change?
Predictive confidence	How strongly does the state support a future outcome?

13.16 State Boundaries and Thresholds

Categorical states require thresholds. Thresholds simplify classification but create artificial boundaries. A value just above a cutoff may be nearly identical to a value just below it.

Every threshold should document its rationale, calibration period, units, boundary sensitivity, persistence rule, missing-data behavior, and version. The continuous value should remain available where possible.

Thresholds should not be treated as natural laws merely because software applies them consistently.

- Threshold rationale and calibration sample.
- Entry and exit conditions.
- Sensitivity near boundaries.
- Treatment of missing or stale values.
- Version and effective date.
- Evidence for continued validity.

13.17 Hysteresis and State Stability

Without stabilization rules, classifications may oscillate rapidly near boundaries. Hysteresis addresses this by using separate entry and exit thresholds, persistence requirements, minimum dwell time, or confidence floors.

Hysteresis improves stability but introduces lag. Excessive stabilization can conceal genuine rapid change. Insufficient stabilization can produce noisy state switching.

The design must make the trade-off explicit and test it against the intended purpose.

> **Stability-Responsiveness Principle:** State stability and state responsiveness must be balanced explicitly.

13.18 Time Horizon and Nested States

A market may simultaneously experience intraday stress, intermediate structural balance, and a positive long-horizon trend. These descriptions are not contradictory if they refer to different horizons.

Every state should identify its observation horizon, sampling interval, effective time, update cadence, universe, and model version. The phrase "the market is stressed" is incomplete without scale.

Nested states can support richer reasoning, but they should not be forced into one category. Short-horizon stress may remain local, or it may become early evidence of broader transition.

> **Nested-State Principle:** A state at one horizon does not automatically determine the state at another.

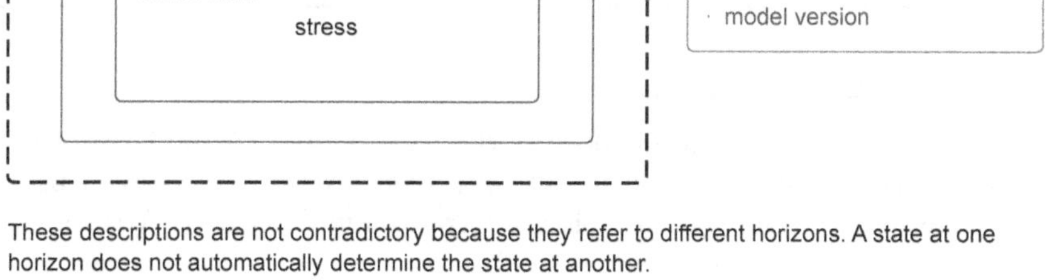

Figure 13.5 — Nested States Across Horizons

13.19 State Dependence

The response to new information depends on the configuration receiving it. A modest earnings disappointment may produce limited movement in a liquid, lightly positioned market but a large decline in a crowded, illiquid market.

State representations support conditional reasoning by summarizing the receiving configuration. They do not guarantee the response, identify all relevant variables, or establish causation.

The state should therefore be used to frame scenarios and expectations, not to convert conditional sensitivity into certainty.

> **State-Dependence Principle:** A state describes the conditions under which an event occurs; it does not determine the event's outcome.

13.20 State Persistence and Duration

States may be momentary, emerging, persistent, mature, deteriorating, or transitioning. Duration can increase descriptive confidence, but a long-lasting state is not necessarily stable or resilient. Fragile configurations can persist for extended periods.

State duration should be measured from the governed effective time, not inferred from retrospective visual inspection. The method should preserve entry time, dwell time, revisions, and exits.

Temporal label	Meaning
Momentary	Detected briefly; low persistence.
Emerging	Evidence is accumulating but not mature.
Persistent	Conditions remain present across the required horizon.
Mature	The state has persisted and is broadly established under the method.
Deteriorating	The state remains assigned while supporting components weaken.
Transitioning	Evidence supports movement toward a different state.

13.21 State Validation

Validation must match the purpose of the state model. A model that summarizes current evidence accurately may not forecast future returns. A stable classification may be too slow for transition detection. A responsive model may switch too often.

Validation should therefore separate descriptive validity, discriminant validity, stability, transition detection, predictive value, and decision usefulness.

Validation type	Question
Descriptive	Does the state accurately summarize current evidence?
Discriminant	Are different states meaningfully distinct?

Validation type	Question
Stability	Does the model avoid excessive noise?
Transition	Does it detect meaningful changes with acceptable lag?
Predictive	Does the state add information about future outcomes?
Decision usefulness	Does it improve a stated decision process after costs and constraints?

13.22 State Calibration

Calibration asks whether expressed confidence and classifications correspond reasonably with observed evidence over time. High-confidence states should generally be more reliable than low-confidence states under the defined evaluation criterion.

Calibration requires a clear definition of correctness. For a descriptive state, correctness may mean faithful representation of component evidence. For transition detection, it may mean persistence and reduced false switching. For forecasting, it requires separately defined outcomes and horizons.

- Compare high- and low-confidence classifications.
- Measure immediate reversal frequency.
- Review transitional and indeterminate labels.
- Track stale or unavailable component rates.
- Test calibration across instruments and periods.

13.23 State Drift

A state model may lose relevance even if its code remains unchanged. Market structure, participant behavior, regulation, data sources, volatility distributions, and strategy crowding can alter the meaning of its components and thresholds.

Drift should be detected through periodic review, performance monitoring, component-distribution analysis, and comparison with alternative methods. A state model should be revised or retired when its assumptions no longer hold.

> **Drift Principle:** A stable calculation does not guarantee a stable meaning.

13.24 Composite-State Risk

A single state label can conceal opposing domains, unequal confidence, missing measurements, threshold sensitivity, model disagreement, horizon mismatch, and concentration. Composite states are most dangerous when their simplicity is mistaken for completeness.

Every composite should preserve component values, quality states, timestamps, weights, thresholds, and version. Missing values should never be silently replaced by neutral values unless the rule is justified and disclosed.

> **Decomposability Principle:** A state representation may compress evidence, but it must remain decomposable into component measurements, assumptions, quality states, and confidence.

13.25 Worked Example: Directional Strength with Structural Sensitivity

Consider a market with a positive intermediate trend, narrowing breadth, concentrated leadership, contained realized volatility, rising short-dated implied volatility, normal visible spreads, slower downside-depth replenishment, and model-dependent evidence of concentrated positioning.

A defensible vector interpretation might classify trend as positive, liquidity as functional but asymmetric, positioning as concentrated with moderate confidence, volatility as contained in realized terms but elevated in short-horizon implied terms, breadth as weak, resilience as moderate, fragility as elevated, data quality as mixed, and overall configuration confidence as moderate.

The confirmed structural summary could state: "The market remains directionally positive but increasingly concentrated and adjustment-sensitive. Liquidity is functional under observed conditions, while weaker downside replenishment and narrow participation reduce structural balance. Positioning-based fragility remains model-dependent."

A fast trajectory observation might add: "Recent trajectory shows further breadth deterioration and short-horizon volatility expansion, but persistence requirements for a confirmed structural-state change have not yet been satisfied."

13.26 State Representation and Decision Boundaries

The same state can support different actions for different participants. A market maker may alter inventory and spread, a long-term investor may make no change, a risk manager may reduce leverage, and a tactical trader may wait for confirmation.

The difference arises from objective, horizon, mandate, capital, risk tolerance, execution constraints, and existing exposure. The state supplies context; it does not determine a universal response.

> **Decision-Boundary Principle:** State supports decision context; objectives, constraints, horizon, and risk capacity determine action.

13.27 Common Misuses

The following errors convert a useful representation into false certainty.

Misuse	Why it is misleading
Treating the state as the market itself	The representation is selective.
Treating state as forecast	Description is not prediction.
Treating trajectory as confirmed state	Fast movement may not persist.
Treating missing as neutral	Absence is not balance.
Treating a composite score as explanation	Components and mechanisms are concealed.
Treating thresholds as natural laws	Boundaries are designed.
Ignoring horizon	States may differ by scale.
Treating state as universal action guidance	Decisions depend on participant context.
Treating confidence as certainty	Confidence remains conditional.
Preserving an outdated state	Configuration and data may have changed.

13.28 State Governance

A formal state model should be governed as an analytical system. Governance protects against undocumented changes, inconsistent interpretation, and silent degradation.

The specification should identify purpose, horizon, universe, component measurements, normalization, weights, thresholds, missing-data rules, confidence logic, persistence and hysteresis, update cadence, validation evidence, version, effective date, known limitations, and retirement criteria.

Governance does not make the state correct. It makes the state inspectable, reproducible, and accountable.

- Purpose and intended use.
- Horizon, universe, and effective time.
- Components, sources, and calculations.
- Normalization, weights, and thresholds.
- Missingness, freshness, and quality states.
- Confidence, persistence, and hysteresis.
- Validation, calibration, and drift monitoring.
- Version, approval, limitations, and retirement criteria.

Chapter Summary

A market configuration is the detailed arrangement of observable and inferred conditions across liquidity, positioning, volatility, trend, and related evidence. A market state is a controlled, higher-level representation of selected features of that configuration for a stated purpose, horizon, universe, and method.

State representations reduce complexity but do not eliminate it. They are selective, provisional, model-dependent, and subject to measurement uncertainty. A state is not the market itself, a signal, forecast, decision, or permanent regime.

The Structural State Vector provides a decomposable representation of multidomain conditions. The Market Compass provides a visual communication layer. Neither should replace the measurements, assumptions, quality states, and confidence underlying the representation.

Confirmed structural state should remain distinct from faster trajectory observations. Fast observations may identify rotation or emerging change, while confirmed state requires designated evidence-quality and persistence conditions.

Responsible state representation preserves mixed evidence, missingness, staleness, model dependence, horizon, thresholds, versioning, and uncertainty. Its purpose is to improve understanding and monitoring, not to create artificial certainty.

Established Knowledge

The concepts in this chapter draw upon established work in state-space modeling, hidden Markov models, regime-switching methods, clustering, latent-state inference, dynamic systems, control theory, signal processing, classification, change-point detection, financial-regime analysis, systemic-risk indicators, composite indexes, calibration, and model governance.

The Institute does not claim originality for the general concepts of state, regime, vector representation, or classification. Its proposed contribution lies in integrating the four observational domains, separating configuration from state, preserving decomposition and quality states, distinguishing confirmed state from fast trajectory, and treating state as provisional and decision-neutral.

Institute Perspective

The Institute treats a market state as a governed representation rather than a discovered certainty. Its value depends on clarity of purpose, component quality, transparency of construction, and the ability to revise the representation when evidence changes.

The Market Compass and Structural State Vector should therefore function as inspectable implementations of a measurement and reasoning discipline, not as authoritative labels or automated opinions.

Questions for Reflection

1. What distinguishes a market configuration from a market state?
2. Why is a state representation necessarily selective?
3. Why can two valid state models classify the same market differently?
4. What distinguishes a state from a regime?
5. Why is a state not automatically a signal or forecast?
6. What information may be lost when a configuration is compressed?
7. What is the purpose of the Structural State Vector?
8. Why must a vector remain decomposable?
9. What is the proper role of the Market Compass?
10. Why should continuous values remain available beneath categorical labels?
11. What distinguishes confirmed structural state from fast trajectory?
12. How can an adverse trajectory coexist with an unchanged confirmed state?
13. Why should mixed evidence not be averaged automatically into neutral?
14. Why is a missing component not neutral?
15. Why is a stale component not current?
16. What confidence dimensions should accompany a state?
17. How do thresholds create artificial boundaries?
18. What trade-off does hysteresis create?
19. How can states differ across time horizons without contradiction?
20. What does state dependence mean?
21. Why can a fragile state persist for a long time?
22. How should descriptive validation differ from predictive validation?
23. What is state drift?
24. Why is composite-state decomposability essential?
25. Why does a state not prescribe universal action?
26. What evidence would justify retiring a state model?

Questions for Reflection

Chapter 14. Market Transitions

How Configurations Change Through Time

Chapter Purpose

Financial markets change continuously. Some changes are minor and temporary. Others represent meaningful reorganization across liquidity, positioning, volatility, trend, breadth, resilience, and stress sensitivity.

The analytical challenge is not merely to observe movement. It is to determine whether that movement is noise, ordinary variation, local disturbance, emerging transition, confirmed transition, false transition, stabilization, reversal, or structural reorganization.

This chapter establishes a framework for describing market transitions without assuming that every change is a regime shift. It distinguishes configuration change, transition evidence, trajectory, confirmation, stabilization, reversal, and failure. It also establishes requirements for timing, persistence, hysteresis, confidence, validation, calibration, and governance.

Learning Objectives

- Distinguish configuration change from state transition.
- Explain why transition detection is method- and horizon-dependent.
- Distinguish early indication, emerging transition, confirmation, maturity, failure, and reversal.
- Evaluate magnitude, persistence, breadth, coherence, speed, acceleration, and reversibility.
- Distinguish trigger, structural precondition, transition pathway, feedback, and destination.
- Understand the balance between responsiveness, lag, false transitions, and hysteresis.
- Distinguish transition confidence from destination and predictive confidence.
- Construct scenario-based transition pathways with signposts and invalidation conditions.
- Validate, calibrate, govern, and retire transition models.

14.1 From State to Transition

Chapter 13 asks how selected features of the current market configuration should be represented. Chapter 14 asks how that configuration is changing and whether the change is material and persistent enough to alter the governed state representation.

The controlled sequence is current configuration, measurable configuration change, emerging transition evidence, confirmed transition, and new state representation. Each stage should remain traceable to measurements and quality states.

The sequence is not irreversible. Emerging evidence can fade, a confirmed transition can fail, and a new state can stabilize, deteriorate, or reverse.

> **Transition Hierarchy:** Current configuration leads to configuration change, emerging evidence, possible confirmation, and a revised state representation. Confirmation remains provisional.

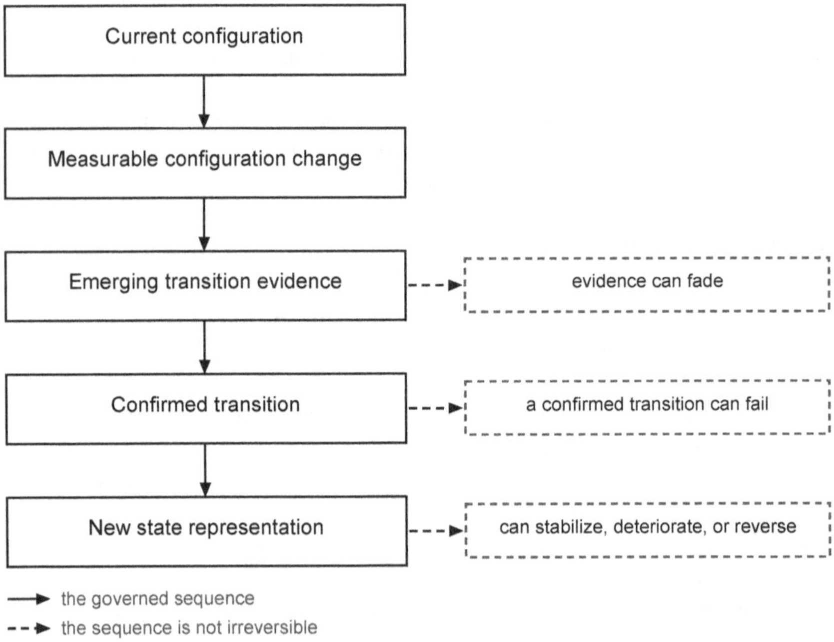

Figure 14.1 — Configuration Change to Confirmed Transition

14.2 What Is a Market Transition?

A market transition is a material reorganization of selected market-configuration features through time, evaluated relative to a stated baseline, horizon, and classification method.

A state transition is the governed classification event that occurs when the reorganization satisfies defined materiality, persistence, quality, and threshold requirements. The market process and the classification event are related but not identical.

A transition may be gradual or abrupt, orderly or disorderly, broad or concentrated, temporary or persistent, complete or incomplete, and reversible or sustained.

> **Governing Definition:** A market-state transition is a sufficiently persistent and material change in selected configuration features that causes the governed state representation to move from one classified condition to another under a stated method.

14.3 What a Transition Is Not

Transition language is often applied too quickly. The following distinctions limit overstatement.

A transition may be	A transition is not automatically
A material configuration change	Every price move
A multidomain reorganization	A universal regime shift
An emerging process	A guaranteed destination
A method-defined classification change	A natural boundary visible to everyone
A provisional conclusion	A permanent label
A monitored pathway	A forecast
A reversible development	Irreversible
Decision-relevant context	A universal trading instruction

14.4 Change, Disturbance, Transition, Regime Shift, and Structural Break

Change is any measurable difference through time. A disturbance is a short-lived or localized disruption. A transition is a material reorganization moving the configuration toward a different state representation.

A regime shift is a relatively persistent and statistically meaningful change in the environment or governing relationships. A structural break occurs when the underlying process changes enough that prior relationships become less reliable.

Every regime shift includes transition, but not every transition becomes a regime shift. A one-session volatility event may be a disturbance, while a multi-month change in inflation, policy, and correlation structure may represent a regime shift.

Concept	Meaning
Change	Any measurable difference through time.
Disturbance	Short-lived or localized disruption.
Transition	Material reorganization toward a different state representation.
Regime shift	Relatively persistent change in the broader environment or relationships.
Structural break	Change that weakens the validity of prior process assumptions.

Classification Principle: All state transitions involve configuration change, but most configuration changes do not become confirmed state transitions.

14.5 Transition Evidence

Transition evidence may arise from domain changes, cross-domain interactions, threshold breaches, reduced resilience, failed stabilization, altered relationships, or changes in model confidence. No single observation should define transition unless the method explicitly justifies it.

A price decline alone establishes direction and magnitude. It does not establish liquidity impairment, forced selling, structural deterioration, or a new state. Stronger transition evidence combines relevant, timely, and sufficiently independent observations.

- Material component changes.
- Persistence across the defined horizon.
- Breadth across instruments or domains.
- Coherent cross-domain interaction.
- Threshold or boundary movement.
- Changes in resilience and feedback.
- Quality and confidence sufficient for classification.

14.6 Dimensions of Transition

Transitions should be evaluated across multiple dimensions because no single dimension fully describes change.

Dimension	Question
Magnitude	How large is the change?
Persistence	How long has it remained?

Dimension	Question
Breadth	How widely is it distributed?
Coherence	Do domains support a common interpretation?
Speed	How rapidly is the configuration changing?
Acceleration	Is the rate of change increasing or decreasing?
Depth	How structurally significant is the change?
Reversibility	How easily could the configuration return?
Confidence	How strongly does evidence support the transition interpretation?

14.7 Transition Maturity

Transition maturity describes the evidentiary development of a change. It does not guarantee a destination or imply that every transition follows a fixed sequence.

An isolated observation may become emerging evidence, then developing and confirmed change. A confirmed transition may mature, stabilize, reverse, or fail.

Maturity label	Meaning
Isolated	A brief or local change with limited support.
Emerging	Several observations begin to support material change.
Developing	Magnitude, breadth, or persistence is increasing.
Confirmed	Governed transition requirements are satisfied.
Mature	The new configuration has persisted and broadened.
Stabilizing	The rate of change is slowing.
Reversing	Evidence supports movement back or toward another state.
Failed	The transition does not persist under the method.

> **Maturity Principle:** Transition maturity describes evidentiary development, not certainty about the eventual destination.

14.8 Early Indication and Confirmation

Early indication emphasizes responsiveness. Confirmation emphasizes reliability. A system that reacts too quickly may classify ordinary variation as structural change. A system that waits too long may describe a transition only after it has become obvious and operationally irrelevant.

An early indication is recent evidence suggesting possible configuration change. An emerging transition requires several related observations. A confirmed transition satisfies the designated materiality, persistence, quality, and classification requirements.

Post-confirmation monitoring then evaluates whether the new state is stable, maturing, reversing, or failing.

Stage	Primary meaning
Early indication	Possible change; limited persistence.
Emerging transition	Related evidence is accumulating.
Confirmed transition	Governed requirements are satisfied.
Post-confirmation monitoring	Stability, continuation, reversal, or failure is evaluated.

Responsiveness-Reliability Principle: Early evidence improves responsiveness; confirmation improves reliability. A governed design must balance both.

14.9 Fast Trajectory and Confirmed Structural Transition

The distinction between fast trajectory and confirmed structural phase is central to any governed transition design. Observations taken over implementation-defined sampling intervals may describe recent rotation. The confirmed structural evaluation horizon, with its implementation-defined persistence and confirmation requirements, governs confirmation.

Fast trajectory should not automatically override the confirmed state. Instead, it should identify emerging movement, divergence, and monitoring needs. A confirmed transition occurs only after the designated structural rules are satisfied.

Both outputs should be available together so that responsiveness does not erase structural context and structural stability does not conceal emerging change.

Current implementation example: In one WallStreetDelta implementation, five- and ten-minute observations describe fast trajectory, while a thirty-minute evaluation horizon governs the confirmed structural transition. These values are implementation parameters, not universal market laws.

Fast trajectory	Confirmed structural transition
Short-horizon movement	Governed structural reclassification
Responsive	More persistent
Noise-sensitive	Stability-oriented
Supports monitoring	Supports state update
Not confirmation	Not prediction

Fast-Path Principle: Fast trajectory identifies emerging rotation. Confirmed transition identifies a governed change in structural state.

BOTH OUTPUTS AVAILABLE TOGETHER

FAST TRAJECTORY	CONFIRMED STRUCTURAL TRANSITION
Short-horizon movement	Governed structural reclassification
Responsive	More persistent
Noise-sensitive	Stability-oriented
Supports monitoring	Supports state update
Not confirmation	Not prediction

Fast trajectory identifies emerging rotation. Confirmed transition identifies a governed change in structural state. Fast trajectory should not automatically override the confirmed state.

Figure 14.2 — Fast Trajectory Versus Confirmed Structural Transition

14.10 Transition Lag

Confirmation requires evidence, and evidence requires time. Sampling intervals, lookback windows, persistence rules, data delays, missing values, hysteresis, model recalculation, and review can all create lag.

Lag is not always a defect. It may be the cost of avoiding false transitions. Excessive lag, however, can make a state representation too slow for its intended purpose.

The acceptable lag should be validated relative to the purpose, instrument, horizon, and cost of false positives and false negatives.

> **Lag Principle:** Lag is the cost of requiring evidence, but excessive lag can make the representation operationally irrelevant.

14.11 False Transitions

A false transition occurs when evidence briefly approaches or satisfies transition criteria but the configuration returns toward the prior state. False transitions can arise from temporary event risk, low-liquidity spikes, data error, expiration effects, short covering, boundary oscillation, or model sensitivity.

A false transition should not be hidden from evaluation. It reveals the tradeoff between responsiveness and reliability and may identify weaknesses in persistence, hysteresis, or data-quality controls.

Not every failed transition is a model error. Some genuine changes begin and then reverse because participants adapt.

- Temporary event-driven change.
- Data error or timestamp misalignment.

- Boundary oscillation.
- Isolated component movement.
- Expiration or rebalancing effect.
- Genuine transition that later reverses.

14.12 Hysteresis and Transition Control

Hysteresis reduces unstable switching near boundaries by requiring different evidence to enter, remain in, exit, or reverse a state. Controls may include separate entry and exit thresholds, minimum dwell time, confirmation counts, confidence floors, stronger reversal evidence, or cooldown periods.

These controls improve label stability but can delay detection. Transition-control rules should therefore be transparent and tested against rapid genuine change as well as ordinary noise.

Control	Effect
Separate entry and exit thresholds	Reduces immediate boundary reversal.
Persistence minimum	Requires evidence across time.
Minimum dwell time	Prevents rapid reclassification.
Confidence floor	Blocks transitions supported by weak evidence.
Stronger reversal rule	Requires more evidence to reverse direction.
Cooldown	Limits repeated switching after a transition.

> **Control Principle:** Transition-control rules should reduce noise without concealing genuine rapid change.

14.13 Transition Velocity

Transition velocity describes the rate at which selected configuration components are changing over a defined interval. It may be measured through spread deterioration per minute, breadth loss per hour, change in volatility structure, or trend-slope deterioration.

Velocity must identify the component, units, window, and smoothing method. A rapidly changing noisy measure may appear more important than a slower but structurally meaningful shift.

> **Velocity Principle:** Transition velocity describes the speed of configuration change, not the destination or certainty of transition.

14.14 Transition Acceleration

Transition acceleration describes whether the rate of configuration change is itself increasing or decreasing. Liquidity may be worsening faster, volatility may be rising at an increasing rate, or breadth deterioration may be slowing.

Acceleration can provide information about transition intensity and stabilization, but second-order estimates are sensitive to noise, sampling, and smoothing. They require stronger uncertainty controls than level measures.

14.15 Gradual and Abrupt Transitions

Gradual transitions develop through slow reorganization, such as narrowing breadth, increasing concentration, declining liquidity resilience, volatility compression, or long-horizon trend deterioration.

Abrupt transitions develop rapidly after events such as policy shocks, funding disruption, liquidation, exchange impairment, or sudden loss of bids. Abrupt transitions may be easier to observe but harder to classify before they mature.

The same destination can be reached through different pathways, and the same trigger can produce gradual or abrupt change depending on the receiving configuration.

Gradual transition	**Abrupt transition**
Slow accumulation of evidence	Rapid multidomain change
Often easier to monitor	Often greater detection lag relative to movement
May involve concentration and resilience erosion	May involve shock, liquidation, or discontinuity
Destination can remain uncertain	Destination can remain uncertain

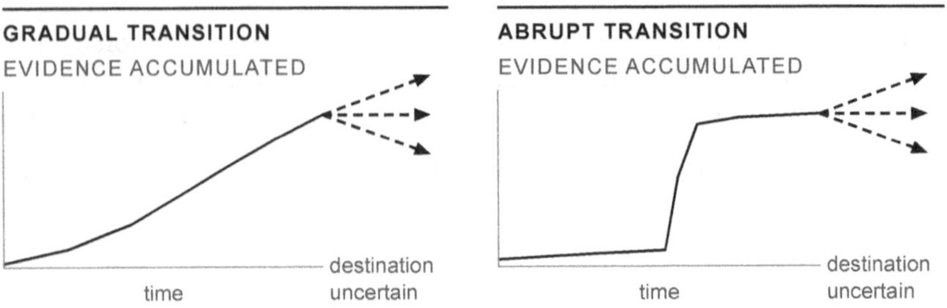

Slow accumulation of evidence	Rapid multidomain change
Often easier to monitor	Often greater detection lag relative to movement
May involve concentration and resilience erosion	May involve shock, liquidation, or discontinuity

The same destination can be reached through different pathways, and the same trigger can produce gradual or abrupt change depending on the receiving configuration. Curves are schematic.

Figure 14.3 — Gradual Versus Abrupt Transition

14.16 Orderly and Disorderly Transitions

An orderly transition occurs while exchange remains functional, spreads remain proportionate, depth replenishes, adjustment is distributed, and volatility remains interpretable relative to the event.

A disorderly transition involves severe liquidity deterioration, expanding price impact, spread gaps, forced activity, volatility dislocation, or impaired market function.

A large move is not necessarily disorderly, and a small move can occur under impaired conditions. Orderliness concerns the quality of adjustment, not only magnitude.

> **Orderliness Principle:** The size of a price move does not by itself determine whether the transition is orderly or disorderly.

14.17 Trigger and Transition

A trigger is the event associated with initiation or timing. Examples include an earnings announcement, policy decision, economic release, margin event, or geopolitical shock.

The trigger does not explain the full transition. Magnitude and pathway depend on liquidity, positioning, volatility, trend, leverage, confidence, and participant response.

The trigger helps explain when change began; the receiving configuration helps explain how change propagated.

> **Trigger Principle:** The trigger helps explain timing; the market configuration helps explain transmission and scale.

14.18 Structural Preconditions

Some configurations are more sensitive to disturbance. Concentrated exposure, leverage, weak liquidity, narrow leadership, unstable volatility structure, poor resilience, strategy crowding, and funding dependence may increase the probability or severity of transition.

These conditions are contributory and conditional. They do not guarantee transition, establish direction, or identify timing.

A fragile configuration may persist until a trigger arrives, or it may repair without a major event.

- Concentrated or leveraged exposure.
- Thin or asymmetric liquidity.
- Narrow leadership.
- Unstable volatility structure.
- Weak replenishment and resilience.
- Funding or collateral sensitivity.
- Crowded strategy use.

14.19 Reinforcing Transition Pathways

Reinforcing pathways amplify change. A downside pathway may begin with adverse price movement, followed by risk reduction, liquidity consumption, greater price impact, volatility expansion, tighter limits, additional selling, trend deterioration, and further repositioning.

The actual sequence may differ, several steps may occur simultaneously, and balancing forces may interrupt the loop. The pathway is an analytical representation of interaction, not a directly observed object.

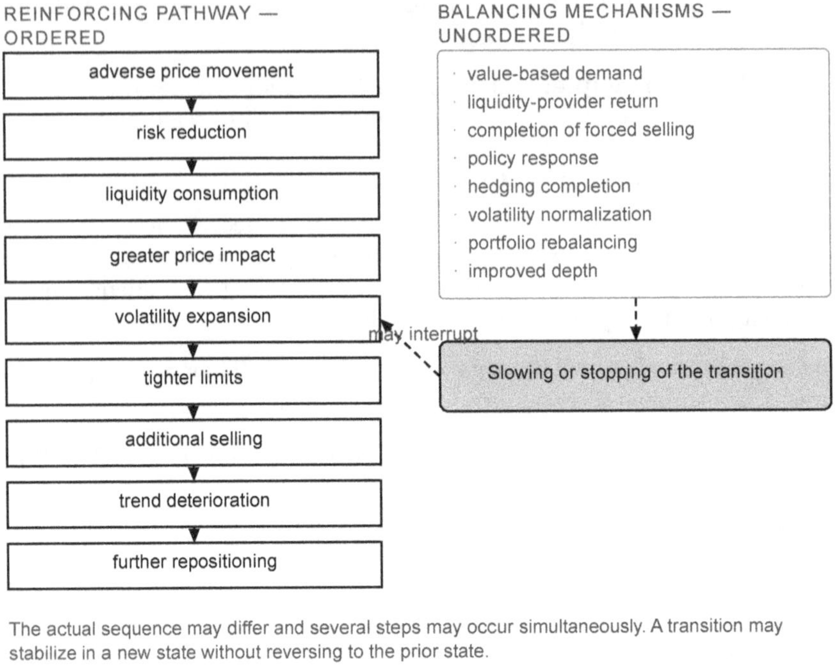

Figure 14.4 — Reinforcing and Balancing Transition Pathways

14.20 Balancing Transition Pathways

Balancing pathways oppose change and support stabilization. Value-based demand, liquidity-provider return, completion of forced selling, policy response, hedging completion, volatility normalization, portfolio rebalancing, and improved depth may slow or stop a transition.

Stabilization does not require a return to the prior state. The market may settle into a new balanced configuration after substantial reorganization.

> **Balancing Principle:** A transition may stabilize in a new state without reversing to the prior state.

14.21 Incomplete Transitions

An incomplete transition occurs when some components change materially while others do not. Volatility may expand while trend holds. Breadth may deteriorate while liquidity remains resilient. Positioning may concentrate without visible stress.

Incomplete transitions should be labeled as partial, uneven, domain-specific, unresolved, or stalled rather than forced into a complete state change.

The unaligned components may later confirm, repair, or remain structurally divergent.

14.22 Failed Transitions

A failed transition is an emerging or confirmed change that does not persist under the governing method and moves back toward the prior state. Examples include a reversed breakdown, normalized volatility spike, repaired breadth deterioration, absorbed liquidity stress, or exhausted squeeze.

Failure does not necessarily mean the original evidence was invalid. It may mean that balancing mechanisms became dominant or that the pathway changed.

Failed transitions are valuable research cases because they identify which signposts distinguish persistence from reversal.

> **Failure Principle:** A failed transition may represent a real but nonpersistent change, not merely an analytical mistake.

14.23 Reversal

A reversal is not merely a temporary move against the prevailing direction. A confirmed reversal may require sustained opposing movement, breadth confirmation, leadership change, altered volatility and liquidity structure, positioning change, and persistence beyond a temporary disturbance.

The exact requirements depend on the state model and horizon. An intraday reversal can occur within an unchanged intermediate trend.

Countertrend movement should therefore be described first as movement; reversal should be reserved for governed evidence of state change.

> **Reversal Principle:** Countertrend movement is not automatically a state reversal.

14.24 Stabilization

Stabilization means the rate of adverse change slows or stops. Evidence may include spreads ceasing to widen, depth beginning to replenish, volatility no longer accelerating, breadth ceasing to deteriorate, forced selling declining, and price impact falling.

Stabilization does not necessarily imply recovery, favorable direction, or restored resilience. It means that deterioration has stopped intensifying under the observed measures.

14.25 Recovery

Recovery describes movement toward a more functional or resilient configuration. It may involve liquidity restoration, volatility normalization, broader participation, improved trend structure, reduced concentration, and higher confidence.

Recovery may lead back to the prior state, produce a new state, or stall in a range-bound condition. The destination remains an empirical question.

> **Recovery Principle:** Stabilization means deterioration has slowed; recovery means selected conditions have improved. The two should not be confused.

14.26 Transition Across Time Horizons

Transitions can differ across scales. An intraday transition to stress may occur while the intermediate structural state and long-horizon regime remain unchanged.

Every transition should identify observation horizon, confirmation horizon, effective time, update cadence, universe, and model version. A transition at one horizon should not be projected automatically onto another.

Nested horizons can provide early context, but they can also create apparent contradiction. The contradiction should be preserved and explained.

> **Horizon Principle:** A transition at one horizon does not automatically imply transition at another.

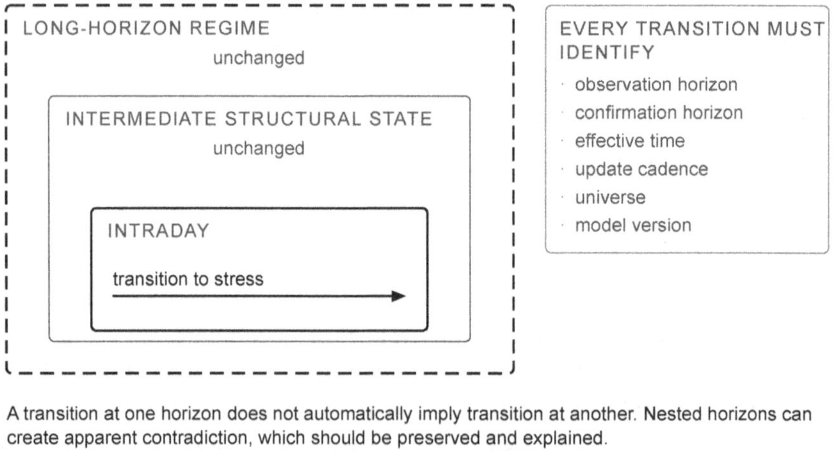

Figure 14.5 — Nested Transitions Across Horizons

14.27 Cross-Domain Transition Coherence

A transition gains support when several domains change in a mutually consistent manner. Liquidity may weaken, positioning may become adjustment-sensitive, volatility may expand, trend may deteriorate, and breadth may contract.

Coherence is not the same as independence. Several measures may respond to the same event or share the same data. Dependency mapping remains necessary.

Partial coherence may indicate an incomplete transition rather than analytical failure.

14.28 Domain-Led Transitions

Transitions may begin in different domains. A liquidity-led transition begins with impaired exchange capacity. A positioning-led transition begins with exposure adjustment. A volatility-led transition begins with changing variability or option repricing. A trend-led transition begins with deteriorating directional structure.

Information-led transitions begin with new information that changes valuation or expectations. The initiating domain should not be treated automatically as the sole cause. Other domains determine propagation and stabilization.

Transition lead	**Illustrative first evidence**
Liquidity-led	Depth loss, spread widening, impact increase.
Positioning-led	Forced adjustment, concentration, hedge demand.
Volatility-led	Rapid realized or implied variability change.
Trend-led	Breadth and directional structure deterioration.
Information-led	Repricing after new information.

14.29 Cross-Market Transmission

Transitions may spread across equities, rates, credit, currencies, commodities, volatility markets, and funding markets. Transmission channels include collateral, common ownership, derivative hedging, portfolio rebalancing, leverage reduction, funding stress, index relationships, and volatility targeting.

Cross-market co-movement does not by itself identify the channel. Timing, balance-sheet relationships, common exposures, and alternative explanations must be evaluated.

- Collateral and margin.
- Common ownership and balance sheets.
- Derivative hedging.
- Portfolio rebalancing.
- Leverage and funding.
- Index, ETF, and basis relationships.

- Volatility targeting and risk limits.

14.30 Transition Confidence

Transition confidence should remain separate from confidence in the current state, destination, cause, and forecast. The evidence may strongly support that the configuration is changing while the destination remains uncertain.

A useful assessment might state: high confidence that configuration is changing, moderate confidence that a confirmed transition is underway, low confidence regarding destination, and low predictive confidence regarding price outcome.

Confidence dimension	Question
Evidence-quality	Are the transition inputs current and valid?
Trajectory	Is the direction of change clear?
Transition classification	Have materiality and persistence requirements been met?
Destination	Which new state is most likely?
Causal	Which mechanisms materially contributed?
Predictive	What future outcomes are supported?

14.31 Transition Destination Uncertainty

A transition can be clear while its destination remains uncertain. A deteriorating positive state may return to the prior state, enter balance, become stressed, reverse direction, or stabilize in a new configuration.

Destination uncertainty should not be concealed by naming a transition after its most feared or desired outcome. “Emerging deterioration” is more defensible than “bear market beginning” when the destination remains unresolved.

> **Destination Principle:** Confidence in transition does not imply confidence in destination.

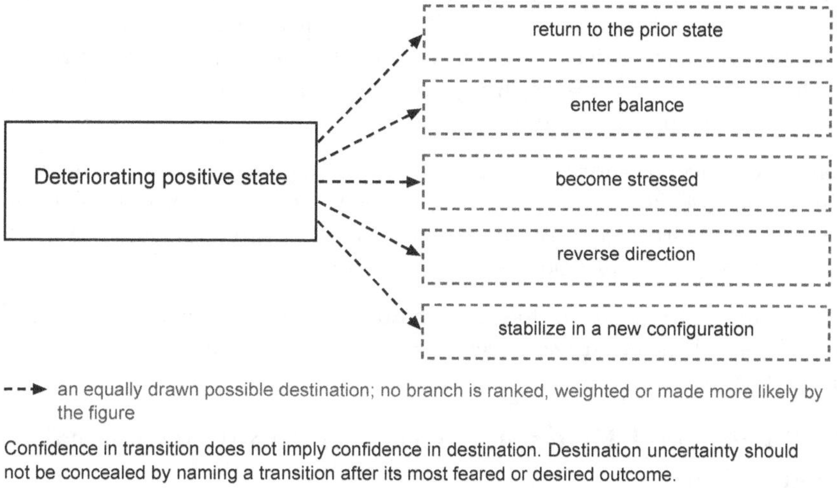

Figure 14.6 — Transition Branching and Destination Uncertainty

14.32 Scenario-Based Transition Analysis

Scenarios organize possible transition pathways without claiming that one must occur. Each scenario should identify the starting configuration, trigger or initiating condition, pathway, signposts, invalidation conditions, possible destination, horizon, and confidence.

Probabilities should be assigned only when the method is defined and calibrated. Otherwise, scenarios should remain conditional and descriptive.

Scenario field	Required content
Starting configuration	What state is currently represented?
Initiating condition	What may begin or accelerate change?
Pathway	How may domains evolve?
Signposts	What observations support the pathway?
Invalidation	What would weaken it?
Possible destination	What state may emerge?
Horizon and confidence	When and with what support?

14.33 Worked Example: Positive Trend to Fragile Transition

Initial configuration: intermediate trend positive, breadth moderate, volatility low, liquidity functional, and positioning increasingly concentrated. The confirmed structural state remains directionally positive.

Emerging evidence: breadth narrows, downside depth replenishes more slowly, short-dated implied volatility rises, leadership concentration increases, and fast trajectory deteriorates. The appropriate interpretation is that the market remains in a positive confirmed state but is becoming more concentrated and less resilient.

Later evidence: breadth deteriorates further, spreads widen, price impact rises, trend weakens, positioning estimates indicate greater downside sensitivity, and persistence criteria are met. The governed state then transitions toward a fragile, adjustment-sensitive condition.

The confirmed transition does not establish that a major decline must follow. It establishes that the selected configuration features have reorganized under the method.

14.34 Worked Example: Stress Without Structural Transition

Consider a sharp intraday decline accompanied by realized-volatility expansion, higher implied volatility, and surging volume. The event appears severe.

However, spreads remain proportionate, depth replenishes, broad forced selling does not emerge, the intermediate trend remains intact, and conditions normalize by the close.

The disciplined assessment is that the market experienced a short-horizon disturbance and temporary stress, but the evidence did not satisfy the requirements for a confirmed structural transition.

14.35 Transition Validation

Validation should measure whether the model detects meaningful transitions without excessive noise or unacceptable delay. Different purposes require different trade-offs.

Validation should be conducted across instruments, periods, event types, data-quality conditions, and out-of-sample environments.

Validation dimension	Question
Detection sensitivity	Can meaningful transitions be identified?
False-transition rate	How often is temporary change classified as structural?
Detection lag	How long after change does confirmation occur?
State stability	Does the model oscillate excessively?
Horizon consistency	Are classifications coherent across scales?
Component attribution	Which domains drive transition?

Validation dimension	Question
Missing-data robustness	How does the model behave with incomplete evidence?
Out-of-sample validity	Does performance persist elsewhere?

14.36 Transition Calibration

Calibration asks whether expressed confidence corresponds with observed transition behavior. High-confidence transitions should generally persist or meet the defined criterion more often than low-confidence transitions.

Calibration should track the failure rate of early indications, the reversal rate of confirmed transitions, destination accuracy where applicable, detection lag, and variation across instruments.

Calibration cannot be assessed until correctness, horizon, and evaluation criteria are defined.

- Persistence by confidence level.
- Failure rate of emerging transitions.
- Immediate reversal rate after confirmation.
- Destination classification performance.
- Lag distribution.
- Instrument and regime differences.

14.37 Transition Drift

Transition models may lose relevance as market structure, liquidity patterns, participant behavior, instruments, data sources, and volatility distributions change. Widely followed thresholds may also alter participant response.

Drift monitoring should examine component distributions, transition frequency, false-transition rate, lag, missingness, and calibration. A model should be revised or retired when its assumptions no longer hold.

> **Drift Principle:** A transition model must be governed through time because the market process and the data environment both change.

14.38 Common Misuses

Transition analysis becomes misleading when early evidence is presented as certainty or when designed thresholds are treated as natural boundaries.

Misuse	Why it is misleading
Treating every move as transition	Most variation is not structural.
Treating early indication as confirmation	Evidence may not persist.

Misuse	Why it is misleading
Treating confirmation as prediction	State change does not determine future path.
Treating destination as known	Transitions may branch or fail.
Ignoring horizon	Different scales may disagree.
Ignoring false transitions	Reliability becomes overstated.
Treating threshold crossing as natural law	Boundaries are designed.
Ignoring missing data	Confidence becomes inflated.
Confusing stabilization with recovery	Change may stop without improvement.
Confusing reversal with countertrend movement	Persistence and structure matter.

14.39 Transition Governance

A governed transition model should document its transition definition, starting-state definition, horizon, universe, components, materiality rules, persistence rules, breadth requirements, thresholds, hysteresis, confirmation logic, fast-path logic, missing-data behavior, confidence calculation, validation, version, effective date, limitations, and retirement criteria.

Governance should also preserve every transition event, revision, false transition, and model change for later calibration and failure analysis.

The purpose of governance is not to eliminate uncertainty. It is to prevent uncertainty and design judgment from being concealed.

- Transition and starting-state definitions.
- Horizon, universe, and effective time.
- Components, materiality, breadth, and persistence.
- Entry, exit, reversal, and hysteresis logic.
- Fast-path and confirmation logic.
- Missingness, freshness, and confidence.
- Validation, calibration, and drift monitoring.
- Version, approval, limitations, and retirement criteria.

Chapter Summary

Market configurations change continuously, but most changes do not become confirmed state transitions. A state transition is a material and sufficiently persistent reorganization of selected configuration features under a stated method, horizon, and classification framework.

Transition analysis requires attention to magnitude, persistence, breadth, coherence, speed, acceleration, reversibility, and evidence quality. Early indications improve responsiveness, while confirmation improves reliability.

The balance between them creates unavoidable trade-offs between lag and false transitions.

Transitions may be gradual or abrupt, orderly or disorderly, complete or incomplete, reinforcing or balancing, reversible or persistent. The trigger helps explain timing, while the receiving configuration helps explain transmission, amplification, and scale.

Fast trajectory should remain distinct from confirmed structural transition. A short-horizon path may identify emerging rotation without satisfying the persistence and quality requirements for structural reclassification.

Confidence in transition should remain separate from confidence in destination. A market may clearly be changing while the final state remains uncertain. Responsible transition analysis therefore preserves alternatives, signposts, missingness, model dependence, and revision conditions.

Established Knowledge

The concepts in this chapter draw upon established work in change-point detection, state-space modeling, hidden Markov models, regime-switching methods, transition matrices, dynamic and nonlinear systems, early-warning indicators, control theory, signal detection, sequential analysis, contagion, volatility clustering, liquidity spirals, leverage cycles, market microstructure, stress testing, resilience, and model calibration.

The Institute does not claim originality for the general concept of state transition. Its proposed contribution lies in integrating transition analysis with the four observational domains, separating configuration change from state transition, distinguishing fast trajectory from confirmed structural change, preserving confidence and missingness, and treating destination as uncertain.

Institute Perspective

The Institute treats transition as a governed evidentiary classification rather than an inevitable market narrative. Its framework separates indication, emergence, confirmation, maturity, stabilization, reversal, and failure while preserving the measurements and assumptions beneath each classification.

A transition model should help observers understand how the configuration is moving. It should not convert early change into deterministic prediction or substitute an automated label for judgment.

Questions for Reflection

1. What distinguishes configuration change from state transition?
2. Why does most market change not become structural transition?
3. What makes a transition material?

4. How should persistence be defined?
5. What is the difference between disturbance and transition?
6. Why is transition method-dependent?
7. What distinguishes early indication from confirmation?
8. Why does confirmation create lag?
9. What is a false transition?
10. How does hysteresis reduce unstable classification?
11. What is transition velocity?
12. What is transition acceleration?
13. How can gradual and abrupt transitions reach the same destination?
14. What distinguishes orderly from disorderly transition?
15. Why is a trigger different from the transition process?
16. How do structural preconditions affect sensitivity?
17. What is a reinforcing transition pathway?
18. What is a balancing transition pathway?
19. What distinguishes incomplete transition from failed transition?
20. Why is countertrend movement not automatically reversal?
21. What distinguishes stabilization from recovery?
22. Why can transitions differ across time horizons?
23. What is a domain-led transition?
24. How can transition spread across markets?
25. Why should transition confidence remain separate from destination confidence?
26. How should false-transition rate be evaluated?
27. What evidence would justify changing a confirmed structural state?
28. Why should a transition model remain decomposable and versioned?

Part IV. Market Judgment and Research

Chapter 15. Decision Quality Under Uncertainty

From Market Understanding to Responsible Action

Chapter Purpose

Financial analysis does not end when the current market configuration has been described. Participants must decide whether to act, wait, reduce exposure, seek additional evidence, hedge, rebalance, change execution, or preserve optionality. Yet no market assessment determines one universally correct action. The same evidence may justify different decisions for participants with different objectives, liabilities, mandates, horizons, risk capacities, and alternatives.

This chapter defines decision quality, distinguishes judgment from decision and action, formalizes the Decision Environment, explains how uncertainty should affect commitment, and establishes standards for evaluating decisions independently from their realized outcomes. Its purpose is not to prescribe trades. Its purpose is to show how market understanding can be translated into responsible, reviewable action without concealing uncertainty or participant dependence.

Learning Objectives

- distinguish market assessment, judgment, decision, action, outcome, and review;
- define decision quality independently from outcome quality;
- construct a Decision Environment using objectives, constraints, alternatives, uncertainty, horizon, risk capacity, implementation conditions, and authority;
- explain how uncertainty should influence commitment, timing, reversibility, and monitoring;
- distinguish risk tolerance, risk capacity, risk appetite, and risk limits;
- use scenarios, sensitivity analysis, decision margins, and decision records without creating false precision;
- evaluate decisions ex ante and ex post while preserving contemporaneous evidence;
- recognize the roles of incentives, group dynamics, automation, ethics, and governance in decision quality.

15.1 From Market Understanding to Decision

Chapters 10 through 14 developed a framework for describing market configurations, constructing state representations, and evaluating transitions. Those activities improve understanding, but understanding alone does not specify what any participant should do. Decision requires an additional layer containing objectives, constraints, alternatives, uncertainty, and responsibility.

A complete decision chain can be represented as: phenomenon → data → measurement → evidence → interpretation → assessment → judgment → decision → action → outcome → review. Each layer has a different purpose. Evidence supports interpretation; interpretation supports assessment; assessment informs judgment; judgment helps compare alternatives; decision selects a course of action; action implements it; outcome reveals one realized path; review updates knowledge and process.

Confusing these layers creates serious errors. A state label may be mistaken for a trading instruction. A forecast may be treated as a certainty. An action may be defended because its outcome happened to be favorable. A loss may be treated as proof that the original reasoning was irrational. The discipline of decision quality begins by preserving the boundaries among these layers.

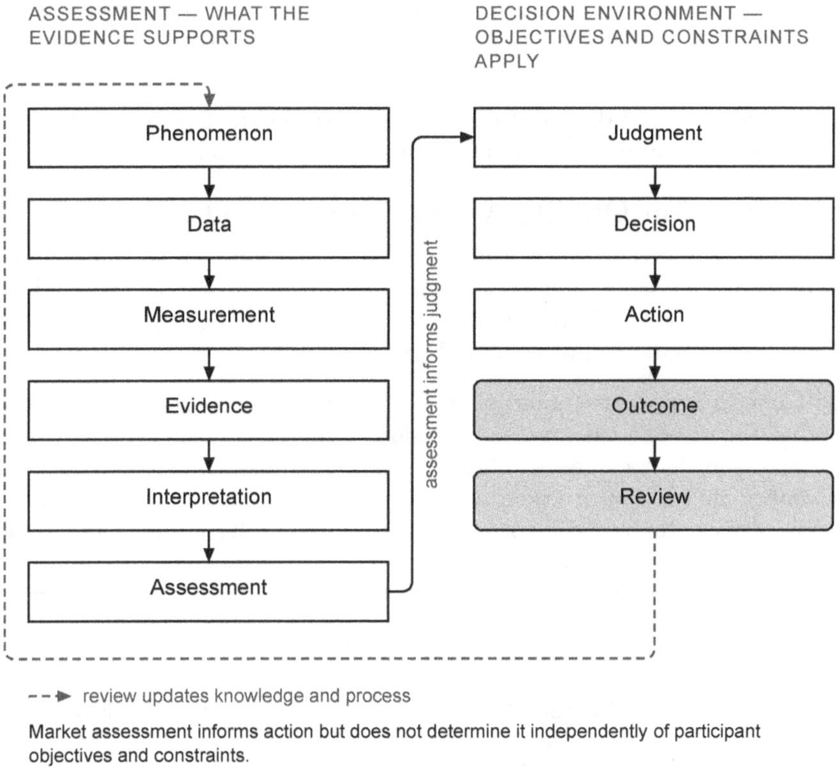

Figure 15.1 — From Market Understanding to Decision and Review

> **Assessment–Decision Principle:** Market assessment informs action but does not determine it independently of participant objectives and constraints.

15.2 What Is Decision Quality?

Decision quality is the degree to which a choice is made through a coherent, evidence-informed, objective-aligned, constraint-aware, uncertainty-conscious, and reviewable process. It concerns how the decision was formed, not merely whether the realized outcome was favorable.

A high-quality process generally defines the decision question, identifies the responsible decision maker, states objectives, records constraints, compares realistic alternatives, uses relevant evidence, expresses uncertainty honestly, calibrates the degree of commitment, plans implementation, specifies monitoring conditions, and preserves a contemporaneous record.

Decision quality does not require perfect information. In many markets, delay itself is costly and information is incomplete by design. The standard is not omniscience. The standard is whether the process was proportionate to the stakes, used the best reasonably available evidence, and remained open to revision.

> **Decision-Quality Principle:** Evaluate the quality of the process separately from the favorability of the outcome.

15.3 Decision Quality Versus Outcome Quality

Financial decisions are made before the future is known and evaluated after an outcome is visible. This asymmetry encourages hindsight bias and outcome bias. A profitable result can make weak reasoning appear intelligent; a loss can make disciplined risk reduction appear foolish.

Outcome and process should therefore be evaluated separately and then studied together across repeated decisions. One outcome is evidence, but it is rarely sufficient evidence. Repeatedly poor outcomes may reveal faulty assumptions, poor calibration, model drift, execution weakness, or unrealistic objectives. Repeated favorable outcomes may reflect skill, luck, hidden risk, or a combination of all three.

Decision process	Outcome	Interpretation
Sound	Favorable	Good process, favorable realization
Sound	Unfavorable	Good process, adverse realization
Poor	Favorable	Poor process, favorable luck
Poor	Unfavorable	Poor process, adverse realization

> **Outcome Principle:** One favorable or unfavorable outcome is insufficient to establish decision quality.

15.4 Assessment, Judgment, Decision, Action, Outcome, and Review

Assessment asks what the evidence supports about current conditions. Judgment asks what conclusions are defensible for the stated purpose. Decision selects among available alternatives. Action implements the selected course. Outcome is what follows from the action and the environment. Review examines the process, implementation, realized outcome, and lessons.

These categories overlap in practice, but their conceptual separation improves accountability. A participant may agree with an assessment yet choose a different action because constraints differ. A sound decision may be implemented poorly. An excellent execution may carry out a weak decision. A favorable outcome may follow from both.

Layer	Central question
Assessment	What does the evidence support?
Judgment	What conclusions are defensible for this purpose?
Decision	Which alternative should be selected?
Action	How will the choice be implemented?
Outcome	What happened?
Review	What should be learned or revised?

15.5 The Decision Environment

A Decision Environment is the structured combination of objectives, constraints, alternatives, information, uncertainty, horizon, risk capacity, implementation conditions, and responsibility relevant to a particular choice.

The concept prevents market analysis from being converted directly into generic action labels. The same market state can support different rational decisions because the decision maker, mandate, liabilities, time horizon, and ability to absorb loss differ. The relevant question is not simply whether the market appears favorable or unfavorable. It is whether a particular action fits a particular participant in a particular environment.

A complete Decision Environment should identify the decision maker, the decision question, objectives, constraints, alternatives, current market understanding, uncertainties, horizon, risk capacity, implementation conditions, reversibility, review conditions, and authority.

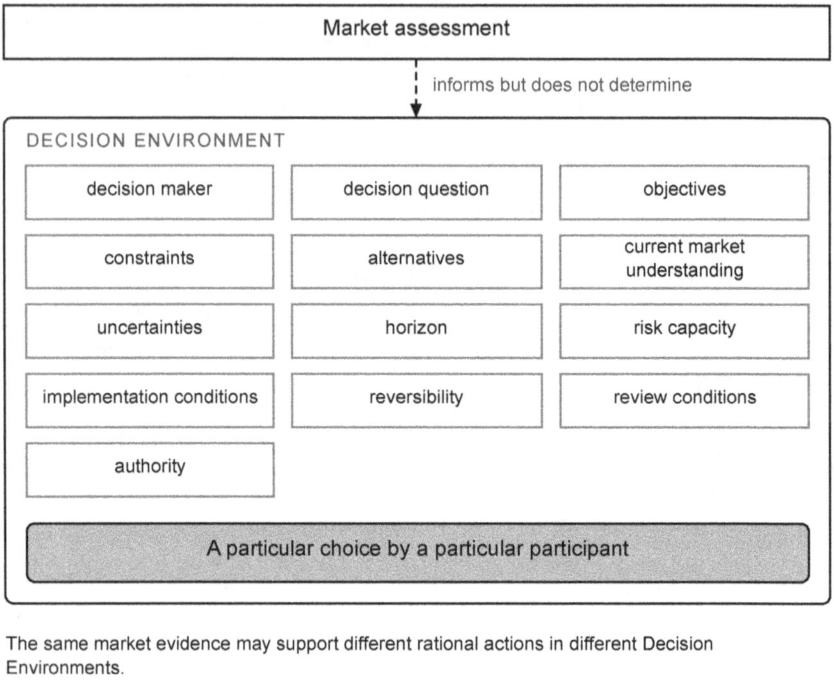

Figure 15.2 — The Decision Environment

> **Participant-Dependence Principle:** The same market evidence may support different rational actions in different Decision Environments.

15.6 Objectives

A decision cannot be evaluated without knowing what it is intended to achieve. Possible objectives include maximizing expected return, preserving capital, meeting liabilities, tracking a benchmark, maintaining liquidity, reducing volatility, hedging a known exposure, generating income, or satisfying a legal or fiduciary requirement.

Objectives frequently conflict. Greater return may require lower liquidity. Faster action may reduce evidence quality. Protection may impose ongoing cost. Benchmark tracking may conflict with absolute drawdown control. Responsible decision design makes these conflicts explicit rather than hiding them inside a single score.

Objectives should be specific enough to guide comparison but not so narrow that important consequences disappear. A narrow return objective that ignores survival, client suitability, or legal constraints can produce decisions that are numerically attractive and institutionally irresponsible.

> **Objective Principle:** A decision is not good in the abstract; it is good or poor relative to defined objectives and constraints.

15.7 Constraints

Constraints determine which alternatives are feasible. They may arise from capital, leverage, liquidity, mandate, regulation, taxes, time, concentration limits, operational capacity, execution access, knowledge, funding, collateral, authority, or psychological tolerance.

A theoretically attractive action may be unavailable in practice. A strategy that depends on continuous liquidity may be unsuitable for a participant who must exit rapidly under stress. A hedge may be too expensive, too illiquid, or prohibited by mandate. An option may exist conceptually but not operationally.

Constraints should be distinguished from preferences. A preference can sometimes be traded off; a hard legal, fiduciary, funding, or survival constraint cannot.

> **Constraint Principle:** An unavailable or infeasible alternative is not a genuine decision option.

15.8 Alternatives and the Status Quo

A decision process should compare realistic alternatives rather than a preferred action against an undefined opposite. Alternatives may include acting now, acting gradually, waiting, gathering more information, hedging, reducing exposure, changing instrument, choosing a more reversible structure, delegating, or abstaining.

The status quo is itself an alternative. Maintaining an existing position, holding cash, or postponing a change has consequences and opportunity costs. Treating the status quo as neutral hides those consequences and can bias the process toward inertia.

Inaction may be deliberate or accidental. Deliberate deferral states why waiting is valuable, what information is expected, and when the decision will be revisited. Passive nondecision results from fear, unclear authority, process failure, or avoidance of accountability.

15.9 Opportunity Cost

Every choice excludes or delays alternatives. Opportunity cost may include foregone return, lost liquidity, capital lockup, reduced flexibility, hedging expense, research time, execution capacity, or missed alternatives.

Opportunity cost is often less visible than realized loss. Avoiding a visible decline may appear successful even if an overly defensive choice causes a larger long-run shortfall. Conversely, pursuing incremental return may consume liquidity or risk capacity needed for a more important obligation.

Opportunity costs are rarely known with certainty because the unchosen path is not fully observable. They should be treated as estimates, not facts.

15.10 Decision Horizon

The decision horizon should be distinguished from the measurement horizon, market-state horizon, forecast horizon, holding period, review interval, and liability horizon. These may differ materially.

A short-horizon stress transition may matter greatly to an intraday leveraged trader and very little to an unleveraged long-term owner. A pension fund may care less about one-day price movement than about whether liquidity will remain available when liabilities come due. A market maker may react to seconds or minutes because inventory and execution risk change rapidly.

Horizon mismatch is a common source of error. A valid short-horizon observation can still be irrelevant to a long-horizon decision, and a long-horizon thesis can still be inadequate for a short-horizon risk-control choice.

> **Horizon Principle:** Evidence should be translated into decisions only after the analytical horizon is matched to the decision horizon.

15.11 Information Available at the Time

A defensible decision record should preserve what was known, what was estimated, what was assumed, what was unavailable, what was stale, what was expected, and what uncertainty remained when the decision was made.

This contemporaneous record protects against hindsight reconstruction. After an outcome occurs, people naturally remember warning signs as more obvious, reinterpret ambiguous evidence, and forget alternatives that once seemed plausible. A preserved record allows ex ante reasoning to be reviewed without contamination from later knowledge.

The record should also distinguish information that was available but ignored from information that was genuinely unavailable. The first may reveal process failure; the second may represent ordinary uncertainty.

> **Record Principle:** Material decisions should preserve the information, assumptions, alternatives, and reasoning available at the time.

15.12 Dimensions of Decision Uncertainty

Uncertainty in decisions is multidimensional. Data may be incomplete. Measurements may be noisy. Models may disagree. The current state may be uncertain. A transition may be real but its destination unclear. The causal mechanism may be contested. Execution may differ from expectation. External conditions may change after action.

Collapsing these forms into one confidence score can conceal important distinctions. A participant may have high confidence in the current state, moderate confidence that a transition is underway, low confidence in its destination, and high confidence that the existing exposure exceeds risk capacity. That combination can still justify action.

Uncertainty should therefore be attached to specific claims and decision components rather than expressed as a vague overall feeling.

Uncertainty type	Central issue
Data	Are observations complete, current, and reliable?
Measurement	How sensitive are calculated values to method and noise?
Model	Would alternative specifications change the conclusion?
State	How secure is the current classification?
Transition	Is material change actually underway?
Causal	Are the mechanisms understood?
Outcome	Which future path will occur?
Decision	Which alternative best serves the objectives?
Implementation	Can the action be executed as intended?
Environmental	What may change outside the model?

15.13 Risk and Uncertainty

Across disciplines, risk and uncertainty are defined in different ways. In this chapter, risk refers to exposure evaluated under an explicit probability or scenario framework, while uncertainty includes limitations in probabilities, outcomes, models, and information. This distinction is analytical rather than universal.

A decision may contain measurable risk and deep uncertainty simultaneously. Historical loss distributions may estimate ordinary variation while saying little about a structural break. Scenario ranges may be useful even when exact probabilities are unreliable. Responsible practice does not force every uncertainty into a probability merely to make the analysis appear quantitative.

15.14 Probability and Confidence

Probability should not be used as decoration. A meaningful probability requires a defined event, horizon, reference class, model, data, calibration process, and model version. A number without those elements can create false precision.

Confidence is not identical to probability. A model may assign a 60 percent probability while confidence in the model itself is low. An analyst may have high confidence that liquidity has deteriorated but low confidence about whether prices will fall further. These claims should not be merged.

Qualitative judgments can be rigorous when definitions, evidence, and calibration are clear. Numerical judgments can be weak when assumptions are hidden or reference classes are inappropriate.

> **Probability Principle:** A numerical probability is not automatically more rigorous than a qualitative judgment; rigor depends on definition and calibration.

15.15 Expected Value

Expected value compares actions by weighting possible outcomes by assigned probabilities and values. In simplified form, $\mathrm{EV(a)} = \Sigma\ \mathrm{p}_i \mathrm{u}(\mathrm{o}_i \mid \mathrm{a})$, where a is an action, o_i is a possible outcome, p_i is the assigned probability, and u represents the value or utility of that outcome.

Expected value is useful, but it is not a complete definition of rationality. Its result depends on probability estimates, utility assumptions, horizon, and the range of outcomes considered. It may ignore path dependence, liquidity, model error, correlation, survival constraints, and the difference between repeated and one-time decisions.

A favorable expected value can coexist with unacceptable ruin risk. Conversely, a negative expected financial value may be rational for insurance when it protects an essential obligation.

15.16 Utility and Participant Dependence

Two participants may assign different values to the same market outcome. Utility may reflect wealth, liabilities, drawdown limits, mandate, consumption needs, career consequences, survival, optionality, or ethical obligations.

This participant dependence explains why no state representation can prescribe one universal action. A ten percent decline has a different meaning for a fully funded long-term investor, a leveraged trader near a margin threshold, and a fiduciary responsible for near-term distributions.

Market outcomes are common observations. Their decision value is participant-dependent.

15.17 Asymmetry

Decision quality often depends more on asymmetric consequences than on a single forecast. The relevant questions include the plausible upside, plausible downside, survivability of adverse outcomes, reversibility, permanent impairment, and whether one side of the payoff is capped or open-ended.

A modest expected gain may be unattractive if the downside threatens essential obligations. A low-probability hedge may be valuable when it protects against a catastrophic outcome. Delay may improve asymmetry by allowing information to arrive, or worsen it by allowing risk to accumulate.

Asymmetry should be evaluated across the participant's full environment, not only within the instrument being considered.

15.18 Risk Tolerance, Capacity, Appetite, and Limits

Risk tolerance is willingness to experience variability or loss. Risk capacity is the ability to absorb loss without violating essential objectives. Risk appetite is the chosen level of risk the participant is prepared to assume. A risk limit is a governed boundary that constrains exposure regardless of current belief.

These concepts are frequently conflated. A participant may tolerate volatility emotionally but lack financial capacity to absorb it. An institution may have capacity but adopt a lower appetite because of fiduciary obligations. A trader may remain confident in a thesis but still be required to reduce exposure when a limit is reached.

Risk capacity should generally dominate preference when survival or essential obligations are at stake.

Concept	Meaning
Risk tolerance	Willingness to experience variability or loss
Risk capacity	Ability to absorb loss without violating essential objectives
Risk appetite	Chosen level of risk the participant is prepared to assume
Risk limit	Governed boundary that constrains exposure regardless of belief

> **Survival Principle:** Favorable expected value does not justify exposure that threatens essential obligations or survival.

15.19 Robust Decisions

A robust decision performs acceptably across several plausible scenarios rather than optimally under one fragile forecast. Robustness may involve smaller commitment, diversification, staging, hedging, liquidity preservation, reversible structures, or reduced dependence on one assumption.

Optimization can be valuable when the model is stable and probabilities are well estimated. Under substantial model uncertainty, however, an apparently optimal choice may fail sharply when one assumption changes. Robustness trades some base-case efficiency for greater resilience across alternatives.

Robustness should not become an excuse for permanent indecision. It is a design principle for choosing actions that remain acceptable when the future differs from the preferred forecast.

> **Robustness Principle:** Under model uncertainty, acceptable performance across plausible scenarios may matter more than optimality under one forecast.

15.20 Reversibility and Optionality

Decisions differ in how easily they can be revised. Transaction cost, depth, lockup, path dependence, tax consequences, legal commitment, and information arrival all affect reversibility.

A reversible decision permits learning after partial commitment. Staged entry, limited exposure, liquid instruments, or explicit review points may preserve the ability to adapt. This flexibility has value when uncertainty is expected to resolve through time.

Optionality is not free. Reversible structures may cost more, produce lower immediate return, or delay commitment. Their value should be compared with the cost of being wrong under an irreversible action.

> **Optionality Principle:** Reversible actions and preserved flexibility can have value when uncertainty is unresolved.

15.21 Value of Information

Additional information has value when it can change the selected action enough to justify its cost and delay. More data are not automatically better. Information may arrive too late, be unreliable, duplicate existing evidence, or fail to affect the choice.

A value-of-information inquiry asks which uncertainty the information could reduce, whether the decision would change, how costly delay is, whether the source is credible, and whether the opportunity will remain available.

When the decision margin is narrow and delay is inexpensive, additional information may be valuable. When action is urgent or the information cannot alter the choice, waiting may reduce decision quality.

Information Principle: Additional information is valuable only when it can improve the decision enough to justify its cost and delay.

15.22 Act, Wait, Investigate, Hedge, or Abstain

Action is not binary. A participant may act fully, act partially, wait, investigate, hedge, or abstain. Each can be rational under the appropriate Decision Environment.

Acting may be appropriate when evidence and asymmetry justify commitment. Partial action may fit when direction is supported but uncertainty remains material. Waiting may preserve value when delay is inexpensive. Investigation is useful when new information could alter the choice. Hedging can reduce consequences when the underlying exposure must remain. Abstention is appropriate when alternatives fail minimum standards.

Choice	Appropriate when
Act	Evidence and asymmetry justify commitment
Act partially	Evidence supports direction but uncertainty remains material
Wait	Delay preserves value without excessive opportunity cost
Investigate	Additional information could materially change the choice
Hedge	Exposure must remain but adverse consequences should be reduced
Abstain	Available alternatives do not meet minimum standards

15.23 Commitment and Position Size

Commitment includes position size, timing, duration, leverage, and irreversibility. Size should reflect downside, risk capacity, liquidity, correlation, model uncertainty, horizon, and portfolio interaction—not confidence alone.

A high-confidence judgment can still justify small size if adverse consequences are severe or liquidity is poor. A lower-confidence judgment can justify a hedge when the cost is acceptable and the exposure threatens an essential objective.

Uncertainty should affect the degree and reversibility of commitment, not merely the language used to describe the decision.

Uncertainty–Commitment Principle: Uncertainty should affect the magnitude, timing, and reversibility of commitment.

15.24 Staging and Sequential Decisions

Many decisions need not be made all at once. A participant may enter gradually, reduce gradually, condition later action on signposts, or use checkpoints that allow learning before further commitment.

Sequential decisions are especially useful when uncertainty will resolve through time, actions are partially reversible, information arrival is expected, or market impact matters. They can reduce the cost of being wrong while preserving participation if the thesis develops.

Staging also creates complexity. It may produce inconsistent execution, increase transaction costs, or become a disguised form of indecision. A staged plan should specify what evidence governs each subsequent step.

15.25 Decision Rules and Judgment

Rules improve consistency, speed, and auditability. Judgment permits context, exception handling, and recognition of conditions not captured by the rule. Either can fail when used alone.

Rigid rules may become obsolete, ignore structural breaks, or force action under poor data quality. Unconstrained judgment may become inconsistent, self-serving, or vulnerable to emotion and incentives. A governed process can combine predefined rules, documented exceptions, escalation thresholds, human challenge, and post-decision audit.

Rules should constrain arbitrary judgment without pretending that every relevant condition can be specified in advance.

15.26 Decision Thresholds

A decision threshold defines the minimum evidence or desirability required before action. Thresholds may depend on expected value, confidence, downside, reversibility, cost, urgency, risk capacity, and evidence quality.

As with state and transition thresholds, decision thresholds are designed boundaries rather than natural laws. They should be documented, tested, and reviewed. A value just above the threshold may not be meaningfully different from one just below it.

Thresholds may also require hysteresis or persistence to prevent repeated switching. The cost of stability is slower response; the cost of responsiveness is greater susceptibility to noise.

> **Threshold Principle:** Decision thresholds are designed rules and must be documented, tested, and revised.

15.27 Scenario-Based Decision Analysis

Scenario analysis evaluates plausible pathways rather than forcing one forecast. Each scenario should state the starting configuration, possible pathway, signposts, consequences for objectives, candidate responses, and invalidation conditions.

Scenarios are not predictions and need not be exhaustive. Their value lies in exposing conditional logic: if the market follows this pathway, what does it imply for the participant and what response becomes appropriate?

A scenario set should include both confirming and disconfirming possibilities. Otherwise it becomes a narrative designed to defend the preferred action.

Scenario	Market pathway	Participant consequence	Candidate response
Orderly continuation	Trend persists with stable liquidity	Opportunity remains; moderate risk	Maintain or stage exposure
Fragile continuation	Direction persists with concentration	Gains possible; sensitivity elevated	Reduce size or hedge
Stress transition	Liquidity weakens and volatility expands	Loss and execution risk rise	Reduce, hedge, or preserve liquidity
Repair	Breadth and resilience improve	Prior concern weakens	Reassess defensive action
Indeterminate	Evidence remains mixed	Decision confidence low	Wait or gather information

15.28 Decision Trees and Branching Choices

A decision tree can represent choice nodes, uncertain events, conditional actions, outcome values, and review points. It makes branching logic visible and can expose where assumptions enter.

Yet a tree may create false completeness. Unknown pathways, model interactions, and feedback effects can be omitted simply because they are difficult to draw. The representation should therefore be treated as a map of considered alternatives, not proof that all relevant possibilities have been captured.

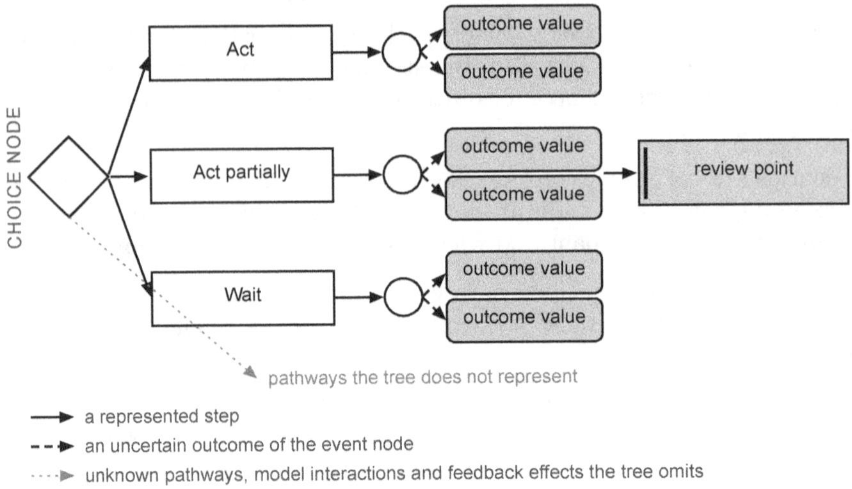

Figure 15.3 — Scenario and Decision Branching

15.29 Sensitivity Analysis

Sensitivity analysis tests whether the preferred action changes when probabilities, costs, expected returns, loss severity, liquidity, correlation, horizon, or model assumptions change.

The central question is whether a small assumption change reverses the decision. If it does, the choice is fragile. A fragile decision may justify further information, smaller commitment, staging, or a more robust alternative.

Sensitivity analysis should focus on assumptions that are both uncertain and decision-relevant. Testing many irrelevant parameters can create the appearance of rigor without improving the choice.

15.30 The Decision Margin

The decision margin is the degree by which the preferred alternative exceeds the next-best alternative under the stated objectives, constraints, assumptions, and scenario weights. It is an Institute framework intended to make choice sensitivity more visible.

A wide decision margin suggests that moderate assumption changes are unlikely to alter the preferred action. A narrow margin indicates greater sensitivity, higher value of information, and possible benefit from delay or partial commitment.

The decision margin is not the same as confidence. Confidence concerns support for claims; the decision margin concerns the relative attractiveness of alternatives.

15.31 Confidence, Decision Margin, and Commitment

Confidence, decision margin, and commitment should remain separate. Confidence describes the strength of support for an assessment. Decision margin describes the difference between alternatives. Commitment describes the magnitude and irreversibility of action.

High confidence can coexist with a narrow decision margin when alternatives have similar value. Moderate confidence can coexist with a large decision margin when one action protects against severe downside. Low confidence can still justify an urgent hedge when risk capacity is limited. High confidence may still require small commitment when liquidity is poor.

Keeping these concepts separate prevents confidence from becoming a universal position-sizing variable.

Confidence	the strength of support for an assessment
Decision margin	the difference between the preferred alternative and the next-best alternative
Commitment	the magnitude and irreversibility of action

COMBINATIONS THE CHAPTER RECORDS

COMBINATION	BECAUSE
High confidence with a narrow decision margin	alternatives have similar value
Moderate confidence with a large decision margin	one action protects against severe downside
Low confidence with an urgent hedge	risk capacity is limited
High confidence with small commitment	liquidity is poor

The three are kept separate so that confidence does not become a universal position-sizing variable. No mapping between them is asserted.

Figure 15.4 — Confidence, Decision Margin, and Commitment

15.32 Common Decision Biases

Decision biases are recurring patterns that can distort evidence selection, probability judgment, action, or evaluation. Evidence biases include confirmation bias, anchoring, selective attention, and availability. Probability biases include overconfidence, base-rate neglect, representativeness, and neglect of tail outcomes.

Action biases include action bias, omission bias, inertia, escalation of commitment, and the sunk-cost effect. Evaluation biases include hindsight bias, outcome bias, self-serving attribution, and survivorship bias. Social and organizational biases include groupthink, authority pressure, mandate ambiguity, and incentive distortion.

A bias label should not substitute for analysis. The reviewer should identify which evidence was ignored, which assumption became distorted, or which alternative was excluded.

15.33 Emotion and Decision Quality

Emotion should not be treated as simply irrational. Fear, excitement, regret, and stress may reflect perceived stakes, but they can also distort attention, time horizon, risk perception, and action urgency.

The goal is not emotional elimination. It is governance. Precommitment, checklists, cooling periods, independent review, position limits, decision logs, and escalation rules can reduce the risk that temporary emotional states dominate high-stakes choices.

Emotional awareness can itself be evidence. A strong urge to act may signal that exposure, incentives, or identity have become entangled with the decision.

15.34 Incentives and Conflicts

Decision quality can be distorted by compensation, career risk, benchmark pressure, marketing incentives, client retention, institutional politics, performance periods, personal ownership, or model sponsorship.

A technically sophisticated process can still be compromised when the decision maker benefits from one conclusion or bears asymmetric consequences. Material conflicts should therefore be disclosed in the decision record and considered during review.

Governance should examine not only whether a model was followed, but also whether the objectives and incentives surrounding its use were appropriate.

> **Incentive Principle:** A technically sophisticated decision process can still be compromised by misaligned incentives.

15.35 Group Decisions

Groups can improve decisions by combining expertise and challenging assumptions. They can also create diffusion of responsibility, groupthink, dominance, conformity, hidden information, and compromise without coherence.

Useful controls include independent initial estimates, explicit dissent, designated challenge, clear decision authority, documented rationale, and preservation of minority views. A group should know who advises, who challenges, who decides, and who is accountable.

Consensus is not always evidence of quality. It may reflect shared data and sound reasoning, or common incentives and social pressure.

15.36 Human Judgment and Automated Systems

Automated systems can organize evidence, enforce limits, monitor thresholds, calculate exposures, compare scenarios, preserve records, and execute actions consistently. These capabilities can improve speed and discipline.

Automation does not eliminate model risk, objective ambiguity, unknown conditions, ethical responsibility, or governance responsibility. A system can optimize the wrong objective, act on stale data, or execute a poorly governed rule with great consistency.

Human oversight should not mean informal override without accountability. Overrides, exceptions, and model changes should be documented and reviewable.

> **Responsibility Principle:** Automation may support or execute decisions, but responsibility for objectives, models, and consequences remains human and institutional.

15.37 Decision Records

A decision record converts reasoning into an auditable object. It should identify the decision, time, decision maker, authority, question, objectives, constraints, alternatives, current market assessment, evidence, confidence, scenarios, expected consequences, selected action, commitment, implementation plan, monitoring signposts, review time, invalidation conditions, conflicts, and assumptions.

The record should be proportionate to stakes. A routine low-risk decision may require a compact template; a material institutional allocation or risk-limit change requires more detail. The purpose is not paperwork. It is to preserve what mattered when the choice was made.

A good record also makes future calibration possible. Without structured records, organizations tend to remember outcomes and forget the original uncertainty.

The Decision Record

FIELD	REQUIRED CONTENT
Decision question	What choice must be made?
Decision maker	Who has authority and responsibility?
Objectives	What is the action intended to achieve?
Constraints	What limits feasible choices?
Alternatives	What realistic actions are available?
Market assessment	What does the evidence currently support?
Confidence	How strong is support by claim type?
Scenarios	What plausible pathways are considered?
Consequences	What happens to objectives under each pathway?
Risk capacity	What adverse outcomes can be absorbed?
Reversibility	How easily can the action be changed?
Selected action	Which alternative was chosen?
Commitment	What size, timing, and irreversibility?
Monitoring	Which signposts require attention?
Revision	What would change or invalidate the decision?
Review	When and how will process and outcome be evaluated?

The record should be proportionate to the stakes. Its purpose is to preserve what mattered when the choice was made.

Figure 15.5 — The Decision Record

Field	**Required content**
Decision question	What choice must be made?
Decision maker	Who has authority and responsibility?
Objectives	What is the action intended to achieve?
Constraints	What limits feasible choices?
Alternatives	What realistic actions are available?
Market assessment	What does the evidence currently support?
Confidence	How strong is support by claim type?
Scenarios	What plausible pathways are considered?
Consequences	What happens to objectives under each pathway?
Risk capacity	What adverse outcomes can be absorbed?
Reversibility	How easily can the action be changed?
Selected action	Which alternative was chosen?
Commitment	What size, timing, and irreversibility?
Monitoring	Which signposts require attention?
Revision	What would change or invalidate the decision?
Review	When and how will process and outcome be evaluated?

15.38 Pre-Mortem and Red-Team Review

A pre-mortem asks participants to assume the decision failed and identify plausible causes. This reverses the usual tendency to defend the preferred action and can reveal hidden dependencies, implementation weaknesses, or omitted scenarios.

Red-team review assigns an independent person or process to challenge evidence, assumptions, alternatives, causal claims, probability estimates, implementation, and hidden exposures. The challenge must be capable of changing the decision; otherwise it becomes procedural theater.

Challenge should be proportionate to stakes and time. Urgent decisions may require a compact challenge protocol, but urgency should not eliminate dissent entirely.

15.39 Monitoring and Revision

A decision is not complete at implementation. Monitoring should specify expected signposts, contrary evidence, state changes, transition changes, execution quality, risk-limit use, time-based review, and model drift.

Revision is not inconsistency when the evidence changes. A disciplined process commits to an objective and method, not to defending an outdated conclusion. The decision record should identify what evidence would increase, reduce, or reverse commitment.

Continuous revision can also become instability. Monitoring rules should distinguish ordinary variation from information that materially changes the rationale.

> **Revision Principle:** Revising a decision when evidence changes is disciplined adaptation, not inconsistency.

15.40 Exit, Invalidation, Review, and Risk Limits

An exit condition requires termination or reduction of an action. An invalidation condition indicates that the original rationale no longer holds. A review condition requires reassessment. A risk limit constrains exposure regardless of belief.

These concepts should not be merged. A risk limit may require reduction even when the thesis remains valid. A review may occur without action. An invalidation may change the thesis before an exit is operationally possible. Clear definitions reduce discretionary reinterpretation after losses.

Exit and review conditions should be established before commitment where practical, while allowing documented changes when circumstances materially evolve.

15.41 Decision Failure Analysis

After an unfavorable outcome, reviewers should distinguish evidence failure, reasoning failure, model failure, calibration failure, decision-design failure, implementation failure, risk-control failure, unforeseeable realization, and ordinary adverse variance.

The same analysis should follow favorable outcomes. A profit may conceal ignored evidence, excessive size, poor execution, or an unrecognized tail exposure. Learning requires examining process regardless of whether the result feels rewarding.

Failure analysis should seek correction rather than blame. Blame-centered review encourages concealment and hindsight narratives; process-centered review improves future decisions while preserving accountability.

Failure category	Illustrative question
Evidence failure	Was material information missing, stale, or ignored?
Reasoning failure	Did the inference exceed what the evidence supported?
Model failure	Was the model inappropriate or unstable?
Calibration failure	Was confidence systematically overstated?
Decision-design failure	Were alternatives, constraints, or asymmetries poorly framed?
Implementation failure	Was the action executed differently from the plan?
Risk-control failure	Were limits absent, ignored, or ineffective?
Adverse variance	Was the outcome plausible despite a sound process?

15.42 Decision Calibration

Decision calibration evaluates repeated choices rather than isolated anecdotes. Possible measures include confidence versus outcome frequency, forecast calibration, loss distribution, decision reversals, threshold effectiveness, false-action rates, delayed-action cost, limit breaches, execution slippage, and process compliance.

Calibration should be segmented by market state, decision type, horizon, instrument, confidence, and model version. Aggregate results can conceal that a process works in one environment and fails in another.

Calibration is not limited to predictive accuracy. A risk-reduction decision may be well calibrated if it consistently keeps losses within capacity even when it lowers average return.

15.43 Counterfactual Evaluation

Counterfactual analysis asks what might have happened under an unchosen action. It supports learning but remains uncertain because the alternative outcome is generally not observable.

A hedge may appear unnecessary because the adverse event did not occur. An avoided investment may later rise. A stopped position may recover. A delayed action may miss an opportunity. None of these observations proves that the original decision was poor without considering the information and objectives at the time.

Counterfactuals should be modeled as estimates, with assumptions and ranges, rather than presented as facts.

15.44 Decision Governance

A governed decision system should document permitted decision types, objectives, authority, evidence standards, model use, thresholds, limits, exception handling, monitoring, review, record retention, escalation, audit, and retirement of obsolete rules.

Governance should make discretion visible rather than pretending to eliminate it. Exceptions may be necessary under unusual conditions, but they should identify who authorized them, why the standard process was inadequate, and how the result will be reviewed.

Governance also includes model retirement. A rule that once improved decisions may become harmful when market structure, data quality, or participant behavior changes.

15.45 Ethics and Responsibility

Decision quality includes more than profitability. It may involve fiduciary duty, fairness, market integrity, client suitability, disclosure, conflicts, use of confidential information, and broader organizational consequences.

A decision can be profitable and still be irresponsible. An action that exploits a client's information disadvantage, violates mandate, conceals conflicts, or transfers unacceptable risk to others does not become high quality because it earns money.

Responsibility begins with how objectives are defined, whose interests are represented, which consequences are considered, and who bears the downside.

> **Responsibility and Ethics Principle:** Decision quality includes responsibility for how objectives are defined, whose interests are represented, and which consequences are considered.

15.46 Worked Example: Concentrated Advance Under Rising Fragility

Consider a capitalization-weighted index that continues to advance while breadth narrows, leadership becomes concentrated, short-dated implied volatility rises, and liquidity remains functional but increasingly asymmetric. Positioning estimates suggest possible adjustment sensitivity, though those estimates remain model-dependent. Descriptive confidence is moderate; predictive confidence is low.

A long-term unleveraged investor may maintain exposure, rebalance concentration, and monitor transition evidence because the horizon is long and loss capacity is relatively high. A leveraged short-horizon trader may reduce size, tighten limits, or wait for broader confirmation because margin and drawdown constraints are tighter. A market-neutral options portfolio may adjust hedge frequency or reduce short convexity because the relevant exposure is volatility and nonlinear risk rather than index direction.

The market assessment is common. The rational actions differ because the Decision Environments differ. The example demonstrates why a state label cannot be converted directly into a universal buy, sell, or risk-on instruction.

15.47 Worked Example: Sound Process, Adverse Outcome

A risk manager reduces concentrated exposure because liquidity is deteriorating, volatility is expanding, downside sensitivity is increasing, and the institution's loss capacity is limited. The market rebounds immediately after the reduction.

The rebound does not prove the decision was wrong. The evidence was current, the assessment was reasonable, the exposure exceeded capacity, and the action reduced tail risk. The review should nevertheless examine whether the reduction was too large, whether staging would have improved the decision, whether thresholds were calibrated, and whether execution cost was excessive.

A sound process can produce an adverse outcome because uncertainty remains. Decision quality is not immunity from loss.

15.48 Worked Example: Poor Process, Favorable Outcome

A participant takes an oversized position based on an unverified social-media claim without checking liquidity, downside, conflicting evidence, or risk capacity. The asset rises sharply.

The favorable outcome does not validate the information source, the sizing, the absence of risk controls, or the reasoning process. Interpreting luck as skill can make the next decision more dangerous because the participant becomes more confident in a weak method.

The appropriate review separates the profit from the process and asks whether the same method would remain acceptable across repeated decisions and adverse realizations.

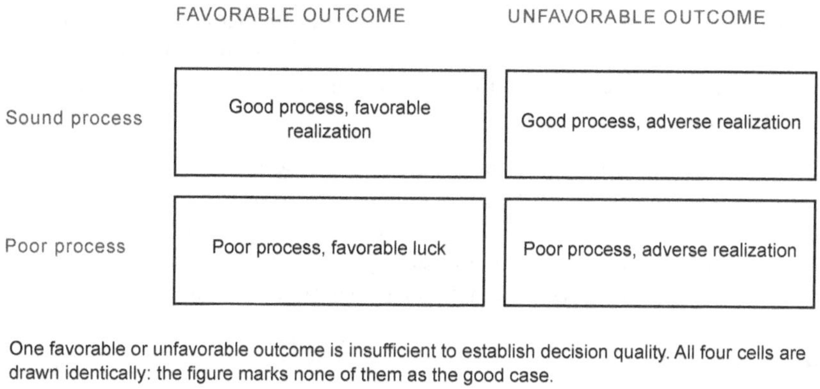

Figure 15.6 — Decision Quality Versus Outcome Quality

Chapter Summary

Market understanding does not determine action independently of the participant. A decision requires objectives, constraints, alternatives, uncertainty, horizon, risk capacity, implementation conditions, and responsibility. Together these elements form the Decision Environment.

Decision quality should be distinguished from outcome quality. A sound process can produce an unfavorable result, while a poor process can benefit from favorable luck. Outcomes remain important, but they should be evaluated alongside the information and reasoning available when the decision was made.

Uncertainty should influence commitment, position size, timing, reversibility, monitoring, and the value assigned to additional information. Under substantial model uncertainty, robust and reversible actions may be preferable to fragile optimization around one forecast.

The same market assessment can support different rational actions because participants differ in objectives, constraints, liabilities, mandates, and risk capacity. Market states and transition assessments therefore provide decision context, not universal instructions.

Responsible decision systems preserve contemporaneous records, alternatives, assumptions, confidence, signposts, invalidation conditions, conflicts, and authority. Decisions should be reviewed for evidence quality, reasoning, design, implementation, risk control, outcome, and calibration.

Established Knowledge

This chapter draws on established work in decision theory, expected utility theory, behavioral economics, bounded rationality, Bayesian decision theory, robust decision-making, operations research, control theory, portfolio theory, risk management, game theory, organizational decision-making, prospect theory, value of information, real options, human factors, model risk management, judgment and forecasting, cognitive-bias research, and fiduciary and governance standards.

The Institute does not claim originality for expected value, utility, decision trees, scenario analysis, Bayesian updating, pre-mortems, decision journals, robust optimization, risk limits, or outcome bias. Its contribution is the integration of these ideas into the market-systems architecture and the formal separation of market assessment from participant action.

Institute Perspective

The Institute's proposed contribution is the Decision Environment: a controlled framework that embeds objectives, constraints, alternatives, uncertainty, horizon, risk capacity, implementation, reversibility, review, and responsibility around a specific choice. The chapter also distinguishes confidence, decision margin, and commitment; links uncertainty to optionality; treats inaction as a possible deliberate decision; and connects decision records to later calibration and research.

The term decision margin is introduced as an Institute framework for comparing the preferred alternative with the next-best alternative under stated assumptions. It should be treated as a transparent analytical device rather than an established universal term.

Questions for Reflection

1. What distinguishes market assessment from judgment?
2. What distinguishes judgment from decision?
3. What distinguishes decision from action?
4. Why does a market state not prescribe one universal action?
5. What is a Decision Environment?
6. Why must objectives be defined before decision quality can be evaluated?
7. How do constraints alter the available alternatives?
8. Why should the status quo be treated as an alternative?
9. What is opportunity cost?
10. Why should the decision horizon be distinguished from the market-state horizon?
11. What information should be preserved contemporaneously?
12. What forms of uncertainty affect a market decision?

13. How does risk differ from broader uncertainty?
14. Why is confidence not identical to probability?
15. What assumptions are embedded in expected value?
16. Why can two participants assign different utility to the same outcome?
17. What is asymmetric decision exposure?
18. What distinguishes risk tolerance from risk capacity?
19. Why can survival constraints override expected value?
20. What makes a decision robust?
21. Why can reversibility have value?
22. When is additional information worth seeking?
23. When may waiting be the best decision?
24. Why is inaction not always the absence of a decision?
25. What factors should influence commitment or position size?
26. Why may staged action improve decision quality?
27. How should rules and judgment be combined?
28. What is a decision threshold?
29. What is the decision margin?
30. Why should confidence, decision margin, and commitment remain separate?
31. How can a favorable outcome result from a poor process?
32. How can an unfavorable outcome follow a sound decision?
33. What role should a pre-mortem play?
34. Why must counterfactual evaluation remain qualified?
35. How should automated decision support be governed?
36. What should a decision record contain?
37. What evidence should cause a decision to be revised?
38. How should decisions be calibrated across repeated cases?
39. How can incentives degrade decision quality?
40. Why does responsibility extend beyond profitability?

Chapter 16. Research Method

Investigating Markets as Evolving Systems

Chapter Purpose

Financial-market research faces an unusual combination of scientific and practical difficulties. Markets cannot normally be isolated in a laboratory. Participants learn, adapt, and respond to published findings. Institutions, technologies, rules, and instruments change. Data are selected, revised, delayed, and produced through market structure. Relationships that appear stable in one period may weaken, reverse, or disappear in another.

This chapter establishes a disciplined research method for investigating markets under those conditions. It defines the research object, distinguishes exploratory from confirmatory work, formalizes claims and hypotheses, requires governed measurement design, addresses nonstationarity and adaptive behavior, and establishes standards for validation, reproducibility, replication, documentation, negative results, and revision. Its purpose is not to prescribe one statistical technique. Its purpose is to provide a research architecture within which different methods can be used transparently and appropriately.

Learning Objectives

- define market research as a systematic, documented, and reviewable process;
- distinguish research objects, claim types, hypotheses, predictions, and revision conditions;
- separate exploratory discovery from confirmatory evaluation;
- design governed research protocols with explicit universe, horizon, sampling, data, and measurement definitions;
- identify look-ahead bias, survivorship bias, dependence, nonstationarity, endogeneity, and multiple-testing risk;
- evaluate measurement validity, reliability, provenance, missingness, and transformation lineage;
- use baselines, robustness tests, sensitivity analysis, negative controls, and out-of-sample validation;
- distinguish reproducibility, replication, implementation validation, and decision usefulness;

- maintain a Research Ledger that preserves protocol versions, deviations, results, review, limitations, and disposition;
- update the knowledge state in response to null results, failed replications, structural change, and independent challenge.

16.1 From Decision Review to Research Method

Chapter 15 established that decisions should be reviewed for evidence quality, reasoning, design, implementation, risk control, and outcome. Research begins when a learning question is transformed into a governed investigation that other people can examine, reproduce, challenge, and revise.

The research cycle can be represented as: phenomenon → research question → claim type → hypothesis → design → data → measurement → analysis → result → interpretation → validation → replication → revision. Each link matters. A sophisticated model cannot repair an ill-defined question, and a persuasive interpretation cannot compensate for invalid measurements.

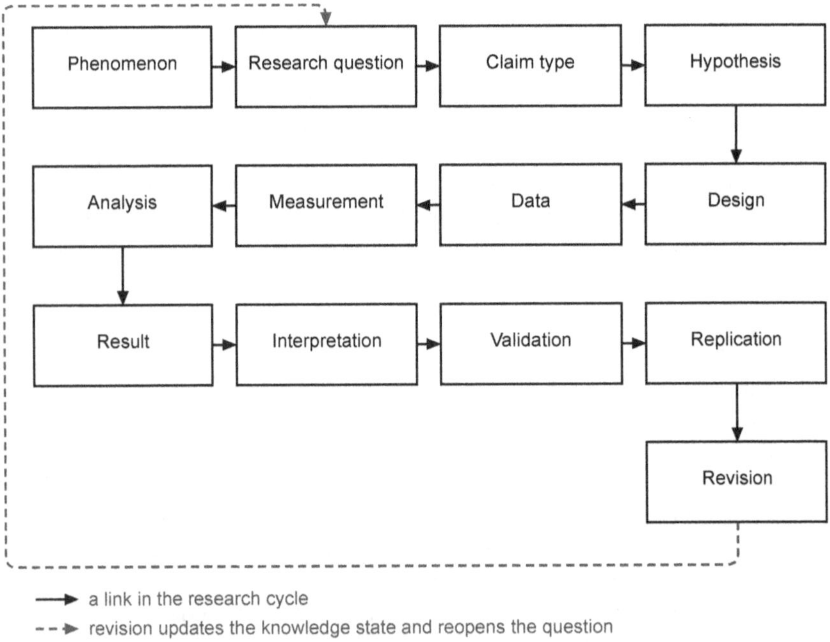

Figure 16.1 — The Market Systems Research Cycle

16.2 What Is Research?

Research is a systematic, documented, and reviewable process for investigating a question, evaluating claims against evidence, and refining knowledge in response to results. It is not merely the accumulation of data, the calculation of indicators, the fitting of a model, the discovery of a correlation, or the production of a backtest.

A research result becomes meaningful only through its connection to a defined question, a suitable design, governed measurements, explicit assumptions, appropriate analysis, and a qualified interpretation. The process must also preserve what failed, what changed, what remains unknown, and what evidence would alter the conclusion.

> **Research Principle:** Research connects question, method, evidence, inference, limitation, and revision in one reviewable chain.

16.3 Research in an Evolving System

Markets are evolving systems. Their participants respond to prices, policies, technology, information, forecasts, and one another. Trading rules change. New instruments appear. Data collection improves. Strategies become crowded. A relationship can weaken because the environment changed, because participants adapted, or because the original result was sample-specific.

This does not make disciplined research impossible. It changes the burden of interpretation. Findings should be treated as conditional on a universe, period, horizon, institutional setting, data-generating process, and market configuration. Stability is something to be demonstrated, monitored, and periodically re-evaluated—not assumed.

> **Evolving-System Principle:** Market research investigates a moving system using measurements and models that may themselves evolve.

16.4 The Research Object

The research object is the phenomenon, representation, relationship, process, or system being investigated. Clear identification of the object is essential because different objects require different evidence and methods.

A study of a recorded trade event differs from a study of a liquidity measure. A study of a relationship differs from a study of a latent market state. A state-transition classifier requires different validation from a decision process or an operational implementation.

Research object	Illustrative question
Observation	What market activity was recorded?
Measurement	Does the measure validly represent the intended phenomenon?

Research object	Illustrative question
Relationship	Are two measurements associated under stated conditions?
Configuration	Which measurements commonly coexist?
State	Does a representation summarize meaningful configuration differences?
Transition	Can material configuration change be identified reliably?
Mechanism	Through what pathway may the effect arise?
Forecast	Does current evidence improve future-outcome estimates?
Decision process	Does the process improve a specified decision objective?
Implementation	Does the operational system reproduce the intended method?

16.5 The Research Question

A strong research question specifies the phenomenon, population or universe, timeframe, horizon, comparison, outcome, claim type, and intended use. "Does liquidity matter?" is too broad to guide a design. "Under what intraday configurations is declining displayed depth associated with increased short-horizon price impact in highly liquid U.S. equities?" is more useful because it defines observable elements and scope.

A precise question does not guarantee a valid answer, but an imprecise question almost always produces ambiguous evidence. The wording should also avoid claiming causation before the design can support it.

> **Research-Object Principle:** Method should follow the research question and the nature of the research object, not the researcher's preferred tool.

16.6 Claim Types and Research Requirements

Research claims differ in strength. A descriptive claim characterizes what occurred. An associative claim evaluates whether variables move together. A predictive claim asks whether information improves estimates of a defined future outcome. A mechanistic claim investigates a plausible pathway. A causal claim asks whether changing one factor would alter another under stated assumptions. A decision claim asks whether information or a process improves a specified objective.

The required evidence becomes stronger as the claim moves from description toward causation and decision usefulness. Temporal sequence or predictive accuracy alone does not establish a causal mechanism.

Claim-Proportionality Principle: The strength of the research design and evidence must be proportional to the strength of the claim.

Claim type	Primary question	Minimum research requirement
Descriptive	What occurred?	Valid observation, coverage, measurement, uncertainty
Associative	What varies together?	Comparison, dependence analysis, confound consideration
Predictive	What improves future estimates?	Out-of-sample design, baseline, leakage control, calibration
Mechanistic	Through what pathway?	Temporal ordering, process evidence, alternatives
Causal	What would change if a factor changed?	Identification assumptions, counterfactual design, sensitivity
Decision-related	Does this improve a stated objective?	Operational costs, constraints, utility, robustness

16.7 Claims, Hypotheses, and Predictions

A claim is a proposition. A hypothesis is a proposition structured for evaluation. A prediction is an observable result expected under a hypothesis and design. The distinctions matter because vague claims can be protected from contradiction, whereas useful hypotheses create observable implications.

For example, the claim that liquidity resilience deteriorates before certain disorderly transitions can be converted into the hypothesis that slower depth replenishment is associated with greater subsequent price impact under otherwise comparable conditions. A corresponding prediction might state that observations in the lowest replenishment-resilience group will show higher subsequent impact than matched observations in higher-resilience groups.

Hypothesis Principle: A hypothesis becomes scientifically useful when it implies observations that could weaken it.

16.8 Falsifiability and Revision Conditions

Not every useful market proposition can be falsified through one decisive test. Nevertheless, every material research claim should identify observable implications, competing explanations, scope limits, and evidence that would reduce confidence or require reformulation.

Revision conditions may include failure in a holdout period, sensitivity to small threshold changes, contradiction in a relevant market state, absence of the proposed temporal sequence, or successful explanation by a simpler alternative. A claim that cannot be weakened by any conceivable evidence functions as belief rather than research.

> **Revision-Condition Principle:** A research claim should state what evidence would narrow, weaken, or require reformulation of the claim.

16.9 Exploratory Research

Exploratory research is essential for discovering distributions, anomalies, candidate variables, possible state structures, and questions that merit formal testing. It may use visualization, clustering, alternative transformations, and subgroup comparisons.

Exploration also creates selection risk because researchers observe many possibilities and remember the most compelling. Exploratory findings should therefore be labeled as such, the search process should be preserved where practical, and confirmatory language should be avoided until independent evaluation occurs.

16.10 Confirmatory Research

Confirmatory research evaluates a specified hypothesis under a defined design. Before examining the confirmatory result, the study should state the primary hypothesis, outcome, predictors, sample, exclusions, transformations, statistical test, threshold, multiplicity treatment, robustness plan, and criteria for failure.

Preregistration can strengthen this separation, but public preregistration is not always possible in proprietary or operational settings. Internal timestamped protocols, immutable version control, and independent review can still reduce hidden flexibility.

> **Exploration–Confirmation Principle:** Exploration generates hypotheses; confirmation evaluates them. Treating both as one activity inflates confidence.

Exploratory research	**Confirmatory research**
Generates hypotheses	Evaluates specified hypotheses
Allows broad search	Limits researcher degrees of freedom
Uses flexible transformations	Uses declared transformations
Findings are provisional	Findings are tested against failure criteria
Requires later validation	Requires independent or holdout evidence

16.11 The Research Protocol

A research protocol converts a question into a planned investigation. It should be specific enough that an independent reviewer can determine what was intended before results were known and what changed afterward.

The protocol should include a research identifier, motivation, claim type, hypotheses, universe, period, data sources, measurement definitions, inclusion and exclusion rules, analysis plan, robustness plan, expected limitations, version, ownership, and review authority.

Protocol field	**Required content**
Question and motivation	What is being investigated and why?
Claim type and hypothesis	What proposition and evidentiary burden apply?
Universe and period	Which observations and dates are eligible?
Data and measurements	Sources, definitions, transformations, versions
Analysis plan	Comparisons, models, tests, thresholds
Robustness plan	Alternative specifications and sensitivity
Limitations	Known weaknesses and anticipated uncertainty
Governance	Owner, reviewer, version, approval state

The Research Protocol

PROTOCOL FIELD	REQUIRED CONTENT
Question and motivation	What is being investigated and why?
Claim type and hypothesis	What proposition and evidentiary burden apply?
Universe and period	Which observations and dates are eligible?
Data and measurements	Sources, definitions, transformations, versions
Analysis plan	Comparisons, models, tests, thresholds
Robustness plan	Alternative specifications and sensitivity
Limitations	Known weaknesses and anticipated uncertainty
Governance	Owner, reviewer, version, approval state

The protocol should be specific enough that an independent reviewer can determine what was intended before results were known, and what changed afterward.

Figure 16.2 — The Research Protocol

16.12 Universe and Sampling

Research should distinguish the target population, observable universe, sampled universe, and final analysis sample. Each narrowing step can change what the result supports.

Sampling risks include survivorship bias, index-membership bias, liquidity filtering, vendor coverage, missing history, exchange selection, corporate-action treatment, and the exclusion of failed or inactive instruments. The supported conclusion cannot be broader than the represented population.

> **Population Principle:** The population supported by a conclusion cannot be broader than the population represented by the design.

16.13 Time and Event Alignment

Market research depends on temporal integrity. Every study should document timezone, exchange calendar, market session, event-time anchor, timestamp precision, latency, publication delay, revision time, and asynchronous measurements.

Common errors include using information before it was available, aligning vendor and exchange timestamps incorrectly, mixing overnight and regular sessions, or using end-of-period classifications to explain earlier events. These errors can produce impressive but impossible results.

> **Temporal Integrity Principle:** No study may use information before it was reasonably available to the evaluated process.

16.14 Look-Ahead Bias

Look-ahead bias occurs when a study uses information that would not have been available when the evaluated decision or prediction was made. Sources include revised economic data, finalized index membership, future corporate-action knowledge, complete option chains unavailable in real time, and retrospectively assigned state labels.

Preventing look-ahead bias requires point-in-time data, availability timestamps, versioned reference data, and simulation of the actual information boundary. Merely sorting records by date is insufficient.

16.15 Survivorship and Delisting Bias

A dataset containing only currently existing securities can omit bankruptcies, mergers, delistings, inactive contracts, and failed products. This can materially overstate return, liquidity, and persistence.

Research should preserve historical membership and explicitly account for disappearance. If complete histories are unavailable, the limitation should constrain the claim rather than be ignored.

16.16 Measurement Validity

Measurement validity asks whether a variable represents the intended construct. Construct validity addresses the theoretical relationship between the measure and the concept. Content validity asks whether important dimensions are omitted. Criterion validity compares the measure with an external benchmark. Convergent and discriminant validity examine expected agreement and distinction.

A spread measure may be calculated perfectly yet capture only one dimension of liquidity. Reliable computation does not establish conceptual completeness.

> **Measurement Principle:** A statistically sophisticated analysis of poorly governed measurements remains weak research.

16.17 Measurement Reliability

Reliability concerns consistency. A measure should reproduce under the same procedure, remain stable under immaterial implementation changes, and agree across independent implementations within understood tolerances.

Reliability testing should examine vendor corrections, timestamp resolution, rounding, transformation order, and software version. A measure can be reliable but invalid, or valid in principle but unreliable in implementation.

Property	Central question
Validity	Does the measure represent the intended construct?
Reliability	Does the procedure produce consistent results?
Coverage	Where and when is the measure available?
Sensitivity	How much does it change under reasonable implementation choices?
Traceability	Can the result be traced to source data and transformations?

16.18 Data Provenance

Every dataset should identify provider, collection method, fields, schema, timezone, revision policy, coverage, licensing constraints, acquisition date, processing steps, and checksum or version identifier.

Provenance is not administrative overhead. It determines whether a result can be reproduced, audited, and interpreted after data or vendors change. The complete transformation path should be traceable from raw observation to research variable.

> **Provenance Principle:** Data, transformations, code, models, and outputs should maintain traceable lineage.

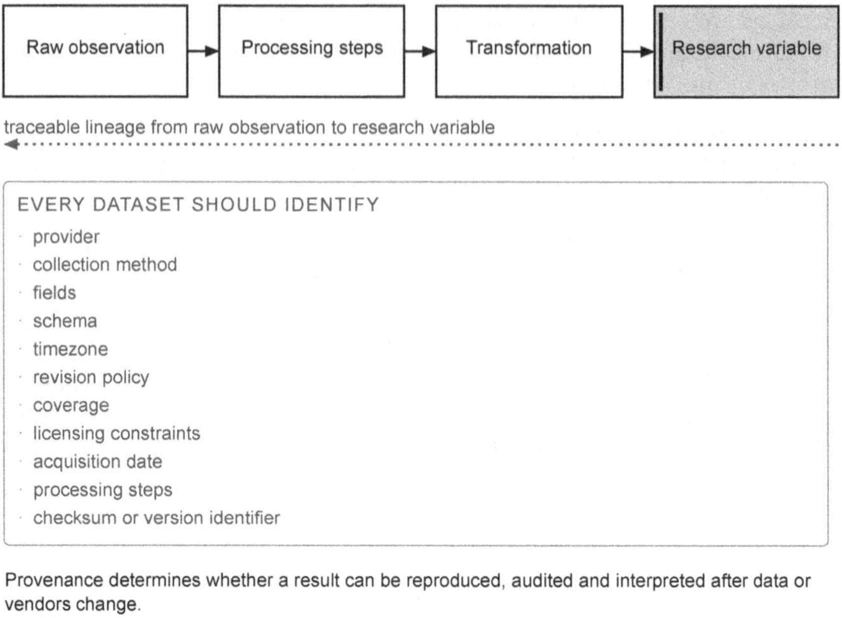

Figure 16.3 — Data Provenance and Transformation Lineage

16.19 Missing Data

Missing data should be classified where possible. A value may be structurally unavailable, absent because the market was closed, missing because of collection failure, filtered by a rule, invalid, delayed, or unknown.

Missing values must not silently become zero, neutral, unchanged, or normal. The treatment should follow the meaning of the missingness and be included in sensitivity analysis.

Missingness status	Interpretation
Structurally unavailable	The field does not exist for this observation
Market closure	No trading session or qualifying event
Vendor missing	Source did not provide the value
Collection failure	Expected data were not captured
Filtered	Removed under a declared rule
Invalid	Observed value failed validation
Unknown	Cause cannot be established

16.20 Outliers and Anomalies

Outliers may be errors, incorrect adjustments, timestamp mismatches, genuine extreme events, or the system behavior of greatest scientific interest.

Automatic deletion can remove exactly the observations needed to understand stress and transition.

Each outlier policy should define detection, investigation, classification, treatment, and sensitivity. Exclusion should be justified by evidence, not by inconvenience to a model.

> **Outlier Principle:** Investigate an outlier before excluding it; extreme observations may be invalid data or important system behavior.

16.21 Data Transformations

Returns, normalization, scaling, smoothing, winsorization, differencing, deseasonalization, volatility adjustment, ranks, and aggregation all change interpretation. A smoothed variable may improve stability while concealing abrupt transitions. A rank may support comparison while discarding magnitude.

Transformations should be documented in order, with parameters and version. Research should distinguish transformations required by the phenomenon from those selected to improve a result.

16.22 Baselines and Comparisons

A result requires a meaningful comparison. Baselines may include unconditional history, the same time of day, a matched instrument, the prior state, a simple model, a random strategy, or an alternative specification.

A complex model should not be evaluated only against no model. The baseline should reflect the intended use and the simplest credible alternative.

16.23 Dependence and Effective Sample Size

Market observations are rarely independent. Dependence arises from time series, overlapping windows, common macro events, index membership, shared ownership, repeated contracts, and cross-sectional correlation.

The number of rows in a dataset can substantially exceed the effective information. Standard errors, confidence intervals, and validation designs should reflect clustering, serial dependence, and overlap.

> **Dependence Principle:** Statistical precision should reflect the dependence structure, not merely the number of observations.

16.24 Nonstationarity

Nonstationarity means that relevant properties of the data-generating process change through time. The mean, variance, correlation, tail behavior, participant mix, microstructure, policy environment, or measurement process may change.

Stationarity should not be treated as all-or-nothing. Some relationships may be locally stable within a configuration and unstable across configurations. Research should test stability over time and define the scope within which a model is intended to operate.

> **Nonstationarity Principle:** Relationships should be assumed capable of changing unless stability is demonstrated.

16.25 Structural Breaks

Structural breaks may arise from regulation, tick-size changes, market fragmentation, new trading technology, monetary-policy shifts, product innovation, crises, or data-source changes.

A model spanning a structural break without acknowledging it may produce an average that describes no actual period. Break detection, segmented analysis, and versioned model eras can be more informative than one full-sample estimate.

16.26 Adaptation and Reflexivity

Participants respond to prices, forecasts, public research, model outputs, and each other. Once a relationship becomes widely used, it may weaken, reverse, migrate to another horizon, or alter execution conditions.

Reflexivity does not imply that every discovered relationship disappears. It means the act of observation, publication, and adoption may change the system to which the finding applies. Model decay should therefore be monitored rather than treated as a surprise.

> **Adaptation Principle:** Research findings may alter the system through participant response and adoption.

16.27 Market States as Research Context

Market-state representations can serve as research context. A relationship may differ across liquidity, positioning, volatility, trend, breadth, resilience, or fragility conditions.

State conditioning must remain cautious because state labels are themselves estimated. Misclassification, threshold design, and model version can create apparent conditional effects. Studies should test whether findings survive alternative state definitions and preserve confidence in the state assignment.

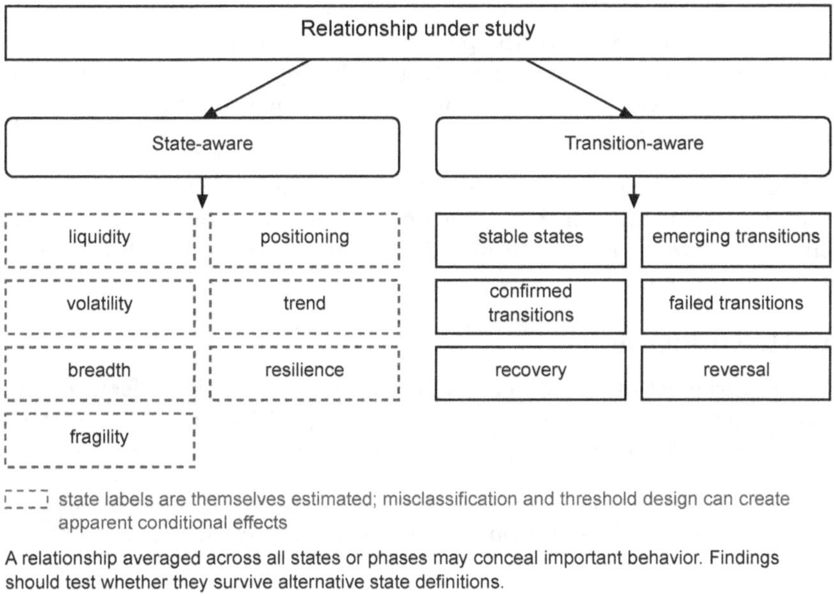

Figure 16.4 — State-Aware and Transition-Aware Research

16.28 Transition-Aware Research

Transition-aware research distinguishes stable states, emerging transitions, confirmed transitions, failed transitions, recovery, and reversal. A relationship averaged across all phases may conceal important behavior.

For example, a liquidity measure may have limited predictive value in stable conditions yet become highly informative during emerging stress. Conversely, a signal that appears useful during one transition episode may fail across repeated transitions.

16.29 Mechanisms and Pathways

A mechanism specifies a plausible sequence through which an effect may arise. Concentrated exposure may interact with adverse movement, risk reduction, liquidity consumption, greater price impact, and volatility expansion.

Mechanistic evidence may come from temporal sequence, participant constraints, cross-market transmission, microstructural observations, interventions, or natural experiments. A mechanism is stronger than a narrative but does not establish causation unless the design supports the counterfactual claim.

16.30 Confounding

A confound influences both the proposed explanatory variable and the outcome. Higher volume may coincide with volatility because both respond to information arrival. Apparent liquidity effects may reflect an unobserved market-wide shock.

Matching, stratification, controls, fixed effects, instrumental variables, and natural experiments can reduce particular confounds, but no method eliminates confounding automatically. Assumptions should be stated and sensitivity examined.

16.31 Endogeneity

Market variables often influence one another. Volatility affects liquidity while liquidity affects volatility. Prices affect positioning while positioning affects prices. Forecasts affect actions while actions affect outcomes.

Regression direction is not causal direction. Research should consider simultaneity, feedback, selection, and measurement error when interpreting coefficients.

16.32 Statistical Significance

Statistical significance is evidence relative to a statistical model and null hypothesis. It is not equivalent to economic importance, causal validity, predictive stability, or decision usefulness.

A small effect can be statistically significant in a very large sample yet operationally irrelevant. A large effect can remain uncertain in a small but important sample. Researchers should report effect size, uncertainty, design assumptions, and context—not only a threshold crossing.

16.33 Economic, Structural, and Decision Significance

Research results should be evaluated across several dimensions. Economic significance concerns magnitude relative to cost and value. Structural significance concerns system function, breadth, persistence, and state dependence. Decision significance concerns whether the information can improve a specified action under real constraints.

These dimensions may disagree. A statistically detectable effect may be too small after costs. A rare structural effect may matter greatly for risk even when average predictive value is modest.

> **Significance Principle:** Evaluate statistical, economic, structural, and decision significance separately.

16.34 Multiple Testing and Researcher Degrees of Freedom

Testing many variables, thresholds, horizons, transformations, and subgroups increases false-discovery risk. The selected result may reflect the search process rather than a stable relationship.

Controls include preregistration, holdout samples, false-discovery procedures, family-wise adjustments, full search disclosure, nested validation, and independent replication. No single correction removes all selection bias.

16.35 Overfitting

Overfitting occurs when a model captures noise or sample-specific structure rather than a repeatable relationship. Warning signs include excessive complexity, unstable parameters, large in-sample performance, weak out-of-sample results, sensitivity to small sample changes, and dependence on one unusual period.

Mechanistic plausibility, simplicity, regularization, and external validation can reduce overfitting risk, but the decisive test remains performance on genuinely unseen conditions.

16.36 Training, Validation, and Test Sets

The training set is used to fit the model. The validation set is used to select features, tune parameters, and compare candidate models. The test set is reserved for final evaluation.

Repeatedly consulting the test set turns it into another validation set. In time-dependent research, chronological separation is usually more defensible than arbitrary random splitting when the intended use is future prediction.

16.37 Walk-Forward Analysis

Walk-forward analysis repeatedly fits a model using past data and evaluates it on a subsequent unseen interval before advancing the window. It approximates historical deployment more closely than one static split.

It does not eliminate data-mining history, publication bias, unavailable real-time data, implementation differences, or structural change. The researcher must still preserve the true information boundary and model-selection history.

16.38 Cross-Validation in Time-Dependent Data

Random cross-validation can leak future information or break temporal dependence. Blocked, rolling, expanding, purged, and embargoed methods may better reflect the information structure.

The appropriate method depends on the prediction horizon, overlap among labels, update cadence, and deployment process. Cross-validation should simulate intended use rather than follow a default software setting.

16.39 Backtesting

A backtest is a historical simulation under declared assumptions. It is not a live experiment, proof of future profitability, or substitute for a plausible mechanism.

A governed backtest should include point-in-time data, costs, slippage, impact, liquidity, latency, position limits, borrow, funding, corporate actions, survivorship, parameter selection, and out-of-sample evaluation. It should also identify where assumptions are idealized.

Backtest requirement	Research question
Information timing	Was every input available at the simulated decision time?
Execution	Can the assumed orders be filled at stated prices and size?
Costs	Are spread, fees, impact, borrow, funding, and tax addressed?
Capacity	Does performance survive realistic capital deployment?
Selection	Were parameters chosen without contaminating the test?
Validation	Does the result survive unseen periods and configurations?

16.40 Transaction Costs and Capacity

Predictive accuracy may not survive implementation. Spread, fees, slippage, impact, borrow, funding, hedging, latency, and taxes can dominate a small statistical edge.

Capacity asks how much capital can use the method before the method changes its own execution conditions. A finding may be valid at small scale and unusable at larger scale.

16.41 Robustness Analysis

Robustness analysis asks whether the interpretation survives reasonable alternatives: nearby thresholds, alternative definitions, different periods, instruments, controls, cost assumptions, state definitions, and simpler models.

A result that survives only one exact specification should be described as fragile. Robustness does not prove truth, but it reduces the chance that the conclusion depends on an arbitrary choice.

> **Robustness Principle:** Findings should be tested across reasonable definitions, assumptions, periods, and configurations.

16.42 Sensitivity Analysis

Sensitivity analysis intentionally varies assumptions such as lookback, horizon, threshold, normalization, missing-data treatment, transaction cost, sample, model form, and state definition.

The goal is not to find one setting that preserves the result. It is to map where the conclusion is stable, where it changes, and which assumptions dominate.

> **Sensitivity Principle:** A result is more credible when its interpretation survives reasonable changes in assumptions.

16.43 Placebo and Falsification Tests

Placebo and falsification tests challenge a claim by examining conditions where the proposed effect should not appear. Examples include shifting timestamps, randomizing labels, testing an irrelevant outcome, using a pre-event period, or applying the mechanism to a market where it should not operate.

A placebo result similar to the main result may reveal leakage, common trends, or design artifact.

16.44 Negative and Positive Controls

A negative control should not show the hypothesized effect. A positive control should show an effect already expected under the design. Together they help determine whether the method can distinguish signal from artifact.

Controls should be chosen from the mechanism and measurement structure, not added cosmetically after the result is known.

16.45 Replication

Replication asks whether a comparable finding appears with new data, another period, a different market, or an independent implementation. Exact, temporal, cross-market, conceptual, and independent replications answer different questions.

A failed replication should trigger investigation of scope, implementation, data, power, structural change, and selection. It should not be concealed or dismissed solely because the original result was compelling.

> **Replication Principle:** A finding becomes stronger when it survives new data, independent implementation, or a different setting.

16.46 Reproducibility

Reproducibility asks whether the same result can be regenerated from the same data, code, environment, and protocol. A reproducible package may include the protocol, source data or access instructions, data dictionary, transformations, environment specification, code, outputs, checksums, model version, and known deviations.

Licensing and confidentiality may limit data sharing. In those cases, the method, access constraints, and internal reproduction process should still be documented.

Reproducibility	**Replication**
Same data and procedure	New data, period, market, or implementation
Checks execution consistency	Challenges generality and stability
Requires lineage and environment	Requires comparable design and independence
Can succeed while finding is narrow	Can fail because scope or system changed

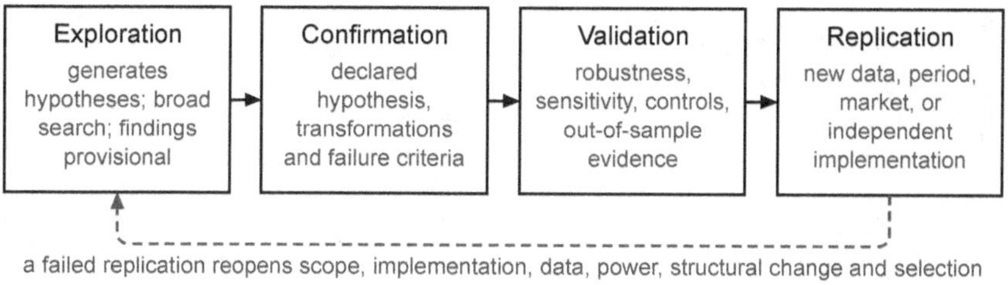

REPRODUCIBILITY	REPLICATION
Same data and procedure	New data, period, market, or implementation
Checks execution consistency	Challenges generality and stability
Requires lineage and environment	Requires comparable design and independence
Can succeed while finding is narrow	Can fail because scope or system changed

Reproducibility establishes that the procedure can be repeated. Replication addresses whether the finding is more general and credible.

Figure 16.5 — Exploration, Confirmation, Validation, and Replication

16.47 The Research Ledger

The Research Ledger is the governed record of a study's evolution. It preserves what was planned, what was executed, what changed, what was found, how the work was challenged, and the current disposition.

The ledger should include the research identifier, question, hypothesis, claim type, owner, protocol version, data versions, code version, analysis runs, deviations, results, review comments, replication status, limitations, disposition, and revision history.

> **Ledger Principle:** Material research should preserve protocol, execution, deviation, review, and disposition as one traceable history.

The Research Ledger

- research identifier
- question
- hypothesis
- claim type
- owner
- protocol version
- data versions
- code version
- analysis runs
- deviations
- results
- review comments
- replication status
- limitations
- disposition
- revision history

The ledger preserves what was planned, what was executed, what changed, what was found, how the work was challenged, and the current disposition — as one traceable history.

Figure 16.6 — The Research Ledger

16.48 Protocol Deviations

Research rarely proceeds exactly as planned. A deviation record should state what changed, why, when, who approved it, whether the change occurred before or after results were observed, and how interpretation is affected.

Undocumented flexibility creates hidden researcher degrees of freedom. A justified deviation is not misconduct; an undisclosed result-driven deviation weakens trust.

16.49 Research Review

Review should examine question clarity, claim strength, measurement validity, sample construction, dependence, design, analysis, robustness, interpretation, limitations, reproducibility, and conflicts.

Review must be capable of changing the conclusion. A checklist completed after approval has already been decided is not meaningful challenge.

16.50 Independent Challenge and Red-Team Research

Independent challenge may attempt to reproduce the result, identify leakage, vary assumptions, test competing explanations, locate structural breaks, search for failed periods, and evaluate implementation realism.

A research claim becomes stronger when it survives competent attempts to weaken it. The goal is not adversarial theater but discovery of hidden fragility.

> **Challenge Principle:** Research claims should be exposed to competent attempts at disconfirmation.

16.51 Model Validation

When research produces a model, validation should examine conceptual soundness, data quality, implementation accuracy, performance, stability, sensitivity, limitations, monitoring, and governance.

A model may reproduce its code and still fail conceptually. It may perform historically and still be unsuitable for deployment. Chapter 17 develops model architecture; this chapter establishes the research evidence required to support it.

16.52 Research and Decision Use

A statistically credible finding may still be unsuitable for decisions. Decision usefulness depends on timeliness, cost, capacity, risk, horizon, stability, interpretability, and participant constraints.

The boundary established in Chapter 15 must remain intact: research evidence informs a decision environment but does not determine one universal action.

> **Decision-Boundary Principle:** Evidence that supports a research claim does not automatically justify an action.

16.53 Publication Bias

Publication bias favors statistically significant, novel, favorable, and narratively clean results. A research program distorted by selective survival will overstate confidence and underestimate instability.

The Institute should preserve null studies, failed replications, retired models, contradictory evidence, and unresolved questions. Publication status and evidentiary status are not the same.

16.54 Researcher Incentives and Conflicts

Ownership of a strategy, platform marketing, compensation, publication pressure, model sponsorship, and reputational commitment can influence question selection, analysis, interpretation, and disclosure.

Material conflicts should be recorded and governed. Technical sophistication does not neutralize incentives.

16.55 Proprietary Research and Transparency

Not all market data or methods can be public. Research may be internally reproducible, independently auditable, externally replicable, or publicly reproducible. These are distinct transparency levels.

Proprietary status does not excuse undocumented methods. Where disclosure is limited, internal lineage, independent review, access controls, and clear external claims become more important.

16.56 Ethical Research Practice

Ethical research requires lawful data use, respect for privacy and confidentiality, accurate attribution, avoidance of manipulation, and honest presentation of performance and limitations.

A technically correct analysis may still be ethically deficient if it uses confidential information improperly, hides adverse evidence, exaggerates certainty, or misleads participants about risk.

16.57 Research Failure Analysis

A failed study should be classified rather than discarded. Failure may arise from the question, data, measurement, design, implementation, statistics, interpretation, replication, environmental change, or ordinary null results.

A null result is not automatically a research failure. It may be the correct outcome of a well-designed investigation and can materially improve the knowledge state.

Failure category	**Illustrative issue**
Question failure	Question is ambiguous or unanswerable with available evidence
Data failure	Coverage, timing, or provenance is inadequate
Measurement failure	Variable does not represent the intended construct
Design failure	Comparison or identification is unsuitable
Implementation failure	Code or pipeline does not match the method
Statistical failure	Power, dependence, or inference is mishandled
Interpretation failure	Claim exceeds the evidence
Replication failure	Finding does not survive new data or implementation
Environmental change	The system changed materially
Ordinary null result	The hypothesized effect is not supported

16.58 Research Disposition

Research status should not be reduced to pass or fail. Useful dispositions include proposed, exploratory, protocol approved, in progress, analyzed, internally reproduced, independently reviewed, replicated, conditionally supported, unsupported, contradicted, and retired.

Disposition should reflect evidence, scope, replication, and current relevance. A retired model may remain historically valuable.

Disposition	Meaning
Exploratory	Pattern identified; confirmation not completed
Conditionally supported	Evidence supports the claim within stated scope
Replicated	Comparable result obtained with new evidence
Unsupported	Planned test did not support the claim
Contradicted	Evidence materially opposes the claim
Retired	No longer approved for current use

16.59 Knowledge Updating

Research should update confidence, scope, definitions, mechanisms, models, questions, and decision relevance. A result may strengthen one part of a claim while narrowing another.

The knowledge state should preserve prior versions and explain why confidence changed. Correction is not institutional failure; it is the mechanism through which a research program becomes more reliable.

> **Knowledge-Update Principle:** The purpose of research is not to defend the original hypothesis but to improve the quality of the knowledge state.

16.60 Worked Example: Liquidity Resilience and Price Impact

Research question: Is slower displayed-depth replenishment associated with greater subsequent short-horizon price impact under comparable market conditions?

The claim is associative with a possible mechanistic interpretation, not automatically causal. The design defines the universe and event time, calculates replenishment, measures subsequent impact, controls for volatility, volume, spread, time of day, and instrument, stratifies by market state, and preserves a chronological validation period.

Competing explanations include information arrival, hidden liquidity, volatility shock, venue fragmentation, and trade-size composition. Validation uses alternative replenishment definitions, matched samples, state-conditioned analysis, an out-of-sample period, negative controls, and an independent implementation.

A robust association would support liquidity resilience as relevant evidence. It would not alone prove that slower replenishment causes price impact.

16.61 Worked Example: State-Transition Classifier

Research question: Can a multidomain classifier identify meaningful structural transitions more reliably than a simple volatility threshold?

The evaluation includes descriptive validity, discriminant validity, transition lag, false-transition rate, stability, missing-data behavior, out-of-sample performance, state dependence, and model-version comparison. The baseline must be simple enough to interpret and strong enough to be credible.

Even if the classifier performs better, the result does not establish one universal trading action. It supports a research claim about transition representation, not a participant-independent decision.

16.62 Worked Example: Failed Predictive Signal

A signal appears predictive in sample but fails out of sample. Review shows that many thresholds were tested, the best result was selected retrospectively, transaction costs were omitted, the test period overlapped tuning, and performance depended on one unusual episode.

The correct disposition is: unsupported as a stable predictive finding; retained as exploratory evidence and as a case study in selection bias. The failed result remains in the Research Ledger so later researchers do not unknowingly repeat the same search.

Market Systems Research Record

The following record consolidates the chapter's minimum documentation standard. It is a governance template rather than a substitute for domain-specific methods.

Field	Required content
Research question	What is being investigated?
Research object	Observation, measurement, relationship, state, transition, model, or decision process
Claim type	Descriptive, associative, predictive, mechanistic, causal, or decision-related
Hypothesis	What proposition is being evaluated?
Predictions	What observations are expected?
Revision conditions	What would weaken or alter the claim?
Universe	What population and sample are studied?
Time structure	Period, horizon, event alignment, and cadence
Data	Sources, versions, provenance, and licensing
Measurements	Definitions, transformations, and limitations
Design	Comparisons, controls, exclusions, and analysis
Dependence	Temporal and cross-sectional structure
Robustness	Alternative specifications and sensitivity
Validation	In-sample, out-of-sample, walk-forward, and controls
Reproduction	Can the same result be regenerated?
Replication	Has the finding survived new evidence or independent testing?

Field	Required content
Limitations	Known weaknesses and unknowns
Conflicts	Ownership, incentives, or sponsorship
Disposition	Current evidentiary status
Revision history	How the research evolved

Responsible Research Principles

Research-Object Principle: Method should follow the question and research object.

Claim-Proportionality Principle: Design strength must match claim strength.

Configuration Principle: Findings should identify the configurations and horizons in which they were observed.

Temporal Integrity Principle: No study may use information before it was available.

Measurement Principle: Research depends on governed, valid, and traceable measurements.

Exploration–Confirmation Principle: Exploration generates hypotheses; confirmation evaluates them.

Dependence Principle: Precision must reflect dependence, not row count.

Nonstationarity Principle: Relationships should be assumed capable of change unless stability is shown.

Adaptation Principle: Participants may alter a relationship through response and adoption.

Robustness Principle: Findings should survive reasonable alternative assumptions.

Reproducibility Principle: A result should be regenerable from governed data, code, environment, and protocol.

Replication Principle: A finding strengthens when it survives new evidence or independent implementation.

Negative-Evidence Principle: Null results and failed replications belong in the evidence base.

Challenge Principle: Claims should be exposed to competent disconfirmation attempts.

Revision Principle: Research should improve knowledge rather than defend the original hypothesis.

Decision-Boundary Principle: A valid finding does not automatically determine action.

Provenance Principle: Data, transformations, code, models, and outputs require traceable lineage.

Research-Governance Principle: Material studies require protocol, ownership, review, deviation, disposition, and version records.

Chapter Summary

Market research requires more than data collection, statistical significance, or backtesting. It requires a governed connection among question, claim, hypothesis, design, measurement, analysis, interpretation, validation, replication, and revision.

Markets are evolving systems. Participants adapt, institutions change, data-generating processes shift, and discovered relationships may weaken after adoption. Findings should therefore be interpreted relative to universe, horizon, market configuration, transition context, data version, and institutional environment.

Research design should be proportional to claim strength. Descriptive, associative, predictive, mechanistic, causal, and decision claims require different evidence. Temporal sequence and predictive accuracy do not by themselves establish causation.

Measurement validity, provenance, missingness, event alignment, dependence, nonstationarity, structural breaks, selection, and implementation assumptions are part of scientific validity rather than secondary technical details.

Exploration and confirmation should be separated. Robustness, out-of-sample validation, reproducibility, replication, controls, and independent challenge help determine whether a result is stable or sample-specific.

Null results, failed replications, abandoned models, and contradictory evidence should remain in the research record. The purpose of research is not to defend an original hypothesis but to improve the state of knowledge through transparent correction and cumulative learning.

Established Knowledge and Institute Perspective

This chapter draws on established work in philosophy of science, experimental design, observational research, causal inference, econometrics, time-series analysis, market microstructure, statistical learning, machine learning, reproducible research, preregistration, replication science, model validation, robust statistics, structural-break analysis, research ethics, and scientific governance.

The Institute does not claim originality for hypothesis testing, falsifiability, train–validation–test separation, cross-validation, walk-forward analysis, causal inference, significance testing, robustness checks, replication, data lineage, research protocols, or model validation. Its contribution is the integration of these practices with market configuration, transition context, measurement governance, a Research Ledger, versioned knowledge, and explicit separation between research validity and decision use.

Questions for Reflection

1. What distinguishes research from data analysis?
2. What makes market research different from research in a stable laboratory system?
3. Why should the research object be defined before the method?
4. How should research design vary by claim type?
5. What distinguishes a claim, hypothesis, and prediction?
6. What makes a hypothesis open to revision?
7. Why must exploratory and confirmatory work be separated?
8. What should a research protocol contain?
9. How does the target population differ from the analysis sample?
10. What forms of selection bias arise in market data?
11. What is look-ahead bias?
12. How does survivorship bias distort research?
13. What distinguishes measurement validity from reliability?
14. Why is data provenance part of scientific validity?
15. Why should missing values not automatically be treated as zero?
16. Why may outliers be scientifically important?
17. How do transformations change interpretation?
18. Why does every result require a baseline?
19. How does dependence affect effective sample size?
20. What is nonstationarity?
21. What creates structural breaks in markets?
22. How can adaptation change a discovered relationship?
23. Why should research be conditioned on market state where appropriate?
24. What does transition-aware research add?
25. What distinguishes mechanism from association?

26. What is confounding?
27. What is endogeneity?
28. Why is statistical significance different from economic significance?
29. What is multiple-testing risk?
30. How does overfitting arise?
31. Why must training, validation, and test data remain distinct?
32. What does walk-forward analysis approximate?
33. Why can random cross-validation be misleading in time-series research?
34. What assumptions should a governed backtest disclose?
35. Why do transaction costs and capacity matter?
36. What makes a result robust?
37. What is the role of sensitivity analysis?
38. How do placebo and falsification tests challenge a claim?
39. What distinguishes reproducibility from replication?
40. What should a Research Ledger preserve?
41. Why must protocol deviations be documented?
42. What should independent research review examine?
43. How can incentives distort research?
44. Why should negative and null results be retained?
45. What is a research disposition?
46. Why does a valid research finding not automatically justify action?
47. What evidence should cause a research claim to be narrowed?
48. Why should knowledge remain versioned and provisional?

Chapter 17. Frameworks and Models

Constructing Useful Representations of Market Systems

Chapter Purpose

Financial markets are too complex to observe, explain, or govern without abstraction. Researchers and practitioners therefore rely on frameworks, taxonomies, equations, indicators, scores, state representations, simulations, statistical models, machine-learning systems, and decision tools. These abstractions can improve understanding, but they can also conceal assumptions, combine incompatible measurements, create false precision, and encourage users to treat model output as fact.

This chapter defines frameworks and models, distinguishes their purposes and levels, explains how model architecture connects concepts to measurements and outputs, and establishes requirements for decomposition, validation, uncertainty, monitoring, documentation, change control, and retirement. Its purpose is not to prescribe one preferred modeling technique. It is to provide a common architecture for constructing and evaluating many kinds of representations responsibly.

Learning Objectives

- distinguish frameworks, models, indicators, scores, classifications, rules, forecasts, and decision processes;
- define model purpose, scope, intended use, prohibited use, and claim boundaries before selecting a method;
- explain the conceptual, data, measurement, feature, model, output, interpretation, decision-use, and governance layers;
- evaluate conceptual, statistical, machine-learning, rule-based, structural, reduced-form, dynamic, and hybrid models;
- document inputs, features, assumptions, parameters, thresholds, constraints, outputs, uncertainty, and dependencies;
- distinguish verification, validation, benchmarking, calibration, discrimination, robustness, and stress testing;
- govern missing data, drift, feedback, overrides, deployment, incidents, versioning, and retirement;
- construct and use a Governed Model Record without confusing model output with market truth or universal action.

17.1 From Research Evidence to Model Architecture

Chapter 16 established how market claims should be investigated, challenged, reproduced, and revised. A model is one possible product of that research, but it is not the inevitable product of every study. Research may instead produce a measurement definition, a documented empirical relationship, a conceptual mechanism, a classification scheme, or evidence that an earlier model should be narrowed or retired.

A model becomes appropriate when a defined purpose requires selected features of a market system to be represented, transformed, compared, simulated, classified, or projected in a repeatable way. The model should therefore emerge from a clear question and evidence base rather than from attachment to a favored technique.

> **Research-to-Model Principle:** Research supports model construction only when the intended purpose, represented object, evidence, assumptions, and limitations are explicit.

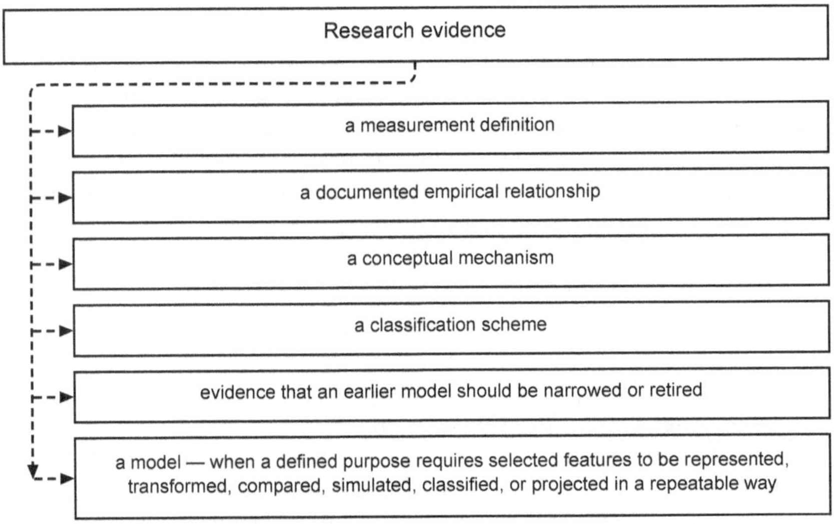

A model is one possible product of research, not the inevitable product of every study. All six outcomes are drawn at equal weight.

Figure 17.1 — From Research Evidence to Model Architecture

17.2 What Is a Framework?

A framework is an organized conceptual structure that identifies relevant objects, relationships, categories, boundaries, and questions for a stated field of inquiry. Frameworks help define terminology, organize evidence, reveal omissions, guide model design, and connect research areas.

The four observational domains, the evidence hierarchy, the market-configuration architecture, the Decision Environment, and the Research Ledger are frameworks. They organize inquiry, but they do not automatically quantify relationships, generate predictions, validate themselves, prove causation, or determine decisions.

17.3 What Is a Model?

A model is a simplified, purpose-specific representation of selected features, relationships, or processes within a defined system. Every model selects some information, imposes structure, and omits other information.

A complete model description should identify the object represented, purpose, scope, universe, horizon, inputs, assumptions, transformations, outputs, uncertainty, validation status, limitations, and version. A model without these boundaries is difficult to interpret and easy to misuse.

> **Representation Principle:** A model represents selected features of the market; it is not the market itself.

17.4 Framework, Model, Indicator, Score, and Rule

These constructs often appear together but perform different roles. Confusing them causes a measurement to be treated as a model, a score to be treated as an explanation, or a rule to be treated as a forecast.

Construct	Primary role	Boundary
Framework	Organizes concepts and inquiry	Does not validate or quantify itself
Model	Represents selected relationships or processes	Purpose- and assumption-dependent
Indicator	Measures or signals a defined feature	May cover only one dimension
Score	Compresses inputs into a numerical or ordinal result	Can conceal dispersion and weighting
Classification	Assigns an observation to a category	Depends on boundaries and labels

Construct	Primary role	Boundary
Rule	Specifies a response under conditions	Does not prove the condition is true
Forecast	Estimates a future outcome	Requires target, horizon, and calibration
Decision process	Selects among actions under objectives and constraints	Participant-dependent

17.5 Models as Selective Representations

Selection occurs through variable choice, time horizon, sampling, aggregation, mathematical form, threshold design, category design, estimation method, and scenario choice. These selections are not necessarily defects; they are how abstraction becomes possible.

The scientific obligation is to make the selections visible and test whether they are appropriate for the stated purpose. Omission is unavoidable. Hidden omission is not.

> **Selection Principle:** Every model is a statement about what the designer believes matters for the stated purpose.

17.6 Model Purpose Taxonomy

A model cannot be judged without knowing what it was designed to do. Descriptive, measurement, classification, explanatory, predictive, simulation, optimization, decision-support, execution, and control models require different evidence and should not be evaluated by one universal standard.

Purpose	Primary task	Typical output	Common misuse
Descriptive	Summarize observed conditions	Profile or state summary	Treated as forecast
Measurement	Estimate a construct	Value with uncertainty	Treated as direct observation
Classification	Assign categories	Class or probability	Treated as natural regime
Explanatory	Represent relationships or mechanisms	Coefficients or pathways	Causation overstated
Predictive	Estimate future outcomes	Forecast distribution	Decision relevance assumed

Purpose	Primary task	Typical output	Common misuse
Simulation	Explore behavior under assumptions	Scenario paths	Simulation treated as reality
Optimization	Select mathematical solution	Optimal allocation or action	Wrong objective mistaken for right answer
Decision support	Compare alternatives	Consequences and margins	Universal action implied
Execution	Guide implementation	Orders or schedules	Market impact understated
Control	Monitor and adjust system	Alerts or adjustments	Automation authority unclear

17.7 Conceptual Models

Conceptual models describe relationships without necessarily producing numerical output. Examples include a liquidity-volatility feedback loop, a positioning-adjustment pathway, the configuration-to-state hierarchy, and the trigger-mechanism-feedback-outcome structure.

Their value lies in organizing mechanisms, identifying variables, generating hypotheses, and exposing assumptions. Their limitations include qualitative ambiguity, difficult calibration, incomplete causal identification, and susceptibility to narrative confirmation.

17.8 Mathematical and Statistical Models

Mathematical and statistical models express relationships through equations, distributions, or estimation procedures. Regression, state-space models, volatility models, hazard models, option-pricing models, transition matrices, and factor models belong to this broad family.

Formal mathematics improves precision when definitions and assumptions are appropriate. It cannot compensate for invalid measurements, omitted dependencies, nonstationarity, or a poorly defined purpose.

> **Mathematical-Form Principle:** Mathematical form can make assumptions more visible, but it does not make them true.

17.9 Machine-Learning Models

Machine-learning systems can represent nonlinear relationships, interactions, and high-dimensional patterns. Their flexibility may improve prediction or classification when the research design, data volume, and validation structure support it.

The same flexibility creates overfitting, leakage, instability, opacity, proxy dependence, distribution-shift risk, and excessive confidence. Machine learning is neither categorically superior nor categorically inferior; it is a family of methods whose value depends on purpose and governance.

Machine learning is not the only family of automated systems now used in market work. Generative and agentic systems—those that produce open-ended output, invoke tools, retrieve external context, or take sequential actions toward a goal—raise governance questions that validation designed for predictive models does not by itself answer. Their output may be non-deterministic, sensitive to context and phrasing, dependent on data the operator does not control, and consequential through action rather than through a score. Where such systems are used, governance should address purpose, permitted use, data provenance, evaluation method, monitoring, human oversight, and failure containment alongside the practices developed in this chapter. Those practices remain necessary for such systems; they should not be assumed sufficient.

17.10 Rule-Based and Expert Models

Rule-based systems encode thresholds, logical relationships, exceptions, and domain expertise. They can be transparent, consistent, auditable, and directly controllable.

They can also become rigid, sensitive to boundaries, incomplete in exceptional conditions, and costly to maintain. Expert assumptions remain model choices even when they are expressed in prose rather than equations.

17.11 Hybrid Models

Hybrid models combine statistical estimation, machine learning, expert rules, structural constraints, and human review. One component may estimate probabilities, another may enforce data-quality gates, a structural layer may combine dimensions, and a human reviewer may handle exceptional states.

Hybridization can improve performance and governance, but only when responsibility and interfaces are explicit. Otherwise, failures can move between components without a clear owner.

Model family	Strengths	Principal risks
Conceptual	Mechanism organization and hypothesis generation	Ambiguity and narrative confirmation
Statistical	Formal estimation and inference	Misspecification and unstable assumptions
Machine learning	Flexible nonlinear representation	Overfitting, leakage, opacity, drift

Model family	Strengths	Principal risks
Rule based	Transparency and operational control	Rigidity and threshold sensitivity
Hybrid	Combines complementary strengths	Boundary and responsibility ambiguity

17.12 Structural and Reduced-Form Models

A structural model attempts to represent mechanisms, constraints, or participant behavior. A reduced-form model represents empirical relationships without fully modeling the underlying mechanism.

A reduced-form model may forecast well without explaining why. A structural model may explain plausibly while forecasting poorly. Explanatory ambition and predictive performance should therefore be evaluated separately.

17.13 Deterministic and Probabilistic Models

A deterministic model produces the same output from the same inputs without explicitly representing outcome probability. A probabilistic model represents uncertainty through distributions or probabilities.

Deterministic output can still be uncertain because inputs are noisy, thresholds are designed, model form may be wrong, and the environment may change. A probabilistic output is not automatically calibrated merely because it contains a number between zero and one.

17.14 Static and Dynamic Models

A static model represents relationships at a point or over a fixed sample. A dynamic model represents change through time using lags, state evolution, transition probabilities, feedback, updating, or persistence.

The state and transition architectures developed in Chapters 13 and 14 are dynamic when they explicitly represent how configuration evolves. Time dependence introduces additional requirements for alignment, lag structure, stability, and drift monitoring.

17.15 Observable and Latent Variables

Price, volume, quotes, trades, and published reports may be directly recorded. Liquidity resilience, crowding, dealer exposure, market state, transition maturity, and participant intent are usually latent or inferred.

Every latent variable should disclose its inference method, proxy assumptions, uncertainty, validation evidence, and competing interpretations.

Latent-Variable Principle: An inferred variable should never be presented with the epistemic status of a directly observed fact.

17.16 The Model Architecture Stack

A governed model should preserve the path from market phenomenon to recorded data, controlled measurements, features, model transformation, output, interpretation, and decision context. A governance layer surrounds the entire chain.

Every layer introduces assumptions, dependencies, and possible failure. A score that appears without this lineage can be persuasive while remaining scientifically weak.

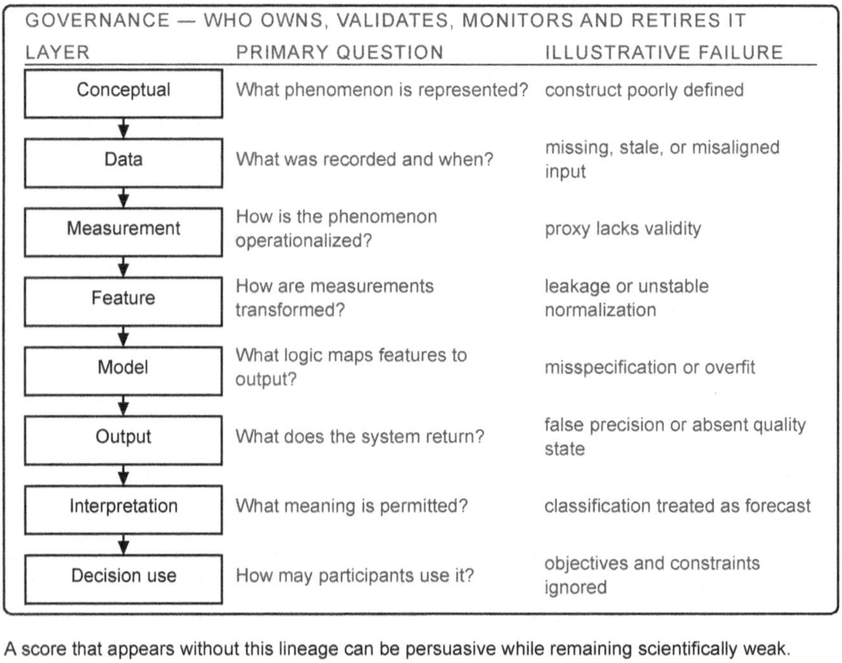

Figure 17.2 — The Model Architecture Stack

Layer	Primary question	Illustrative failure
Conceptual	What phenomenon is represented?	Construct poorly defined
Data	What was recorded and when?	Missing, stale, or misaligned input

Layer	Primary question	Illustrative failure
Measurement	How is the phenomenon operationalized?	Proxy lacks validity
Feature	How are measurements transformed?	Leakage or unstable normalization
Model	What logic maps features to output?	Misspecification or overfit
Output	What does the system return?	False precision or absent quality state
Interpretation	What meaning is permitted?	Classification treated as forecast
Decision use	How may participants use it?	Objectives and constraints ignored
Governance	Who owns, validates, monitors, and retires it?	Uncontrolled change or orphaned model

17.17 Inputs and Input Contracts

Each input should have a contract specifying its name, source, definition, unit, timestamp, expected range, freshness, missingness rule, quality status, and version. Input contracts turn hidden assumptions into testable interfaces.

A model should not silently accept stale values, changed units, schema drift, impossible values, unknown time alignment, or undocumented fallbacks.

17.18 Feature Construction

Features may be raw, transformed, normalized, ranked, aggregated, lagged, differenced, smoothed, state-conditioned, or interaction-based. Feature construction can create more model risk than the final algorithm because it determines what information enters and how it is represented.

A feature is a designed measurement transformation, not a naturally occurring fact.

17.19 Normalization

Normalization supports comparison across instruments, periods, scales, and distributions. Common methods include z-scores, percentiles, ranks, min-max scaling, volatility scaling, and rolling baselines.

Each method changes interpretation. Rolling normalization can make identical raw values imply different relative conditions at different times, while fixed normalization may become obsolete after structural change.

17.20 Aggregation

Aggregation may occur across time, instruments, domains, participants, scenarios, and model outputs. It reduces complexity but can conceal dispersion, contradiction, concentration, missingness, and tail behavior.

An aggregate should preserve access to the components and distributions it compresses.

17.21 Weighting

Weights may be equal, expert-assigned, statistically estimated, optimized, time-varying, or state-dependent. Every method should explain its rationale, estimation period, constraints, normalization, sensitivity, and update frequency.

Equal weighting is not assumption-free. It assigns the same importance by design.

17.22 Thresholds and Boundaries

Thresholds convert continuous variation into categories, alerts, or actions. They may be based on empirical distributions, economic meaning, risk limits, calibration, operational requirements, or expert judgment.

Thresholds introduce discontinuity, boundary sensitivity, oscillation, and path dependence. Entry, exit, persistence, and hysteresis rules should therefore be documented and validated.

17.23 Parameters and Hyperparameters

Parameters are values estimated or assigned within a fitted model. Hyperparameters govern model structure or the fitting process. Both require provenance, tuning method, versioning, sensitivity analysis, and review.

Repeated tuning against a test set weakens the test set's independence and can create hidden overfitting.

17.24 Model Assumptions

Assumptions may concern stationarity, independence, distribution, linearity, liquidity, rationality, data completeness, execution, participant behavior, transaction costs, or causal structure.

Assumptions should be classified as explicit, tested, partially tested, operational, unverifiable, or currently violated. A model limitation often begins as an assumption that is forgotten after deployment.

17.25 Constraints

Constraints can improve realism or governance. Examples include nonnegative weights, leverage caps, monotonicity, bounded probabilities, turnover limits, minimum data quality, economic sign restrictions, and exposure limits.

Constraints are design decisions. They should not be reported as empirical findings merely because they appear in the fitted output.

17.26 Model Outputs

A governed output should contain more than a primary number or class. Depending on purpose, it may need a point estimate, interval, category, confidence, freshness, quality status, contributing components, version, warning state, and missingness status.

Output field	Required meaning
Value or class	Primary result under the model definition
Effective time	When the result applies
Horizon	Interval represented or forecast
Quality status	Validity, freshness, and completeness
Uncertainty	Specific uncertainty attached to the claim
Components	Inputs or contributions supporting decomposition
Version	Exact model and parameter version
Warnings	Scope, fallback, disagreement, or exceptional condition
Permitted interpretation	What the output may legitimately mean

17.27 Confidence and Uncertainty

Uncertainty may arise from data, measurement, parameters, model form, classification, future realization, environment, and implementation. A single confidence score can conceal these distinctions.

Uncertainty should therefore be attached to specific claims and outputs. High confidence in data freshness does not imply high confidence in mechanism, forecast, or decision usefulness.

17.28 Probability Outputs

A probability output should identify the event, horizon, conditioning information, reference class, model version, calibration evidence, uncertainty, and update time.

A probability of transition is incomplete unless transition is formally defined. A probability is a model-conditioned statement, not a property that exists independently of the model and information set.

17.29 Model Explainability

Explainability may involve global structure, local feature contributions, scenario response, sensitivity, counterfactual behavior, rule trace, or component decomposition.

Explainability is purpose-dependent. A developer, validator, regulator, researcher, and end user may require different forms of explanation. A technically available explanation is not useful if it does not answer the user's actual governance question.

17.30 Interpretability and Predictive Performance

Interpretability and performance are not simple opposites. A model may be interpretable and weak, opaque and strong, interpretable and strong, or opaque and unstable.

The relevant requirement is whether interpretability is sufficient for the model's purpose, stakes, criticality, and decision influence.

17.31 Model Ensembles

Ensembles combine several models and may reduce variance or broaden representation. They can also hide common dependence, create false diversification, complicate attribution, and compound complexity.

Several models that use the same data, features, labels, and assumptions do not constitute independent confirmation.

17.32 Model Disagreement

Model disagreement may arise from different horizons, inputs, assumptions, purposes, quality states, or responses to structural change. It may be informative rather than a defect.

Automatically averaging disagreement can conceal the exact conditions in which the models diverge. Governed systems should preserve disagreement, investigate its cause, and distinguish expected diversity from unexpected failure.

17.33 Composite Models

Composite models combine several dimensions into one representation, such as a state score, fragility score, systemic-stress index, or opportunity index.

Composite design should preserve component visibility, weighting rationale, missingness behavior, sensitivity, alternative specifications, and versioning. Compression is useful only when the path back to evidence remains available.

> **Decomposition Principle:** Compressed outputs should remain traceable to inputs, transformations, assumptions, weights, thresholds, and quality states.

17.34 The Structural State Vector as a Model Architecture

The Structural State Vector can be represented as SSV(t) = [L, P, V, T, B, R, F, Q, C], where the components summarize selected liquidity, positioning, volatility, trend, breadth, resilience, fragility, quality, and confidence information.

The vector is not merely a list of direct observations. Each component may contain several measurements, transformations, thresholds, latent estimates, and quality conditions. It is therefore a model architecture for controlled compression, not a self-validating representation of the market.

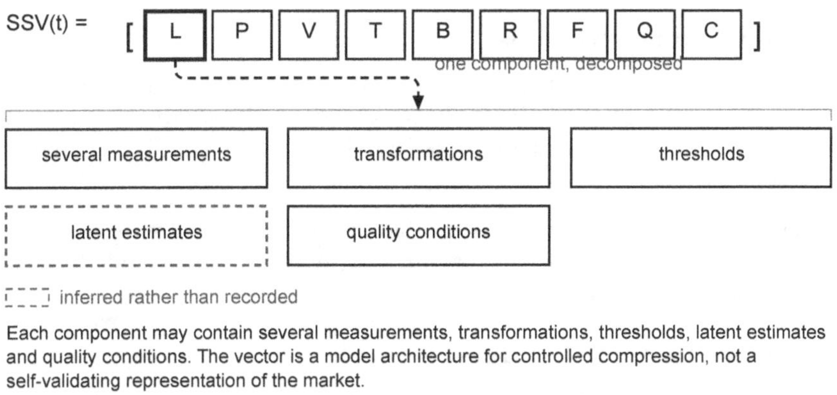

Figure 17.3 — Structural State Vector as a Decomposable Model

17.35 The Market Compass as a Presentation Model

The Market Compass is a presentation model layered above the underlying state architecture. Its purpose is to communicate selected multidomain conditions without replacing the underlying measurements and evidence.

It should not become a separate source of truth, hide component disagreement, imply equal distance or symmetry without validation, or convert market condition into universal action.

> **Presentation Principle:** A visualization may summarize a model, but it should not silently redefine it.

17.36 Transition Models

Transition models may estimate configuration change, transition maturity, state-change probability, persistence, reversal, and false-transition risk.

They must preserve the distinction among current state, fast trajectory, transition evidence, confirmed transition, and destination forecast. A model that collapses these concepts may appear decisive while obscuring important uncertainty.

17.37 Forecasting Models

A forecasting model should define its target, horizon, information set, update cadence, loss function, baseline, calibration, and cost of error.

Forecast quality depends on the intended use. Directional accuracy, magnitude error, tail sensitivity, timing, and asymmetric consequences may matter differently. Statistical improvement over baseline does not automatically imply economic or decision value.

17.38 Scenario Models

Scenario models represent conditional pathways rather than one predicted future. They should state the starting configuration, assumptions, trigger, pathway, signposts, participant responses, invalidation conditions, and possible destination.

Scenarios should not be assigned probabilities merely to create an appearance of precision. Probability requires an explicit model and defensible calibration.

17.39 Simulation Models

Simulations can explore distributions, feedback, stress, liquidity impact, portfolio response, transition pathways, and policy changes.

Their validity depends on behavioral rules, parameter choices, initial conditions, interaction structure, and external assumptions. A simulated outcome is evidence about the model under its assumptions, not direct evidence that the market will behave identically.

17.40 Optimization Models

Optimization models select a mathematical solution under an objective and constraints. They are useful when the problem is well specified and uncertainty is managed.

They can produce unstable estimates, corner solutions, impractical turnover, hidden utility assumptions, and false precision. Optimization finds the best solution to the specified problem, not necessarily the right solution to the real problem.

17.41 Decision-Support Models

Decision-support models may compare alternatives, consequences, decision margins, robustness, exposure, reversibility, and value of information.

They must preserve participant objectives, constraints, risk capacity, authority, ethical duties, and human responsibility. A decision-support model can clarify a choice without selecting one universal action.

17.42 Model Validation

Validation should examine conceptual soundness, data suitability, measurement validity, implementation accuracy, performance, stability, robustness, and appropriateness for intended use. These dimensions should not be compressed into one pass or fail label.

Validation dimension	**Central question**
Conceptual	Does the structure fit the phenomenon and purpose?
Data	Are inputs reliable, timely, and representative?
Measurement	Do features represent the intended constructs?
Implementation	Does code match the approved specification?
Performance	Does the model satisfy its stated task?
Stability	Does behavior remain acceptable through time?
Robustness	Does the conclusion survive reasonable changes?
Use	Is the model suitable for the intended operational context?

Some models are supplied externally rather than developed internally. External provenance changes what can be inspected, but it does not transfer accountability: the institution that deploys a model remains responsible for its purpose, use, and consequences. A supplier's documentation, benchmarks, or client list are evidence about the product, not a substitute for local evaluation of fitness for the intended purpose, data, and population. Where a supplied model is customized, recalibrated, reweighted, or wrapped in overlays, the deployed system differs materially from the product that was evaluated and should be governed as its own version. Limited visibility into proprietary internals raises rather than lowers the importance of outcome monitoring, benchmarking against alternatives, and documented limitations.

17.43 Verification Versus Validation

Verification asks whether the model was implemented correctly according to specification. Validation asks whether the specified model is appropriate and reliable for its intended use.

A model can be correctly implemented and still be conceptually wrong. Conversely, a sound concept can fail because the implementation does not match the specification.

> **Verification–Validation Principle:** Correct implementation does not establish conceptual validity.

17.44 Benchmarking

Every model should be compared with credible baselines, such as naive persistence, historical average, a simple threshold, random classifier, existing model, alternative method, or governed human judgment.

Complexity should earn its place through incremental improvement in the stated purpose, not through sophistication alone.

17.45 Calibration

Calibration asks whether model confidence corresponds with observed frequency or quality. Probability calibration, state confidence, transition confidence, uncertainty bands, and alert severity should be evaluated separately where appropriate.

Calibration may vary by horizon, market, state, instrument, model version, and output range. Good overall calibration can conceal important subgroup failures.

17.46 Discrimination

Discrimination asks whether the model distinguishes relevant cases. A model may rank cases well while assigning inaccurate probabilities, or be well calibrated overall while ranking cases poorly.

Calibration and discrimination answer different questions and should not be treated as substitutes.

17.47 Robustness and Sensitivity

Robustness testing evaluates behavior under changes in inputs, missing data, nearby thresholds, alternative windows, parameter values, market states, structural breaks, vendor sources, and implementation environments.

Sensitivity is not always a defect. Some market processes are genuinely sensitive. The question is whether the sensitivity is understood, appropriate, and governed.

17.48 Stress Testing

Stress testing examines behavior under extreme or unusual conditions, including market stress, data outage, stale inputs, volatility discontinuity, liquidity collapse, schema change, model disagreement, computational delay, and adversarial input.

A model that performs well in ordinary conditions may still be unsuitable if its failure mode during stress is uncontrolled.

17.49 Missing-Data Behavior

The model should define behavior when inputs are unavailable, delayed, stale, invalid, partial, or contradictory. Possible responses include withholding output, degrading confidence, using a documented fallback, preserving a last-good value, marking an estimate, or escalating review.

Missing data must not be silently converted into zero, normal, neutral, or unchanged.

17.50 Model Monitoring

Monitoring should include input distributions, missingness, drift, output frequency, calibration, error, latency, stability, override rate, exception rate, and downstream use.

Monitoring is not only a technical activity. It tests whether the model remains valid for the conditions and uses under which it operates.

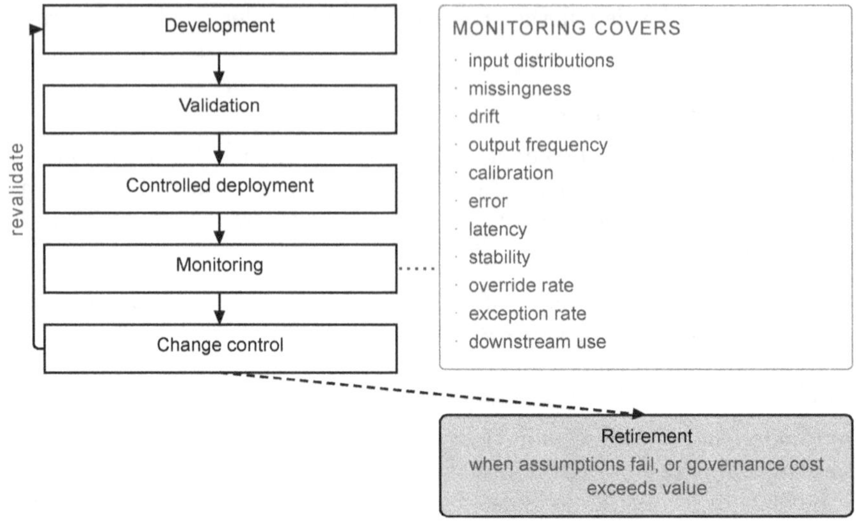

Development, validation, deployment, monitoring, change, incident response and retirement form one governed lifecycle.

Figure 17.4 — Model Lifecycle and Monitoring Loop

17.51 Data Drift, Concept Drift, Label Drift, and Use Drift

Data drift occurs when input distributions change. Concept drift occurs when the relationship between inputs and target changes. Label drift occurs when the outcome or classification distribution changes. Use drift occurs when the model is applied outside its approved context.

These forms of drift should be monitored separately because they require different responses.

Drift type	What changes	Illustrative response
Data drift	Input distribution	Investigate source, normalization, and retraining need
Concept drift	Input–target relationship	Revalidate model logic and performance
Label drift	Target prevalence or classification	Recalibrate and review thresholds
Use drift	Operational context or user behavior	Restrict use, retrain users, or reapprove scope

17.52 Model Decay

Model performance may decay because of participant adaptation, structural change, market evolution, data changes, crowding, policy shifts, technology, or implementation changes.

Decay should be expected as a possibility rather than treated as an exceptional surprise. Stable historical performance is evidence, not a permanent entitlement.

17.53 Feedback and Reflexivity

A deployed market model may become part of the system it attempts to represent. Widespread use can create crowding, earlier response, threshold clustering, reduced edge, amplified movement, self-fulfilling dynamics, or self-defeating signals.

Reflexive effects should be considered during capacity analysis, deployment design, and ongoing monitoring.

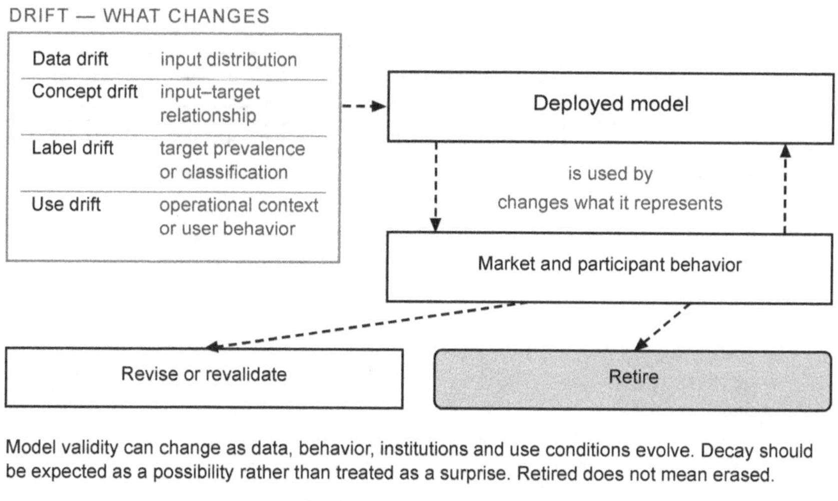

Figure 17.5 — Model Drift, Feedback, and Retirement

17.54 Human Overrides

Human override may be necessary when data are invalid, exceptional context is unrepresented, or model scope has been exceeded. Override also introduces discretion, inconsistency, and bias.

A governed override should record who acted, when, why, which evidence supported the action, how long it remains effective, its impact, and how it will be reviewed.

17.55 Automation and Responsibility

Automation may calculate, classify, monitor, alert, recommend, or execute. The greater the autonomy and consequence, the stronger the required validation, limits, monitoring, fallback, explainability, authority, audit, and incident response.

Responsibility for objectives, model use, and consequences remains human and institutional. Automation changes the mechanism of action; it does not remove accountability.

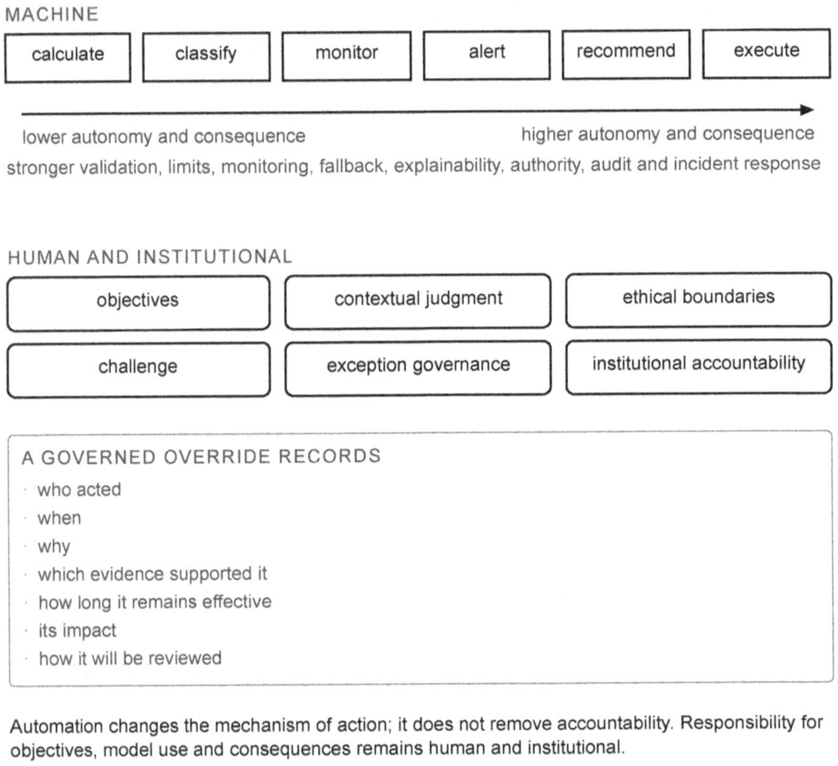

Figure 17.6 — Human–Machine Hybrid Governance

17.56 Model Documentation

A standard model document should include an identifier, name, owner, purpose, intended use, prohibited use, conceptual basis, inputs, features, assumptions, architecture, parameters, outputs, validation, limitations, monitoring, dependencies, change history, approval, and retirement criteria.

This documentation should connect with the manuscript's Model Documentation Standard and remain synchronized with the implemented version.

17.57 Model Inventory

An institution should maintain an inventory of active, experimental, shadow, restricted, and retired models, together with owners, dependencies, criticality, approved uses, and review status.

A model cannot be governed if no responsible function knows that it exists or how it influences downstream systems.

17.58 Model Criticality

Criticality may depend on financial exposure, user reach, automation, decision influence, regulatory significance, replacement difficulty, systemic dependency, and error severity.

Higher criticality should require stronger validation, independent challenge, monitoring, access control, fallback, incident response, and approval.

17.59 Model Change Control

Material changes may involve data sources, features, parameters, thresholds, code, model form, output format, intended use, or deployment environment.

Each change should be classified by materiality, documented, reviewed, tested, and validated to a degree proportional to its risk. Small code changes can have large behavioral effects, while large refactoring may preserve exact model behavior; materiality should be assessed by impact, not line count.

17.60 Versioning

Versioning should preserve the model specification, code, data, parameters, environment, outputs, effective date, approval, and migration path.

A result without a model version is difficult to reproduce, compare, audit, or interpret after the model changes.

17.61 Shadow Testing and Controlled Deployment

A new or materially changed model should often pass through offline validation, historical replay, shadow mode, limited canary, staged rollout, and rollback readiness.

Historical performance alone does not establish deployment readiness because live data, latency, dependencies, user behavior, and operational controls may differ from research conditions.

17.62 Model Incidents

A model incident may include incorrect output, data corruption, stale classification, unapproved use, threshold failure, calibration failure, implementation mismatch, uncontrolled automation, or misleading presentation.

Incident response should include containment, evidence preservation, impact assessment, correction, root-cause analysis, revalidation, and disclosure where appropriate.

17.63 Model Failure Analysis

Model failure should be classified rather than described only as poor performance. Different failure categories require different corrective actions.

Failure category	Illustrative problem
Conceptual	Model structure does not fit the phenomenon
Data	Input is incomplete, stale, or misaligned
Measurement	Feature does not represent intended construct
Estimation	Parameters are unstable or biased
Implementation	Code differs from specification
Calibration	Confidence does not match observed behavior
Scope	Model is used outside approved context
Interpretation	Output is overstated or misunderstood
Decision use	Participant constraints are ignored
Governance	Ownership, change, or monitoring fails
Environmental	Market structure changes materially

17.64 Model Retirement

A model should be retired when its purpose no longer exists, assumptions fail, performance deteriorates, a replacement is superior, data become unavailable, governance cost exceeds value, use becomes unsafe, or architecture becomes obsolete.

Retirement should preserve historical versions, rationale, outputs, incidents, dependencies, and migration records. Retired does not mean erased.

17.65 Framework Revision

Frameworks also require revision. Repeated model failures, new phenomena, evidence of omitted domains, contradictory research, terminology problems, institutional change, and technological change may reveal that the organizing framework itself is incomplete.

A framework should organize inquiry without becoming immune to the evidence generated within it.

17.66 Worked Example: Liquidity-Resilience Model

Purpose: estimate the market's ability to absorb exchange demand under observed conditions. Inputs may include spread, displayed depth, replenishment, price impact, cancellation behavior, trade size, and time of day.

The architecture may normalize component measurements against state-aware baselines, enforce quality filters, combine them into a resilience estimate, and report confidence. Material risks include hidden liquidity, incomplete venue coverage, unstable weights, stress conditions outside the validation range, stale quote data, and structural changes in execution behavior.

An appropriate claim is that the model summarizes selected evidence about liquidity resilience. An inappropriate claim is that it directly measures all available liquidity or guarantees future market stability.

17.67 Worked Example: Market-State Classifier

A market-state classifier compresses selected liquidity, positioning, volatility, trend, breadth, resilience, fragility, quality, and confidence information into a governed state representation.

It requires decomposable components, time alignment, explicit missingness, thresholds, hysteresis, validation, confidence, and versioning. Appropriate uses include description, comparison, transition monitoring, and research stratification. It should not be treated as a universal trade instruction or deterministic forecast.

17.68 Worked Example: Predictive Model With Limited Usefulness

Suppose a model predicts next-period direction with modest statistical improvement over baseline. Turnover is high, transaction costs eliminate the advantage, capacity is limited, performance is concentrated in one period, confidence is poorly calibrated, and losses cluster during stress.

The correct conclusion is not that the model has no information. It may possess limited predictive content but lack sufficient decision and deployment usefulness. Research validity, predictive performance, and operational value should remain distinct.

17.69 Worked Example: Human–Machine Hybrid

A transition model produces current state, trajectory, confidence, and data-quality warnings. A human reviewer evaluates unusual event context, known data limitations, model disagreement, and participant exposure.

The hybrid system should document what the machine determines, what the human may override, when escalation is required, how overrides are reviewed, and who retains responsibility. The human should not become an undocumented substitute for missing model governance.

The Governed Model Record

The Governed Model Record is the principal Institute construct for preserving the purpose, lineage, validation, permitted interpretation, operational status, and lifecycle of a material model.

Field	Required content
Model identifier	Unique name and version
Owner	Responsible person or function
Purpose	Task the model performs
Intended use	Approved operational context
Prohibited use	Contexts in which output must not be used
Framework context	Concepts and domains organizing the model
Inputs	Sources, definitions, freshness, and quality
Features	Transformations and rationale
Architecture	Rules, equations, algorithms, and structure
Assumptions	Tested, operational, and uncertain assumptions
Parameters	Values, estimation, tuning, and constraints
Outputs	Values, categories, confidence, and warnings
Interpretation	Permitted meaning and claim boundaries
Validation	Conceptual, data, implementation, and performance evidence
Benchmark	Simple and alternative comparisons
Robustness	Sensitivity, stress, and missing-data behavior
Monitoring	Drift, calibration, latency, incidents, and use
Dependencies	Data, services, models, and human processes
Governance	Approval, access, and change control
Limitations	Known weaknesses and excluded contexts
Lifecycle	Development, deployment, review, and retirement
History	Versions, changes, incidents, and disposition

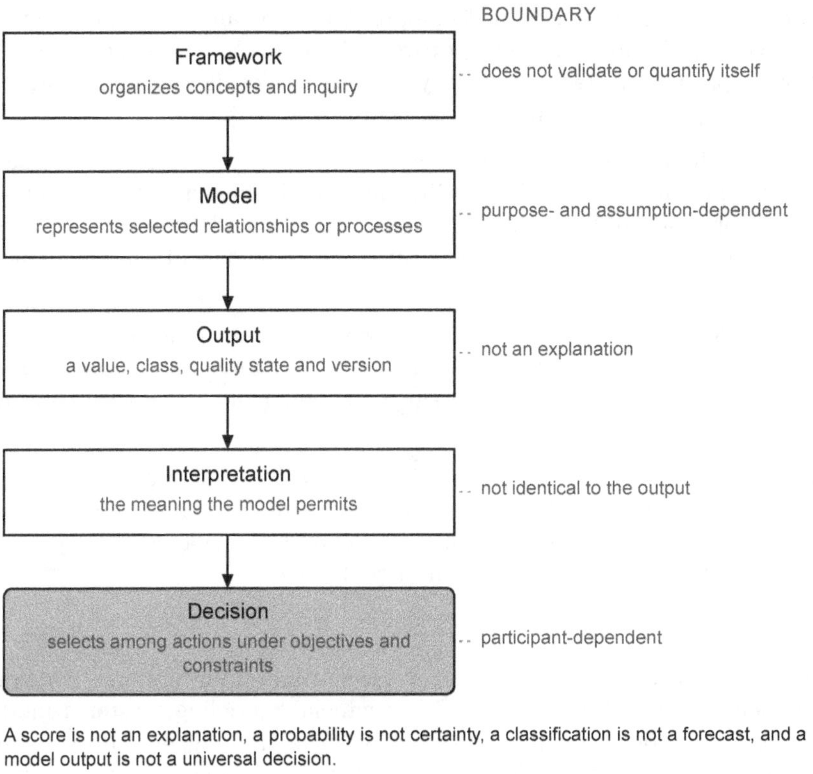

Figure 17.7 — Framework, Model, Output, Interpretation, and Decision

Chapter Summary

Frameworks and models are necessary abstractions for studying complex markets, but neither should be mistaken for the market itself. A framework organizes concepts, relationships, questions, and boundaries. A model represents selected features or processes for a defined purpose under explicit assumptions.

Model purpose must precede model selection. Descriptive, measurement, classification, explanatory, predictive, simulation, optimization, decision-support, execution, and control models require different evidence and should not be evaluated by one universal standard.

A governed model architecture preserves the full path from market phenomenon to data, measurements, features, transformation, output, interpretation, and decision context. Every layer introduces choices, dependencies, uncertainty, and possible failure.

Model outputs should remain decomposable, time-aligned, quality-aware, versioned, and limited to their approved meaning. A score is not an explanation, a probability is not certainty, a classification is not a forecast, and a model output is not a universal decision.

Validation should distinguish conceptual soundness, data quality, measurement validity, implementation verification, performance, stability, robustness, calibration, and suitability for use. Correct code does not establish a correct model, and historical performance does not establish deployment readiness.

Models require lifecycle governance. Monitoring, drift detection, change control, incident response, human override, documentation, inventories, versioning, and retirement are integral to model quality rather than administrative additions.

The strongest model is not necessarily the most complex or the most accurate in sample. It is the model that performs its stated purpose with sufficient validity, robustness, transparency, and governance while preserving the limits of what it can legitimately claim.

Established Knowledge

This chapter draws on established work in philosophy and methodology of modeling, statistics, econometrics, financial modeling, systems modeling, control theory, machine learning, artificial intelligence, decision science, simulation, optimization, model risk management, software verification, validation science, explainable artificial intelligence, human factors, operational risk, lifecycle governance, and systems engineering.

The Institute does not claim originality for regression, factor models, state-space models, machine learning, ensembles, optimization, scenario analysis, simulation, calibration, sensitivity analysis, stress testing, model documentation, model inventories, model validation, change control, drift monitoring, or model retirement.

Institute Perspective

The Institute contribution lies in integration: embedding model architecture within the full chain from observation to decision; distinguishing framework, model, output, interpretation, and use; requiring decomposability across multidomain state models; integrating measurement quality, state confidence, and transition uncertainty; treating the Structural State Vector as a governed architecture rather than a self-validating score; treating the Market Compass as a presentation model; formalizing the Governed Model Record; connecting lifecycle governance to research evidence and decision quality; preserving human responsibility in automated systems; and treating framework revision as part of scientific progress.

Responsible Modeling Principles

1. Representation Principle: A model represents selected features of the market; it is not the market itself.

2. Framework–Model Principle: A framework organizes inquiry, while a model performs a defined representational task within that structure.

3. Purpose Principle: Model purpose must be defined before model selection or evaluation.

4. Selection Principle: Every model reflects choices about what to include, transform, weight, and omit.

5. Decomposition Principle: Compressed outputs should remain traceable to inputs, transformations, assumptions, and quality states.

6. Output–Interpretation Principle: A model output is not identical to its interpretation or decision use.

7. Claim-Boundary Principle: A model should not make stronger claims than its design and validation support.

8. Assumption Principle: Assumptions should remain explicit, testable where possible, and monitored through time.

9. Complexity Principle: Additional complexity should be justified by meaningful improvement in the stated purpose.

10. Latent-Variable Principle: Inferred variables should not be presented with the status of directly observed facts.

11. Uncertainty Principle: Model uncertainty should be attached to specific outputs and claims.

12. Dependency Principle: Several models using common inputs or assumptions do not provide independent confirmation.

13. Verification–Validation Principle: Correct implementation does not establish conceptual validity.

14. Benchmark Principle: Complex models should be evaluated against credible simpler alternatives.

15. Drift Principle: Model validity can change as data, behavior, institutions, and use conditions evolve.

16. Reflexivity Principle: A deployed model may become part of the system it represents.

17. Use Principle: Approved use, prohibited use, and user responsibility should be explicit.

18. Lifecycle Principle: Development, validation, deployment, monitoring, change, incident response, and retirement form one governed lifecycle.

19. Responsibility Principle: Automation does not remove human and institutional responsibility.

20. Framework-Revision Principle: Frameworks and models should remain open to correction when evidence reveals omission or failure.

Questions for Reflection

1. What distinguishes a framework from a model?
2. Why is a framework not automatically a predictive system?
3. Why must model purpose be defined before model selection?
4. What makes every model a selective representation?
5. How does a model differ from an indicator?
6. How does a model differ from a score?
7. How does a model differ from a decision rule?
8. What distinguishes descriptive, explanatory, and predictive models?
9. What distinguishes structural and reduced-form models?
10. Why does mathematical form not make assumptions true?
11. What are the strengths and limitations of machine-learning models?
12. What are the strengths and limitations of rule-based systems?
13. What makes a hybrid model governable?
14. Why should observable and latent variables remain distinct?
15. What should a model architecture document?
16. What belongs in an input contract?
17. Why is feature construction a source of model risk?
18. How can normalization change interpretation?
19. What information can aggregation conceal?
20. Why is equal weighting still a model choice?
21. Why are thresholds designed boundaries rather than natural laws?
22. What distinguishes parameters from hyperparameters?
23. Which model assumptions require monitoring?
24. How can constraints improve or distort a model?
25. What should accompany a model's primary output?
26. Why should uncertainty not be collapsed into one score?
27. What information must accompany a probability output?
28. What forms of explainability may be required?
29. Why are interpretability and predictive performance not simple opposites?

30. Why may an ensemble provide false diversification?
31. What can model disagreement reveal?
32. What safeguards should govern composite models?
33. Why is the Structural State Vector a model architecture rather than a natural object?
34. Why should the Market Compass remain a presentation layer?
35. What distinctions should a transition model preserve?
36. What makes a forecasting target well defined?
37. What are the limitations of scenario and simulation models?
38. Why can optimization solve the wrong problem?
39. Why does a decision-support model not determine one universal action?
40. What distinguishes verification from validation?
41. Why should a complex model be compared with a simple benchmark?
42. What is calibration?
43. What is discrimination?
44. What does model stress testing examine?
45. How should a model behave when inputs are missing or stale?
46. What should model monitoring include?
47. What distinguishes data drift from concept drift?
48. How can model deployment create reflexive effects?
49. When is a human override appropriate?
50. What should a model document contain?
51. Why is a model inventory necessary?
52. How should model criticality affect governance?
53. What changes require model revalidation?
54. Why must every output preserve a model version?
55. What role do shadow testing and staged deployment play?
56. What constitutes a model incident?
57. How should model failure be classified?
58. When should a model be retired?
59. What evidence should cause a framework to be revised?
60. Why does automation not transfer responsibility away from people and institutions?

Chapter 18. The Future of Market Systems Science

An Open Research Program for Understanding Evolving Markets

Chapter Purpose

Volume I has developed a structured way to observe, measure, interpret, represent, investigate, and govern financial-market phenomena. It has treated markets as evolving systems rather than as collections of isolated indicators, and it has emphasized that knowledge about those systems is always mediated by data, measurement, inference, models, and institutional practice.

This final chapter does not attempt to convert that architecture into a finished doctrine. Its purpose is to define Market Systems Science as an open research program: one that can accumulate evidence, preserve disagreement, support reproducibility, incorporate new methods, revise its own concepts, and retire claims that no longer withstand scrutiny. The future of the field depends less on the number of models it creates than on the quality of the questions it asks and the discipline with which it handles uncertainty, evidence, technology, and institutional responsibility.

> **Open-Program Principle:** Market Systems Science should remain open to criticism, replication, competing models, negative evidence, and revision.

Learning Objectives

- define Market Systems Science as an open research program rather than a finished doctrine;
- distinguish what Volume I establishes from what it does not establish;
- state criteria for progress and criteria for failure in a research program;
- organize a first generation of research around questions rather than products;
- outline research agendas for measurement, liquidity, positioning, volatility, trend, and domain interaction;
- explain how participant heterogeneity, institutional context, and reflexivity condition research findings;
- evaluate the role of artificial intelligence and of the complete human–machine system in market research;

- identify the standards and infrastructure that make research cumulative, covering data, measurement, state and transition, model and AI governance, reproducibility, and replication;
- separate research, model, product, and marketing claims;
- state the limits of generalization and the conditions under which the framework itself should be revised.

18.1 Completing Volume I

The chapters of Volume I form a governed reasoning architecture. They begin with observable market phenomena, move through controlled measurement and evidentiary reasoning, represent multidomain configurations and transitions, and then connect those assessments to decisions, research, and model governance. The sequence is not a rigid pipeline. Analysts may move backward as evidence is challenged, measurements are revised, models fail, or new questions emerge.

The complete architecture can be expressed conceptually as: market phenomenon → observation → recorded data → controlled measurement → contextual evidence → inference → interpretation → assessment → market configuration → state representation → transition analysis → judgment → decision → action → outcome → review → research → model or framework revision. At every step, some information is selected, transformed, compressed, or interpreted. The responsibility of the discipline is to keep those transformations visible enough to be challenged.

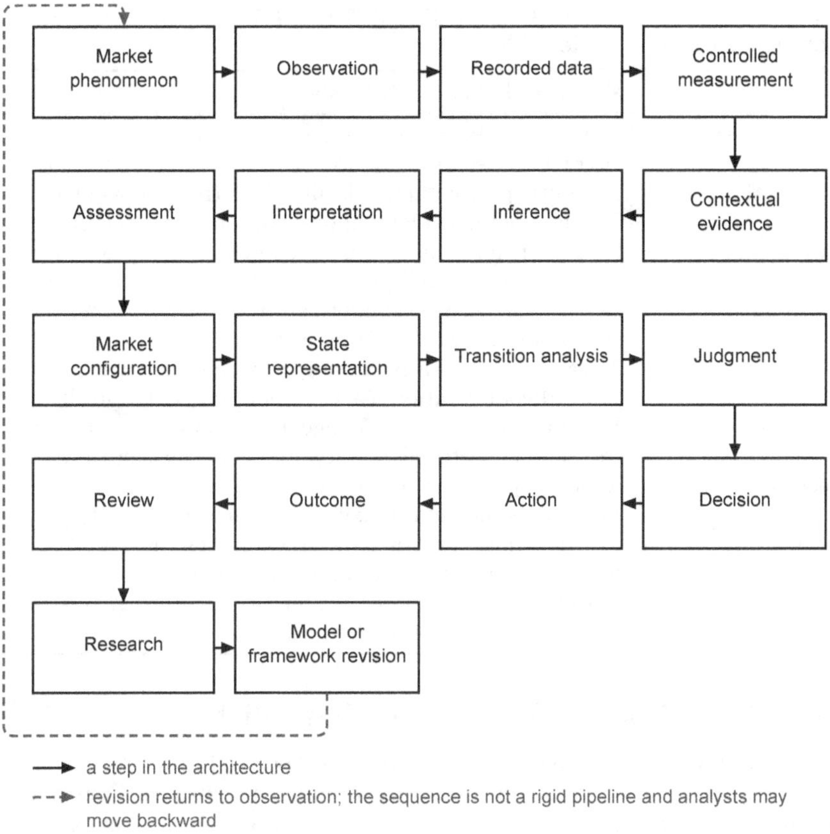

Figure 18.1 — The Complete Market Systems Science Architecture

18.2 What Volume I Establishes

Volume I establishes a coherent vocabulary and a set of methodological boundaries. Conceptually, it treats financial markets as evolving systems shaped by interaction, feedback, adaptation, heterogeneity, and nonlinear response. Observationally, it organizes inquiry around four foundational domains—liquidity, positioning, volatility, and trend—while recognizing that these domains interact and do not exhaust every possible determinant of market behavior.

Epistemically, the volume separates observation, measurement, evidence, inference, interpretation, assessment, judgment, and decision. It requires uncertainty, missingness, model dependence, and claim strength to remain explicit. Operationally, it introduces market configuration, state representation, transition analysis, the Decision Environment, the Research Ledger, and the Governed Model Record as structures for making complex work more traceable and reviewable.

Area	**What Volume I establishes**
Systems view	Markets can be studied as evolving systems with interaction, feedback, adaptation, and nonlinear behavior.
Observation	Liquidity, positioning, volatility, and trend provide a foundational multidomain observational architecture.
Measurement	Measurements require controlled definitions, provenance, time alignment, and quality states.
Reasoning	Evidence must be distinguished from inference, interpretation, causal claim, and decision.
State	A market state is a purpose-specific representation of selected configuration features, not the market itself.
Transition	Material configuration change can be evaluated through governed persistence, quality, and confirmation rules.
Decision	Action depends on participant-specific objectives, constraints, horizon, risk capacity, and uncertainty.
Research	Claims require proportional research designs, reproducibility, replication, and revision.
Models	Models require purpose, validation, monitoring, versioning, change control, and retirement.

18.3 What Volume I Does Not Establish

The boundaries of a contribution are part of the contribution. Volume I does not establish a complete theory of financial markets, a final domain taxonomy, universal state categories, universal thresholds, a causal hierarchy among all market forces, a guaranteed forecasting advantage, or one correct decision method. It does not claim that latent constructs such as positioning, fragility, or state can be observed without modeling assumptions.

Nor does the framework establish that multidomain integration will always outperform simpler approaches. Some problems may be explained adequately by one measurement, one domain, or one carefully defined statistical relationship. The framework earns its place only when the added structure improves understanding, measurement, prediction, decision quality, or governance enough to justify its complexity.

> **Incompleteness Principle:** Scientific credibility requires stating clearly what the framework does not explain, establish, or guarantee.

18.4 Market Systems Science as an Open Research Program

Market Systems Science is best understood as an open research program for investigating financial markets as evolving systems through governed observation, measurement, evidence, multidomain representation, transition analysis, decision reasoning, and model revision. "Open" refers first to epistemic openness. Claims must remain open to criticism, competing explanations, new data, independent implementation, failed replication, and narrowing of scope.

Epistemic openness does not require that every dataset, algorithm, or proprietary implementation be publicly released. Data licenses, confidentiality, security obligations, and competitive constraints may limit disclosure. What openness does require is that the evidentiary status of a claim not depend solely on institutional authority or proprietary mystique. Where public replication is impossible, internal reproducibility, independent audit, controlled external review, or replicated analysis under agreement can still strengthen credibility.

18.5 Criteria for Progress

A research program should define progress in terms that are more demanding than growth in publications, terminology, or model count. Progress may mean clearer definitions, stronger measurement validity, better reproducibility, more stable classification, improved calibration, lower false-transition rates, more informative uncertainty, stronger cross-market replication, fewer uncontrolled model incidents, and more disciplined decision records.

Progress can also occur when a claim is narrowed or retired. If a broad relationship fails outside one period but survives under specific configurations, the revised statement is scientifically stronger even though it is less ambitious. If a complex state model adds no value beyond a simpler benchmark, recognizing that fact is progress because it reduces unnecessary complexity.

> **Evidence-Progress Principle:** Progress should be measured by improvements in knowledge quality, reproducibility, calibration, and learning rather than by accumulation alone.

18.6 Criteria for Failure

A field also needs ways to recognize failure. The program should be concerned if its definitions cannot be operationalized consistently, if measurements cannot be reproduced, if model outputs add no value over simple baselines, if transition systems are chronically too noisy or too late, or if classifications become detached from observable evidence.

Institutional failure can also occur when governance becomes ceremonial: negative findings disappear, conflicts are concealed, product incentives determine scientific conclusions, models are retained after their assumptions fail, or framework language becomes so flexible that no observation can count against it. A healthy research program should detect those failures in itself.

Progress signal	Failure signal
Definitions become more precise and reproducible.	Terms become broader or less falsifiable.
Measurements gain validity across settings.	Measures work only under undocumented conditions.
Models improve over credible baselines.	Complexity grows without incremental value.
Replication narrows uncertainty.	Failed replication is ignored or hidden.
Corrections improve the knowledge base.	Institutional consistency is valued above correction.
Governance changes behavior.	Governance exists only as documentation.

18.7 The Foundational Research Questions

The first generation of research should be organized around questions rather than products. For observation, the field must ask which market phenomena are directly recorded, which are inferred, and how latency, missingness, and data revision affect the evidence. For domains, it must test whether liquidity, positioning, volatility, and trend are sufficiently distinct to organize inquiry and whether their measurements contribute independent information.

For configuration and state, the central questions concern representation: which dimensions are necessary, which can be measured reliably, how contradictions should be preserved, and whether states remain stable enough to support comparison. For transitions, the program must evaluate early indications, confirmation lag, false transitions, reversals, and uncertainty about destination. For decisions, it must ask whether the additional structure actually improves participant-specific decision quality under stated objectives and constraints.

Research area	Illustrative question
Observation	Which phenomena are directly observed, and which require inference?
Domains	Do the four domains remain distinct and useful across asset classes and horizons?
Configuration	Which multidomain combinations are persistent and structurally meaningful?

Research area	Illustrative question
State	Can state representations be descriptively valid, stable, and decomposable?
Transition	Which indicators improve detection without unacceptable lag or false alarms?
Decision	Do state and transition frameworks improve decisions for defined participants?
Models	Which representations remain robust as markets, data, and participant behavior evolve?

18.8 Measurement Research Agenda

The next stage of the discipline depends on measurement research. Candidate areas include liquidity resilience, hidden and latent liquidity, positioning proxies, dealer-exposure uncertainty, crowding, volatility structure, breadth and concentration, trend persistence, cross-domain dependency, data freshness, and measurement confidence.

Every candidate measure should be studied for construct validity, reliability, sensitivity, horizon dependence, market dependence, missing-data behavior, and failure conditions. A measure that behaves well in highly liquid U.S. equities may not transport to fragmented credit markets, thin futures contracts, or digital assets. Measurement standards should therefore include scope as part of the definition rather than as an afterthought.

18.9 Liquidity Research Agenda

Future liquidity research should move beyond static spread and depth snapshots toward capacity and resilience. Important questions include how quickly displayed depth replenishes, how hidden liquidity interacts with visible books, how venue fragmentation affects apparent capacity, how price impact changes with order size, and how liquidity migrates across instruments during stress.

The central discipline remains conditionality. Liquidity is not a fixed asset property. It depends on size, horizon, venue, urgency, market state, and the behavior of other participants. Research should therefore avoid universal labels such as "liquid" or "illiquid" without specifying the conditions under which exchange capacity is being evaluated.

18.10 Positioning Research Agenda

Positioning is among the most difficult domains because meaningful exposure is often latent, delayed, netted, or model-dependent. Future research should examine ownership concentration, leverage, funding dependence, derivative sensitivities, convexity, crowding, forced-adjustment pathways, cross-market exposure, and the uncertainty embedded in dealer-positioning estimates.

The goal should not be to pretend that the market's true positioning can be reconstructed perfectly. Instead, research should quantify which proxies are informative, under what conditions they fail, how uncertainty propagates into state assessments, and when positioning evidence adds incremental value beyond price, volatility, and liquidity measurements.

18.11 Volatility Research Agenda

Volatility research should preserve the distinction between observed variability and implied pricing. Future work may examine realized versus implied structure, horizon-specific uncertainty, volatility-of-volatility, skew, tail pricing, liquidity–volatility feedback, state dependence, and option-market information.

The field should resist reducing volatility to fear or treating implied volatility as a pure forecast. Option prices reflect supply, demand, risk transfer, convexity, funding, inventory, and model assumptions in addition to expectations. The research question is therefore not simply whether implied volatility predicts realized volatility, but how different volatility structures behave under different market configurations and participant constraints.

18.12 Trend Research Agenda

Trend research should focus on directional persistence under explicit methods and horizons. Important topics include breadth, leadership, rotation, scale dependence, trend maturity, trend failure, cross-asset confirmation, and the interaction of directional persistence with liquidity, positioning, and volatility.

A key unresolved issue is how much of apparent trend is persistent information and how much reflects temporary flow, mechanical rebalancing, crowding, or delayed adjustment. Research should also distinguish trend description from extrapolation. A persistent historical direction is evidence about the path that occurred, not by itself proof of continued future direction.

18.13 Interaction Research Agenda

The greatest promise of a systems approach lies in interaction research, but this is also where causal overstatement is most dangerous. Candidate topics include liquidity–volatility feedback, positioning–liquidity sensitivity, positioning–volatility interaction, breadth–fragility relationships, trend–positioning reinforcement, stabilizing mechanisms, cross-domain lead–lag structure, and nonlinear amplification.

Several domains may move together because they share data, respond to a common event, or are linked through one mechanism. Co-movement therefore does not establish independent confirmation. Future studies should map shared dependencies explicitly and compare multidomain models with simpler alternatives to determine whether interaction modeling adds real information.

18.14 Market Configuration Research

Market configuration research should investigate which combinations of measurements provide a meaningful description of the current environment. The central challenge is to preserve contradiction while still producing usable representations. A configuration may contain positive trend, narrowing breadth, stable displayed spreads, rising short-dated implied volatility, and uncertain positioning at the same time.

Research should test whether selected configuration dimensions are comparable across instruments, whether configuration distance can be defined meaningfully, and whether particular configurations are associated with resilience, fragility, or transition. Any such association should remain conditional on horizon, measurement method, and data quality.

18.15 Market-State Research

State research should test the descriptive and operational validity of higher-level representations. Questions include whether continuous dimensions are more stable than categories, whether state confidence is calibrated, how mixed and indeterminate conditions should be handled, and whether hysteresis reduces classification noise without creating excessive lag.

The Structural State Vector should remain a research architecture for controlled compression rather than a declared natural object. Its components, weights, thresholds, and even dimensions should remain open to evidence-driven revision. A state model earns credibility through decomposition, validation, and repeated use—not through elegance alone.

18.16 Transition Research

Transition research should distinguish change from confirmed structural reclassification. Important topics include early indication, transition maturity, confirmation delay, false-transition rate, stabilization, recovery, reversal, destination uncertainty, cross-domain coherence, and horizon nesting.

A central future question is how to improve responsiveness without sacrificing reliability. Faster detection may create more false transitions; stronger confirmation may arrive too late to be useful. The correct balance may vary by participant and use case, which means transition models should be validated against their intended purpose rather than against one universal threshold.

18.17 Resilience and Fragility

Resilience and fragility deserve a cross-domain research program because they describe how systems respond to disturbance rather than merely where current measurements stand. Resilience can be understood as capacity to absorb disturbance, continue functioning, replenish, adapt, or recover. Fragility can be understood as sensitivity to disturbance, amplification, constraint activation, or loss of function.

The concepts should not be assumed to be exact opposites. A market can appear resilient under ordinary conditions while retaining latent fragility to a particular funding or positioning shock. Future research should test measures of resilience and fragility across horizons and identify what distinguishes latent vulnerability from active stress.

18.18 Cross-Market and Network Research

Markets are connected through ownership, funding, collateral, derivatives, indexes, volatility, currencies, policy, clearing, information, and automated strategies. Network analysis may help represent these dependencies through exposure graphs, common ownership, transmission pathways, and concentration measures.

The visual appeal of network diagrams can create false confidence. An observed connection does not establish causal transmission, and incomplete exposure data can distort centrality measures. Network research should therefore preserve uncertainty, data coverage, directionality, timing, and alternative mechanisms.

18.19 Participant Heterogeneity

Market behavior emerges from participants with different objectives, horizons, liabilities, technologies, mandates, funding structures, and risk capacities. Research that assumes a representative participant may miss the very heterogeneity that creates liquidity, disagreement, and forced adjustment.

Future work should ask who supplies liquidity, who consumes it, who can wait, who must rebalance, who responds mechanically, who benefits from volatility, and who is constrained by funding. These questions may be difficult because participant identities and inventories are often incomplete, but the limitations should motivate careful inference rather than simplification.

18.20 Institutions, Regulation, and Technology

Market relationships are embedded in institutions. Exchange design, tick sizes, settlement cycles, margin rules, clearing, reporting, fragmentation, passive investment, algorithmic execution, tokenization, and artificial intelligence can alter the data-generating process itself.

Future research should therefore treat institutional context as part of model scope. A relationship estimated before a major rule change may not remain valid afterward. Structural breaks should not be treated solely as statistical anomalies; they may reflect genuine changes in how the market system operates.

18.21 Reflexivity and Model Adoption

A deployed model may become part of the system it attempts to represent. If many participants use similar signals, thresholds, or risk controls, their coordinated actions may alter price impact, timing, volatility, or the persistence of the relationship that made the model useful.

Research priorities include signal crowding, threshold clustering, strategy decay, publication effects, model-induced synchronization, self-reinforcing execution, and self-defeating forecasts. A successful model can weaken its own future performance by changing participant behavior.

> **Reflexivity Principle:** A deployed market model may alter the system it represents; model validity must therefore be treated as potentially endogenous to adoption.

18.22 Artificial Intelligence in Market Research

Artificial intelligence will increasingly support market research, documentation, software development, education, and model operations. Appropriate uses may include literature organization, code assistance, test generation, anomaly review, research documentation, hypothesis enumeration, model comparison, and natural-language interfaces.

The risks are equally material. AI systems can fabricate evidence, produce plausible but unsupported causal narratives, obscure source dependence, leak confidential information, drift between versions, and encourage automation bias. Fluency is not evidence. An explanation that sounds coherent is not scientifically stronger unless its observations, measurements, claims, and sources can be traced and challenged.

AI-supported activity	**Primary governance requirement**
Drafting and summarization	Source traceability and human review.
Code generation	Testing, code review, dependency control, and reproducibility.
Hypothesis generation	Clear exploratory label and independent confirmation.

AI-supported activity	Primary governance requirement
Measurement generation	Validation against governed definitions and known benchmarks.
Model output generation	Versioning, calibration, monitoring, and failure handling.
Recommendations	Participant-specific authority, constraints, and human responsibility.
Autonomous execution	Strict validation, limits, audit, fallback, and incident response.

AI Instrument Principle: AI may accelerate inquiry, but evidence, provenance, validation, and responsibility cannot be delegated to fluency.

18.23 Human–Machine Collaboration

The future should not be framed as a contest between humans and machines. Machines are strong at scale, consistency, rapid comparison, monitoring, and structured search. Humans remain responsible for objectives, contextual judgment, ethical boundaries, challenge, exception governance, and institutional accountability.

Humans also make systematic errors, and automated systems may reveal those errors through consistency checks and calibration. The correct unit of evaluation is therefore the complete human–machine system: its data, models, interfaces, authority boundaries, incentives, controls, and review process.

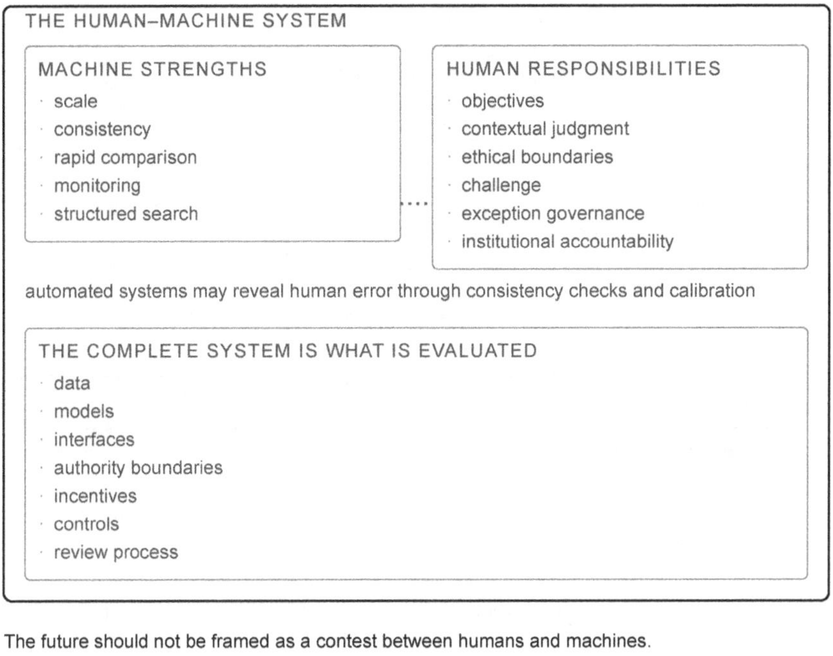

Figure 18.2 — Human–Machine Research and Governance

18.24 Technical Architecture for Cumulative Research

Cumulative research requires technical infrastructure that preserves scientific lineage. At minimum, the system should support governed data intake, provenance tracking, immutable source preservation, controlled transformations, versioned measurements, experiment registration, reproducible environments, model registries, validation records, shadow deployment, incident records, and publication lineage.

The purpose of this architecture is epistemic integrity, not technological prestige. A sophisticated platform that cannot reproduce how an output was produced is weaker scientifically than a simpler system with reliable lineage. Technical design should therefore prioritize traceability, repeatability, and challengeability.

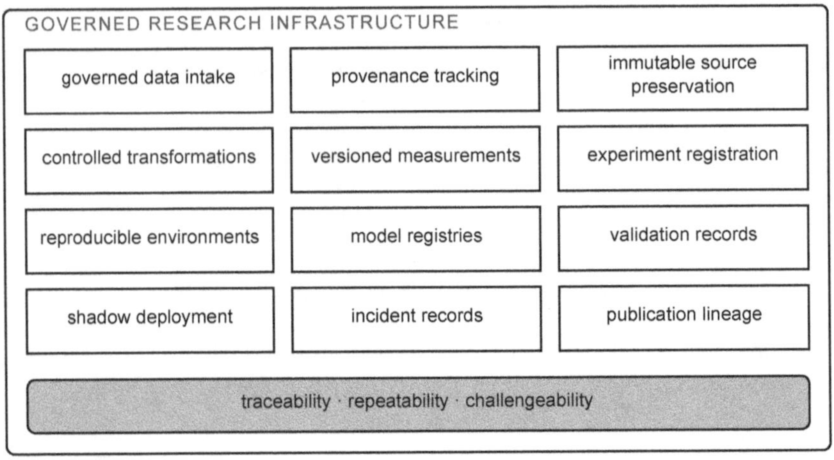

The purpose of this architecture is epistemic integrity, not technological prestige. A sophisticated platform that cannot reproduce how an output was produced is weaker scientifically than a simpler system with reliable lineage.

Figure 18.3 — Technical Architecture for Cumulative Market Research

18.25 Data Standards

Shared data semantics are a prerequisite for replication. Future standards should define identifiers, timestamps, timezones, units, venues, session labels, missingness categories, revision status, source quality, corporate actions, model-effective time, and lineage. Two researchers may use the same field name while referring to different effective times or adjustment conventions; without explicit semantics, apparent replication can be illusory.

18.26 Measurement Standards

A measurement standard should specify the construct, formula, source, transformation, horizon, universe, exclusions, missing-data rule, calibration, quality state, version, and known limitations. The appendices of Volume I should be treated as operational foundations for these standards rather than as administrative supplements.

Standardization should not freeze innovation. New measures may be introduced, but they should enter with clear versioning and validation status. When definitions change, historical results should retain the version under which they were produced.

18.27 State and Transition Standards

State and transition standards should define minimum metadata for every output: effective time, horizon, component quality, confidence, thresholds, hysteresis, confirmation logic, revision status, destination uncertainty, false-transition treatment, and model version. A classification without these fields is difficult to interpret or compare.

18.28 Model and AI Governance Standards

Future governance standards should cover intended use, prohibited use, criticality, ownership, validation, explainability, monitoring, change control, incident response, override, security, retirement, and disclosure of AI-generated content where material. The level of governance should scale with consequence and autonomy.

A research assistant that drafts prose does not require the same control as a system that generates market measurements, assigns state classifications, recommends actions, or executes trades. Governance should distinguish these roles rather than treating "AI use" as one category.

18.29 Reproducibility Infrastructure

The field should support versioned protocols, checksums, environment lockfiles, data snapshots where licensing permits, synthetic reproducibility datasets, code archives, machine-readable model records, result manifests, and automated validation. These mechanisms allow a study to be reconstructed after its authors, software, or vendors have changed.

Reproducibility should not be confused with truth. A flawed study can be perfectly reproducible. Reproducibility establishes that the procedure can be repeated; replication and methodological challenge address whether the finding is more general and credible.

18.30 Replication Networks

Independent replication is especially important for a field developed partly within one institution. Universities, independent researchers, practitioners, exchanges, data providers, regulators, technology organizations, and professional societies may all contribute different data, incentives, and methodological perspectives.

Replication networks should preserve disagreement rather than forcing consensus. Exact, temporal, cross-market, conceptual, and independent-implementation replications can each reveal different failure modes. Negative replications should remain visible in the knowledge base.

18.31 Open and Proprietary Research

Market research often operates under legitimate constraints: proprietary data licenses, confidentiality, privacy, security, and competitive research.

These constraints create several transparency levels rather than a binary choice between open and closed research.

Transparency level	Characteristics
Public and reproducible	Data or sufficient access, code, protocol, and environment available for public reproduction.
Externally auditable	Qualified reviewers can inspect governed evidence and methods under access controls.
Independent replication under agreement	A separate party can test the claim using controlled data or implementation access.
Internally reproducible	The institution can regenerate the result from versioned evidence, code, and environment.
Restricted but governed	Access is limited, but provenance, ownership, review, and limitations remain documented.

Proprietary-Research Principle: Proprietary status may constrain disclosure, but it cannot justify undocumented claims or unreviewable evidence.

18.32 Publication Standards

A Market Systems Science publication should disclose the research question, claim type, universe, period, data, measurements, model, assumptions, limitations, conflicts, robustness, replication status, version, and decision-use boundary. Where performance is discussed, costs, capacity, selection, and out-of-sample status should be explicit.

Publication language should distinguish exploratory, conditionally supported, replicated, contested, and retired findings. The goal is to prevent rhetorical certainty from outrunning evidentiary status.

18.33 Negative Results and Retractions

A cumulative field must preserve null findings, failed replications, invalidated measurements, model retirements, corrected publications, retractions, and incident reports. Removing failed work from view creates survivorship bias in the knowledge base and encourages repeated mistakes.

Correction should be treated as evidence of a functioning research program. The discipline should value correction over institutional consistency and refinement over institutional pride.

Correction Principle: Correction, narrowing, retirement, and retraction are signs of a functioning research program when evidence warrants them.

18.34 A Living Knowledge Base

The future knowledge base should separate established findings, conditionally supported findings, exploratory hypotheses, contested claims, unsupported claims, retired models, and unresolved questions. Each item should carry scope, evidence, confidence, version, review date, owner, and revision history.

This structure prevents old statements from surviving merely because they once appeared in an approved document. A claim can remain historically important while being scientifically retired. Conversely, an exploratory idea can be preserved without being presented as established knowledge.

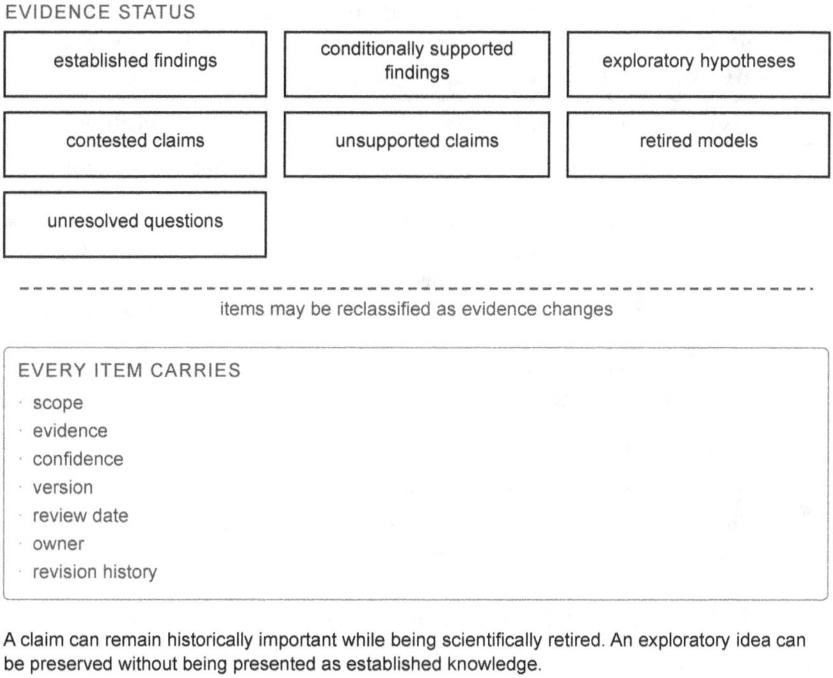

Figure 18.4 — The Living Knowledge Base

18.35 The Role of the WallStreetDelta Institute

The WallStreetDelta Institute may serve as framework steward, research coordinator, standards developer, educational institution, platform builder, publication host, replication sponsor, and archival custodian. These roles can help the field develop coherently, but they also create conflicts if the institution becomes the sole validator of its own claims.

Credibility therefore requires external review, independent replication, conflict disclosure, documented dissent, correction mechanisms, and separation of research approval from commercial incentives where practical. The Institute's strongest role is stewardship of process rather than ownership of truth.

Independence Principle: A research program becomes stronger when its claims can survive competent review outside the institution that introduced them.

18.36 Research–Product Separation

WallStreetDelta products may operationalize research, but several claim layers must remain distinct. A research claim states what evidence supports. A model claim states what a validated model can represent. A product claim states what the deployed system actually provides. A marketing claim states what is communicated to users.

Claim layer	Primary question	Required discipline
Research	What does the evidence support?	Claim type, scope, limitations, replication status.
Model	What can the validated model represent or estimate?	Purpose, validation, uncertainty, approved use.
Product	What does the deployed system actually deliver?	Implementation verification, monitoring, availability, user context.
Marketing	What is communicated externally?	No stronger than underlying research, model, and product evidence.

Research–Product Principle: No product or marketing claim should be stronger than the research, validation, and implementation evidence beneath it.

18.37 Education and Credentialing

Education should be part of the scientific program because the framework depends on precise distinctions. Learners should be trained to separate observation from inference, measurement from evidence, association from mechanism, state from forecast, transition from destination, confidence from probability, model output from decision, and decision quality from outcome quality.

If credentials are developed, they should emphasize applied reasoning, evidence discipline, documentation, and challenge rather than memorization of Institute terminology. A credential should indicate demonstrated competence under governed standards, not allegiance to a doctrine.

18.38 Professional Practice

A mature field may eventually develop professional practices around scope statements, claim discipline, contemporaneous records, model documentation, conflict disclosure, uncertainty representation, revision obligations, incident reporting, and continuing education. These standards should evolve from evidence and practical need rather than being declared prematurely.

18.39 Ethical Boundaries

Future development should address market manipulation, misuse of confidential information, discriminatory proxy use, surveillance, misleading performance claims, unsuitable automation, privacy, concentration of technological power, systemic feedback, and downstream harm. A model can be statistically effective and ethically unacceptable.

Ethical quality is therefore not reducible to profitability or predictive performance. Responsible use requires attention to whose objectives are served, whose risks are externalized, which rights are affected, and what institutional obligations apply.

18.40 Security and Operational Resilience

Security is part of scientific integrity because research depends on trusted data, code, credentials, models, and environments. Manipulated data can invalidate measurement. Compromised code can invalidate reproducibility. Stolen credentials can undermine provenance. Unauthorized model changes can invalidate version control. Outages can alter what evidence is available at decision time.

A trustworthy research infrastructure therefore requires access control, credential governance, software provenance, dependency security, environment isolation, backups, recovery, monitoring, incident response, and business continuity. These are not merely information-technology concerns; they protect the epistemic chain from source to conclusion.

> **Security–Integrity Principle:** A research or model system cannot be trusted if its data, code, models, credentials, or operational environment cannot be trusted.

18.41 Regulatory and Public-Interest Research

Market Systems Science may eventually contribute to public-interest questions such as market stability, systemic-risk monitoring, transparency, investor education, policy evaluation, market-design analysis, and operational resilience. Such work should remain careful about institutional mandate and should never imply regulatory endorsement without explicit evidence.

18.42 Global and Cross-Asset Applicability

The framework should be tested across equities, fixed income, credit, foreign exchange, commodities, derivatives, digital assets, private markets, and funding markets. Transfer should not be assumed. Market structure, data availability, participant composition, legal rules, and trading conventions differ materially across asset classes and jurisdictions.

Some concepts may generalize well while specific measurements fail. Liquidity as conditional exchange capacity may remain useful across markets, for example, while the relevant observable measures differ dramatically. Cross-asset research should therefore distinguish conceptual portability from measurement portability.

18.43 Limits of Generalization

The scope of a conclusion should not exceed the scope of the evidence. A finding from U.S. large-cap equities during regular trading hours using one vendor, one state classifier, and one volatility period should not be generalized automatically to other instruments, sessions, countries, or regimes.

Generalization should be earned through replication, theoretical justification, and explicit evaluation of structural differences. When transport fails, the correct response may be to narrow the claim rather than to force universality.

> **Scope Principle:** The scope of a conclusion should not exceed the markets, periods, horizons, and conditions represented by the evidence.

18.44 Future Volumes

Future volumes may extend the foundation into advanced market measurement, state and transition models, market microstructure, cross-market systems, decision science, quantitative research governance, artificial intelligence and automation, empirical case studies, or institutional and systemic risk. These should be treated as possible directions rather than fixed publication promises.

Each future volume should add empirical depth or methodological capability rather than merely repeat the vocabulary of Volume I. The foundation is useful only if later work tests, refines, and sometimes contradicts it.

18.45 The Market Systems Science Research Charter

The principal institutional construct proposed in this chapter is the Market Systems Science Research Charter. The Charter should define how the research program governs its mission, scope, standards, conflicts, corrections, and amendments. It should function as a constitutional research document rather than as a marketing statement.

Charter field	**Required content**
Mission	Why the research program exists and what kinds of questions it seeks to improve.
Scope	Markets, phenomena, and activities inside and outside the program.
Foundational propositions	Current organizing ideas, explicitly marked as revisable.
Open questions	Unresolved research priorities and known limitations.
Claim standards	Requirements for descriptive, predictive, mechanistic, causal, and decision claims.
Measurement standards	Provenance, definitions, quality, time, versioning, and limitations.
Research methods	Protocol, review, reproduction, replication, and deviation requirements.
Model governance	Validation, monitoring, change control, incident response, retirement.
AI-use standards	Permitted roles, evidence requirements, authority boundaries, audit.
Conflict policy	Disclosure and governance of commercial, personal, and institutional incentives.
Publication standards	Minimum disclosure, correction, retraction, and version requirements.
Amendment process	How definitions, standards, and framework architecture may be revised.

The Market Systems Science Research Charter

CHARTER FIELD	REQUIRED CONTENT
Mission	Why the research program exists and what kinds of questions it seeks to improve.
Scope	Markets, phenomena, and activities inside and outside the program.
Foundational propositions	Current organizing ideas, explicitly marked as revisable.
Open questions	Unresolved research priorities and known limitations.
Claim standards	Requirements for descriptive, predictive, mechanistic, causal, and decision claims.
Measurement standards	Provenance, definitions, quality, time, versioning, and limitations.
Research methods	Protocol, review, reproduction, replication, and deviation requirements.
Model governance	Validation, monitoring, change control, incident response, retirement.
AI-use standards	Permitted roles, evidence requirements, authority boundaries, audit.
Conflict policy	Disclosure and governance of commercial, personal, and institutional incentives.
Publication standards	Minimum disclosure, correction, retraction, and version requirements.
Amendment process	How definitions, standards, and framework architecture may be revised.

The Charter should function as a constitutional research document rather than as a marketing statement.

Figure 18.5 — The Market Systems Science Research Charter

18.46 A Long-Horizon Research Agenda

A long-horizon agenda is better organized by maturity than by rigid calendar promises. In a foundation stage, the priority is terminology, measurement standards, data lineage, reproducibility, and credible baselines. In a validation stage, the emphasis shifts toward cross-period studies, cross-market replication, state validity, transition performance, and calibration.

An integration stage can then examine multidomain systems, cross-market transmission, human–machine collaboration, and decision-quality effects. An institutional stage may develop external review networks, standards, educational programs, professional practice, and public-interest research. Progress through these stages should depend on evidence rather than schedule.

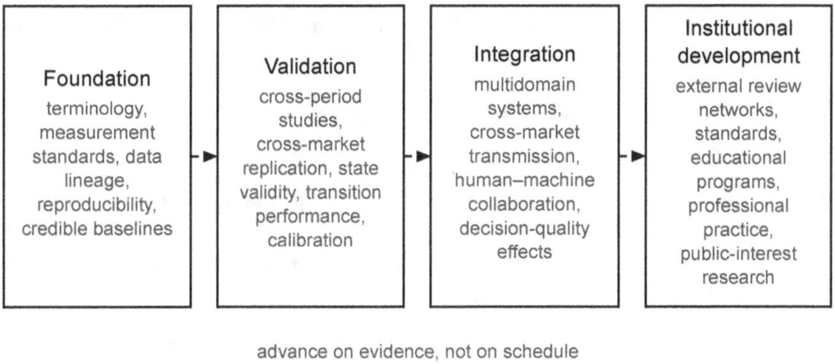

Stages, not dates. The agenda is organized by maturity rather than by calendar promises, and progress through these stages should depend on evidence rather than schedule.

Figure 18.6 — Foundation, Validation, Integration, and Institutional Development

18.47 Worked Example: From Research Question to Open Program

Consider the question: does declining liquidity resilience contribute useful evidence about disorderly transition risk? A one-off study could test one measure over one period, but an open research program treats the question cumulatively.

1. Define liquidity resilience precisely and specify its observable and inferred components.
2. Validate the measurements for timestamp integrity, sensitivity, and market coverage.
3. Establish simple baselines and unconditional distributions.
4. Test association with subsequent price impact and disorderly transition outcomes.
5. Investigate plausible mechanisms such as replenishment failure and forced adjustment.
6. Condition results on market configuration, horizon, and volatility state.
7. Compare transition models with simpler alternatives and measure lag and false alarms.
8. Replicate across periods, instruments, venues, and independent implementations.
9. Evaluate whether the evidence improves participant-specific decisions after costs and constraints.
10. Publish null results, failed replications, and scope restrictions.
11. Revise, narrow, or retire the claim as the evidence accumulates.

The example illustrates the intended culture of the field: one question can support a sequence of studies, models, replications, disagreements, and revisions without any single result being treated as final.

18.48 Worked Example: AI-Generated Market Explanation

Suppose an AI system produces a persuasive explanation for a sharp market decline. It attributes the move to crowded positioning, dealer hedging, weakening liquidity, and rising uncertainty. The narrative is coherent, but coherence alone does not establish evidence.

A responsible review asks which sources were used, whether the observations were current, which statements are measurements and which are inferred, whether dealer ownership assumptions are valid, whether trigger has been distinguished from structural condition, whether alternative hypotheses were considered, whether uncertainty is preserved, and whether the narrative can be reproduced from the cited evidence.

If the explanation cannot answer those questions, it remains an unverified narrative regardless of fluency. AI can accelerate synthesis, but the evidentiary chain must remain inspectable.

18.49 Worked Example: Framework Revision

Suppose repeated studies across several markets show that funding and collateral conditions explain important variation in stress transmission that cannot be represented adequately within the existing domain boundaries. The framework would then face a genuine revision question.

Possible responses include treating funding as a subdimension of an existing domain, representing it as a cross-domain structural condition, revising domain definitions, adding a fifth domain, or narrowing the scope of the four-domain framework. No answer should be selected because it preserves institutional simplicity. The decision should follow evidence, conceptual clarity, measurement validity, and replication.

> **Domain-Revision Principle:** The four-domain architecture is foundational, but it is not immune to evidence-driven revision when additional structure is needed.

18.50 Closing Perspective

Markets will continue to change faster than any fixed framework can fully capture. New instruments, regulations, technologies, participant behaviors, and institutional structures will alter both the phenomena being studied and the measurements available to study them. The task of Market Systems

Science is therefore not to eliminate uncertainty or freeze market behavior into permanent categories.

Its task is to improve how market phenomena are observed, measured, interpreted, challenged, represented, and revised. It should make uncertainty more visible rather than hiding it, make models more accountable rather than more authoritative, and make decisions more reviewable rather than merely more automated.

The discipline should ultimately be judged not by whether it always predicts correctly, but by whether it produces clearer questions, more trustworthy measurements, more defensible claims, more transparent models, more responsible decisions, and a stronger capacity to learn from error.

> **Final Principle:** The discipline values correction over consistency, refinement over institutional pride, and cumulative learning over claims of final certainty.

Chapter Summary

Volume I is not converted into a finished doctrine. Market Systems Science is defined instead as an open research program: one that can accumulate evidence, preserve disagreement, support reproducibility, incorporate new methods, revise its own concepts, and retire claims that no longer withstand scrutiny. Openness here is first epistemic. Claims remain open to criticism, competing explanations, new data, independent implementation, failed replication, and narrowing of scope, and that does not require every dataset, algorithm, or proprietary implementation to be publicly released.

The volume establishes a coherent vocabulary and a set of methodological boundaries: a systems view of markets shaped by interaction, feedback, adaptation, heterogeneity, and nonlinear response; a foundational multidomain observational architecture of liquidity, positioning, volatility, and trend; controlled measurement; the separation of observation, measurement, evidence, inference, interpretation, assessment, judgment, and decision; and the operational structures of market configuration, state representation, transition analysis, the Decision Environment, the Research Ledger, and the Governed Model Record. It does not establish a complete theory of financial markets, a final domain taxonomy, universal state categories, universal thresholds, a causal hierarchy among all market forces, a guaranteed forecasting advantage, or one correct decision method.

Progress is defined in terms more demanding than growth in publications, terminology, or model count. It may mean clearer definitions, stronger measurement validity, better reproducibility, more stable classification, improved calibration, lower false-transition rates, more informative uncertainty, and more disciplined decision records, and narrowing or retiring a claim can itself be progress. Failure has its own signals: definitions that cannot be operationalized consistently, measurements that cannot be reproduced, model outputs that add no value over simple baselines, classifications detached from observable evidence, and governance that has become ceremonial.

The research agenda is organized around questions rather than products. It spans measurement, the four domains and their interaction, market configuration, state, transition, resilience and fragility, cross-market and network structure, participant heterogeneity, and institutional and technological change. Cumulative work depends on shared data, measurement, state and transition, and model and AI governance standards, on technical infrastructure that preserves scientific lineage, and on replication networks that preserve disagreement rather than forcing consensus. Null findings, failed replications, retired models, and corrections belong in the record.

Artificial intelligence will increasingly support market research, but fluency is not evidence, and provenance, validation, and responsibility cannot be delegated to it. The correct unit of evaluation is the complete human–machine system, including its data, models, interfaces, authority boundaries, incentives, controls, and review process. Institutional credibility requires external review, independent replication, conflict disclosure, documented dissent, and correction mechanisms; product and marketing claims should not be stronger than the research, validation, and implementation evidence beneath them; and security is part of scientific integrity, because research depends on trusted data, code, credentials, models, and environments.

The scope of a conclusion should not exceed the scope of the evidence, and the framework itself remains open to evidence-driven revision when additional structure is needed. The discipline should ultimately be judged not by whether it always predicts correctly, but by whether it produces clearer questions, more trustworthy measurements, more defensible claims, more transparent models, more responsible decisions, and a stronger capacity to learn from error.

Established Knowledge

The future research program described in this chapter builds upon established work in systems science, complexity science, economics and finance, market microstructure, econometrics, network science, decision science, model risk management, reproducible research, open science, replication studies, artificial-intelligence governance, human factors, research ethics, operational resilience, cybersecurity, institutional governance, and educational science.

Market Systems Science should not claim originality for research programs, scientific charters, replication, open-science practices, model inventories, data lineage, artificial-intelligence governance, model validation, incident response, research ethics, network analysis, or operational resilience. Its contribution lies in integrating these disciplines around a governed architecture for market observation, measurement, evidence, configuration, state, transition, decision, research, and model lifecycle management.

Institute Perspective

The WallStreetDelta Institute proposes Market Systems Science as an integrated research orientation rather than a finished universal theory. Its distinctive contribution is the combination of systems thinking, the four-domain observational architecture, controlled measurement, evidence and claim discipline, market configuration and state, transition analysis, decision quality, research governance, model lifecycle governance, technical provenance, education, and institutional correction.

The Institute's stewardship role should therefore be evaluated by its ability to preserve challenge and revision. The strongest proof of stewardship will not be consistency of conclusions, but the existence of processes that allow definitions to change, models to be retired, dissent to remain visible, and external evidence to alter the framework.

Principles for the Future Research Program

Principle	Meaning
Open-Program Principle	Remain open to criticism, replication, competing models, and revision.
Incompleteness Principle	State clearly what the framework does not explain or establish.
Evidence-Progress Principle	Measure progress through improved validity, reproducibility, calibration, and learning.
Failure-Testing Principle	Test the framework for where it fails, adds no value, or requires narrowing.
Domain-Revision Principle	Treat the four-domain architecture as foundational but revisable.
Scope Principle	Do not generalize beyond the markets, periods, horizons, and conditions represented by evidence.
Independence Principle	Support review and replication outside the originating institution.
Research–Product Principle	Do not allow product or marketing claims to exceed underlying research and validation.

Principle	Meaning
Provenance Principle	Preserve traceable data, code, measurement, model, and publication lineage.
Negative-Result Principle	Retain null findings, failed replications, and model retirements.
Correction Principle	Treat correction and retraction as part of scientific functioning.
AI Instrument Principle	Use AI as a research instrument rather than an epistemic authority.
Human-Responsibility Principle	Preserve human and institutional responsibility under automation.
Security–Integrity Principle	Protect the integrity of data, code, models, credentials, and operational systems.
Education Principle	Teach disciplined reasoning and challenge rather than doctrinal repetition.
Ethical-Boundary Principle	Do not equate profitability or predictive performance with responsible use.
Living-Knowledge Principle	Maintain evidence status, version, review date, and revision history for material claims.
Framework-Stewardship Principle	Preserve the field's capacity to challenge and revise the framework itself.

Questions for Reflection

1. What does it mean to describe Market Systems Science as an open research program?
2. What has Volume I established?
3. What has Volume I explicitly not established?
4. Why should the framework identify its own failure conditions?
5. What should count as progress in the field?
6. How can the research program distinguish growth from unnecessary complexity?
7. Why should the four domains remain open to revision?
8. What evidence could justify adding or redefining a domain?
9. What are the most important unresolved measurement questions?
10. Why must liquidity research remain conditional on size, horizon, and market condition?
11. Why is positioning especially difficult to observe?
12. What future questions remain about volatility?
13. How should trend be researched across horizons?
14. Why are multidomain interactions difficult to validate?
15. What makes a market configuration scientifically useful?
16. How should state representations be validated?

17. What makes transition research different from ordinary prediction?
18. How should resilience and fragility be distinguished?
19. What can network research contribute to market-systems analysis?
20. Why does participant heterogeneity matter?
21. How can institutional and technological change alter research findings?
22. What is reflexivity in deployed models?
23. How might a successful model undermine its own stability?
24. Which research tasks may AI support appropriately?
25. Why should AI-generated explanations remain traceable to evidence?
26. What distinguishes AI assistance from AI decision authority?
27. What technical infrastructure supports cumulative research?
28. Why are shared data semantics important?
29. What should a measurement standard contain?
30. What should state and transition standards contain?
31. What is the difference between reproducibility and truth?
32. Why are independent replication networks valuable?
33. How can proprietary research remain disciplined?
34. What should publication standards disclose?
35. Why should null findings and retractions be preserved?
36. What belongs in a living knowledge base?
37. What responsibilities should the WallStreetDelta Institute assume?
38. Why should the Institute not be the sole validator of its claims?
39. How should research and product claims remain separated?
40. What should an educational program teach?
41. What professional standards may emerge from the field?
42. What ethical boundaries should govern model use?
43. Why is cybersecurity part of scientific integrity?
44. How may the framework apply differently across asset classes?
45. Why should conclusions remain scoped to evidence?
46. What should a Market Systems Science Research Charter contain?
47. How should amendments to the framework be governed?
48. What would justify retiring a claim or model?
49. How should future volumes extend rather than repeat Volume I?
50. By what standards should Market Systems Science ultimately be judged?

Appendix A. Glossary

Canonical terminology for Volume I

This glossary consolidates the principal terms used throughout Volume I. Definitions are intentionally bounded: where a term has a narrower technical meaning in a specific chapter, the chapter definition governs.

Action — Implementation of a selected decision. Action should be distinguished from the judgment and decision that preceded it.

Adaptation — Change in participant behavior, institutional practice, or model use in response to information, incentives, constraints, or prior outcomes.

Assessment — A structured synthesis of evidence, alternatives, contradiction, uncertainty, and confidence for a stated analytical purpose.

Association — A relationship in which variables vary together under defined conditions; association alone does not establish causation.

Baseline — A defined comparison state, period, model, distribution, or reference against which a measurement or result is evaluated.

Breadth — The degree to which market movement or participation is distributed across the defined universe rather than concentrated in a small subset.

Calibration — Evaluation of whether expressed probabilities, confidence levels, classifications, or forecasts correspond with observed outcomes or defined correctness criteria over repeated cases.

Causal claim — A claim that changing one factor would alter an outcome under stated assumptions; it requires stronger design than description, association, or temporal sequence.

Claim boundary — The limit of what a measurement, model, result, or analysis is justified in asserting.

Configuration — See Market configuration.

Confidence — The strength of support for a specific claim or output. Confidence is multidimensional and should not be treated as a universal property of an analysis.

Confirmation — The point at which governed evidence, quality, persistence, and classification requirements are satisfied for a stated claim or transition.

Constraint — A condition that limits feasible actions, model solutions, interpretations, or research designs.

Contextual evidence — A measurement interpreted relative to a defined question, proposition, universe, horizon, and baseline.

Contradictory evidence — Evidence that conflicts with, weakens, or complicates a proposed explanation, classification, or hypothesis.

Data — Recorded or processed representations of observations. Data are not identical to the underlying market phenomenon.

Data drift — A change in the distribution or characteristics of model inputs through time.

Decision — Selection among available alternatives within a Decision Environment.

Decision Environment — The structured combination of objectives, constraints, alternatives, information, uncertainty, horizon, risk capacity, implementation conditions, reversibility, authority, and responsibility relevant to a choice.

Decision margin — An Institute term for the degree by which a preferred alternative exceeds the next-best alternative under stated assumptions and objectives.

Decision quality — The quality of the process used to choose an action under uncertainty, evaluated separately from the favorability of the realized outcome.

Decomposability — The ability to trace a compressed output back to component measurements, assumptions, transformations, quality states, and confidence.

Discrimination — The ability of a model or classification to distinguish relevant cases, separate from calibration.

Domain — A foundational observational category used to organize evidence. Volume I uses liquidity, positioning, volatility, and trend as the initial domain architecture.

Emergence — System-level behavior arising from interactions among components that is not fully described by any single component in isolation.

Error — A value, calculation, implementation, or assertion that is incorrect; error should be corrected rather than merely labeled as uncertainty.

Evidence — A measurement or observation evaluated as relevant to a particular question, proposition, comparison, or hypothesis.

Evidence dependency — Dependence among apparently separate pieces of evidence caused by shared data, transformations, models, or mechanisms.

Expected value — A decision-theoretic representation of probability-weighted value across possible outcomes; useful but dependent on probabilities, utility, model assumptions, and feasibility.

Fast trajectory — A short-horizon description of recent multidomain movement or rotation relative to a confirmed structural state.

Feature — A designed transformation of one or more inputs used by a model; a feature is not a naturally occurring fact.

Feedback — A process in which the output or consequence of an interaction influences subsequent behavior of the system.

Forecast — An estimate or statement about a possible future outcome under a defined target, horizon, information set, and method.

Framework — An organized conceptual structure identifying relevant objects, relationships, categories, boundaries, and questions for a stated field of inquiry.

Fragility — Sensitivity to disturbance, amplification, constraint activation, or loss of function under specified conditions.

Governed Model Record — The Institute model-documentation construct preserving purpose, lineage, assumptions, validation, permitted use, monitoring, changes, incidents, and lifecycle status.

Hierarchy — An ordered conceptual relationship among analytical layers. A hierarchy should not be interpreted as implying that later layers are inherently more truthful than earlier ones.

Horizon — The time scale over which a measurement, state, forecast, decision, or research claim is defined.

Hypothesis — A proposed explanation or relationship structured so that evidence can increase, reduce, or revise confidence in it.

Implementation validation — Evidence that an operational system reproduces the intended method under the approved environment and use conditions.

Indicator — A measurement or signal about a defined feature; an indicator may be only one component of a broader model or framework.

Inference — A proposition that extends beyond direct observation or measurement through reasoning and assumptions.

Information — A general term for data or measurements organized to make relationships or context easier to examine. In Volume I it is not a separate formal epistemic tier.

Interpretation — An organized account of what evidence may mean in context, explicitly bounded by assumptions and alternatives.

Judgment — A reasoned conclusion formed for a stated purpose. Judgment is distinct from the participant-specific decision that may follow.

Knowledge — A provisional state of justified understanding supported by evidence and reasoning that have survived an appropriate degree of examination for the scope of the claim.

Latency — Delay between an underlying event, its recording, its availability to a user or system, and any subsequent calculation.

Liquidity — The market's capacity for exchange under specified size, horizon, venue, and market conditions; it is multidimensional rather than a single universal quantity.

Market Compass — An Institute presentation model for communicating selected multidomain state components while preserving decomposition, freshness, and confidence.

Market configuration — The detailed, time-specific arrangement of observable and inferred conditions across domains and other relevant evidence at a stated scale.

Market phenomenon — An event, condition, interaction, or process in the market that exists independently of the representation used to study it.

Market state — A controlled, higher-level representation of selected features of a market configuration for a stated purpose, horizon, universe, and method.

Measurement — A controlled representation constructed from data according to a defined method and purpose.

Mechanism — A proposed process or pathway through which observed conditions may contribute to an outcome.

Missingness — The state in which potentially relevant evidence is unavailable, absent, invalid, delayed, or structurally unobservable. Missingness is not equivalent to neutrality.

Model — A simplified, purpose-specific representation of selected features, relationships, or processes within a defined system.

Model drift — Change through time in the meaning, performance, or approved applicability of a model.

Model risk — The possibility of adverse conclusions or actions arising from conceptual, data, measurement, estimation, implementation, calibration, interpretation, use, or governance failures.

Nonlinearity — A relationship in which proportional changes in inputs do not necessarily produce proportional changes in outcomes.

Nonstationarity — Change through time in relevant statistical or structural properties of the process being studied.

Null result — A research result that does not support the proposed effect or relationship under the defined design; it is evidence and should be preserved.

Observation — A recorded or otherwise identified representation of market activity under defined source and timing conditions.

Outcome — What occurs after a decision and action within the evolving environment; outcome quality should be evaluated separately from decision quality.

Positioning — The distribution of exposure, sensitivity, leverage, concentration, and potential adjustment requirements across participants or instruments, much of which may be latent or model-dependent.

Prediction — A stated expectation about a future outcome. Predictive success does not by itself establish mechanism, causation, or understanding.

Principle of Provisional Knowledge — The principle that market understanding represents the current best-supported account permitted by available evidence, models, assumptions, and scope, and remains open to revision.

Probability — A quantified representation of uncertainty about a defined event under a stated model, information set, horizon, and reference class.

Provenance — Traceable lineage showing where data, measurements, code, models, transformations, and published claims originated and how they changed.

Recorded observation — A value or event reported by an identified source under a specified timestamp, schema, and context.

Replication — Testing whether a comparable finding survives new data, another period, another market, or an independent implementation.

Reproducibility — The ability to regenerate the same result using the same data, code, environment, and procedure.

Research Ledger — The Institute research-governance construct preserving the research question, protocol, versions, deviations, results, review, replication status, limitations, disposition, and revision history.

Resilience — Capacity to absorb disturbance, continue functioning, replenish, adapt, or recover under specified conditions.

Risk capacity — The ability to absorb adverse outcomes without violating essential objectives or obligations.

Scenario — A conditional pathway describing how events or configurations may evolve under stated assumptions and signposts; a scenario is not automatically a forecast.

Signal — A rule-generated indication intended to inform a decision; a signal is distinct from a state, forecast, or universal action instruction.

State representation — A controlled representation of selected configuration features at a stated horizon and purpose.

Structural break — A material change in the underlying process such that previously estimated relationships may become less reliable.

Structural State Vector — An Institute decomposable representation of selected domain and cross-domain state variables, illustratively SSV(t) = [L, P, V, T, B, R, F, Q, C].

System — A set of interacting components whose collective behavior depends on relationships, feedback, constraints, and evolution through time.

Threshold — A designed boundary used to convert continuous variation into a category, alert, decision rule, or state change.

Trajectory — The direction and pattern of recent change in selected configuration components.

Transition — A material and sufficiently persistent reorganization of selected configuration features under a stated method, horizon, and classification framework.

Transition confidence — Confidence that a material configuration change is underway; distinct from confidence in the eventual destination.

Trend — Sustained directional persistence identified under a stated method and horizon; trend is not an independent causal force or deterministic forecast.

Uncertainty — Incomplete confidence about a claim, outcome, model, measurement, or future condition.

Validation — Evaluation of whether a method, model, measurement, classification, or implementation is appropriate and reliable for its stated purpose.

Verification — Evaluation of whether an implementation conforms to its documented specification.

Volatility — The degree and structure of variability observed or implied in market prices over a specified horizon and method; one expression of uncertainty, sensitivity, information processing, and adjustment.

Appendix B. Principles

Canonical principles of Market Systems Science

This appendix consolidates the governing principles that recur across Volume I. The chapter text remains authoritative where a principle is defined more narrowly or with additional conditions.

1. Systems Perspective

Study relationships, feedback, adaptation, constraints, and emergence as carefully as isolated observations.

2. Observation Principle

A recorded observation establishes what an identified source reported, not the complete meaning or cause of the event.

3. Measurement Principle

Measurements are controlled representations, not the phenomena themselves.

4. Evidence Principle

A measurement becomes evidence only in relation to a defined question or proposition.

5. Inference Principle

Claims extending beyond measurement require explicit reasoning and assumptions.

6. Alternative-Explanation Principle

A plausible explanation does not eliminate competing or null explanations.

7. Scope Principle

Claims should specify the universe, horizon, method, and conditions under which they are intended to hold.

8. Confidence Principle

Confidence should remain proportional to evidence quality and appropriate to the claim type.

9. Provisional-Knowledge Principle

Market understanding remains open to revision when evidence, measurements, models, assumptions, or conditions change.

10. Correction Principle

Correction is evidence that disciplined inquiry is functioning.

11. Liquidity Conditionality

Liquidity should be described relative to size, horizon, venue, and prevailing market conditions.

12. Positioning Uncertainty

Positioning evidence should preserve ownership assumptions, leverage, aggregation, netting, and model dependence.

13. Volatility Interpretation

Volatility describes the degree and structure of variability; implied volatility is model-dependent and should not be treated as pure fear or a pure forecast.

14. Trend Horizon Principle

Trend exists only relative to a stated method, universe, and horizon.

15. Interaction Principle

Domain interactions may create system-level behavior that cannot be inferred from one domain alone.

16. Measurement Governance

Every material measurement should preserve definition, source, units, time, transformation, version, quality state, and limitations.

17. Dependency Principle

Several measurements or models using common inputs or assumptions do not constitute independent confirmation.

18. Language-Proportionality Principle

Claim language should not exceed the strength and scope of supporting evidence.

19. Machine-Reasoning Principle

Automated narratives should be trusted only to the extent that claims, sources, timestamps, versions, assumptions, uncertainty, and revision conditions can be inspected.

20. Configuration-to-State Principle

The market possesses a configuration; the analyst or model assigns a state representation to selected features of that configuration.

21. Compression Principle

A state may compress evidence but must not destroy traceability.

22. Vector Principle

The Structural State Vector is a governed representation of selected evidence, not a self-validating description of the entire market.

23. Compass Principle

The Market Compass communicates selected state components; it is not the market state itself.

24. Trajectory Principle

Fast observations describe trajectory; confirmed state requires the designated evidence-quality and persistence conditions.

25. Decomposability Principle

A state representation may compress evidence but must remain decomposable into component measurements, assumptions, quality states, and confidence.

26. Transition Principle

All confirmed state transitions involve configuration change, but most configuration changes do not become confirmed transitions.

27. Indication–Confirmation Principle

Early evidence improves responsiveness; confirmation improves reliability.

28. Destination-Uncertainty Principle

Confidence that a transition is underway does not imply confidence in its destination.

29. Trigger–Configuration Principle

A trigger may explain timing; the receiving configuration helps explain transmission and scale.

30. State-Horizon Principle

A transition at one horizon does not automatically imply transition at another.

31. Assessment–Decision Principle

Market assessment informs action but does not determine it independently of participant objectives and constraints.

32. Decision-Quality Principle

Evaluate the quality of the decision process separately from the favorability of the outcome.

33. Participant-Dependence Principle

The same market evidence may support different rational actions in different Decision Environments.

34. Uncertainty–Commitment Principle

Uncertainty should affect the magnitude, timing, and reversibility of commitment.

35. Survival Principle

Favorable expected value does not justify exposure that threatens essential obligations or survival.

36. Robustness Principle

Under model uncertainty, acceptable performance across plausible scenarios may matter more than optimization under one forecast.

37. Optionality Principle

Reversible actions and preserved flexibility can have value when uncertainty remains unresolved.

38. Research-Object Principle

Method should follow the research question and the nature of the research object.

39. Claim-Proportionality Principle

The strength of research design and evidence should be proportional to the strength of the claim.

40. Temporal Integrity Principle

No study should use information before it was reasonably available.

41. Exploration–Confirmation Principle

Exploration generates hypotheses; independent confirmation evaluates them.

42. Dependence Principle

Statistical precision should reflect dependence structure, not merely row count.

43. Nonstationarity Principle

Relationships should be assumed capable of change unless stability is demonstrated.

44. Reproducibility Principle

A result should be regenerable from governed data, code, environment, and protocol.

45. Replication Principle

A finding becomes stronger when it survives new data, independent implementation, or a different setting.

46. Negative-Evidence Principle

Null results and failed replications belong in the evidence base.

47. Challenge Principle

Research claims should be exposed to competent attempts at disconfirmation.

48. Representation Principle

A model represents selected features of the market; it is not the market itself.

49. Framework–Model Principle

A framework organizes inquiry, while a model performs a defined representational task within that structure.

50. Purpose Principle

Model purpose must be defined before model selection or evaluation.

51. Selection Principle

Every model reflects choices about what to include, transform, weight, and omit.

52. Output–Interpretation Principle

A model output is not identical to its interpretation or decision use.

53. Complexity Principle

Additional complexity should be justified by meaningful improvement in the stated purpose.

54. Verification–Validation Principle

Correct implementation does not establish conceptual validity.

55. Benchmark Principle

Complex models should be evaluated against credible simpler alternatives.

56. Drift Principle

A stable calculation does not guarantee a stable meaning.

57. Reflexivity Principle

A deployed model may become part of the system it attempts to represent.

58. Lifecycle Principle

Development, validation, deployment, monitoring, change, incident response, and retirement form one governed lifecycle.

59. Open-Program Principle

Market Systems Science should remain open to criticism, replication, competing models, negative evidence, and revision.

60. Incompleteness Principle

The framework should state clearly what it does not explain or establish.

61. Failure-Testing Principle

The framework should be tested for where it fails, adds no value, or requires narrowing.

62. Independence Principle

Claims should be capable of review and replication outside the originating institution.

63. Research–Product Principle

Product and marketing claims should not exceed the research and validation beneath them.

64. AI Instrument Principle

AI may support inquiry but should not be treated as an epistemic authority.

65. Security–Integrity Principle

Research integrity depends on the integrity of data, code, models, credentials, and operational systems.

66. Living-Knowledge Principle

Material claims, models, and standards should retain evidence status, version, review date, and revision history.

67. Framework-Stewardship Principle

Stewardship requires preserving the field's capacity to challenge and revise the framework itself.

Appendix C. Hierarchies

Canonical analytical architectures and boundaries

The hierarchies in this appendix are analytical architectures rather than claims that later layers are inherently more truthful. They show how representations and responsibilities change as inquiry moves from observation toward action, research, and governance.

C.1 Market Inquiry Chain

Market phenomenon

↓

Recorded observation / data

↓

Controlled measurement

↓

Contextual evidence

↓

Inference and reasoning

↓

Interpretation

↓

Assessment

↓

Judgment

↓

Decision

↓

Action

↓

Outcome and review

↓

Revised questions, measurements, models, or decisions

C.2 Measurement-to-Evidence Architecture

Phenomenon

↓

Source record

↓

Processing / normalization

↓

Measurement

↓

Quality state

↓

Contextual evidence

↓

Claim-specific interpretation

C.3 Multidomain Representation Architecture

Controlled measurements

↓

Contextual evidence

↓

Domain assessment

↓

Market configuration

↓

Market state

↓

Trajectory / transition assessment

C.4 Decision Architecture

Assessment

↓

Judgment

↓

Decision Environment

↓

Alternatives

↓

Decision

↓

Commitment / implementation

↓

Outcome

↓

Review and calibration

C.5 Research Cycle

Research object

↓

Question

↓

Claim type

↓

Hypothesis

↓

Protocol / design

↓

Data and measurements

↓

Analysis

↓

Result

↓

Interpretation

↓

Validation

↓

Reproduction

↓

Replication

↓

Revision / disposition

C.6 Model Architecture Stack

Conceptual layer

↓

Data layer

↓

Measurement layer

↓

Feature layer

↓

Model layer

↓

Output layer

↓

Interpretation layer

↓

Decision-use layer

↓

Governance layer

C.7 Model Lifecycle

Proposed

↓

Research / development

↓

Verification

↓

Validation

↓

Shadow testing

↓

Approved deployment

↓

Monitoring

↓

Change control

↓

Incident response

↓

Revalidation

↓

Retirement

C.8 Claim Escalation

Recorded observation

↓

Measurement statement

↓

Descriptive claim

↓

Associative claim

↓

Temporal-sequence claim

↓

Mechanistic claim

↓

Causal claim

↓

Predictive claim

↓

Decision-use claim

C.9 Transparency Levels for Proprietary Research

Internally reproducible

↓

Independently auditable

↓

Externally replicable under agreement

↓

Publicly reproducible

C.10 Knowledge Status

Exploratory

↓

Conditionally supported

↓

Supported within scope

↓

Contested

↓

Unsupported

↓

Contradicted

↓

Retired

C.11 Important Boundary Notes

- Evidence, inference, interpretation, assessment, judgment, and decision are not interchangeable.
- A hypothesis is not a "higher fact"; it is a proposition structured for evaluation.
- A market state is not a forecast, signal, or universal action instruction.
- A transition classification does not determine its future destination.
- A research finding does not automatically justify a decision.
- Correct implementation does not establish conceptual validity.
- Reproducibility does not establish truth; replication and challenge address generality.

Appendix D. Notation

Notation conventions used in Volume I

Notation in Volume I is intentionally limited. Symbols are illustrative unless a chapter specifies a formal model. No symbol should be interpreted as a universal market quantity independent of the definition, horizon, universe, source, and version used.

Symbol	Meaning	Required qualification
t	Time or effective timestamp.	The relevant clock, timezone, and session should be specified.
Δt	Time interval or sampling horizon.	May represent seconds, minutes, days, or another defined interval.
P_t	Price or index level at time t.	Specify instrument and price convention.
r_t	Return over a defined interval.	Arithmetic or log return must be stated.
b_t, a_t	Best bid and best ask at time t.	Venue and market scope must be stated.
m_t	Quoted midpoint, commonly (a_t + b_t)/2.	A midpoint is a measurement, not executable price.
s_t	Quoted spread, commonly a_t − b_t.	Absolute, relative, or basis-point form must be identified.
σ	Volatility or dispersion parameter.	The estimator, horizon, and whether realized or implied must be stated.
IV	Implied volatility.	A model-dependent derived estimate from option prices and assumptions.
p(E | I)	Probability of event E conditional on information set I.	Requires event, horizon, reference class, model, and calibration.
EV(a)	Expected value of action a.	May be written as Σ p_i u(o_i | a); utility and probabilities must be defined.
u(o)	Utility or value assigned to outcome o.	Participant- and objective-dependent.

Symbol	Meaning	Required qualification
SSV(t)	Structural State Vector at time t.	Institute representation; components and version must be specified.
L	Liquidity condition component of SSV.	Not a universal scalar of all liquidity.
P	Positioning condition component of SSV.	May be proxy- or model-dependent.
V	Volatility condition component of SSV.	Specify realized/implied structure and horizon.
T	Trend condition component of SSV.	Specify method, horizon, and breadth.
B	Breadth and leadership component of SSV.	Specify universe and weighting.
R	Resilience component of SSV.	Specify disturbance and recovery definition.
F	Fragility or stress-sensitivity component of SSV.	Specify inference method and dependencies.
Q	Data-quality state component of SSV.	May include freshness, completeness, and validity.
C	Confidence component of SSV.	Should be claim-specific and calibrated where possible.
x	Generic observation or measurement.	Definition and units must accompany use.
x̄	Sample mean of x.	Dependence may reduce effective sample size.
Var(x)	Variance of x.	Estimator and sample must be specified.
Corr(x,y)	Correlation between x and y.	Association does not establish causation.
β	Generic estimated sensitivity or coefficient.	Meaning depends on the model specification.
θ	Generic parameter vector.	Parameters and estimation method must be versioned.

D.1 Structural State Vector

SSV(t) = [L, P, V, T, B, R, F, Q, C]

This representation is illustrative and decomposable. It does not imply that the components are directly observable, independent, equally weighted, universally sufficient, or predictive.

D.2 Return Convention

When returns are used, the manuscript should state the convention. Illustratively, a log return may be written r_t = ln(P_t / P_{t-1}). An arithmetic return may be written $R_t = P_t/P_{t-1} - 1$. The chosen form, horizon, adjustment policy, and price field should be documented.

D.3 Expected Value Convention

Illustratively, $EV(a) = \Sigma_i p_i u(o_i \mid a)$, where a is an action, p_i is the assigned probability of outcome i, and u represents the participant-specific value or utility of that outcome. Expected value is one decision tool rather than a universal definition of rationality.

D.4 Notation Governance

- Define every symbol at first material use.
- State units, horizon, universe, and time convention.
- Distinguish observed variables from latent or estimated variables.
- Do not reuse the same symbol for materially different constructs without explicit qualification.
- Version model-specific notation when definitions change.
- Prefer clarity over unnecessary mathematical compression.

Appendix E. Research Standards

Minimum standards for governed Market Systems Science research

These standards operationalize the research-method requirements of Volume I. They define a minimum governance baseline, not a substitute for domain-specific statistical, econometric, causal, or engineering methods.

E.1 Research question and object

- State the research question.
- Identify the research object: observation, measurement, relationship, configuration, state, transition, mechanism, forecast, decision process, model, or implementation.
- Define universe, period, horizon, and intended claim.

E.2 Claim classification

- Classify the primary claim as descriptive, associative, predictive, mechanistic, causal, or decision-related.
- Use a design proportional to claim strength.
- State revision conditions and competing explanations.

E.3 Protocol

- Record research identifier, owner, version, question, hypothesis, primary outcomes, data, exclusions, transformations, analysis plan, robustness plan, and limitations.
- Separate exploratory changes from confirmatory commitments.
- Record deviations, timing, rationale, and approval.

E.4 Data provenance

- Identify provider, collection method, schema, timezone, coverage, revision policy, acquisition date, and licensing constraints.
- Preserve checksums or version identifiers where practical.
- Document corporate-action and survivorship treatment where relevant.

E.5 Temporal integrity

- Use only information available at the evaluated decision or prediction time.

- Document event-time alignment, latency, publication delay, session boundaries, and timestamp precision.
- Prevent look-ahead and retrospective state-label leakage.

E.6 Measurement governance

- Define construct, formula, units, source, transformation, horizon, exclusions, missing-data behavior, outlier policy, version, and limitations.
- Separate measurement reliability from construct validity.
- Treat implied, latent, or proxy variables as model-dependent where appropriate.

E.7 Sampling and dependence

- Define target population, observable universe, sampled universe, and analysis sample.
- Assess survivorship, selection, availability, and coverage bias.
- Account for temporal, cross-sectional, overlapping-window, and cluster dependence.

E.8 Exploration and multiplicity

- Label exploratory work explicitly.
- Preserve the search space where practical.
- Address multiple testing, researcher degrees of freedom, and repeated threshold selection.
- Use independent validation for confirmatory claims.

E.9 Validation

- Compare against credible baselines.
- Use out-of-sample or walk-forward evaluation when future prediction is the purpose.
- Test robustness across periods, instruments, states, thresholds, and reasonable alternative definitions.
- Use placebo, falsification, negative-control, or positive-control tests where appropriate.

E.10 Implementation realism

- Include transaction costs, latency, liquidity, capacity, funding, slippage, and market impact where decision usefulness is evaluated.
- Distinguish historical simulation from live deployment evidence.
- Document operational constraints and failure modes.

E.11 Reproducibility and replication

- Preserve code version, environment, data version, protocol, and outputs.
- Distinguish reproduction of the same study from replication in new data or settings.
- Retain failed replications and null results.

E.12 Interpretation

- Match language to evidence strength.
- Distinguish association, temporal sequence, mechanism, contribution, and causation.
- Disclose contradiction, missingness, model dependence, and inferential distance.
- Do not convert a research finding directly into a universal action.

E.13 Review and challenge

- Require review capable of changing the conclusion.
- Preserve dissent and competing explanations.
- Use independent challenge for material claims where practical.
- Disclose conflicts, ownership, sponsorship, and product incentives.

E.14 Disposition and knowledge update

- Assign a research disposition: exploratory, conditionally supported, supported within scope, unsupported, contradicted, or retired.
- Update confidence, scope, model use, and open questions.
- Preserve negative results and failure analysis in the Research Ledger.

E.15 Minimum Research Acceptance Checklist

Control	Minimum expectation
Question and object defined	Required
Claim type and scope defined	Required
Data provenance documented	Required
Measurement definitions versioned	Required
Temporal integrity checked	Required
Dependence and sampling risks assessed	Required
Exploratory/confirmatory status disclosed	Required
Baseline and validation plan present	Required
Robustness / sensitivity assessed	Material studies
Replication status recorded	Material claims
Conflicts disclosed	Required
Limitations and revision conditions recorded	Required
Research Ledger updated	Required

Appendix F. Research Ledger Template

Governed record for market-systems research

The Research Ledger preserves the complete evidentiary history of a study: what was proposed, what was executed, what changed, what was found, how the work was challenged, and the current disposition.

F.1 Identity and ownership

Field	Entry
Research ID	
Title	
Owner	
Reviewers	
Protocol version	
Start date	
Current disposition	

F.2 Research question and claim

Field	Entry
Research question	
Research object	
Claim type	
Primary hypothesis	
Alternative hypotheses	
Null / minimal explanation	
Revision conditions	

F.3 Scope

Field	Entry
Universe / population	
Sample	
Period	
Horizon	

Field	Entry
Market session / timezone	
Configuration or state context	
Exclusions	

F.4 Data and measurement

Field	Entry
Data sources	
Data versions / checksums	
Licensing / access constraints	
Measurements	
Transformations	
Missing-data rules	
Outlier rules	
Known data limitations	

F.5 Design and analysis

Field	Entry
Analysis design	
Baseline / comparison	
Controls / matching	
Primary outcome	
Statistical / analytical method	
Multiplicity treatment	
Robustness plan	
Sensitivity plan	

F.6 Validation

Field	Entry
Training period	
Validation period	
Test / holdout period	
Walk-forward design	
Placebo / falsification tests	
Negative / positive controls	
Implementation realism assumptions	

F.7 Execution history

Field	Entry
Run ID / timestamp	
Code version	
Environment	
Data version	
Result summary	
Artifacts	

F.8 Protocol deviations

Field	Entry
Deviation ID	
What changed	
Why	
When	
Observed results before change?	
Approval	
Effect on interpretation	

F.9 Results and interpretation

Field	Entry
Primary result	
Uncertainty	
Supporting evidence	
Contradictory evidence	
Competing explanations	
Claim language	
Scope limits	

F.10 Review and challenge

Field	Entry
Reviewer	
Challenge performed	
Findings	
Required correction	
Disposition	

F.11 Reproducibility and replication

Field	Entry
Internal reproduction	
Independent reproduction	
Temporal replication	
Cross-market replication	
Conceptual replication	
Failed replication details	

F.12 Final disposition

Field	Entry
Current status	
Decision-use boundary	
Model impact	
Publication status	
Next review date	
Retirement / supersession condition	
Revision history	

Appendix G. Model Documentation Standard

Governed Model Record and lifecycle requirements

This standard defines the minimum documentation required for material models, classifiers, scores, simulations, forecasting systems, and automated decision-support components used within the Market Systems Science framework.

Field	Required documentation
Model identifier	Unique name, version, and effective date.
Owner	Responsible person or function.
Purpose	The specific task the model performs.
Intended use	Approved context, users, instruments, horizons, and decisions supported.
Prohibited use	Contexts in which the output must not be used.
Framework context	Concepts, domains, and research findings organizing the model.
Represented object	Observed, measured, latent, state, transition, forecast, or decision construct.
Inputs	Source, definition, units, timestamps, freshness, expected range, quality state.
Features	Transformations, normalization, aggregation, interaction terms, and rationale.
Architecture	Rules, equations, algorithms, model family, and dependency structure.
Assumptions	Tested, partially tested, operational, unverifiable, and currently violated assumptions.
Parameters	Values, estimation method, training period, tuning process, constraints.
Thresholds	Entry/exit boundaries, hysteresis, persistence, and calibration rationale.
Outputs	Values, categories, probabilities, confidence, quality state, warnings.
Interpretation	Permitted meaning and claim boundaries.
Uncertainty	Data, measurement, parameter, model-form, classification, and environmental uncertainty.
Validation	Conceptual, data, measurement, implementation, performance, stability, and use validation.
Benchmarks	Credible simpler and alternative models.

Field	Required documentation
Calibration / discrimination	Defined correctness, reliability, ranking, and subgroup performance.
Robustness	Sensitivity to definitions, periods, parameters, thresholds, missingness, and state.
Stress testing	Extreme market, data, operational, and adversarial conditions.
Missing-data behavior	Withhold, degrade confidence, fallback, last-good retention, escalation, or other governed behavior.
Monitoring	Input drift, concept drift, calibration, latency, output frequency, overrides, incidents.
Dependencies	Data feeds, services, libraries, models, human processes, infrastructure.
Human override	Authority, permitted conditions, evidence, duration, review.
Criticality	Financial exposure, user reach, automation, regulatory or operational impact.
Security / integrity	Access, provenance, change authorization, environment trust, audit evidence.
Change control	Materiality classification, review, testing, approval, migration.
Deployment	Offline validation, replay, shadow, canary, staged rollout, rollback readiness.
Incidents	Containment, evidence preservation, impact, root cause, correction, revalidation.
Limitations	Known weaknesses, excluded contexts, unresolved unknowns.
Lifecycle	Development, validation, deployment, review, suspension, retirement.
Retirement criteria	Conditions requiring withdrawal or replacement.
History	Versions, changes, incidents, approvals, and disposition.

G.1 Model Validation Standard

- Conceptual validation: the structure and assumptions fit the represented phenomenon and purpose.
- Data validation: inputs are reliable, appropriately scoped, and time-aligned.
- Measurement validation: features represent the intended constructs.
- Verification: implementation conforms to the documented specification.
- Performance validation: the model satisfies the defined purpose relative to baselines.
- Stability validation: behavior remains acceptable through time and across relevant configurations.

- Robustness validation: conclusions survive reasonable specification changes.
- Use validation: the model is appropriate for the intended operational context and user population.

G.2 Minimum Output Contract

Output element	Minimum requirement
Primary estimate / category	Clearly defined and versioned.
Effective time	Timestamp and horizon.
Quality state	Freshness, completeness, validity.
Confidence / uncertainty	Attached to the relevant claim, not a generic certainty.
Component decomposition	Available where the output is composite.
Warnings	Stale, degraded, unavailable, out-of-scope, or exceptional conditions.
Model version	Visible or recoverable for audit.
Interpretation boundary	What the output does and does not establish.

Appendix H. Claim Taxonomy

Types of market claims and their evidentiary requirements

Claims should be classified before evidence is evaluated. The design, language, confidence, and permitted decision use should be proportional to the type and inferential distance of the claim.

Claim type	Meaning	Inferential distance	Minimum evidentiary burden	Preferred language
Recorded observation	States what an identified source reported.	Low	Source integrity, timestamp, schema, context.	"The exchange reported..."
Measurement statement	Reports a value produced under a defined method.	Low–moderate	Definition, units, horizon, transformation, quality.	"Realized volatility increased under the stated estimator."
Descriptive claim	Characterizes observed conditions.	Moderate	Valid measurements, baseline, coverage, uncertainty.	"Breadth is narrower than its recent baseline."
Associative claim	States that variables vary together.	Moderate	Comparison, dependence assessment, robustness, confound awareness.	"Lower depth is associated with higher subsequent impact."
Temporal-sequence claim	States that one condition tends to precede another.	Moderate–high	Time integrity, lag definition, leakage controls, repeated evidence.	"Depth deterioration often precedes impact expansion in this sample."
Mechanistic claim	Proposes a process connecting observations.	High	Temporal sequence, pathway evidence, alternatives, participant constraints.	"Forced risk reduction may transmit through liquidity consumption."

Claim type	**Meaning**	**Inferential distance**	**Minimum evidentiary burden**	**Preferred language**
Contributory claim	States that a factor contributed to an outcome.	High	Mechanistic support, alternatives, scope, sensitivity.	"Concentrated positioning likely contributed to amplification."
Causal claim	States that changing a factor would alter an outcome.	Very high	Design capable of causal identification plus assumptions and sensitivity.	"Under the design assumptions, the intervention caused..."
Predictive claim	States that information improves prediction of a defined target.	Variable	Target, horizon, baseline, out-of-sample validation, calibration, costs if used.	"The model improves 30-minute transition classification versus baseline."
State / classification claim	Assigns an observation to a governed category or state.	Moderate–high	Definition, thresholds, confidence, missingness, calibration, version.	"The confirmed structural state is fragile under model vX."
Transition claim	States that material configuration change satisfies governed criteria.	High	Prior state, change magnitude, persistence, quality, horizon, false-transition analysis.	"A confirmed transition is underway under the stated method."
Decision-use claim	States that evidence improves a participant-specific decision process.	High	Decision Environment, utility / objective, risk, constraints, implementation evidence.	"The framework improved decision calibration for this use case."
Universal action claim	Prescribes one action independent of participant context.	Generally inappropriate	Would require implausibly broad evidence and participant assumptions.	Avoid.

H.1 Language Proportional to Evidence

Evidence condition	Preferred language
Direct and well bounded	records, shows, establishes the measured fact
Supported but not proven	indicates, supports, is consistent with, increases confidence in
Limited or indirect	may reflect, could indicate, is compatible with, remains possible
Unresolved	cannot be determined, evidence is mixed, data are unavailable, conclusion remains provisional

H.2 Decision Boundary

A valid market claim does not automatically determine one universal action. Decision use requires participant-specific objectives, constraints, horizon, risk capacity, alternatives, implementation conditions, and responsibility.

Appendix I. Historical Timeline

Selected milestones relevant to Market Systems Science

This timeline is selective rather than exhaustive. It highlights developments in probability, economics, financial theory, market microstructure, decision science, complexity, computation, and governance that help situate the interdisciplinary perspective of Volume I.

Period	Selected milestone
1654	Pascal and Fermat's correspondence helps formalize mathematical probability (Gorroochurn 2014).
1688	Joseph de la Vega publishes Confusión de Confusiones, an early account of trading behavior in Amsterdam (de la Vega 1688).
1900	Louis Bachelier's Théorie de la spéculation develops an early mathematical treatment of price variation (Bachelier 1900).
1933	Cowles Commission-era work challenges the reliability of market-forecasting claims and advances empirical econometrics (Cowles 1933).
1944	von Neumann and Morgenstern publish Theory of Games and Economic Behavior, formalizing strategic interaction and expected utility (von Neumann and Morgenstern 1944).
1952	Harry Markowitz publishes "Portfolio Selection," formalizing mean–variance portfolio analysis (Markowitz 1952).
1954	Leonard J. Savage publishes The Foundations of Statistics, a foundational treatment of subjective probability and decision (Savage 1954).
1963	Benoit Mandelbrot documents heavy-tailed behavior in cotton-price changes, challenging simple Gaussian assumptions (Mandelbrot 1963).
1965	Paul Samuelson formalizes a martingale-style model of properly anticipated prices (Samuelson 1965).
1970	Eugene Fama's review article organizes the efficient-markets literature (Fama 1970).
1973	Black and Scholes, and independently Merton, publish foundational option-pricing models (Black and Scholes 1973; Merton 1973).

Period	Selected milestone
1979	Kahneman and Tversky publish prospect theory, documenting systematic departures from expected-utility behavior (Kahneman and Tversky 1979).
1982	Robert Engle introduces ARCH models for time-varying conditional volatility (Engle 1982).
1985	Albert Kyle and Glosten–Milgrom publish influential market-microstructure models of informed trading and price formation (Kyle 1985; Glosten and Milgrom 1985).
1986	Tim Bollerslev introduces GARCH, extending conditional-volatility modeling (Bollerslev 1986).
1987	The October 1987 market crash intensifies research into market structure, dynamic hedging, liquidity, and systemic feedback (Presidential Task Force on Market Mechanisms 1988).
1990s	Research in market microstructure, agent-based modeling, and complexity economics expands (O'Hara 1995; Arthur et al. 1997).
1995	Maureen O'Hara publishes Market Microstructure Theory, synthesizing information, inventory, and trading-process models (O'Hara 1995).
2004	Andrew Lo articulates the Adaptive Markets Hypothesis, emphasizing competition, adaptation, and changing market efficiency (Lo 2004).
2007–2009	The global financial crisis accelerates research on leverage, liquidity spirals, systemic risk, funding, interconnectedness, and model governance (Financial Crisis Inquiry Commission 2011; Brunnermeier and Pedersen 2009).
2010	The May 6 Flash Crash highlights high-speed interaction, fragmented liquidity, feedback, and operational market resilience (U.S. Commodity Futures Trading Commission and U.S. Securities and Exchange Commission 2010).
2011	U.S. supervisory guidance SR 11-7 formalizes expectations for model risk management in banking organizations (Board of Governors of the Federal Reserve System and Office of the Comptroller of the Currency 2011).
2010s	Machine learning and increasingly automated forms of market analysis and execution become more prominent in financial research and practice (Financial Stability Board 2017).
2020	Pandemic-era market disruption provides a major natural experiment in liquidity, volatility, policy response, and cross-market transmission (Financial Stability Board 2020).

Period	Selected milestone
2020s	Generative AI and foundation models accelerate research assistance, software creation, synthesis, and automated analysis while raising new provenance and governance risks (Financial Stability Board 2024; National Institute of Standards and Technology 2023).
2026	*(Institute milestone.)* Foundations of Market Systems Science, Volume I proposes an integrated, provisional research architecture organized around systems thinking, multidomain observation, evidence, market state, transition, decision quality, research governance, and model lifecycle management.

The timeline should be read as intellectual context rather than as a claim that Market Systems Science follows one linear historical lineage. Many disciplines contributed independently and often disagreed about market behavior, information, rationality, causation, and modeling.

Appendix J. Suggested Reading

A curated interdisciplinary reading guide

The readings below are selected to help readers explore the established disciplines that inform Volume I. Inclusion does not imply agreement with every argument, nor does omission imply lack of importance.

Systems, complexity, and adaptation

- von Bertalanffy, Ludwig. General System Theory.
- Simon, Herbert A. The Sciences of the Artificial.
- Holland, John H. Hidden Order: How Adaptation Builds Complexity.
- Arthur, W. Brian. Complexity and the Economy.
- Mitchell, Melanie. Complexity: A Guided Tour.

Probability, uncertainty, and decision

- Knight, Frank H. Risk, Uncertainty and Profit.
- Savage, Leonard J. The Foundations of Statistics.
- von Neumann, John, and Oskar Morgenstern. Theory of Games and Economic Behavior.
- Kahneman, Daniel, and Amos Tversky. "Prospect Theory: An Analysis of Decision under Risk."
- Howard, Ronald A., and James E. Matheson, eds. Readings on the Principles and Applications of Decision Analysis.

Financial economics and market behavior

- Markowitz, Harry. "Portfolio Selection."
- Fama, Eugene F. "Efficient Capital Markets: A Review of Theory and Empirical Work."
- Shiller, Robert J. "Do Stock Prices Move Too Much to Be Justified by Subsequent Changes in Dividends?"
- Lo, Andrew W. "The Adaptive Markets Hypothesis."
- Mandelbrot, Benoit B. "The Variation of Certain Speculative Prices."

Market microstructure and liquidity

- O'Hara, Maureen. Market Microstructure Theory.
- Hasbrouck, Joel. Empirical Market Microstructure.
- Kyle, Albert S. "Continuous Auctions and Insider Trading."

- Glosten, Lawrence R., and Paul R. Milgrom. "Bid, Ask and Transaction Prices in a Specialist Market with Heterogeneously Informed Traders."
- Brunnermeier, Markus K., and Lasse Heje Pedersen. "Market Liquidity and Funding Liquidity."

Volatility, derivatives, and risk

- Black, Fischer, and Myron Scholes. "The Pricing of Options and Corporate Liabilities."
- Merton, Robert C. "Theory of Rational Option Pricing."
- Engle, Robert F. "Autoregressive Conditional Heteroscedasticity with Estimates of the Variance of United Kingdom Inflation."
- Bollerslev, Tim. "Generalized Autoregressive Conditional Heteroskedasticity."
- Taleb, Nassim Nicholas. Dynamic Hedging.

Causal inference and empirical research

- Angrist, Joshua D., and Jörn-Steffen Pischke. Mostly Harmless Econometrics.
- Imbens, Guido W., and Donald B. Rubin. Causal Inference for Statistics, Social, and Biomedical Sciences.
- Pearl, Judea. Causality.
- Gelman, Andrew, et al. Bayesian Data Analysis.
- Harvey, Campbell R., Yan Liu, and Heqing Zhu. "...and the Cross-Section of Expected Returns."

Modeling, validation, and model risk

- Box, George E. P. "Science and Statistics."
- Board of Governors of the Federal Reserve System and Office of the Comptroller of the Currency. Supervisory Guidance on Model Risk Management (SR 11-7 / OCC 2011-12; superseded in 2026, and read with the revised guidance below).
- Board of Governors of the Federal Reserve System, Federal Deposit Insurance Corporation, and Office of the Comptroller of the Currency. Revised Guidance on Model Risk Management (SR 26-2 / OCC Bulletin 2026-13; the current U.S. supervisory framework).
- Breiman, Leo. "Statistical Modeling: The Two Cultures."
- Molnar, Christoph. Interpretable Machine Learning.
- NIST. Artificial Intelligence Risk Management Framework (AI RMF 1.0).

Reproducibility, open science, and research integrity

- National Academies of Sciences, Engineering, and Medicine. Reproducibility and Replicability in Science.
- Munafò, Marcus R., et al. "A Manifesto for Reproducible Science."
- Ioannidis, John P. A. "Why Most Published Research Findings Are False."
- Popper, Karl. The Logic of Scientific Discovery.
- Kuhn, Thomas S. The Structure of Scientific Revolutions.

References

Angrist, Joshua D., and Jörn-Steffen Pischke. 2009. *Mostly Harmless Econometrics: An Empiricist's Companion.* Princeton University Press.

Arthur, W. Brian. 2015. *Complexity and the Economy.* Oxford University Press.

Arthur, W. Brian, Steven N. Durlauf, and David A. Lane, eds. 1997. *The Economy as an Evolving Complex System II.* Santa Fe Institute Studies in the Sciences of Complexity. Addison-Wesley.

Bachelier, Louis. 1900. "Théorie de la spéculation." *Annales Scientifiques de l'École Normale Supérieure*, 3rd series, vol. 17: 21–86. https://doi.org/10.24033/asens.476.

Black, Fischer, and Myron Scholes. 1973. "The Pricing of Options and Corporate Liabilities." *Journal of Political Economy* 81 (3): 637–54.

Board of Governors of the Federal Reserve System, Federal Deposit Insurance Corporation, and Office of the Comptroller of the Currency. 2026. *Revised Guidance on Model Risk Management.* Supervisory Letter SR 26-2 / OCC Bulletin 2026-13. Board of Governors of the Federal Reserve System. https://www.federalreserve.gov/supervisionreg/srletters/SR2602.htm.

Board of Governors of the Federal Reserve System, and Office of the Comptroller of the Currency. 2011. *Supervisory Guidance on Model Risk Management.* Supervisory Letter SR 11-7 / OCC Bulletin 2011-12. Board of Governors of the Federal Reserve System. https://www.federalreserve.gov/supervisionreg/srletters/sr1107.htm.

Bollerslev, Tim. 1986. "Generalized Autoregressive Conditional Heteroskedasticity." *Journal of Econometrics* 31 (3): 307–27. https://doi.org/10.1016/0304-4076(86)90063-1.

Box, George E. P. 1976. "Science and Statistics." *Journal of the American Statistical Association* 71 (356): 791–99. https://doi.org/10.1080/01621459.1976.10480949.

Breiman, Leo. 2001. "Statistical Modeling: The Two Cultures." *Statistical Science* 16 (3): 199–231. https://doi.org/10.1214/ss/1009213726.

Brunnermeier, Markus K., and Lasse Heje Pedersen. 2009. "Market Liquidity and Funding Liquidity." *The Review of Financial Studies* 22 (6): 2201–38. https://doi.org/10.1093/rfs/hhn098.

Cowles, Alfred. 1933. "Can Stock Market Forecasters Forecast?" *Econometrica* 1 (3): 309–24. https://doi.org/10.2307/1907042.

de la Vega, Joseph Penso. 1688. *Confusión de Confusiones.* Amsterdam.

Engle, Robert F. 1982. "Autoregressive Conditional Heteroscedasticity with Estimates of the Variance of United Kingdom Inflation." *Econometrica* 50 (4): 987–1007. https://doi.org/10.2307/1912773.

Fama, Eugene F. 1970. "Efficient Capital Markets: A Review of Theory and Empirical Work." *The Journal of Finance* 25 (2): 383–417. https://doi.org/10.1111/j.1540-6261.1970.tb00518.x.

Financial Crisis Inquiry Commission. 2011. *The Financial Crisis Inquiry Report.* U.S. Government Printing Office. https://www.govinfo.gov/app/details/GPO-FCIC/.

Financial Stability Board. 2017. *Artificial Intelligence and Machine Learning in Financial Services: Market Developments and Financial Stability Implications.* Financial Stability Board. https://www.fsb.org/uploads/P011117.pdf.

Financial Stability Board. 2020. *Holistic Review of the March Market Turmoil.* Financial Stability Board. https://www.fsb.org/uploads/P171120-2.pdf.

Financial Stability Board. 2024. *The Financial Stability Implications of Artificial Intelligence.* Financial Stability Board. https://www.fsb.org/uploads/P14112024.pdf.

Gelman, Andrew, John B. Carlin, Hal S. Stern, David B. Dunson, Aki Vehtari, and Donald B. Rubin. 2013. *Bayesian Data Analysis.* 3rd ed. CRC Press.

Glosten, Lawrence R., and Paul R. Milgrom. 1985. "Bid, Ask and Transaction Prices in a Specialist Market with Heterogeneously Informed Traders." *Journal of Financial Economics* 14 (1): 71–100. https://doi.org/10.1016/0304-405X(85)90044-3.

Gorroochurn, Prakash. 2014. "Thirteen Correct Solutions to the 'Problem of Points' and Their Histories." *The Mathematical Intelligencer* 36 (3): 56–64. https://doi.org/10.1007/s00283-014-9461-5.

Harvey, Campbell R., Yan Liu, and Heqing Zhu. 2016. "... and the Cross-Section of Expected Returns." *The Review of Financial Studies* 29 (1): 5–68.

Hasbrouck, Joel. 2007. *Empirical Market Microstructure: The Institutions, Economics, and Econometrics of Securities Trading.* Oxford University Press.

Holland, John H. 1995. *Hidden Order: How Adaptation Builds Complexity.* Addison-Wesley.

Howard, Ronald A., and James E. Matheson, eds. 1989. *Readings on the Principles and Applications of Decision Analysis.* Strategic Decisions Group.

Imbens, Guido W., and Donald B. Rubin. 2015. *Causal Inference for Statistics, Social, and Biomedical Sciences: An Introduction.* Cambridge University Press.

Ioannidis, John P. A. 2005. "Why Most Published Research Findings Are False." *PLoS Medicine* 2 (8): e124. https://doi.org/10.1371/journal.pmed.0020124.

Kahneman, Daniel, and Amos Tversky. 1979. "Prospect Theory: An Analysis of Decision under Risk." *Econometrica* 47 (2): 263–91.

Knight, Frank H. 1921. *Risk, Uncertainty and Profit.* Houghton Mifflin.

Kuhn, Thomas S. 1962. *The Structure of Scientific Revolutions.* University of Chicago Press.

Kyle, Albert S. 1985. "Continuous Auctions and Insider Trading." *Econometrica* 53 (6): 1315–35.

Lo, Andrew W. 2004. "The Adaptive Markets Hypothesis: Market Efficiency from an Evolutionary Perspective." *The Journal of Portfolio Management* 30 (5): 15–29. https://doi.org/10.3905/jpm.2004.442611.

Mandelbrot, Benoit B. 1963. "The Variation of Certain Speculative Prices." *The Journal of Business* 36 (4): 394–419.

Markowitz, Harry. 1952. "Portfolio Selection." *The Journal of Finance* 7 (1): 77–91. https://doi.org/10.1111/j.1540-6261.1952.tb01525.x.

Merton, Robert C. 1973. "Theory of Rational Option Pricing." *The Bell Journal of Economics and Management Science* 4 (1): 141–83.

Mitchell, Melanie. 2009. *Complexity: A Guided Tour.* Oxford University Press.

Molnar, Christoph. 2022. *Interpretable Machine Learning: A Guide for Making Black Box Models Explainable.* 2nd ed.

Munafò, Marcus R., Brian A. Nosek, Dorothy V. M. Bishop, et al. 2017. "A Manifesto for Reproducible Science." *Nature Human Behaviour* 1: 0021. https://doi.org/10.1038/s41562-016-0021.

National Academies of Sciences, Engineering, and Medicine. 2019. *Reproducibility and Replicability in Science.* The National Academies Press. https://doi.org/10.17226/25303.

National Institute of Standards and Technology. 2023. *Artificial Intelligence Risk Management Framework (AI RMF 1.0).* NIST AI 100-1. National Institute of Standards and Technology. https://doi.org/10.6028/NIST.AI.100-1.

O'Hara, Maureen. 1995. *Market Microstructure Theory.* Blackwell.

Pearl, Judea. 2009. *Causality: Models, Reasoning, and Inference.* 2nd ed. Cambridge University Press.

Popper, Karl R. 1959. *The Logic of Scientific Discovery.* Hutchinson.

Presidential Task Force on Market Mechanisms. 1988. *Report of the Presidential Task Force on Market Mechanisms.* U.S. Government Printing Office.

Samuelson, Paul A. 1965. "Proof That Properly Anticipated Prices Fluctuate Randomly." *Industrial Management Review* 6 (2): 41–49.

Savage, Leonard J. 1954. *The Foundations of Statistics.* John Wiley & Sons.

Shiller, Robert J. 1981. "Do Stock Prices Move Too Much to Be Justified by Subsequent Changes in Dividends?" *The American Economic Review* 71 (3): 421–36.

Simon, Herbert A. 1996. *The Sciences of the Artificial.* 3rd ed. MIT Press.

Taleb, Nassim Nicholas. 1997. *Dynamic Hedging: Managing Vanilla and Exotic Options.* John Wiley & Sons.

U.S. Commodity Futures Trading Commission, and U.S. Securities and Exchange Commission. 2010. *Findings Regarding the Market Events of May 6, 2010.* Report of the Staffs of the CFTC and SEC to the Joint Advisory Committee on Emerging Regulatory Issues. U.S. Securities and Exchange Commission. https://www.sec.gov/news/studies/2010/marketevents-report.pdf.

von Bertalanffy, Ludwig. 1968. *General System Theory: Foundations, Development, Applications.* George Braziller.

von Neumann, John, and Oskar Morgenstern. 1944. *Theory of Games and Economic Behavior.* Princeton University Press.

Index

Page references are to the printed page. Locators were converted from the approved editorial index's chapter locators against the frozen print candidate; the term set is unchanged.

Index convention: cross-references use *see* and *see also*.

A

B

C

D

E

F

G

H

I

J

K

L

M

N

O

P

Q

R

U

V

W

www.ingramcontent.com/pod-product-compliance
Lightning Source LLC
LaVergne TN
LVHW010710061126
851857LV00014B/1124